WITHDRAWN BY
WHITMAN COLLEGE LIBRARY

Contemporary Canadian Politics

Recent Titles in
Bibliographies and Indexes in Law and Political Science

Scottish Nationalism and Cultural Identity in the Twentieth Century: An Annotated Bibliography of Secondary Sources
Gordon Bryan, compiler

Edwin S. Corwin and the American Constitution: A Bibliographical Analysis
Kenneth D. Crews

Political Risk Assessment: An Annotated Bibliography
David A. Jodice, compiler

Human Rights: An International and Comparative Law Bibliography
Julian R. Friedman and Marc I. Sherman, compilers and editors

Latin American Society and Legal Culture
Frederick E. Snyder, compiler

Congressional Committees, 1789-1982: A Checklist
Walter Stubbs, compiler

Criminal Justice Documents: A Selective, Annotated Bibliography of U.S. Government Publications Since 1975
John F. Berens, compiler

Terrorism, 1980-1987: A Selectively Annotated Bibliography
Edward F. Mickolus, compiler with Peter A. Flemming

Guide to the *Archiv für Sozialwissenschaft und Sozialpolitik* Group, 1904-1933
Regis A. Factor

Contemporary Canadian Politics

An Annotated Bibliography, 1970–1987

Compiled by
Gregory Mahler

Bibliographies and Indexes in Law and Political Science, Number 10

Greenwood Press
New York • Westport, Connecticut • London

Library of Congress Cataloging-in-Publication Data

Mahler, Gregory S., 1950-
   Contemporary Canadian politics.

   (Bibliographies and indexes in law and political science, ISSN 0742-6909 ; no. 10)
   Includes index.
   1. Canada—Politics and government—1945—
Bibliography. I. Title. II. Series.
Z1385.M35   1988   [F1034.2]   016.320971   88-21357
ISBN 0-313-25510-5 (lib. bdg. : alk. paper)

British Library Cataloguing in Publication Data is available.

Copyright © 1988 by Gregory Mahler

All rights reserved. No portion of this book may be reproduced, by any process or technique, without the express written consent of the publisher.

Library of Congress Catalog Card Number: 88-21357
ISBN: 0-313-25510-5
ISSN: 0742-6909

First published in 1988

Greenwood Press, Inc.
88 Post Road West, Westport, Connecticut 06881

Printed in the United States of America

The paper used in this book complies with the Permanent Paper Standard issued by the National Information Standards Organization (Z39.48-1984).

10 9 8 7 6 5 4 3 2 1

Contents

Preface	vii
Introduction: The Study of Canadian Politics	ix
How to Use This Annotated Bibliography	xv
1. General Sources	3
2. The Constitution and the Legal System	7
3. Federalism, Finance, and Public Policy	31
4. Regionalism and Local Politics	93
5. English Canada and Political Culture	123
6. French Canada and Quebec	137
7. Public Opinion and Citizen Participation	167
8. Political Parties, Ideology, and Elections	185
9. The Executive	217
10. The Legislature	225
11. The Administrative Process	241
12. General Works on Foreign Policy	273
13. "High" Foreign Policy Issues: Traditional Diplomacy and National Security	287
14. "Low" Foreign Policy Issues: Quality of Life	319
Index	359

Introduction: The Study of Canadian Politics

Scope

As those who have done research in Canadian politics know very well, there has been a tremendous increase in the volume of the literature in this field in recent years. To some extent this has been a result of a needed increase in the awareness of Canada on the part of American academics, generally. Beyond this, however, and certainly substantially responsible for the proliferation of the literature dealing with Canadian politics, has been the systematic support of Canadian Studies in Canada, the United States, Europe, and indeed all over the world, by the Government of Canada.

Whatever the source of the growth of this literature, there has been substantial growth. This volume covers literature of the period from 1970 through 1987, and the differential in annual production by scholars in the field is both illustrative of this proliferation and worthy of note.

This Annotated Bibliography of Canadian Politics is an attempt to respond to the rapid expansion of the amount of literature in the field. The goal behind the creation of this volume is to facilitate the necessary process of discovering source material while doing research in this area of scholarship.

Purpose

Although many of us undertake to encourage and inspire our students by telling them tale after tale of the excitement and stimulation of the research process, it is nonetheless regrettably true that at times the research process is tedious, and even boring. The process of poring over index after index, searching for references to material needed for a research project, is definitely not the most exciting part of the overall research process, and anything that can cut some of the tedium out of the process should be a welcome contribution.

That, in essence, is the goal of a bibliography such as this one. The purpose of the effort spent in the compilation of this volume was not to "short cut" the overall research process, but rather was to allow the researcher to spend more time in the more meaningful and important parts of the research process -- reading, reflecting, and writing -- and less time in the tedious and mechanical aspects of the research process, composing lists of sources.

Contents

Every bibliography that is anything other than a purely mechanical exercise of compiling a vast list of source material is a reflection of both the time of its creation and the perceptions of its compiler. It is regrettable, although perhaps unavoidable, that inadvertent omissions have undoubtedly been made of material that should have been included here; as well, it should openly be noted at the outset, there was some material which was intentionally left out of this volume.

To those whose work has been left out of this volume intentionally I would say only that it was simply not possible to include in this bibliography absolutely all of the possible sources which deal in any way with Canadian politics. One of the tasks of a compiler in an undertaking such as this one is to make some necessary decisions related to the degree to which a given source -- whether it was a book, an article, or a document -- focused clearly upon the political aspects of the world (as distinct from the historical, sociological, or economic aspects of the world, for example), and the relative value of that source as an additional entry in this volume. Obviously, it was not my intention to leave out any essential references, and and I am aware that most authors are inclined to consider their works "essential."

Some of the general categories of materials which were intentionally left out of this Bibliography include "pure" biographies, political histories which are more historical than political, studies of political sociology and political economics which are more sociological and economic (respectively) than political, collections of political cartoons, and many government documents and reports which are either heavily data-based, or are not likely to be of direct use for the researcher. Sources in the latter category, government documents, can easily be found in indexes of government (Canadian, American, and other) documents, in any case, and the researcher interested in using this kind of primary resource -- something which is to be encouraged and commended -- is better served simply by starting off with an index of government periodicals.

To those whose work has been inadvertently left out of this volume, I apologize, and add only that every effort was made to be sure to include all of the sources which met the subjective criteria used here, specifically articles falling within the time period, and focusing upon "political" questions.

One problem in the assembling of this bibliography involved the factor of time. There was, as will be clear to those who have undertaken any kind of bibliographic search in the past, a problem with access to the most con-

Introduction   xi

temporary sources. Even the most timely indexes often do not appear until many months, even a year, after a book, journal, or document appears, and although the goals of this undertaking were to make the Bibliography as timely and comprehensive as possible, there was a limit to what was possible in terms of those books and journals which could be examined individually, and the degree to which it was necessary to rely upon other resources. At some point it is invariably necessary to say "This is as far as we can go," and go to press.

Themes

Although there has been a proliferation of literature in the field of Canadian politics, most of what could be described as the general themes covered by the literature have corresponded to traditional areas of scholarly interest. This Bibliography has endeavored, where possible, to follow these traditional lines of inquiry on a chapter-by-chapter basis.

Certainly one of the oldest aspects of the study of politics is that involving the study of law and the legal and constitutional system of the nation-state. This is as true in the study of Canadian politics as it is in other areas. There had been, traditionally, a limited degree to which the "constitution" of Canada could be analyzed, to a large extent because so much of the Canadian constitution wasn't "written," but rather was a function of unwritten traditions, customs, and interpretation by the courts.

The process of the "patriation" of the Canadian Constitution during the 1980-1982 period gave scholars much to write about, and a good deal of the literature in the period covered by this bibliography deals with the new Charter of Rights and Freedoms, the various proposed amending formulae for a new constitution, the relationship between a new constitution and the Canadian federal arrangement, and the impact that a new constitution would have on Canadian society.

The issue of federalism is another traditional concern of students of Canadian politics. Debates over the precise nature of the Canadian federal formula have taken place since prior to the moment of confederation; scholars and politicians have argued over the nature of the social compact, the implications of specific federal-provincial arrangements in terms of power and policy jurisdiction, and how the federal agreement -- whatever it might or might not mean -- could be changed. The question of which level of government, Ottawa or the individual province, has legislative (policymaking) jurisdiction in a variety of substantive policy areas has been seen as a critically important issue, both for the provincial governments and for the central government in Ottawa. This "federal question" is one that has absolutely permeated the literature in the last decade, as can be seen by the relative length of the third chapter here.

Similarly, regionalism is a traditional theme in the study of Canadian politics. Regionalism as an issue predated the Canadian confederation, and issues of regional interests -- West versus East, local versus central -- have been the focus of concern of many scholars in recent years. Part of this concern has been exacerbated by the federal issue referred to above, but another part of the issue is more a function of Canada's very nature as a "community of communities,"[1] a "mosaic,"[2] a "tapestry,"[3] or whatever image we prefer. Local politics and regionalism have been a significant theme in Canadian politics in recent years.

Two other themes related to the "regional" issue are the subjects of chapters here, English Canada and Political Culture, and French Canada and Quebec. These chapters are not entirely geographically-focused, but instead are directed at the literature which deals with the intersection of cultural and political issues. The literature on French Canada and Quebec includes a substantial component dealing with nationalism, as well as the sovereignty-association movement, cultural hegemony, and the continuation of a French-Canadian minority in an English majority population. The literature on English Canada deals with regional cultures, multiculturalism, nationalism, ethnicity, and the nature of a bilingual-bicultural society. Although these themes may be perceived as not strictly speaking "political," sources included in these chapters focus upon political dimensions of these issues.

Traditional political science includes the study of public opinion and political participation, as well as analysis of political parties, ideologies, and elections and voting behavior. Two chapters in this bibliography focus upon these areas of inquiry. A chapter on public opinion and citizen participation includes literature dealing with interest groups, rates of participation, the role of women in politics, the relationship between public opinion and public policy, the concept of political support, the role of aboriginal groups in politics, and the like. The study of political parties, ideology, and elections includes a wide range of examinations of these dimensions of political behavior, including analysis of the development and roles of individual political parties over time, ideological issues in Canada, and electoral and voting studies.

The chapter on the executive includes analysis of both the office of the prime minister and the position of the governor-general. This literature is much smaller in quantity than some of the other institutional literature, and includes study of the individual prime ministers, the growth and development of the prime ministers' position in

---

1. This is the image prefered by former Prime Minister and current Foreign Minister Joe Clark.

2. This is the image offered by John Porter in his classic work The Vertical Mosaic (Toronto: University of Toronto Press, 1965).

3. This is the image preferred by Robert Jackson, Doreen Jackson, and Nicolas Baxter-Moore in Politics in Canada (Scarborough: Prentice-Hall of Canada, 1986).

Canadian politics, and the relationship between the prime minister and his cabinet. The position of governor general has received even less attention than that of the prime minister, and tends to be more historical in nature.

Another "traditional" structure of political regimes that has been a major focus of research in the study of Canadian politics has been the legislature. This chapter includes literature dealing not only with both houses of the federal legislature in Ottawa, but also literature dealing with any of the provincial legislatures. Parliamentary tradition, bicameralism, reform of the Senate and the House of Commons, the relationship between the legislature and the prime minister, parliamentary committees, and a wide range of policy-oriented topics are all among the subjects included in the broad coverage of the literature dealing with the legislative institution here.

The administrative process and the bureaucracy is the subject of a quite substantial body of literature in recent years. This is to some degree the result of growth in the bureaucracy itself, coupled with the proliferation of journals interested in this area of scholarship. Journals such as Canadian Public Administration, Administration, Public Administration Review, and the like, have given scholars and practitioners in this area a number of outlets for the publication of their research activities. This literature discusses oversight, efficiency, the policy process, reform, and a wide range of highly important and salient issues.

The last section of this bibliography deals with the scholarship focusing upon Canadian foreign policy. This literature is so substantial that the decision was made to divide it into three chapters. The first of these chapters includes general works on foreign policy, which encompass textbooks on foreign policy, broad studies of Canada's role in the world, bibliographies of Canadian foreign policy, and general analyses of the Canadian foreign policy infrastructure and policymaking process. The chapter on "high" foreign policy issues: traditional diplomacy and national security includes the vast literatures dealing with what can be called the "traditional" diplomatic concerns, such as defense, armaments, warfare and international relations of a formal nature such as diplomatic relations between countries, negotiation, and so on. The chapter on "low" foreign policy issues: quality of life issues deals with other aspects of diplomacy, such as foreign aid, international environmental issues, "continentalism" in North America, and free trade.

* * * * * *

This introduction began with a statement of the massive increase in the literature dealing with Canadian politics in the period since 1970, and it should be clear to anyone who examines the nearly 4,000 entries here that there is, indeed, quite a substantial literature. This Bibliography of Canadian Politics does not claim to be exhaustive, but rather seeks to provide a point of entrance to the literature for the student or scholar beginning research in this area.

The goal of this _Bibliography_ is to respond to the problem of source proliferation by making available to those studying the Canadian political system a readily accessible index of publications dealing with the Canadian political world. The comprehensiveness of this resource will save the individual doing research on Canada a great deal of time at the early phase of the research process: searching for materials for study. Thereby, it is hoped, this resource will encourage further inquiry into the study of Canadian politics.

How to Use This Annotated Bibliography

This Annotated Bibliography of Canadian Politics is organized so that it can provide entry to the quite substantial literature dealing with the study of Canadian politics in two ways. First, the contents of the Bibliography are grouped into fourteen "chapters" on the basis of subject matter. For many of the sources this grouping was both obvious and easy; for others it was much less so. Since each source could be included in the Bibliography only once, a decision had to be reached as to the primary focus of the source, and it was placed accordingly. Thus a reader interested in Canadian political parties, generally, will find most material with political parties as a primary focus in Chapter Eight ("Political Parties, Ideology, and Elections"), but may find other material involving political parties in chapters dealing with public policy, regionalism and local politics, the legislature, and so on. A reader with a specific interest in a particular political party, on the other hand, may choose to use an alternative means of finding a source, the keyword index.

As a second point of entry to the literature, this Bibliography uses a structure that is used in many indexes in the study of political science, a keyword index. The keyword index is based upon the idea that a given source may appear in the index any number of times, depending upon the subjects it covers and the breadth of its coverage. All key terms and concepts in the title of the source are indexed; as well, often terms and concepts not in the title of the source, but which are central to the analysis and discussion in the source, are also indexed.

The Index of the Bibliography is easy to use. The user simply looks up the terms or concepts in which he or she is interested, and finds an appropriate entry followed by a series of entry numbers, ranging from 1 to 3,738. These entry numbers refer to individual references -- books, articles, and documents -- which are listed in the first part of the Bibliography. The user simply needs to note the relevant entry numbers found after the keyword in which he or she is interested, and then turn to the bibliography itself and look up the entry or entries concerned.

Contemporary Canadian Politics

1
General Sources

1. Albinski, Henry S. *Canadian and Australian Politics in Comparative Perspective*. New York: Oxford University Press, 1973. Study of the major political structures of the two nations and how, with the many structures which they share from their common "Westminster Model" heritage they still have some significant differences in their political institutions.

2. Banting, Keith G. *State and Society: Canada in Comparative Perspective*. Toronto: University of Toronto Press, 1986.

3. Byers, R.B., ed. *Canadian Annual Review of Politics and Public Affairs, 1982*. Toronto: University of Toronto Press, 1984. Single volume discussion of major events of the 1982 year, including the passage of the Canada Act by the British Parliament.

4. Byers, R.B., ed. *Canadian Annual Review of Politics and Public Affairs, 1985*. Toronto: University of Toronto Press, 1985. Annual review of politics, including discussion of the selection as prime minister of Brian Mulroney.

5. Campbell, Colin. *Canadian Political Facts 1945-1976*. Toronto: Methuen, 1977. A compendium of lists, tables, and charts covering the executive, parliament, elections, political parties and pressure groups, the judiciary, the provinces, federal-provincial relations, the economy, and demographics of Canada.

6. Dawson, Robert MacGregor, and Ward, Norman. *The Government of Canada*. Toronto: University of Toronto Press, 1970. Introductory textbook dealing with Canadian politics with a very strong structural orientation. Chapters on the Constitution, the executive, the administration, the legislature, the judiciary, and political parties.

4   Contemporary Canadian Politics

7.   Dickerson, Mark, and Flanagan, Thomas. <u>An Introduction to Government and Politics: A Conceptual Approach</u>. Toronto: Methuen, 1982.

8.   Dreijmanis, John. <u>Canadian Politics, 1950-1975: A Selected Research Bibliography</u>. Monticello, Ill.: Council of Planning Librarians, 1976.

9.   Forsey, Eugene. <u>How Canadians Govern Themselves</u>. Ottawa: Government of Canada, 1980.

10.   Fox, Paul W. <u>Politics: Canada; Culture and Process</u>. 5th Edition. Toronto: McGraw-Hill Co. of Canada, 1982. Collection of scholarly and news articles dealing with the Constitution, federalism, regionalism, biculturalism, public opinion, political parties, the electoral process, voting behavior, the Crown, the executive structures, the legislative process in both the House of Commons and the Senate, the administrative process, the judicial process, civil rights, and provincial election results.

11.   Fry, Earl H. <u>Canadian Government and Politics in Comparative Perspective</u>. Washington, D.C.: University Press of America, 1978. Introductory textbook on Canadian government which approaches its subject from a comparative perspective, emphasizing similarities to and differences from American political structures.

12.   Hockin, Thomas A. <u>Government in Canada</u>. Toronto: McGraw-Hill Ryerson, 1976. Discussion of the development of Canadian government, the development of the public service, and discussion of the role of parliament, political parties, leadership, and the executive in the Canadian political world.

13.   Jackson, Robert J., Jackson, Doreen, and Baxter-Moore, Nicolas, eds. <u>Contemporary Canadian Politics: Readings and Notes</u>. Scarborough, Ontario: Prentice-Hall Canada, 1987. Up-to-date collection of essays, many previously published in journals, covering a wide range of political structures and aspects of political behavior in Canada.

14.   Jackson, Robert J., Jackson, Doreen, and Baxter-Moore, Nicolas. <u>Politics in Canada: Culture, Institutions, Behaviour, and Public Policy</u>. Scarborough, Ont.: Prentice-Hall Canada, 1986. A substantial text covering political structures, political behavior, and foreign policy in Canada.

15.   Jarman, Frederick, and Hux, Allan. <u>Political Decisions in Canada</u>. Toronto: Wiley of Canada, 1980. High-school level text describing how political decisions are made in Canada. Includes some discussion of governmental structures, federalism, decision-makers, and interest groups.

16. Jenson, Jane, and Tomlin, Brian W. *Canadian Politics: An Introduction to Systematic Analysis*. Toronto: McGraw-Hill Ryerson, 1977. Introduction to the methodology of political measurement, and subsequent analysis of data related to Canadian politics, dealing with political culture, voting behavior, political parties and interest groups, legislatures and the cabinet, the courts, the bureaucracy, and political attitudes of Canadians related to nationalism, Canadian-American relations, and foreign aid.

17. Kruhlak, O.M. *The Canadian Political Process*. Toronto: Holt, Rinehart and Winston, 1970.

18. Landes, Ronald G., ed. *Canadian Politics: A Comparative Reader*. Scarborough, Ontario: Prentice-Hall Canada, 1985. Collection of essays comparing the Canadian political system and political structures with the American and British political systems and political structures.

19. Landes, Ronald G. *The Canadian Polity: A Comparative Introduction*. Prentice-Hall, 1983.

20. McInnis, Edgar. *Canada: A Political and Social History*. Toronto: Holt, Rinehart, and Winston of Canada, 1982.

21. McMenemy, John. *The Language of Canadian Politics: A Guide to Important Terms and Concepts*. Toronto: Wiley of Canada, 1980.

22. Mallory, J. R. *The Structure of Canadian Government*. Toronto: Macmillan of Canada, 1971. Textbook with treatment of the constitution, the formal executive and the political executive, the bureaucracy, the electorate, the parliament, the courts and the legal system, and federalism.

23. Merritt, Allen S, and Brown, George W. *Canadians and Their Government*. Toronto: Fitzhenry and Whiteside, 1983.

24. Miller, John A., and Hurst, Donald A. *Exercising Power: Government in Canada*. Don Mills, Ont.: Longman Canada, 1977. High school level text discussing the prime minister and parliament and how they operate together.

25. Redekop, John Harold, ed. *Approaches to Canadian Politics*. Scarborough, Ont.: Prentice-Hall of Canada, 1978. Introductory textbook with sections dealing with the Canadian political environment, foreign policy, ideology, federalism, major institutional political structures, political parties and elections, and leadership and political elites.

26. Ricker, John, and Saywell, John. *How Are We Governed?* Toronto: Clarke, Irwin, 1980. Elementary introductory textbook dealing with basic institutions and procedures of Canadian politics, including political parties, federalism, provincial and municipal government, political leaders, and the legal system.

27. Schultz, Richard, Kruhlak, Orest M., Terry, John C., eds. *The Canadian Political Process.* 3d ed. Toronto: Holt, Rinehart and Winston of Canada, 1979. Collection of essays dealing with political culture and attitudes, political parties, interest groups and elections, government agencies, and decision-making processes in government.

28. Stewart, Gordon T. *The Origins of Canadian Politics: A Comparative Approach.* Vancouver: University of British Columbia Press, 1986.

29. Van Loon, Richard, and Whittington, Michael. *The Canadian Political System: Environment, Structure, and Process.* Toronto: McGraw Hill Ryerson, 1981. Introductory textbook on Canadian politics which focuses upon political structures and political behavior in the environment.

30. Vaughan, Frederick, Kyba, Patrick, and Dwivedi, O.P., ed. *Contemporary Issues in Canadian Politics.* Scarborough, Ont.: Prentice Hall of Canada, 1970. Essays dealing with federalism, constitutional issues, parliament and the executive, the public service, and the judiciary.

31. White, Walter Leroy, Wagenberg, R. H., and Nelson, R. C. *Introduction to Canadian Politics and Government.* 3rd ed. Toronto: Holt, Rinehart and Winston of Canada, 1981. Introductory text including discussion of the physical and ideological setting of Canadian politics, the constitutional framework, the political process including political parties and elections, and formal governmental institutions and processes.

32. Whittington, Michael, and Williams, Glen, eds. *Canadian Politics in the 1980's.* Toronto: Methuen, 1981. Essays covering the political agenda for the 1980's, sociocultural issues in Canadian politics, the party system, elections and voting, and political structures including constitutional reform, federalism, and regulatory agencies.

2
The Constitution and the Legal System

Books

33. Abel, Albert S. <u>Towards a Constitutional Charter for Canada</u>. Toronto: University of Toronto Press, 1980. A proposal for a new Canadian constitution put forward by Albert Abel, assembled from his writings after his death.

34. Anisman, Philip, and Linden, Allen M., eds. <u>The Media, the Courts, and the Charter</u>. Toronto: Carswell, 1986.

35. Asch, Michael. <u>Home and Native Land: Aboriginal Rights and the Canadian Constitution</u>. Toronto: Methuen, 1984.

36. Banting, Keith, and Simeon, Richard, eds. <u>Redesigning the State: The Politics of Constitutional Change</u>. Collection of articles focusing upon recent constitutional changes in a variety of political systems including Spain, Belgium, Canada, the United States, the United Kingdom, West Germany, and Poland, as well as some broader theoretical chapters.

37. Beaudoin, Gérald. <u>Le partage des pouvoirs</u>. [The Separation of Powers] Ottawa: Éditions de l'Université d'Ottawa, 1980. 2nd ed, 1982. Study of the articles of the British North America Act and how they limit governmental powers, with detailed citation of constitutional legal precedent.

38. Beaudoin, Gerald A. <u>Essais sur la Constitution</u>. [<u>Essays on the Constitution</u>] Ottawa: Éditions de l'Université d'Ottawa, 1979.

39. Beaupre, Remi Michael. <u>Interpreting Bilingual Legislation</u>. 2nd ed. Toronto: Carswell, 1986.

40. Beck, Stanley, and Bernier, Ivan, eds. *Canada and the New Constitution*. 2 vols. Montreal: Institute for Research on Public Policy, 1983. Volume One includes essays on justice, constitutional reform, human rights, and language rights. Volume Two includes papers on energy policy, natural resources, environmental protection, and external affairs.

41. Beckton, Clare. *The Law and the Media in Canada*. Toronto: Carswell, 1982. Discussion of the legal system and how it affects the concepts of defamation, contempt, copyright, obscenity, privacy, and freedom of information.

42. Beckton, Claire, and Mackay, A. Wayne, eds. *The Courts and the Charter*. Toronto: University of Toronto Press, 1985. Discussion of the Charter of Rights and Freedoms, the role of the Supreme Court, the equality provisions of the Charter of Rights and Freedoms and government institutions, and the problem of Section 96 of the Constitution Act, 1867.

43. Bennett, William Andrew Cecil. *Opening Statement of the Province of British Columbia to the Constitutional Conference, Victoria, June 14 to 16, 1971*. Victoria: Government of British Columbia, 1971.

44. Bennett, William Andrew Cecil. *Proposals of the Province of British Columbia to the Working Sessions of the Constitutional Conference and Federal-Provincial Conference, Ottawa, September 14 to 16, 1970*. Victoria: Government of British Columbia, 1970.

45. Bennett, William Andrew Cecil. *What Is British Columbia's Position on the Constitution of Canada?* Victoria: K. M. MacDonald, Queen's Printer, 1976.

46. Berger, Thomas R. *Fragile Freedoms: Human Rights and Dissent in Canada*. Toronto: Clarke Irwin, 1981.

47. Bernier, Ivan, amd Lajoie, Andree. *Family Law and Social Welfare Legislation in Canada*. Toronto: University of Toronto Press, 1986.

48. Bernier, Ivan, and Lajoie, Andree. *Labour Law and Urban Law in Canada*. Toronto: University of Toronto Press, 1986.

49. Bernier, Ivan, and Lajoie, Andree. *The Supreme Court of Canada as an Instrument of Political Change*. Buffalo: University of Toronto Press, 1986.

50. Boldt, Menno, and Long, J. Anthony. *The Quest for Justice: Aboriginal Peoples and Aboriginal Rights*. Toronto: University of Toronto Press, 1985. Essays on aboriginal rights, including constitutional, historical, legal, political, and social analysis.

51. Bonenfant, Jean C. La constitution. [The Constitution] Montreal: La Presse, 1976.

52. British Columbia. British Columbia's Constitutional Proposals: Presented to the First Ministers' Conference on the Constitution, October, 1978. Victoria: Province of British Columbia, 1979.

53. British Columbia. British Columbia's Constitutional Proposals. Victoria: Province of British Columbia, 1978.

54. Brun, Henri, and Tremblay, Guy. Droit constitutionnel. [Constitutional Law] Cowansville, Québec: Les Éditions Y. Blais, 1982.

55. Cairns, Alan, and Williams, Cynthia, eds. Constitutionalism, Citizenship, and Society in Canada. Toronto: University of Toronto Press, 1985. Essays discussing the relationship between constitutionalism and citizenship, the evolution of constitutionalism, the changing nature of citizen rights, and nation-building and the Charter of Rights.

56. Canada. Labour Canada. Library and Information Services. Human Rights in Canada, 1977: Legislative Analysis. Ottawa: Labour Canada: Printing and Publishing Supply and Services Canada, 1976.

57. Canada. Parliament. House of Commons. Sub-Committee on Equality Rights. Toward Equality: The Response to the Report of the Parliamentary Committee on Equality Rights. Ottawa: Communications and Public Affairs, Department of Justice Canada, 1986.

58. Canada. Parliament. Special Joint Committee of the Senate and of the House of Commons on the Constitution of Canada. Final Report. Ottawa: ueen's Printer for Canada, 1972.

59. Canadian Intergovernmental Conference Secretariat. Proposals on the Constitution, 1971-1978. Ottawa: Canadian Intergovernmental Conference Secretariat, 1978.

60. Cheffins, Ronald I., and Tucker, Ronald N. The Constitutional Process in Canada. Toronto: McGraw-Hill Ryerson, 1976. Constitutional history of Canadian politics, with emphasis upon the evolution of the Canadian constitution. Discusses the fundamental principles and the assorted machinery of the Canadian constitutional system, major issues of discussion, the Crown, the judiciary, and the federal-provincial consultative process.

61. Colas, Emile. La troisieme voie: une nouvelle constitution. [The Third Path: A New Constitution] Montréal: Éditions de l'Homme, 1978.

62. Craig, Richard G., and Noonan, Randy J. *Two Nations: Problems and Prospects: Understanding Canada's Constitutional Crisis*. Vancouver: New Star Books, 1979.

63. Daniels, Harry W. *Declaration of Metis and Indian Rights*. Ottawa: Native Council o Canada, 1979.

64. Davenport, Paul, and Leach, Richard, eds. *Reshaping Confederation: The 1982 Reform of the Canadian Constitution*. Durham, N.C.: Duke University Press, 1984. A collection of articles, originally published in volume 45:4 of *Law and Contemporary Problems*, analyzing the 1982 reform of the Constitution. Articles discuss historical context, Quebec public opinion, economics, sharing of wealth and resources in Canada, implications for federalism, language and education rights, criminal rights, and the amendment process of the new Constitution.

65. Davis, Henry Francis. *The Constitutional Review, 1968-1971: Secretary's Report*. Ottawa: Canadian Intergovernmental Conference Secretariat, 1974.

66. Doerr, Audrey, and Carrier, Micheline, eds. *Women and the Constitution in Canada*. Ottawa: Canadian Advisory Council on the Status of Women, 1981. A collection of articles covering the entrenchment of rights for women, applications of the Constitution to family law, and economic and social issues facing women.

67. Dussault, R. *Traité de droit administratif: canadien et québeécois*. [*Treatise on Administrative Law: Canadian and Quebecois*] Québec: Les Presses de l'Université Laval, 1974. 2 vols.

68. Dworaczek, M. *Human Rights Legislation in Canada: A Bibliography*. Toronto: Ontario Ministry of Labour Library, 1982.

69. Foucher, Pierre. *Constitutional Language Rights of Official-Language Minorities in Canada: A Study of the Legislation of the Provinces and Territories Respecting Education Rights of the Official-Language Minorities and Compliance withh Section 23 of the Canadian Charter of Rights and Freedoms*. Ottawa: Canadian Law Information Council, 1985.

70. Gaffney, R.E., Gould, G.P., and Semple, A.J. *Broken Promises: The Aboriginal Constitutional Conferences*. Fredericton, N.B.: New Brunswick Association of Métis and Non-Status Indians, 1984.

71. Gall, Gerald. *Studies in Civil Liberties*. Toronto: Butterworths, 1981.

72. Gall, Gerald, ed. *Civil Liberties in Canada: Entering the 1980's*. Toronto: Butterworths, 1982. Collection of articles describing civil liberties in Canada, including historical analysis, and specific discussion of a number of current issues related to civil liberties.

73. Griffiths, C.T., et al. *Criminal Justice in Canada*. Toronto: Butterworths, 1980.

74. Heyman, R. P. *Constitutional Law*. Vancouver: International Self-Counsel Press, 1977.

75. Hill, Karen. *Social Policy and the Constitution of Canada*. Ottawa: Canadian Council of Social Development, 1980.

76. Hogg, Peter. *Constitutional Law of Canada*. Toronto: Carswell, 1985. Analysis of trends in constitutional law with texts of many cases included.

77. Hogg, Peter W. *Constitutional Law of Canada: Canada Act 1982 Annotated*. Toronto: Carswell, 1982.

78. Hogg, Peter W. *Cases on Constitutional Law*. Toronto: Osgoode Hall Law School, York University, 1977. Study of classic cases of Canadian constitution law with emphasis upon analysis of cases and court decisions. Textbook includes discussion of basic concepts of constitutional law, analysis of the distribution of powers, and examination of law relating to civil liberties.

79. Kelly, W., and Kelly, N. *Policing in Canada*. Toronto: Macmillan, 1976.

80. Kenniff, P., et al. *Le contrôle politique des tribunaux administratifs*. [Political Control of Administrative Courts] Québec: Les Presses de l'Université Laval, 1978.

81. Kerr, Robert William. *Legislation Against Discrimination in Canada*. Fredericton, N.B.: New Brunswick Human Rights Commission, 1975.

82. Kome, Penney. *The Taking of Twenty-Eight: Women Challenge the Constitution*. Toronto, Ontario: Women's Press, 1983.

83. LaForest, G.V. *The Allocation of Taxing Power Under the Canadian Constitution*. Toronto: Canadian Tax Foundation, 1981.

84. Lang, Otto E. *Constitutional Reform: Canadian Charter of Rights and Freedoms*. Ottawa: Canadian Unity Information Office, 1978.

85. Lang, Otto E. *Constitutional Reform: The Supreme Court of Canada*. Ottawa: Canadian Unity Information Office, 1978. Description of the role of the Supreme Court in a new Canadian federal system.

86. Laskin, Bora. *Canadian Constitutional Law: Cases, Text and Notes on Distribution of Legislative Power*. Toronto: Carswell, 1973.

87. Laskin, Bora, and Abel, Albert S. *Laskin's Canadian Constitutional Law: Cases, Text, and Notes on Distribution of Legislative Power*. Toronto: Carswell Co., 1975.

88. Laskin, Bora, and Finkelstein, Neil. *Laskin's Canadian Constitutional Law*. Toronto: Carswell, 1986.

89. Law Society of Upper Canada. *The Constitution and the Future of Canada*. Toronto: R. De Boo, 1978.

90. Leavy, James. *Mise à jour 1967-1982 de la Cour suprême et la Constitution [de] Jacques Brossard*. [Update 1967-1982 of the Supreme Court and the Constitution, Jacques Brossard] Montréal: Presses de l'Université de Montréal, 1983. Brings up to date Brossard's study of the Canadian Supreme Court and its constitutional jurisprudence, and his description of judicial organization.

91. Lederman, William. *Continuing Canadian Constitutional Dilemmas: Essays on the Constitutional History, Public Law, and Federal System of Canada*. Toronto: Butterworths, 1980. A collection of most of Lederman's major essays written between 1953 and 1979 which had appeared in numerous journals and anthologies. Essays focus upon the nature of constitutions and of legal reasoning, constitutional history of Canada, the development and maturation of the Canadian judicial system, the federal distribution of power in Canada, and human rights and freedoms in Canada.

92. Lyon, J. Noel, and Atkey, Ronald G., eds. *Canadian Constitutional Law in a Modern Perspective*. Toronto: University of Toronto Press, 1970. A massive study of Canadian constitutional law including discussion of basic issues, the institutional framework, constitutional procedures, fundamental rights, the separation of powers, federalism, and constitutional reform.

93. McConnell, W.H. *Commentary on the British North America Act*. Toronto: Macmillan of Canada, 1977. Analysis of components of B.N.A. Act in relation to executive power, legislative power, provincial constitutions, distribution of legislative power and federalism, and judicature.

94. Macdonald, R. St. J., and Humphrey, J.P., eds. The Practice of Freedom: Canadian Essays on Human Rights and Fundamental Freedoms. Toronto: Butterworths, 1979.

95. McKerral, Cal. Human Rights in Canada 1978: Legislative Analysis. Hull, Québec: Labour Canada, 1978.

96. McNairn, Colin H. Governmental and Intergovernmental Immunity in Australia and Canada. Canberra: Australian National University Press, 1978. Cross-national comparison of the Canadian and Australian approaches to questions of governmental immunity. Includes discussion of governmental immunity from statutes, federalism and governmental immunity, immunity of the crown, and taxation.

97. MacPherson, James C. Developments in Constitutional Law. Vancouver, B.C.: Continuing Legal Education Society of British Columbia, 1978. Analysis of recent case law in Canada with text of many court decisions.

98. McWhinney, Edward. Canada and the Constitution, 1979-1982: Patriation and the Charter of Rights. Toronto: University of Toronto Press, 1982. Examines the process by which the Canadian Constitution was "patriated," the Constitutional-legal arguments made, the political deals that developed, and the final Constitutional package which was approved.

99. McWhinney, Edward. Constitution-Making: Principles, Process, Practice. Toronto: University of Toronto Press, 1981.

100. McWhinney, Edward. Quebec and the Constitution, 1960-1978. Toronto: University of Toronto Press, 1979. Examines Quebec's demands since 1960 for social, economic, and political self-determination, and the implementations of those demands for the federal system. Also examines the roles of the Senate and the Supreme Court in the Quebec issue.

101. Magnet, Joseph E. Constitutional Law of Canada: Cases, Notes, and Materials. Toronto: Carswell, 1983.

102. Mann, E., and Lee, J.A. The RCMP vs. the People. Don Mills, Ont.: General Publishing, 1979.

103. Meekison, J. Peter, Romanow, Roy, and Moull, William. The Origins and Meaning of Section 92a: The 1982 Constitutional Amendment on Resources. Montreal: Institute for Research on Public Policy, 1985. Analysis of the effects that the new Section 92a of the Constitution will have on public policy and federal-provincial relations.

104. Millar, P.S., and Baar, C. *Judicial Administration in Canada*. Montreal: McGill-Queen's University Press, 1981.

105. Milne, David. *The New Canadian Constitution*. Toronto: Lorimer, 1982. Examines the process by which the Canadian constitution was developed and ultimately approved by nine of the ten provinces.

106. Moore, Kermot. *The Will to Survive: Native People and the Constitution*. Val d'Or, Quebec: Hyperborea, 1984.

107. Mullan, D.J. *The Federal Court Act: A Study of the Court's Administrative Law Jurisdiction*. Ottawa: Law Reform Commission, 1978.

108. Nurgitz, Nathan, and Segal, Hugh. *No Small Measure: The Progressive Conservatives and the Constitution*. Ottawa, Ontario: Deneau Publications, 1983. Study of the role played by the Progressive Conservative party in the construction and ultimate adoption of the 1982 Constitution.

109. Olling, R.D., and Westmacott, M.W. *The Confederation Debate: The Constitution in Crisis*. Dubuque Iowa: Kendall/Hunt Publishing Company, 1980.

110. Orban, Edmond, et al. *Mecanismes pour une nouvelle constitution*. [*Mechanisms for a New Constitution*] Ottawa: Éditions de l'Université d'Ottawa, 1981.

111. Paul, Victor, ed. *Le Dossier de la crise constitutionnelle, 1981: O' Canada vs. Je me souviens*. [*Record of the Constitutional Crisis, 1981: Oh Canada vs. I Remember*] Victoriaville, Québec: Publications Vic, 1981.

112. Peck, S. R. *Constitutional Law 1977-78*. Downsview, Ont.: York University, Osgoode Hall Law School, 1977.

113. Quebec: Ministry of Intergovernmental Affairs. *Dossier sur les discussions constitutionnelles, 1978-1979*. [*Record of Constitutional Discussions: 1978-1979*.] Quebec: Government of Quebec, Ministry of Intergovernmental Affairs, 1979.

114. Quebec: Ministry of Intergovernmental Affairs. *Les Positions traditionnelles du Quebec sur le partage des pouvoirs, 1900-1976*. [*Traditional Positions of Quebec on the Division of Powers, 1900 - 1976*] Québec: Ministry of Intergovernmental Affairs, 1978.

115. Quebec: Office of Information and Publicity. *The Government of Quebec and the Constitution*. Québec, Office of Information, 1978.

116. Quebec: Ministry of Intergovernmental Affairs. Dossier sur les discussions constitutionnelles, 1978-1979. [Dossier on Constitutional Discussions, 1978-1979] Québec: Government of Quebec, 1979.

117. Rankin, T. Murray. Freedom of Information in Canada: Will the Doors Stay Shut?: A Research Study Prepared for the Canadian Bar Association. Ottawa: Canadian Bar Association, 1977.

118. Roberts, Roda P., ed. L'interpretation aupres des tribunaux: actes du mini-colloque tenu les 10 et 11 avril 1980 a l'Universite d'Ottawa. [Court Interpreting: Parts of a Mini-Colloquium Held April 10 and 11, 1980, at the University of Ottawa] Ottawa, Ontario: University of Ottawa, 1981. Collection of papers dealing with the role of court interpreting and the work of court interpreters.

119. Romanow, Roy, Whyte, John, and Leeson, Howard. Canada, Notwithstanding: The Making of the Constitution, 1976-1982. Toronto: Methuen, 1984.

120. Rowat, Donald Cameron, ed. The Right to Know: Essays on Governmental Publicity and Public Access to Information. Ottawa: Carleton University, 1981.

121. Rowat, Donald Cameron. Public Access to Government Documents: A Comparative Perspective. Toronto: Commission on Freedom of Information and Individual Privacy, 1978.

122. Russell, Peter, ed. Leading Constitutional Decisions: Cases on the British North America Act. Ottawa: Carleton University Press, 1982. Collection of cases and Court opinions dealing with the division of powers, rights and freedoms, and constitutional change.

123. Sallot, J. Nobody Said No: The Real Story About How the Mounties Always Get Their Man. Toronto: Lorimer, 1979.

124. Schwartz, Bryan. First Principles: Constitutional Reform with Respect to the Aboriginal People of Canada, 1982-1984. Kingston, Ont.: Institute of Intergovernmental Relations, 1985. Analysis of constitutional reform in Canada with respect to aboriginal peoples, and focus from 1982 through 1984. Examines the constitutional mechanisms for self-government, fiscal arrangements, and the federal and provincial governmental positions.

125. Scott, Francis R. Essays on the Constitution: Aspects of Canadian Law and Politics. Toronto: University of Toronto Press, 1977. Essays on federalism, legal and constitutional rights, Quebec, human rights, and the end of dominion status.

16   Contemporary Canadian Politics

126.   Sheppard, Robert, and Valpy, Michael. The National Deal: The Fight for a Canadian Constitution. Toronto: Fleet Books, 1982.

127.   Simeon, Richard. A Citizen's Guide to the Constitutional Question. Toronto: Gage, 1980.

128.   Smiley, Donald V. The Freedom of Information Issue: A Political Analysis. Toronto: Commission on Freedom of Information and Individual Privacy, 1978.

129.   Smith, D.G., ed. Canadian Indians and the Law: Selected Documents, 1663-1972. Toronto: McClelland and Stewart, 1975.

130.   Snell, James G., and Vaughan, Frederick. The Supreme Court of Canada: History of the Institution. Toronto: University of Toronto Press, 1985. Historical analysis of the founding and growth of the Supreme Court of Canada, its relationship to the Judicial Committee of the Privy Council, and its eventual promotion to be final authority on the Canadian Constitution.

131.   Tarnopolsky, Walter S. The Canadian Bill of Rights. Toronto: McClelland and Stewart, 1975.

132.   Tarnopolsky, Walter, and Gérald-A. Beaudoin, eds. The Canadian Charter of Rights and Freedoms. Toronto: Carswell, 1982. Collection of essays covering comparison of the Charter of Rights and Freedoms with the Bill of Rights, discussion of interpretations and applications of the Charter, and specific analysis of different rights covered in the Charter.

133.   Tarnopolsky, Walter S., et al. Newspapers and the Law. Ottawa: Royal Commission on Newspapers, 1981. Discussion of freedom of expression, and legally designated limits upon freedom of expression in Canada, including blasphemy, obscenity, national security, defamation, and contempt.

134.   Turner, J. The Federal Court of Canada: A Manual of Practice. Ottawa: Information Canada, 1971.

135.   Western Premiers' Task Force on Constitutional Trends. Second Report: Western Premiers' Task Force on Constitutional Trends. Victoria, B.C.: Province of British Columbia, Office of the Premier, 1978.

136.   Western Premiers' Task Force on Constitutional Trends. Report of the Western Premiers' Task Force on Constitutional Trends. Victoria, B.C.: K.M. MacDonald, Queen's Printer, 1977.

137.   White, R. D. Law, Capitalism, and the Right to Work. Toronto: Garamond Press, 1986.

138. Whyte, John D., and Lederman, William R. Canadian Constitutional Law: Cases, Notes and Materials on the Distribution and Limitation of Legislative Powers Under the Constitution of Canada. Toronto: Butterworth & Co. (Canada), 1977.

139. Wiktor, Christian L., and Tanguay, Guy. Constitutions of Canada, Federal and Provincial. Dobbs Ferry, N.Y.: Oceana Publications, 1978.

Articles

140. "Access to Official Information -- Canada." Indian Journal of Public Administration 25:4 (1979): 1280-1283. Draft of the Privy Council's Freedom of Information Bill introduced in the House of Commons in October, 1979.

141. Ajzenstat, Jane. "Comment: The Separation of Powers in 1867." [Comment on Resnick, Philip. "Montesquieu Revisited, or the Mixed Constitution and the Separation of Powers in Canada."] Canadian Journal of Political Science 20:1 (1987): 117-120.

142. Allen, J. Garfield. "Canada's Constitutional Time-Bomb I: The Divisive Effects of Trudeau's Approach." Round Table 281 (1981): 15-32. Criticism of the Liberal Party's policies on the Constitution.

143. Anderson, Ellen. "The Saskatchewan Indians and Canada's New Constitution." Journal of International Affairs 36:1 (1982): 125-148. Brief political history of relationships between the Saskatchewan Indians and the federal government, with discussion of some of their special rights.

144. Asplund, C.T. "Mr. Trudeau's Constitution: Going in Style." Queen's Quarterly 87:4 (1980): 584-587. Critique of Trudeau that claims Canadians should write the Constitution and not rely on the British colonial past or American public-relations manufactured symbolic present.

145. Axworthy, Christopher. "Recent Developments in Consumer Law in Canada." International and Comparative Law Quarterly 29:2 (1980): 346-388.

146. Axworthy, Thomas. "Colliding Visions: The Debate Over the Canadian Charter of Rights and Freedoms, 1980-1981." Journal of Commonwealth and Comparative Politics 24:3 (1986): 239-253. Studies the relationships between the positions adopted by Brian Mulroney and those held by Pierre Trudeau, and looks to the future to suggest those constitutional changes most needed.

147. Bartke, Richard W. "Marital Property Law Reform: Canadian Style." *American Journal of Comparative Law* 25:1 (1977): 46-85. Historical analysis of law relating to marriage, with discussion of constitutional and other legal bases, discussion of recent reforms, and comparison with American law.

148. Bartke, Richard W. "Community Property Law Reform in the United States and in Canada -- A Comparison and Critique." *Tulane Law Review* 50:2 (1976): 213-265. Traces the history of law related to common property in marriage in the United States and Quebec.

149. Batshaw, H. "A Landmark Decision Against Discrimination in Canada." *Revue des Droits de l'Homme* 4:2-3 (1971): 207-211.

150. Bazillion, Richard. "Freedom of Information: A Canadian Dilemma." *The Round Table* 288 (1983): 382-394. Westminster-style political systems are not consistent with the principle of freedom of information. Examines the Access to Information Act of 1983 in terms of cabinet solidarity, ministerial responsibility, and civil-servant anonymity.

151. Beaudoin, Gérald. "Les aspects constitutionnels du référendum." ["Constitutional Aspects of the Referendum"] *Études internationales* 8:2 (1977): 197-207. Raises questions about the 1980 "Sovereignty-Association" referendum held in Quebec supported by the Parti Quebecois.

152. Beaudoin, Gérald. "On the Constitutionality of the 1975 Anti-Inflation Law in Canada." *Revue juridique et politique Indépendance et Coopération* 31:4 (1977): 1121-1127.

153. Boadway, R.W., and Norrie, K.H. "Constitutional Reform Canadian-Style: An Economic Perspective." *Canadian Public Policy* 6:3 (Summer, 1980): 492-505.

154. Boldt, Menno, and Long, J. Anthony. "Tribal Philosophies and the Canadian Charter of Rights and Freedoms." *Ethnic and Racial Studies* 7:4 (1984): 478-493.

155. Boyd, Susan, and Sheehy, Elizabeth. "Canadian Feminist Perspectives on Law." *Journal of Law and Society* 13:3 (1986): 283-320.

156. Breton, Albert. "An Analysis of Constitutional Change, Canada, 1980-1982." *Public Choice* 44:1 (1984): 251-265. Interprets the 1980-1981 constitutional history of Canada in light of the general significance of constitutions in the political life of countries.

157. Brown, Susan V. "The Enforcement of Marital Contracts in the United States, Great Britain, France, and Quebec." Boston College International and Comparative Law Review 6:2 (1983): 475-507. Examination of current legal attitudes toward marriage in four settings. Suggests an alternative model for American marriage contracts based upon French and Quebec civil law systems.

158. Cairns, Alan. "Comment [On Vaughn, Frederick. "Critics of the Judicial Committee of the Privy Council: The New Orthodoxy and an Alternative Explanation."] Canadian Journal of Political Science 19:3 (1986): 521-530.

159. Cairns, Alan. "The Judicial Committee and Its Critics." Canadian Journal of Political Science 4:3 (1971): 301-345. Study of the role of the Judicial Committee of the Queen's Privy Council for Canada and its impact on the evolution of political institutions and political behavior.

160. Cairns, Alan. "The Living Canadian Constitution." Queen's Quarterly 77:4 (1970): 483-498.

161. Cairns, Alan. "Recent Federalist Constitutional Proposals: A Review Essay." Canadian Public Policy 5:3 (Summer, 1979): 348-365.

162. Cairns, R. "The Constitution as Regulation: The Case of Natural Resources." Canadian Public Policy 7:1 (Winter, 1981): 66-74.

163. Careless, Anthony, and Stevenson, Donald. "Canada: Constitutional Reforms as a Policy Making Instrument." Publius 12:3 (1982): 85-98. Analyzes recent major constitutional reforms in the context of how public policy is made and enacted.

164. Cassidy, R. Gordon. "A Systems Approach to Planning and Evaluation in Criminal Justice Systems." Socio-Economic Planning Sciences 9:6 (1975): 301-312. Discussion of the total criminal justice process, suggesting criteria for the planning, implementation, and evaluation of new criminal justice programs and policies.

165. Christian, Timothy. "Sweeping Constitutional Changes in Canada." International and Comparative Law Quarterly 36:1 (1987): 139-142.

166. Close, David. "Politics and Constitutional Reform in Canada: A Study in Political Opposition." Publius 15:1 (1985): 161-176. Examines mobilization of opposition to the Canadian Constitution Act as a case study of how the Opposition behaves in a federal political system.

167. Courchene, Thomas J. "The Political Economy of Canadian Constitution-Making: The Canadian Economic-Union Issue." Public Choice 44:1 (1984): 201-249. Economic emphasis of the new Constitution, and the federal government's attempt to "secure the `Canadian economic union' in the Constitution."

168. Croisat, Maurice. "La Loi Constitutionnelle Canadienne de 1981, Droit Legal, Convention et Convenance Politique." ["The 1981 Canadian Constitutional Law, Legal Law, Convention, and Political Convenience"] Revue juridique et politique Indépendance et Coopération 37:4 (1983): 706-722. Compares the 1981 Constitution with other sources of Canadian law and suggests that Quebec's failure to approve the new constitutional plan may have important consequences for the future of politics.

169. Davenport, Paul. "The Constitution and the Sharing of Wealth in Canada." Law and Contemporary Problems 45:4 (1982): 109-148.

170. Days, Drew S. III. "Civil Rights in Canada: An American Perspective." American Journal of Comparative Law 32:2 (1984): 307-338. Analysis of 1982 Constitution and its impact upon civil rights in Canada. Includes historical analysis, and discussion of new Charter of Rights and Freedoms.

171. Decter, Michael. "Political Rights: A Manitoba Perspective." Canadian Public Administration 29:4 (1986): 668-669.

172. Dellinger, Walter. "The Amending Process in Canada and the United States: a Comparative Perspective." Law and Contemporary Problems 45:4 (1982): 283-302.

173. Devall, W.B. "Support for Civil Liberties Among English-Speaking Canadian University Students." Canadian Journal of Political Science 3:3 (1970): 433-449. Attitudes towards civil liberties among English-speaking Canadian university students and analysis of social determinants of these attitudes.

174. Dobell, Peter C. "Constitutional and Political Confrontation in Canada." World Today 37:6 (1981): 223-234. Discussion of the factors underlying constitutional debate.

175. Dobkin, Donald. "Civil Liberties and the Canadian Bill of Rights." Policy Studies Journal 4:2 (1976): 167-170.

176. Engelmann, Frederick. "A Prologue to Structural Reform of the Government of Canada." Canadian Journal of Political Science 19:4 (1986): 667-678. Discusses changes not made in the constitutional changes of 1982.

177. England, Geoff. "Loss of Jobs in Strikes: The Position in England and Canada Compared." _International and Comparative Law Quarterly_ 25:3 (1976): 583-610.

178. Fischer, Hugo. "The Human Rights Covenants and Canadian Law." _Canadian Yearbook of International Law_ 15 (1977): 42-83. Analysis of the implementation of the Human Rights Covenants in Canada and the problems it poses.

179. Flanagan, Thomas. "Insurance, Human Rights, and Equality Rights in Canada:: When is Discrimination `Reasonable'?" _Canadian Journal of Political Science_ 18:4 (1985): 715-738. Discussion of the constitutional implications of insurance classifications that rely on demographic information, whether they are discrimintory, and whether that discrimination should be permitted.

180. Forsey, Eugene. "The Constitution Bill." _Queen's Quarterly_ 87:4 (1980): 566-569. Discussion of the 1980 Constitutional proposals and why they were different from previous proposals.

181. Forsey, Eugene. "Constitutional Aspects of the Canadian Economy." _Proceedings of the Academy of Political Science_ 32:2 (1976): 53-62.

182. Fowler, Dulcey B. "The Canadian Bill of Rights - A Compromise Between Parliamentary and Judicial Supremacy," _American Journal of Comparative Law_ 21 (1973): 712-746. Discussion of a bill of rights in Canada, and the effect that "American style" judicial review might have in a parliamentary system.

183. Fox, Richard G. "Young Persons in Conflict with the Law in Canada." _International and Comparative Law Quarterly_ 26:2 (1977): 445-467.

184. "Freedom of Information Bill - Canada." _Indian Journal of Public Administration_ 25:4 (1979): 1284-1304. Text of the Federal Government's "Freedom of Information" Bill introduced in the House of Commons in October, 1979.

185. Garant, Patrice. "Le statut légal des tribunaux administratifs et leur rapports avec le gouvernement." ["The Legal Status of Administrative Courts and Their Relation with the Government."] _Canadian Public Administration_ 27:3 (Fall, 1984): 329-347.

186. Garant, Patrice, and Morin, Véronique. "La nouvelle Charte canadienne des droits et la constitutionnalisation du droit administratif." ["The New Canadian Charter of Rights and the Constitutionalization of Administrative Law."] _Revue français de Droit administratif_ 3:1 (1987): 58-68.

187. Gopalakrishna, K.C. "The Canadian Bill of Rights." *Journal of Constitutional and Parliamentary Studies* 5:2 (1971): 214-226. Discussion of Constitutional backround of fundamental rights, and the importance of the Bill of Rights in relation to the judiciary in Canada.

188. Green, L.C. "The Canadian Charter of Rights and International Law." *Canadian Yearbook of International Law* 20 (1982): 3-23. The relationship between the new Charter of Rights and various aspects of contemporary international law.

189. Guiffault, Didier. "The Arbitration of the Canadian Supreme Court." *Revue du Droit publique et de la Science politique* 5 (1979): 1383-1424.

190. Hadfield, Brigid. "Learning from the Indians? The Constitutional Guarantee Revisited." *Public Law* (1983): 351-365. Study of *Manuel and Others v. Attorney General* an action by 124 Canadian Indian chiefs against the Attorney-General of England based on the course of events leading up to the patriation of the Canadian constitution.

191. Hahn, Randalf. "Canada's Charter of Rights and Freedoms." *Public Law* (1984): 530-538.

192. Hogg, Peter W. "Canada's New Charter of Rights." *American Journal of Comparative Law* 32:2 (1984): 283-305. Discusses principles of parliamentary sovereignty, the history of the idea of a Canadian Charter of Rights and Freedoms, a discussion of the rights guaranteed by the Charter, and limitations on rights.

193. Kersell, J.E. "Statutory and Judicial Control of Administrative Behaviour." *Canadian Public Administration* 19:2 (Summer, 1976): 295-307.

194. Kershaw, Anthony. "The Canadian Constitution and the Foreign Affairs Committee of the U.K. House of Commons, 1980 and 1981." *Parliamentarian* 62:3 (1981): 173-182. Analysis of the Canadian request to the House of Commons in Britain for the patriation of the Canadian Constitution.

195. Kilgour, D. Marc. "Reply: Distributing the Power to Amend Canada's Constitution." *Canadian Journal of Political Science* 18:2 (1985): 385-408.

196. Kilgour, D. Marc. "A Formal Analysis of the Amending Formula of Canada's Constitution Act, 1982." *Canadian Journal of Political Science* 16:4 (1983): 771-778. The amending formula systematically directs greater influence to the citizens of the smaller provinces.

197. Kilgour, D. Marc, and Levesque, Terrence J. "The Canadian Constitutional Amending Formula: Bargaining in the Past and the Future." Public Choice 44:3 (1984): 457-480. Analysi9s of the amending formula of the Constitution Act, 1982, with its implications discussed.

198. Kinsella, N.A. "The Canadian Model for the Protection From Discrimination." Revue des Droits de l'Homme 4:2-3 (1971): 270-277.

199. Knopff, Ranier. "What Do Constitutional Equality Rights Protect Canadians Against?" Canadian Journal of Political Science 20:2 1987): 265-286.

200. Kroll, Shelley. "Beyond Equal Pay for Equal Work: Recent Developments in the United States, Great Britain, and Canada." Boston College International and Comparative Law Review 7:1 (1984): 179-222. Examines new developments in these countries dealing with wage discrimination on the basis of gender.

201. Kropff, Rainer. "Federalism, the Charter, and the Court: Comment on Smith's `The Origins of Judicial Review in Canada'." Canadian Journal of Political Science 16:3 (1983): 145-161.

202. LaSelva, Samuel. "Mandatory Retirement: Intergenerational Justice and the Canadian Charter of Rights and Freedoms." Canadian Journal of Political Science 20:1 (1987): 149-162.

203. Laskin, Bora. "La Cour Suprême du Canada." Revue internationale de Droit comparé 30:1 (1978): 139-148.

204. Laskin, John B. "The Canadian Constitutional Proposals." Public Law (1981): 340-354.

205. LaTouche, Daniel. "Les calculs strategiques derrière le Canada Bill." ["The Strategic Calculations Behind the Canada Bill."] Law and Contemporary Problems 45:4 (1982): 165-176.

206. Lederman, William. "Canadian Constitutional Amending Procedures: 1867-1982." American Journal of Comparative Law 32:2 (1984): 339-359. Review of amendments through 1981, and analysis of the 1981 Supreme Court of Canada decision regarding the "Trudeau Constitution" and "unilateral patriation."

207. Lederman, William. "Canada's Current Constitutional Crisis." Parliamentarian 62:3 (1981): 192-198.

208. Lederman, William. "Continuing Constitutional Dilemmas: The Supreme Court and the Federal Anti-Inflation Act of 1975." Queen's Quarterly 84:1 (1977): 90-98.

209. Leigh, L.H. "Canada's Constitutional Time-Bomb, II: The End of an Unwanted Imperial Obligation." The Round Table 281 (1981): 26-32. An account of the constitutional position of Canada in the face of the attempt by the Canadian government to "patriate" the constitution.

210. Levesque, Terrence J., and Moore, James W. "Citizen and Provincial Power Under Alternative Amending Formulae: An Extension of Kilgour's Analysis." Canadian Journal of Political Science 17:1 (1984): 157-174.

211. McConnell, W.H. "Edward McWhinney: Québec and the Constitution." American Journal of Comparative Law 29:4 (1981): 723-727. Review of Edward McWhinney's book Quebec and the Constitution, 1960-1978.

212. McConnell, W.H. "Cutting the Gordian Knot: The Amending Process in Canada," Law and Contemporary Problems 44 (1981): 195-231.

213. McConnell, W.H. "A Western View of Constitution-Building." Queen's Quarterly 87:4 (1980): 570-576. Analysis of whether the entrenchment of the Supreme Court and a "Charter of Rights and Freedoms" will be a movement toward the American system with increased central powers.

214. MacDougall, Donald V. "The Exclusionary Rule and Its Alternatives -- Remedies for Constitutional Violations in Canada and the United States." Journal of Criminal Law and Criminology 76:3 (1985): 608-665.

215. Mackinnon, Frank. "Half the Constitutional Story is Still to be Told." Canadian Public Administration 26:1 (1983): 113-120.

216. Mackintosh, Gordon H.A. "A Fateful Prorogation: The Death of Constitutional Proposals in Manitoba." Parliamentarian 66:2 (1985): 60-66.

217. Macmillan, C.M. "Language Rights, Human Rights, and Bill 101." Queen's Quarterly 90:2 (1983): 343-361. Essay examines whether language rights share characteristics of "established" human rights. In studying Quebec's Charter of the French Language (Bill 101) finds that it restricts language rights for linguistic minorities in Quebec.

218. McWhinney, Edward. "The Constitutional Patriation Project, 1980-1982." American Journal of Comparative Law 32:2 (1984): 241-267. Discusses historical context within which 1980 and 1981 constitutional discussions took place, and the significance of some of the contents of the new plan.

219. McWhinney, Edward. "International Law and the `Patriation' of the Canadian Constitution." Canadian Yearbook of International Law 21 (1983): 284-301.

220. Mallory, J.R. "The `New' Canadian Constitution: Will the Old Answers Do for New Questions?" Canadian Public Administration 27:1 (1984): 111-119.

221. Mallory, J.R. "The Politics of Constitutional Change." Law and Contemporary Problems 45:4 (1982): 53-70.

222. Mallory, J.R. "Amending the Constitution by Stealth." Queen's Quarterly 82:3 (1975): 394-401.

223. Mans, Rowland. "Canada's Constitutional Crisis: Separatism and Subversion." Conflict Studies 98 (1978): 1-24. The challenge to Canada is to derive strength from a variety of cultures, but economic problems and the Kremlin hinder this.

224. Mazen, Noël. "Le juge civil québécois (Approche comparative d'un système de droit mixte)." ["The Quebec Civil Judge (A Comparative Approach of a System of Mixed Law."] Revue internationale de Droit comparé 34:2 (1982): 375-404.

225. Mezey, Susan Gluck. "Civil Law and Common Law Traditions: Judicial Review and Legislative Supremacy in West Germany and Canada." International and Comparative Law Quarterly 32:3 (1983): 689-707.

226. Miller, D.R. "A Shapley Value Analysis of the Proposed Canadian Constitutional Amendment Scheme." Canadian Journal of Political Science 6:1 (1973): 140-143. Analysis of the distribution of voting power among the ten provinces which would have resulted from the proposed 1971 Canadian constitutional amending plan.

227. Mintz, Eric. "Banzhaf's Power Index and Canada's Constitutional Amending Formula: A Comment on Kilgour's Analysis." Canadian Journal of Political Science 18:2 (1985): 385-397.

228. Mockle, Daniel. "La réforme du statut juridique de l'administration fédérale: Observations critiques sur les causes du blocage actual." ["The Reform of Juridical Statutes of Federal Administration: Critical Observations of the Causes of Actual Blockage."] Canadian Public Administration 29:2 (1986): 282-303.

229. Monopoli, William V. "`Equality Before the Law' and `Equal Protection of the Law': A Comparative View." International Journal of Comparative Sociology 18:1-2 (1977): 102-126.

229a. Morton, F. L. "The Political Impact of the Canadian Charter of Rights and Freedoms." Canadian Journal of Political Science 20:1 (1987): 31-55.

229b. Nossal, Kim. "Les droits de la personne et la politique étrangère canadienne: le cas de l'Indonésie." ["Constraints on the Development of a Canadian Human Rights Policy: The Case of Indonesia."] Études internationales 11:2 (1980): 223-238. Special economic constraints have hampered the Government's ability to always transfer statements of official policy into policy action.

229c. O'Connell, D.P. "Canada, Australia, Constitutional Reform and the Crown." Parliamentarian 60:1 (1979): 5-13.

229d. Onorio, Joel-Benoit. "Le conflit constitutionnel canado-québécois." ["The Canada-Quebec Constitutional Conflict."] Revue internationale de Droit comparé 36:1 (1984): 111-123.

229e. Onorio, Joel-Benoit. "Le Rapatriement de la Constitution Canadienne." ["The Repatriation of the Canadian Constitution."] Revue internationale de Droit comparé 35:1 (1983): 69-108. The process of the repatriation of the Constitution and the federal-provincial discussions at that time.

229f. Pattenden, Rosemary. "Informal Judicial Admissions of Criminal Activity: A Comparative Study of England, Canada, and the United States." International and Comparative Law Quarterly 32:4 (1983): 812-831.

229g. Pattenden, Rosemary. "The Exclusion of Unfairly Obtained Evidence in England, Canada, and Australia." International and Comparative Law Quarterly 29:4 (1980): 664-679.

229h. Philip, Christian. "Quebec and the Repatriation of the Canadian Constitution." Revue du Droit publique et de la Science politique 98 (1982): 1567-1600.

229i. Phillips, O. Hood. "The Canada Act, 1982." International and Comparative Law Quarterly 31:4 (1982): 845-848.

229j. Preece, Rod. "Comment: Montesquieuan Principles of Canadian Politics." [Comment on Resnick, Philip. "Montesquieu Revisited, or the Mixed Constitution and the Separation of Powers in Canada."] Canadian Journal of Political Science 20:1 (1987): 121-125.

230. Pye, A. Kenneth. "The Rights of Persons Accused of Crime Under the Canadian Constitution: A Comparative Perspective." Law and Contemporary Problems 45:4 (1982): 221-248.

231. Ratushny, Ed. "What Are Administrative Tribunals? The Pursuit of Uniformity in Diversity." Canadian Public Administration 30:1 (1987): 1-14.

232. Remillard, Gil. "The Constitution Act, 1982: An Unfinished Compromise." American Journal of Comparative Law 32:2 (1984): 269-281. Significance of 1982 Constitution Act for Quebec, with particular reference to the language issue.

233. Resnick, Philip. "The Mixed Constitution and the Separation of Powers in Canada." Canadian Journal of Political Science 20:1 (1987): 125-129.

234. Resnick, Philip. "Montesquieu Revisited, or the Mixed Constitution and the Separation of Powers in Canada." Canadian Journal of Political Science 20:1 (1987): 97-115.

235. Roberts, Lance. "Some Unanticipated Consequences of Affirmative Action Policies." Canadian Public Policy 5:1 (Winter, 1979): 90-96.

236. Russell, Peter. "Comment" [On Vaughn, Frederick. "Critics of the Judicial Committee of the Privy Council: The New Orthodoxy and an Alternative Explanation."] Canadian Journal of Political Science 19:3 (1986): 531-537.

237. Russell, Peter. "The First Three Years in Charterland." Canadian Public Administration 28:3 (1985): 367-396. An examination of Court decisions during the first three years of the Charter of Rights and Freedoms shows that the Charter has been neither as good as some said it would be nor as bad as some said it would be.

238. Russell, Peter. "The Supreme Court and Federal-Provincial Relations: The Political Use of Legal Resources." Canadian Public Policy 11:2 (198): 161-170. The new Charter of Rights will not diminish the Court's role as arbiter between the Federal Government and the Provinces, but will enhance it and make the Court more visible in politics.

239. Russell, Peter H. "Edward McWhinney: Canada and the Constitution, 1979-1982: Patriation and the Charter of Rights." American Journal of Comparative Law 32:2 (1984): 397-401. Review of Edward McWhinney's book on the Constitutional Patriation process, called Canada and the Constitution, 1979-1982.

240. Russell, Peter H. "The Proposed Charter for a Civilian Intelligence Agency: An Appraisal." Canadian Public Policy 9:3 (1983): 326-337. Compares recommendations of the McDonald Commission with the final legislation which created the Canadian Security Intelligence Service.

241. Russell, Peter H. "The Effect of a Charter of Rights on the Policy-making Role of Canadian Courts." Canadian Public Administration 25:1 (1982): 1-33.

242. Russell, Peter H. "The Anti-Inflation Case: The Anatomy of a Constitutional Decision." Canadian Public Administration 20:4 (Winter, 1977): 632-665.

243. Rutan, Gérard F. "Watergate North: How the Mounties Get Their Men." Civil Liberties Review 5:2 (1978): 17-26. Discussion of conflicts involving the Royal Canadian Mounted Police and charges of illegal activities on their part.

244. Sabetti, Filippo. "The Historical Context of Constitutional Change in Canada." Law and Contemporary Problems 45:4 (1982): 11-32.

245. Scott, Stephen A. "The Canadian Constitutional Amendment Process." Law and Contemporary Problems 45:4 (1982): 249-282.

246. Scott, Stephen A. "Law and Convention in the Patriation of the Canadian Constitution." Parliamentarian 62:3 (1981): 183-191. Study of the British Parliament and the laws and traditions involved in the Canadian constitutional process.

247. Sharman, G.C. "The Police and the Implementation of Public Law." Canadian Public Administration 20:2 (1977): 291-304.

248. Sharp, J.M. "The Public Servant and the Right to Privacy." Canadian Public Administration 14:1 (Spring, 1971): 58-64.

249. Sharp, Mitchell. "Freedom of Information: Have We Gone Too Far?" Canadian Public Administration 29:4 (1986): 571-578.

250. Sharpe, Robert. "The Charter of Rights and Freedoms and the Supreme Court of Canada: The First Four Years." Public Law (Spring, 1987): 48-61.

251. Skogstad, Grace. "Affirmative Action: A Pallative Condemned for the Wrong Reasons?" Canadian Public Administration 26:1 (1983): 105-112.

252. Slattery, Brian. "The Hidden Constitution: Aboriginal Rights in Canada." American Journal of Comparative Law 32:2 (1984): 361-391. Discussion of historical treatment of aboriginal Canadians, with analysis of their rights under the current Constitutional framework.

253. Smiley, Donald. "The Three Pillars of the Canadian Constitutional Order." Canadian Public Policy 12 (1986): 113-121. Review of the Report of the Royal Commssion on the Economic Union and the Development Prospects for Canada, 1985, otherwise known as the MacDonald Report.

254. Smith, Jennifer. "The Origins of Judicial Review in Canada." Canadian Journal of Political Science 16:1 (1983): 115-134.

255. Smith, Peter. "The Ideological Origins of Canadian Confederation." Canadian Journal of Political Science 20:1 (1987): 3-30.

256. Stein, Michael B. "Canadian Constitutional Reform, 1927-1982: A Comparative Case Analysis over Time." Publius 14:1 (1984): 121-140. Examines five factors which were significant in the successful amendment of the Canadian Constitution in 1982.

257. Strayer, B.L. "The Constitutional Processes for Prairie Union." Canadian Public Administration 13:4 (1970): 337-343.

258. Tarnopolsky, Walter. "The New Canadian Charter of Rights and Freedoms as Compared and Contrasted with the American Bill of Rights." Human Rights Quarterly 5:3 (1983): 227-274. Describes the new Charter of Rights and Freedoms, and compares rights it confers with rights in the American Bill of Rights. Describes provisions of the Canadian Charter not found in the American Constitution.

259. Tarnopolsky, Walter. "The Historical and Constitutional Context of the Proposed Canadian Charter of Rights and Freedoms." Law and Contemporary Problems 44:3 (1981): 169-194.

260. Tarnopolsky, W. S. "Emergency Powers and Civil Liberties." Canadian Public Administration 15:2 (Summer, 1972): 194-210.

261. Tetley, William. "Language Rights in Quebec and Canada." Law and Contemporary Problems 45:4 (1982): 177-200.

262. Thibodeau, Marc A. "The Legality of an Independent Quebec: Canadian Constitutional Law and Self-Determination in International Law." Boston College International and Comparative Law Review 3:1 (1979): 99-142. Examines the legitimacy of Quebec's claim to political sovereignty, including discussion of Canadian constitutional law, United Nations principles of self-determination, and other doctrines of international law.

263. Torrelli, M. "Les Indiens du Canada et le droit des traités dans la jurisprudence canadienne." ["The Indians of Canada and the Law of Treaties in Canadian Jurisprudence."] Annuaire français de Droit international 20 (1974): 227-249.

264. Van Dycke, Robert. "Les droits de l'homme et leurs modes d'emploi: à propos de la Charte constitutionnelle de 1982." ["Human Rights and Directions for Their Use: The 1982 Constitutional Charter."] Sociologie et Sociétes 18:1 (1986): 139-151.

265. Vaughan, Frederick. "The Americanization of Canadian Law." Round Table 256 (1974): 445-450.

266. Vaughn, Frederick. "Critics of the Judicial Committee of the Privy Council: The New Orthodoxy and an Alternative Explanation." Canadian Journal of Political Science 19:3 (1986): 495-520.

267. Vipond, Robert C. "Constitutional Politics and the Legacy of the Provincial Rights Movement in Canada." Canadian Journal of Political Science 18:2 (1985): 267-294.

268. Ward, Alan. "Exporting the British Constitution: Responsible Government in New Zealand, Canada, Australia, and Ireland." Journal of Commonwealth and Comparative Politics 25:1 (1987): 3-25.

269. Ward, Norman. "The Realities of Constitutional Change." Queen's Quarterly 86:2 (1979): 237-242. Since 1976 major documents on Canadian constitutional change have become specific, but it is still not clear how the changes are going to be enacted.

270. Watson, Garry D. "Finality and Civil Appeals -- A Canadian Perspective." Law and Contemporary Problems 47:3 (1984): 1-16.

271. Watson, William G. "The Economics of Constitution-Making." Law and Contemporary Problems 45:4 (1982): 87-108.

272. West, E.G., and Winer, S.L. "The Individual, Political Tension, and Canada's Quest for a New Constitution." Canadian Public Policy 6:1 (Winter, 1980): 3-15.

273. Winn, Conrad. "Affirmative Action and Visible Minorities: Eight Premises in Quest of Evidence." Canadian Public Policy 11:4 (1985): 684-700. Although there is some support of income difficulties, the non-monetary claims of discrimination of minorities are generally stronger than the monetary.

3
Federalism, Finance, and Public Policy

Books

274. Aaron, Benjamin, Najita, Joyce M., and Stern, James L., eds. *Public Sector Bargaining*. Washington, D.C.: Bureau of National Affairs, 1988.

275. Albinski, H.S. *Canadian and Australian Politics in Comparative Perspective*. Toronto: Oxford University Press, 1973.

276. Alexander, Judith A. *Equal-Pay-for-Equal-Work Legislation in Canada*. Ottawa, Ontario: Economic Council of Canada, 1984.

277. Atkinson, Michael M., and Chandler, Marsha A. *The Politics of Canadian Public Policy*. Toronto: University of Toronto Press, 1983. Essays focus upon policy-related problems in such areas as health, language, natural resources, legal aid, industrial control, and the like.

278. Babe, R.E. *Canadian Television Broadcasting: Structure, Performance, and Regulation.* Ottawa: Economic Council of Canada, 1979.

279. Bakvis, Herman. *Federalism and the Organization of Political Life: Canada in Comparative Perspective*. Kingston, Ontario: Institute of Intergovernmental Relations, 1981.

279a. Bakvis, Herman, and Chandler, William, eds. *Federalism and the Role of the State*. Toronto: University of Toronto Press, 1987. Collection of articles covering themes, institutions, and policies of modern federalism.

280. Baldwin, J.R. *The Regulatory Agency and the Public Corporation: The Canadian Air Transportation Industry*. Cambridge, Ma.: Ballinger, 1975.

281. Banting, Keith G. The State and Economic Interests. Toronto: University of Toronto Press, 1986.

282. Banting, Keith, and Simeon, Richard, eds. And No One Cheered: Federalism, Democracy, and the Constitution Act. Toronto: Methuen, 1983. Articles discussing the importance and nature of the Constitution Act, 1982. Papers discuss how the new constitution will affect federalism, generally, the role of the courts, and democratic institutions in Canada.

283. Bastien, Richard. Federalism and Decentralization: Where Do We Stand? Ottawa: Minister of Supply and Services, 1981. A brief political history of the evolution of Canadian federalism, from the time of Confederation through 1977. Includes specific discussion of fiscal decentralization.

284. Bercuson, David J., ed. Canada and the Burden of Unity. Toronto: Macmillan of Canada, 1977. Essays which focus upon the subject of national unity and the various pressures challenging that unity. Includes discussion of economic issues, regionalism, and transportation policy, among other issues.

285. Black, Edwin R. Divided Loyalties: Canadian Concepts of Federalism. Montreal: McGill-Queen's University Press, 1975. Presents theories of federal arrangements, with analysis of how concepts of federalism affect federal-provincial relations.

286. Blais, André, Desranleau, Claude, and Vanier, Yves. A Political Sociology of Public Aid to Industry. Toronto: University of Toronto Press, 1986.

287. Bonin, B., ed. Immigration: Policy-Making Process and Results. Toronto: Institute of Public Administration of Canada, 1977.

288. Bregha, François. Bob Blair's Pipeline: The Business and Politics of Northern Energy Development Projects. Toronto: J. Lorimer, 1979. Case study of the 1976-1977 process leading to the Canadian Government's deciding in 1977 to approve the construction of the alaska Highway natural gas pipeline.

289. Breton, A., and Scott, A. The Design of Federations. Montreal: Institute for Research on Public Policy, 1980.

290. Breton, A., and Scott, A. The Economic Constitution of Federal States. Toronto: University of Toronto Press, 1978.

291. Breton, Raymond. The Canadian Condition: A Guide to Research in Public Policy. Montreal: Institute for Research on Public Policy, 1977.

292. Bryden, K. Old Age Pensions and Policy-Making in Canada. Montreal: McGill-Queen's University Press, 1974.

293. Buchan, Robert J., ed. Telecommunications Regulation and the Constitution. Montreal: Institute for Research on Public Policy, 1982.

294. Burns, Ronald M., et al. Political and Administrative Federalism. Canberra: Centre for Research on Federal Financial Relations, Australian National University, 1976.

295. Burton, T.L. Natural Resources Policy in Canada: Issues and Perspectives. Toronto: McClelland and Stewart, 1972.

296. Byers, R. B., and Reford, Robert William, eds. Canada Challenged: The Viability of Confederation. Toronto: Canadian Institute of International Affairs, 1979. Essays on federalism and how Canadian confederation might be continued with so many challenges. Chapters on transportation and energy policy, as well as Quebec, cultural affairs, communications, and the Canadian brand of federalism.

297. Canada. Federal-Provincial Relations Office. Interim Report on Relations Between the Government of Canada and the Canada Federal-Provincial Relations Office. Sovereignty-Association, the Contradictions. Ottawa: Government of Canada, 1978.

298. Canada. Task Force on Broadcasting Policy. Report of the Task Force on Broadcasting Policy. Toronto: Minister of Supply and Services Canada, 1986.

299. Canada. Task Force on Program Review. Improved Program Delivery: A Study Team Report to the Task Force on Program Review. Ottawa: Canadian Government Publication Centre, 1986.

300. Canada. Task Force on Program Review. Management of Government: A Study Team Report to the Task Force on Program Review. Ottawa: Canadian Government Publication Centre, Supply and Services Canada, 1986.

301. Canadian Institute of Resources Law. Resources Law Bibliography. Calgary, Alberta: Canadian Institute of Resources Law, 1980.

302. Careless, Anthony G. S. Initiative and Response: The Adaptation of Canadian Federalism to Regional Economic Development. Montreal: McGill-Queen's University Press, 1977. Study of the effect of Canadian federalism on inter-regional economic differences in Canada, and analysis of programs designed to reduce regional disparities.

303. Cheffins, Ronald, and Johnson, Patricia. *The Revised Canadian Constitution: Politics as Law*. Scarborough, Ontario: McGraw-Hill Ryerson, 1986. Overview of the Canadian constitution and critique of the Constitution Act, 1982.

304. Clement, W., and Drache, D. *A User's Guide to Canadian Political Economy*. Toronto: Lorimer, 1978.

305. Coates, Mary Lou. *Employment Equity: Issues, Approaches, and Public Policy Framework*. Kingston, Ont.: Industrial Relations Centre, Queen's University at Kingston, 1986.

306. Cook, C.E. *Nuclear Power and Legal Advocacy: The Environmentalists and the Courts*. Toronto: D.C. Heath, 1980.

307. Courchene, Thomas J. *Economic Management and the Division of Powers*. Toronto: University of Toronto Press, 1986.

308. De Valk, Alphonse. *Morality and Law in Canadian Politics: The Abortion Controversy*. Dorval, Montreal: Palm Publishers, 1974. Examination of the political policy-making process which created Canadian abortion policy in the late 1960's.

309. Dirks, G.E. *Canada's Refugee Policy: Indifference or Opportunism*. Montreal: McGill-Queen's University Press, 1978.

310. Dobson, Wendy, *Canada's Energy Policy Debate*. Montreal: C.D. Howe Research Institute, 1981.

311. Dobson, Wendy. *The Exchange Rate as a Policy Instrument*. Montreal: C.D. Howe Research Institute, 1980.

312. Doern, G. Bruce. *Government Intervention in the Canadian Nuclear Industry*. Montreal: Institute for Research on Public Policy, 1980.

313. Doern, G. Bruce, ed. *How Ottawa Spends Your Tax Dollars: National Policy and Economic Development, 1982*. Toronto: Lorimer, 1982. Essays dealing with energy, trade, regionalism, transportation, consumer protection, and governmental regulation.

314. Doern, G. Bruce, ed. *The Politics of Economic Policy*. Toronto: University of Toronto Press, 1985. Studies the relationship between economic policy and politics, including the politics of the deficit, politics and natural resources, the problem of income security, and labor market policy and politics.

315. Doern, G.Bruce, ed. The Regulatory Process in Canada. Toronto: Macmillan, 1978.

316. Doern, G. Bruce. Science and Politics in Canada. Montreal: McGill-Queen's University Press, 1972. Describes the evolution of the formal machinery with which scientists and policy formulators interact in Canada.

317. Doern, G. Bruce, and Aucoin, Peter, eds. Public Policy in Canada: Organization, Process, and Management. Toronto: Macmillan of Canada, 1979. Essays providing a basic description of structures and processes of Canadian public policy, including discussion of governmental agencies, economic policies, and processes involved in policy-making.

318. Doern, G. Bruce, and Aucoin, Peter, eds. The Structures of Policy-Making in Canada. Toronto: Macmillan of Canada, 1971. Collection of articles dealing with the executive, the budgetary process, royal commissions, task forces, advisory councils, and white papers.

319. Doern, G. Bruce, and Maslove, Allan M., eds. The Public Evaluation of Government Spending: Proceedings of a Conference Sponsored by the Institute for Research on Public Policy and the School of Public Administration, Carleton University, October 19-21, 1978, Ottawa. Montreal: Institute for Research on Public Policy, 1979.

320. Doern, G. Bruce, and Morrison, R.W., eds. Canadian Nuclear Policies. Montreal: Institute for Research on Public Policy, 1980.

321. Doern, G. Bruce, and Phidd, Richard W. Canadian Public Policy: Ideas, Structure, Process. Toronto: Methuen, 1983. Introductory text on Canadian public policy, with discussion of basic public policy concepts, structures and processes in the public policy system, and a number of specific policy fields.

322. Doern, G. Bruce, and Toner, Glen. The Politics of Energy: The Development and Implementation of the NEP. Toronto: Methuen, 1985.

323. Doern, G. Bruce, and Wilson, V.S., eds. Issues in Canadian Public Policy. Toronto: Macmillan, 1974.

324. Drache, Daniel, and Clement, Wallace, eds. The New Practical Guide to the Canadian Political Economy. Toronto: Lorimer, 1985.

325. Dupré, J.S., et al. Federalism and Policy Development: The Case of Adult Occupational Training in Ontario. Toronto: University of Toronto Press, 1973.

326. Dwivedi, O.P., ed. The Administrative State in Canada: Essays in Honour of J. E. Hodgetts. Toronto: University of Toronto Press, 1982. A collection of essays dealing with administration and public policy, including discussion of regulatory agencies, public corporations, delegated legislation, the cabinet, the accountability of public servants, and public access to official documents.

327. Dwivedi, O.P., ed. Resources and the Environment: Policy Perspectives for Canada. Toronto: McClelland and Stewart, 1980.

328. Feldman, Elliot J., and Goldberg, Michael A. Land Rites and Wrongs: The Management, Regulation, and use of Land in Canada and the United States. Boston: OGH Publications, 1988.

329. Feldman, Elliot, and Milch, Jerome. The Politics of Canadian Airport Development: Lessons for Federalism. Durham, N.C.: Duke University Press, 1983. Three case studies of airport planning in Canada, in Montreal, Toronto, and Vancouver, and how lobbying, intergovernmental relations, and financial considerations affected policy decisions in these cases.

330. Fowke, V.C. Canadian Agricultural Policy: The Historical Pattern. Toronto: University of Toronto Press, 1978.

331. French, Richard D. How Ottawa Decides: Planning and Industrial Policy-Making, 1968-1980. Toronto: Lorimer, 1980. Description of the Cabinet committee system, the budget process, and the various planning systems which are part of long-term fiscal policymaking. This includes discussion of reforms of the system made by the Clark government in 1979.

332. French, R., and Béliveau, A. The RCMP and the Management of National Security. Toronto: Butterworths, 1979.

333. French, Stanley George. Philosophers Look at Canadian Confederation. Montreal: Canadian Philosophical Association, 1979.

334. Gibson, R.B. The Strathcona Sound Mining Project: A Case Study of Decision Making. Ottawa: Science Council of Canada, 1978.

335. Good, D.A. The Politics of Anticipation: Making Canadian Federal Tax Policy. Ottawa: Lorimer, 1980.

336. Gordon, W. Storm Signals: New Economic Policies for Canada. Toronto: McClelland and Stewart, 1975.

337. Gotlieb, Allan Ezra, ed. Human Rights, Federalism and Minorities. Toronto: Canadian Institute of International Affairs, 1970.

338. Guest, D. The Emergence of Social Security in Canada. Vancouver: University of British Columbia Press, 1980.

339. Harrell, Karen Fair. Acid Rain: A Legal and Political Perspective. Monticello, Ill.: Vance Bibliographies, 1983.

340. Hartle, Douglas G. The Expenditure Budget Process in the Government of Canada. Toronto: Canadian Tax Foundation, 1978.

341. Hartle, Douglas G. Public Policy Decision-Making and Regulation Montreal: Butterworth, 1979.

342. Hartley, K., et al. Energy R and D Decision-Making for Canada. Montreal: Institute for Research on Public Policy, 1979.

343. Hawkins, F. Canada and Immigration: Public Policy and Public Concern. Montreal: McGill-Queen's University Press, 1972.

344. Heaver, T.D., and Nelson, J.C. Railway Pricing Under Commercial Freedom: The Canadian Experience. Vancouver: University of British Columbia Press, 1977.

345. Helwig, David, ed. Love and Money: The Politics of Culture. Ottawa: Oberon Press, 1980. Study of Canadian government support for arts and culture.

346. Hiemstra, John. Trudeau's Political Philosophy: Its Implications for Liberty and Progress. Toronto: Institute for Christian Studies, 1983.

347. Hill, O.M. Canada's Salesman to the World: The Department of Trade and Commerce. Montreal: McGill-Queen's University Press, 1977.

348. Hodgins, Barbara. Where the Economy and the Constitution Meet in Canada. Montreal, Quebec: C.D. Howe Institute, 1981.

349. Hodgins, Bruce, Wright, Don, and Heick, W. H., eds. Federalism in Canada and Australia: The Early Years. Waterloo, Ont.: Wilfrid Laurier University Press, 1978. Collection of political and historical articles comparing the development of federalism in these two nations. The articles are not explicitly comparative. Articles on Canada focus on individual provinces and specific political leaders.

350. Information Services Directorate, Central Analytical Services Branch, Labour Canada. Human Rights in Canada, 1977: Legislative Analysis. Ottawa: Labour Canada, 1976.

351. Institute of Intergovernmental Relations. Federalism and Intergovernmental Relations in Australia, Canada, the United States, and Other Countries: a Bibliography. Kingston: Queen's University Press, 1975; Supplemental Bibliography, 1979.

352. Ismael, Jacqueline S., ed. Canadian Social Welfare Policy: Federal and Provincial Dimensions. Montreal: McGill-Queen's University Press, 1985. Collection of essays discussing efforts to reform several different social welfare policy areas including social security reform, pension reform, and the like.

353. Knight, Kenneth W., and Wiltshire, Kenneth W. Formulating Government Budgets: Aspects of Australian and North American Experience. St. Lucia, Queensland: University of Queensland Press, 1977.

354. Knox, P., and Resnick, P., eds. Essays in B.C Political Economy. Vancouver: New Star Books, 1974.

355. Krasnick, Mark R. Case Studies in the Division of Powers. Toronto: University of Toronto Press, 1986.

356. Krasnick, Mark R. Fiscal Federalism. Toronto: University of Toronto Press, 1986.

357. Krasnick, Mark R. Perspectives on the Canadian Economic Union. Toronto: Uiversity of Toronto Press, 1986.

358. Kroeker, H. V. Accountability and Control: The Government Expenditure Process. Montreal: C. D. Howe Research Institute, 1978. Discussion of how the expenditure process works, and the institutional machinery for oversight of governmental expenditures. Includes examination of problems of setting priorities, planning expenditures, and relations between the government and parliament.

359. Lalande, Gilles. In Defence of Federalism: A View from Quebec. Toronto: McClelland and Stewart, 1978. A now-classic essay by a Quebecois federalist on the merits of a federal system for Quebec. This book was originally published in French in 1972.

360. Lang, R. The Politics of Drugs: A Comparative Pressure-Group Study of the Canadian Pharmaceutical Manufacturers Association and the Association of the British Pharmaceutical Industry (1930-1970). London: Saxon House, 1974.

361. Langford, J.W., ed. *Administration of Transport Policy: Emerging Problems and Patterns*. Toronto: Institute of Public Administration of Canada, 1979.

362. Langford, J.W. *Transport in Transition: The Reorganization of the Federal Transport Portfolio*. Toronto: Institute of Public Administration of Canada, 1977.

363. Laux, Jeanne Kirk, and Molot, Maureen Appel. *State Capitalism: Public Enterprise in Canada*. Ithaca: Cornell University Press, 1988.

364. Laxer, James. *Canada's Economic Strategy*. Toronto: McClelland and Stewart, 1981. Analysis of new economic policy in Canada in the 1970's and into the 1980's, with the increase in importance of the "new conservatism."

365. Leach, Richard H. *Perceptions of Federalism by Canadian and Australian Public Servants: A Comparative Analysis*. Canberra: Centre for Research on Federal Financial Relations, Australian National University, 1976.

366. Lee, Sidney S. *Quebec's Health System: A Decade of Change, 1967-77*. Toronto: Institute of Public Administration of Canada, 1979.

367. Leeson, Howard Alfred, and Vanderelst, Wilfried, eds. *External Affairs and Canadian Federalism: The History of a Dilemma*. Toronto: Holt, Rinehart and Winston of Canada, 1973.

368. Leiss, William, ed. *Ecology Versus Politics in Canada*. Toronto: University of Toronto Press, 1979. Essays examining the political dimension of environmental and ecological questions in the formulation and operationalization of Canadian public policy.

369. Leman, Christopher. *The Collapse of Welfare Reform: Political Institutions, Policy, and the Poor in Canada and the United States*. Cambridge, Mass.: M.I.T. Press, 1980. Discussion of the "welfare crisis," proposals for welfare reform, the Canadian Social Security review in the 1970's, and the outlook for the future of social welfare policies in Canada.

370. Leslie, P. *Equal to Equal: Economic Association and the Canadian Common Market*. Kingston: Queen's University Press, 1979.

371. Liboiron, Albert A. *Federalism and Intergovernmental Relations in Canada, Australia, the United States and Other Countries: A Supplementary Bibliography*. Kingston, Ont.: Institute of Intergovernmental Relations, Queen's University, 1976.

372. Lysyk, K. M. *Reshaping Canadian Federalism*. Toronto: Ukranian Professional & Business Club of Toronto, 1979.

373. McCamus, J.D., ed. *Freedom of Information: Canadian Perspectives*. Toronto: Butterworths, 1981

374. MacDonald, Dick, ed. *Confederation Dialogue: The Press and the Confederation Debate*. Toronto: Canadian Daily Newspaper Publishers Association, 1978. Collection of essays on the role of the press during the modern Confederation debates.

375. MacDonald, Wendy. *Constitutional Change and the Mineral Industy in Canada*. Kingston, Ont. Institute for Intergovernmental Relations, 1980. Discussion of the implications that constitutional change in Canada might have for the Canadian mineral industry.

376. McDougall, J.N. *Fuels and the National Policy*. Toronto: Butterworths, 1981.

377. MacEachen, Allan. *Federal-Provincial Fiscal Arrangements in the Eighties*. Ottawa: Department of Finance, Canada, 1981. Discussion of the federal government's proposal to the provinces concerning a five-year federal-provincial financial relationship.

378. McFetridge, D.G. *Canadian Industrial Policy in Action*. Toronto: University of Toronto Press, 1985.

379. McIntosh, Dave. *Ottawa Unbuttoned, or, Who's Running This Country Anyway?* Toronto: Stoddart, 1987.

380. McLaren, Angus, and McLaren, Arlene Tigar. *The Bedroom and the State: The Changing Practices and Politics of Contraception and Abortion in Canada, 1880-1980*. Toronto, Ont.: McClelland & Stewart, 1986.

381. McLaren, R.I. *Civil Servants and Public Policy: A Comparative Study of International Secretariats*. Waterloo: Wilfrid Laurier University Press, 1980.

382. Mahler, Gregory S. *New Dimensions of Canadian Federalism: Canada in a Comparative Perspective*. Rutherford, NJ: Fairleigh Dickinson University Press, 1987. Analysis of the development of federalism in Canada and the manner in which the federal nature of the state makes policymaking more difficult in Canada than is the case in other federal parliamentary regimes.

383. Mahon, Rianne. *The Politics of Industrial Restructuring: Canadian Textiles*. Toronto: University of Toronto Press, 1984. Political analysis of industrial strategy of the 1960's, and how economic problems develop which states ultimately cannot ignore.

384. Mann, W.E., ed. *Poverty and Social Policy in Canada*. Toronto: Copp Clark, 1970.

385. Mans, Rowland. *Canada's Constitutional Crisis: Separatism and Subversion*. London: Institute for the Study of Conflict, 1978.

386. Manzer, Ronald. *Public Policies and Political Development in Canada*. Toronto: University of Toronto Press, 1985. How governments in Canada have utilized political power in a variety of policy areas, including economic development, crime, expansion of educational systems, and human rights.

387. Martin, J. *The Role and Place of Ontario in the Canadian Confederation*. Toronto: Ontario Economic Council, 1974.

388. Maslove, Allan M., ed. *How Ottawa Spends, 1985: Sharing the Pie*. Toronto: Methuen, 1985. Essays on housing, energy, pensions, and taxation policy.

389. Maslove, Allan M., Prince, Michael J., and Doern, G. Bruce. *Federal and Provincial Budgeting*. Toronto: University of Toronto Press, 1986.

390. Meekison, J. Peter, ed. *Canadian Federalism: Myth or Reality*. 3rd Edition. Toronto: Methuen, 1977. Articles focusing upon several dimensions of federalism, the constitution and constitutional reform, intergovernmental relations, regionalism, policy-making, and Quebec's role in the Confederation.

391. Memezes, J., ed. *Decade of Adjustment: Legal Perspectives on Contemporary Social Issues.* Toronto: Butterworths, 1980.

392. Milne, David. *Tug of War: Ottawa and the Provinces under Trudeau and Mulroney*. Toronto: J. Lorimer, 1986.

393. Mitchell, B., and Sewell, W.R.D. *Canadian Resource Policies: Problems and Prospects*. Toronto: Methuen, 1981.

394. Mitchell, Don. *The Politics of Food*. Toronto: J. Lorimer, 1975.

395. Montgovery, R., and Marshall, D.R., eds. *Housing Policy for the 1980's*. Toronto: Lexington Books, 1980.

396. Moscovitch, Allan, and Drover, Glenn, eds. *Inequality: Essays on the Political Economy of Social Welfare*. Toronto: University of Toronto Press, 1981. Essays focus upon the effect of capitalism on inequality, and how social welfare tries to address this inequality.

397. Naylor, C. David. *Private Practice, Public Payment: Canadian Medicine and the Politics of Health Insurance, 1911-1966.* Kingston: McGill-Queen's University Press, 1986.

398. Nelles, H.V. *The Politics of Development: Forests, Mines, and Hydro-Electric Power in Ontario, 1849-1941.* Toronto: Macmillan, 1974.

399. Niosi, J. *The Economy of Canada: A Study of Ownership and Control.* Montreal: Black Rose, 1978.

400. Norrie, K. H., Simeon, Richard, and Krasnick, Mark R. *Federalism and Economic Union in Canada.* Toronto: University of Toronto Press, 1986.

401. Oates, W.E. *Fiscal Federalism.* Don Mills, Ontario: Harcourt Brace Jovanovich, 1972.

402. Oates, W.E., ed. *The Political Economy of Fiscal Federalism.* New York: Princeton University Press, 1977.

403. Ontario Economic Council. *Government Regulation.* Toronto: The Council, 1978.

404. Ontario, Government. *Ontario at the Conference of First Ministers on the Economy, Ottawa, February 13-15, 1978.* Toronto, Ont.: Ontario Govt. Bookstore, 1978.

405. Ostry, Bernard. *The Cultural Connection: An Essay on Culture and Government Policy in Canada.* Toronto: McClelland and Stewart, 1978. Discussion of the role of government in the support of the arts and intellectual life in Canada.

406. Palumbo, D.J., and Harder, M.A. *Implementing Public Policy.* Toronto: D.C. Heath, 1981.

407. Panitch, Leo, ed. *The Canadian State: Political Economy and Political Power.* Toronto: University of Toronto Press, 1977. Articles on the nature of the state, federalism and capitalism, class and social structure, economic and social policy, and ideology.

408. Patry, Réjean M. *La législation linguistique fédérale.* [*Federal Language Legislation*] Québec: Conseil de la langue française, 1981. Analysis of federal language policy leading to "functional bilingualism," the role of the Constitution, and the job of the legislature in this task.

409. Peers, Frank W. *The Public Eye: Television and the Politics of Canadian Broadcasting, 1952-1968.* Toronto: University of Toronto Press, 1979. Study of the role of television in modern Canadian politics and its change over the years.

410. Phidd, Richard W., and Doern, G. Bruce. The Politics and Management of Canadian Economic Policy. Toronto: Macmillan of Canada, 1978. Analysis of management and public policy, with description of the management, operation, and processes of economic policy formulation.

411. No entry

412. Pollard, Bruce G. Managing the Interface: Intergovernmental Affairs Agencies in Canada. Kingston, Ont.: Institute of Intergovernmental Relations, Queen's University, 1986.

413. Ponting, J. Rick, and Gibbins, Roger. Out of Irrelevance: A Socio-Political Introduction to Indian Affairs in Canada. Toronto: Butterworths, 1980.

414. Prévost, J.-P. La crise du fédéralisme canadien. [The Crisis of Canadian Federalism] Paris: Presses universitaires de France, 1972.

415. Rawlyk, George A., Hodgins, Bruce, and Bowles, Richard P. Regionalism in Canada: Flexible Federalism or Fractured Nation? Scarborough, Ont.: Prentice-Hall of Canada, 1979. An examination of regionalism after the 1976 Quebec election of the Parti Québécois. Analysis of culture, economic policy, federalism, and historical background.

416. Rea, K. J., and McLeod, J. T., eds. Business and Government in Canada: Selected Readings. 2nd ed. Toronto: Methuen, 1976. The political context of business, how government promotes and controls business, and how the role has changed in recent years.

417. Remillard, Gil. Le federalisme canadien: elements constitutionnels de formation et d'evolution. [Canadian Federalism: Constitutional Elements of Its Formation and Evolution] Montréal: Québec/Amérique, 1980. 2nd ed. 1983.

418. Resnick, Mark. The Energy Crisis: OPEC and a Canadian Perspective. Montreal: Canada-Israel Committee, 1979.

419. Reuber, Grant L. Canada's Political Economy: Current Issues. Toronto: McGraw-Hill Ryerson, 1980. Includes discussion of a just society, international economic relations, aid to Third World nations, and relations with multinational corporations.

420. Reynolds, Rob. Federalism and Intergovernmental Relations in Canada and Other Countries: A Supplementary Bibliography. Kingston, Ontario: Queen's University Institute of Intergovernmental Relations, 1979.

421. Rose, A. *Canadian Housing Policies, 1935-1980*. Toronto: Butterworths, 1980.

422. Rotstein, Abraham. *Rebuilding From Within: Remedies for Canada's Ailing Economy*. Toronto: Lorimer, 1984.

423. Roy, Nicolas. *Mobility of Capital in the Canadian Economic Union*. Toronto: University of Toronto Press, 1986.

424. Safarian, A.E. *Foreign Direct Investment: A Survey of Canadian Research*. Montreal: Institute for Research on Public Policy, 1985. Discussion of theories of foreign direct investment, economic analysis of these theories, and policy implications of foreign direct investment upon social and economic issues.

425. Saunders, J. Owen, ed. *Managing Natural Resources in a Federal State: Essays from the Second Banff Conference on Natural Resources Law*. Toronto: Carswell, 1986.

426. Savoie, Donald J. *The Canada-New Brunswick General Development Agreement*. Montreal: McGill-Queen's University Press, 1981.

427. Savoie, Donald J., ed. *The Canadian Economy: A Regional Perspective*. Toronto: Methuen, 1986.

428. Scheffer, W.F., ed. *Energy Impacts on Public Policy and Administration*. Toronto: Burns and MacEachern, 1976.

429. Schultz, Richard. *Federalism and the Regulatory Process*. Montreal: Institute for Research on Public Policy, 1979. Study of how federal-provincial relations affect the regulatory agencies and processes in Canada.

430. Schultz, Richard. *Federalism, Bureaucracy, and Public Policy: The Politics of Highway Transport Regulation*. Montreal: McGill-Queen's University Press, 1980. Study of the National Transportation Act, 1967, and how federal-provincial tensions and negotiations prevented policy in this area from being effective.

431. Scott, A., ed. *Natural Resource Revenues: A Test of Federalism*. Vancouver: University of British Columbia Press, 1976.

432. Shaffer, Ed. *Canada's Oil and the American Empire*. Edmonton, Alberta: Hurtig, 1983.

433. Shillington, C.H. *The Road to Medicare in Canada*. Toronto: Del Graphics, 1972.

434. Silverstein, Ben. *Bilingualism in Canada: A Public Policy Bibliography*. Monticello, Ill.: Vance Bibliographies, 1987.

435. Simeon, R., ed. *Confrontation and Collaboration: Intergovernmental Relations in Canada Today*. Toronto: Institute of Public Administration of Canada, 1979.

436. Simeon, Richard. *Division of Powers and Public Policy*. Toronto: University of Toronto Press, 1985. Analysis of economic federalism's impact upon the federal system, constitutional aspects of economic development policy, the nature of the division of powers in Canada, and analysis of how federal and provincial governments work on public policy together.

437. Simeon, Richard. *Federal-Provincial Diplomacy: The Making of Recent Policy in Canada*. Toronto: University of Toronto Press, 1972. Insightful study of how Canada's eleven governments attempt to coordinate their efforts and formulate coherent policy. Case studies of federalism, constitutional reform, pension reform, and financial policy-making.

438. Simeon, Richard, ed. *Intergovernmental Relations*. Toronto: University of Toronto Press, 1985. Analysis of executive federalism, how economic policy can be formulated in a federal state, different theories of Canadian federalism, and the role of municipalities and local governments in Canadian federalism.

439. Simeon, Richard, ed. *Must Canada Fail?* Montreal: McGill-Queen's University Press, 1977.

440. Smiley, Donald. *Canada in Question: Federalism in the Eighties*. Toronto: McGraw Hill Ryerson, 1980. Discussion of major issues of contention in Canadian federalism. Includes discussion of the concept of constitutional reform, executive federalism, and economic and cultural aspects of federalism.

441. Smiley, Donald. *Canada in Question: Federalism in the Seventies*. Toronto: McGraw Hill Ryerson, 1972.

442. Smiley, Donald. *Constitutional Adaptation and Canadian Federalism Since 1945*. Ottawa: Queen's Printer for Canada, 1970. Document prepared for the Royal Commission on Bilingualism and Biculturalism covering postwar Canadian federalism, fiscal relations between the federal government and the provinces, and a discussion of a theory of cooperative federalism.

443. Smiley, Donald, and Watts, Ronald. *Intrastate Federalism in Canada*. Toronto: University of Toronto Press, 1985. Examination of how the Canadian Constitution affects intrastate federalism, how the Canadian version of intrastate federalism compares with other federal systems, and how the executive, the two legislative structures, and the Supreme Court are all affected by, and in their turn affect, intrastate federalism in Canada.

444. Sproule-Jones, M. H. *Public Choice and Federalism in Australia and Canada*. Canberra: Centre for Research on Federal Financial Relations, Australian National University, 1975.

445. Stanbury, W.T. *Business Interests and the Reform of Canadian Competition Policy, 1971-1975*. Toronto: Methuen, 1977.

446. Stanbury, W.T., ed. *Government Regulation: Scope, Growth, Process*. Montreal: Institute for Research on Public Policy, 1980.

447. Stanbury, W.T., ed. *Studies on Regulation in Canada*. Toronto: Butterworths, 1979.

448. Stanbury, W.T., and Thomson Fred. *Regulatory Reform in Canada*. Institute for Research on Public Policy, 1982.

449. Stevenson, Garth. *Unfulfilled Union: Canadian Federalism and National Unity*. Toronto: Macmillan of Canada, 1979. Study of Canadian federalism, including the nature of federalism, economic federalism, fiscal federalism, resolution of intergovernmental conflict, and possible reform of the Constitution.

450. Stewart, Walter. *Uneasy Lies the Head: The Truth About Canada's Crown Corporations*. Toronto: Collins, 1987.

451. Stone, Leroy O., and Marceau, Claude. *Canadian Population Trends and Public Policy Through the 1980s*. Montreal: Published for the Institute for Research on Public Policy by McGill-Queen's University Press, 1977. Analysis of Canadian public policy issues related to population trends, with specific discussion of urban issues.

452. Studnicki-Gizert, K.W., ed. *Issues in Canadian Transport Policy*. Toronto: Macmillan, 1974.

453. Sunahara, Ann G. *The Politics of Racism: The Uprooting of Japanese Canadians During the Second World War*. Toronto: Lorimer, 1981. Study of the decision to relocate Japanese-Canadians, how they were deprived of their possessions and deported, and how they sought their rights and compensation.

454. Sutherland, Sharon L., and Doern, G. Bruce. Le bureaucratie au Canada: controle et reforme. [The Bureaucracy in Canada: Control and Reform] Toronto: Commission royale sur l'union economique et les perspectives de developpement du Canada, 1986.

455. Tanner, Adrian, ed. The Politics of Indianness: Case Studies of Native Ethnopolitics in Canada. St. John's, Nfld.: Institute of Social and Economic Research, 1983. Essays focus upon political behavior of Canadian Indians, both within the Indian community and in relation to federal and provincial governments.

456. Task Force on Canadian Unity. A Future Together: Observations and Recommendations. Ottawa: Task Force on Canadian Unity, 1979.

457. Task Force on Canadian Unity. A Time to Speak: The Views of the Public. Ottawa: Minister of Supply and Services Canada, 1979.

458. Task Force on Canadian Unity. Definir pour choisir: vocabulaire du debat. [Coming to Terms: Vocabulary of the Debate.] Ottawa: Task Force on Canadian Unity, 1979.

459. Taylor, Malcolm Gordon. Health Insurance and Canadian Public Policy: The Seven Decisions That Created the Canadian Health Insurance System. Montreal: McGill-Queen's University Press, 1978. Comprehensive history of the development of the Canadian health insurance system and the political pressure groups and lobbies active in that decision era.

460. Thompson, Fred, and Stanbury, W. T. The Political Economy of Interest Groups in the Legislative Process in Canada. Montreal: Institute for Research on Public Policy, 1979.

461. Thur, O.M., ed. Energy Policy and Federalism. Toronto: Seminar Publication, Institute of Public Administration of Canada, 1980.

462. Trudeau, Pierre Elliott. A Time for Action: Toward the Renewal of the Canadian Federation. Ottawa: Government of Canada, 1978. The now-classic articulation of Prime Minister Trudeau's vision of a new Canadian federal system.

463. Veilleux, G. Les relations intergouvernementales au Canada, 1867-1967: les mécanismes de coopération. [Intergovernmental Relations in Canada, 1867-1967: Mechanisms of Cooperation] Montréal: Presses de l'Université du Québec, 1971.

464. Walker, Michael, ed. <u>Canadian Confederation at the Crossroads: The Search for a Federal-Provincial Balance</u>. Vancouver: Fraser Institute, 1978. Includes discussion of federal-provincial fiscal relations, regulatory power, legal consistency across provinces, education and language policy, law enforcement, and housing and urban development policy.

465. Waller, Harold M., Sabetti, Filippo, and Elazar, Daniel Judah, eds. <u>Canadian Federalism: From Crisis to Constitution</u>. Lanham, MD: University Press of America, 1988.

466. Watkins, G.C., and Walker, M.A., eds. <u>Reaction: The National Energy Program</u>. Vancouver: Fraser Institute, 1981.

467. Waverman, Leonard. <u>The Process of Telecommunications Regulation in Canada</u>. Ottawa: Economic Council of Canada, 1982.

468. Weaver, Sally. <u>Making Canadian Indian Policy: The Hidden Agenda, 1968-1970</u>. Toronto: University of Toronto Press, 1981. Background, processes, and effects of changes in Indian policy as discussed in the 1969 government White Paper.

469. Weeks, K.M. <u>Ombudsmen Around the World: A Comparative Chart</u>. Berkeley: University of California Press, 1978.

470. Weisstub, David N., ed. <u>Law and Policy</u>. Toronto: Osgoode Hall Law School, York University, 1976. A collection of essays and lectures dealing with the interaction of law with public policy.

471. White, W.L. et al. <u>Canadian Confederation: A Decision-Making Analysis</u>. Toronto: Macmillan of Canada, 1979. Study of many of the problems of federalism, shifts in power, and political actions by both the federal government and the provinces. The methodology of this study is to treat confederation as a dependent variable, and to examine those factors influencing it, including political, economic, and sociological variables.

472. White, W.L., and Strick, J.C. <u>Policy, Politics, and the Treasury Board in Canadian Government</u>. Don Mills, Ont.: Science Research Associates, 1970.

473. Williams, Glen. <u>Not for Export: Toward a Political Economy of Canada's Arrested Industrialization</u>. Toronto: McClelland and Stewart, 1983.

474. Wilson, B. <u>Canada's Energy Policy</u>. Toronto: Lorimer, 1980.

475. Wilson, B.F. *The Energy Squeeze: Canadian Policies for Survival.* Toronto: Lorimer, 1980.

476. Wilson, Michael H. *The Canadian Budgetary Process: Proposals for Improvement.* Ottawa: Department of Finance, Canada, 1985.

477. Wilson, V. Seymour. *Canadian Public Policy and Administration: Theory and Environment.* Toronto: McGraw Hill Ryerson, 1981.

478. Wiltshire, Kenneth. *Planning and Federalism: Australian and Canadian Experience.* New York: University of Queensland Press in Association with the Centre for Research on Federal Financial Relations, Australian National University, 1986.

479. Woodrow, R. Brian, et al. *Conflict Over Communications Policy: A Study of Federal-Provincial Relations and Public Policy.* Montreal: C.D. Howe Institute, 1980.

480. Yelaja, S.A., ed. *Canadian Social Policy.* Waterloo: Wilfrid Laurier University Press, 1978.

481. Zukowsky, Ronald J. *Intergovernmental Relations in Canada: The Year in Review, 1980.* Kingston, Ontario: Institute of Intergovernmental Relations, 1981.

Articles

482. Adams, Mark S., and Steiner, Barry. "Energy and the North American Community: Canada, Mexico, and the United States." *Hastings International and Comparative Law Review* 3:3 (1980): 369-434. Need for, and possible organization of, a North American Community, a formal energy alliance among the three North American nations.

483. Adamson, Agar. "The Fulton-Favreau Formula: A Study of Its Development, 1960 to 1966." *Journal of Canadian Studies* 6:1 (1971): 45-55.

484. Allen, J. Garfield. "The Flaw in Canadian Federalism." *Round Table* 278 (1980): 172-176. A study of whether Canada is governable if governance means regaining control of the economy, utilizing resources, and providing channels of participation to the entire public.

485. Anderson, F.J. "Price Formation in the Canadian Crude Oil Sector." *Canadian Public Policy* 2:1 (Winter, 1976): 1-16.

486. Andiappan, P. "Public Policy and Equal Pay: A Comparative Study of Equal Pay Laws in Canada, the U.S.A., and the U.K." International Review of Administrative Sciences 51:1 (1985): 24-32.

487. Armstrong, Christopher. "Federalism and Government Regulation: The Case of the Canadian Insurance Industry, 1927-34." Canadian Public Administration 19:1 (1976): 88-101.

488. Arvay, Joseph. "Newfoundland's Claim to Offshore Mineral Resources: An Overview of the Legal Issues." Canadian Public Policy 5:1 (Winter, 1979): 32-44.

489. Atherton, P.J. "Education: Radical Reform in Nova Scotia." Canadian Public Policy 1:3 (Summer, 1975): 384-392.

490. Atkinson, Michael. "On the Prospects for Industrial Policy in Canada." Canadian Public Administration 27:3 (1984): 454-467.

491. Atkinson, Michael. "Policy Interests of Provincial Backbenchers and the Effects of Political Ambition." Legislative Studies Quarterly 3:4 (1978): 629-646.

492. Aucoin, Peter. "Public Policy Analysis and the Canadian Health Care System." Canadian Public Administration 23:1 (1980): 166-174.

493. Aucoin, Peter, and French, Richard. "The Ministry of State for Science and Technology." Canadian Public Administration 17:3 (1974): 461-481.

494. Auld, Douglas. "Human Resources and Social Support Policy in Canada." Canadian Public Policy 12 (1986): 84-91. Review of the Report of the Royal Commssion on the Economic Union and the Development Prospects for Canada, 1985, otherwise known as the MacDonald Report.

495. Auld, Douglas. "Prediction Accuracy and The Canadian Federal Budget." Futures 16:5 (1984): 513-519.

496. Auld, Douglas. "Social Welfare and Decision-Making in the Public Sector." Canadian Public Administration 16:4 (Winter, 1973): 604-612.

497. Auld, D.A.L. "Stabilization and Harmonization." Canadian Public Policy 8:3 (1983): 307-310.

498. Babe, Robert E. "Public and Private Regulation of Cable Television: A Case Study of Technological Change and Relative Power." Canadian Public Administration 17:2 (Summer, 1974): 187-225.

499. Babe, Robert E. "Regulation of Private Television Broadcasting by the Canadian Radio-Television Commission: A Critique of Ends and Means." Canadian Public Administration 19:4 (1976): 552-586.

500. Baetz, R.C., and Collins, K. "Equity Aspects of Income Security Programs." Canadian Public Policy 1:4 (Autumn, 1975): 487-497.

501. Bailey, Robert H. "Some Considerations Related to Environmental Influence Assessment." Canadian Public Administration 16:3 (Fall, 1973): 370-380.

502. Baldwin, John R. "The Evolution of Transportation Policy in Canada." Canadian Public Administration 20:4 (1977): 600-631.

503. Baldwin, John R. "Transportation Policy and Jurisdictional Issues." Canadian Public Administration 18:4 (Winter, 1975): 630-641.

504. Bale, Gordon. "The Treasury's Proposals for Tax Reform: A Canadian Perspective." Law and Contemporary Problems 48:4 (1985): 151-196.

505. Ballentine, J.G., and Thirsk, W.R. "The Effects of Revenue Sharing on the Distribution of Disposable Incomes." Canadian Public Policy 6:1 (Winter, 1980): 30-40.

506. Balls, Herbert R. "New Techniques in Government Budgeting: Planning, Programming, and Budgeting in Canada." Public Administration 48:3 (1970): 289-306.

507. Barbe, Raoul. "The Control of Enterprises by Canadian Parliament," Canadian Public Administration 12 (1969) 463-481.

508. Barbe, Raoul. "Le domaine public au Canada." ["The Public Domain in Canada."] Revue juridique et politique 24:4 (1970): 879-912. Definition of the public domain, and discussion of the relationship between the federal public domain and provincial public domains.

509. Bartha, Peter. "Organizational Competence in Business-Government Relations: A Managerial Perspective." Canadian Public Administration 28:2 (Summer, 1985): 202-220.

510. Bastien, Richard. "Canadian Federalism and Its Problems." Études (1982): 597-610.

511. Bastien, Richard. "La structure fiscale du fédéralisme canadien: 1945-73." ["The Fiscal Structure of Canadian Federalism."] Canadian Public Administration 17:1 (1974): 96-118.

512. Beckman, M. Dale. "The Problem of Communicating Public Policy Effectively: Bill C-256 and Winnipeg Businessmen." Canadian Journal of Political Science 8:1 (1975): 138-143. Politicians and administrators need to create awareness of new policies or proposed policy changes. A case study.

513. Bédard, Denis. "L'économie publique: Suggestions pour une amélioration des choix politiques." ["The Public Economy: Suggestions for an Improvement of Political Choices."] Canadian Public Administration 16:3 (1973): 483-492.

514. Beigie, C.E. "The Optimum Use of Canadian Resources." Proceedings of the Academy of Political Science 32:2 (1976): 164-175.

515. Bélanger, Gérard. "Les aspéts économiques des programmes de sécurité financière pour les personnes âgées." ["Economic Aspects of Financial Security Programs for Aged Persons."] Canadian Public Administration 26:1 (1983):

516. Bélanger, Marcel. "La rapport Bélanger: dix ans après." ["The Bélanger Report: Ten Years Later."] Canadian Public Administration 19:3 (1976): 457-465.

517. Bella, Leslie. "The Provincial Role in the Canadian Welfare State: The Influence of Provincial Social Policy Initiatives on the Design of the Canada Assistance Plan." Canadian Public Administration 22:3 (1979): 439-452.

518. Bellrichard, Suzanne. "Voices from the Margin." Canadian Journal of Political and Social Theory 10:3 (1986): 1-4.

519. Benjamin, J. "La rationalisation des choix budgétaires: le cas québécois et canadien." ["The Rationalization of Budgetary Choices."] Canadian Journal of Political Science 5:3 (1972): 348-364. "Economic rationality" versus "political rationality" of budgetary theory in th U.S., Canada, and Quebec; the problem lies in determining who ought to define society's needs and objectives.

520. Bennett, S.E. "Do Public Program Clients Understand Public Program Rules? The Manitoba Basic Annual Income Experiment." Canadian Public Administration 29:3 (1986): 462-268.

521. Bergeron, Pierre, and Ferguson, James F. "Anatomy of Planning in the Public Service Commission of Canada." Optimum 10:3 (1979): 48-63. The Public Service Commission has a new systematic and integrated management approach which links many sub-systems into one process.

522. Berkes, Fikret. "Management of Recreational Fisheries in Northern Quebec: Policies Versus Tools." Canadian Public Policy 4:4 (Autumn, 1978): 460-473.

523. Bernard, Jean--Thomas. "La Rente Des Ressources Naturelles." ["Rent of Natural Resources"] Canadian Public Policy 8:3 (1983): 297-299.

524. Berry, G.R. "The Oil Lobby and the Energy Crisis." Canadian Public Administration 14:4 (1974): 600-635.

525. Bird, Richard. "The Incidence of the Property Tax: Old Wine in New Bottles." Canadian Public Policy (Special Issue, 1976): 323-334.

526. Bird, Richard. "Tax Harmonization and Federal Finance: A Perspective on Recent Canadian Discussion." Canadian Public Policy 10:3 (September, 1984): 253-266.

527. Bird, Richard, and Slack, Enid. "Can Property Taxes Be Reformed? Reflections on the Ontario Experience." Canadian Public Administration 24:3 (1981): 469-485.

528. Black, Alexander. "Jurisdiction Over Petroleum Operations in Canada." International and Comparative Law Quarterly 35:2 (1986): 446-455.

529. Black, Erroll. "A New Deal for Paupers(?) -- Report of the Manitoba Task Force on Social Assistance." Contemporary Crises: Crime, Law, and Social Policy 9:3 (1985): 281-296.

530. Black, Erroll. "One Too Many Reports on Poverty in Canada." Canadian Journal of Political Science 5:3 (1972): 439-443. Bibliographic essay dealing with recent studies of Canadian poverty.

531. Blair, David. "Energy Security and Canadian Energy Policy: Collective versus Independent Action." Millennium Journal of International Studies 11:2 (1982): 130-148. Canadian responses to fears of "energy vulnerability" in the 1970's, and the importance of the concept of energy security.

532. Blais, André, Faucher, Philippe, and Young, Robert. "La dynamique de l'aide financière direct du gouvernement fédéral à l'industie manufacturière au Canada." ["Dynamics of Direct Federal Government Financing for the Manufacturing Industry in Canada."] Canadian Journal of Political Science 19:1 (1986): 29-52.

533. Boadway, R., Flatters, F., and LeBlanc, A. "Revenue Sharing and the Equalization of Natural Resource Revenues." Canadian Public Policy 9:2 (June, 1983): 174-180.

534. Boase, Joan. "Regulation and the Paramedical Professions: An Interest Group Study." Canadian Public Administration 25:3 (Fall, 1982): 332-353.

535. Boismenu, Gérard, DuCatenzeiler, Graciela, and Anderson, Frances. "L'aide directe fédérale à l'innovation industrielle." ["Direct Federal Aid for Industrial Innovation."] Politique 8 (1985): 45-76.

536. Bonin, Bernard, and Moran, Patrick. "L'environnement et la portée de l'évaluation." ["The Environment and the Scope of Evaluation."] Canadian Public Administration 24:3 (1981): 387-403.

537. Boucher, M. "La réforme fiscale de l'impôt sur le revenu des particuliers était-elle nécessaire?" ["Fiscal Reform of Taxes on Specific Income: Is it Necessary?"] Canadian Public Policy 1:4 (Autumn, 1975): 527-535.

538. Boyd, Neil. "The Dilemma of Canadian Narcotics Legislation: The Social Control of Altered States of Consciousness." Contemporary Crises: Crime, Law, and Social Policy 7:3 (1983): 257-270.

539. Brachet, B. "La crise du fédéralisme canadien et le problème québécois." ["The Crisis of Canadian Federalism and the Problem of Quebec."] Revue du Droit public et de la Science politique 88:2 (1972): 303-324.

540. Braën, André. "La formation des professionnels de la santé au Nouveau-Brunswick ou l'application du principe de l'inégalité." ["The Development of Health Professionals in New Brunswick, or the Application of the Principle of Inequality."] Canadian Public Administration 26:2 (Summer, 1983): 286-300.

541. Brazeau, J.A.R. "Great Immigration Debate: Special Attention for Refugees." International Perspectives (September/October, 1975): 13-18.

542. Bregha, F. "The Mackenzie Valley Pipeline and Canadian Natural Gas Policy." Canadian Public Policy 3:1 (Winter, 1977): 63-75.

543. Brooks, Stephen. "The State as Entrepreneur: From CDC to CDIC." Canadian Public Administration 26:4 (1983): 525-543. Focuses upon the cases of the Canada Development Corporation and the Canada Development Investment Corporation and provides a critique of the joint stock company as an instrument of public policy.

544. Brown, J. Everett. "Taxation of Farm Lands." Governmental Finance 4:2 (1975): 20-24. British Columbia policy to help low taxes on farm lands and recoup tax incomes elsewhere.

545. Brown, Malcolm C. "The Public Finance of Medical and Dental Care in Newfoundland -- Some Historical and Economic Considerations." *Journal of Social Policy* 10:2 (1981): 209-228.

546. Brown, M. Paul. "Environment Canada and the Pursuit of Administrative Decentralization." *Canadian Public Administration* 29:2 (1986): 218-236.

547. Brown, M. Paul. "Responsiveness Versus Accountability in Collaborative Federalism: The Canadian Experience." *Canadian Public Administration* 26:4 (1983): 629-639. A critique of proposals for a parliamentary solution to the problem of accountability in Canadian federalism.

548. Brown-John, C. Lloyd. "Comprehensive Regulatory Consultation in Canada's Food Processing Industry." *Canadian Public Administration* 28:1 (1985): 70-98.

549. Brown-John, C. Lloyd. "Defining Regulatory Agencies for Analytical Purposes." *Canadian Public Administration* 19:1 (Spring, 1976): 140-157.

550. Brown-John, C. Lloyd. "Membership in Canadian Regulatory Agencies." *Canadian Public Administration* 20:3 (1977): 513-533.

551. Burns, Ronald M. "Intergovernmental Relations in Canada." *Public Administration Review* 33:1 (1973): 14-22. Describes the constitutional basis for intergovernmental relations in Canada, how powers are distributed, and the importance of different types of revenue transfers and conditional grants.

552. Bushnell, S. "The Control of Natural Resources Through the Trade and Commerce Power and Proprietary Rights." *Canadian Public Policy* 6:2 (Spring, 1980): 313-324.

553. Cabatoff, Kenneth. "Radio-Québec: Une institution publique à la recherche d'une mission." ["Radio-Quebec: A Public Institution in Search of a Mission."] *Canadian Public Administration* 19:4 (Winter, 1976): 542-551.

554. Cairns, Alan. "The Governments and Societies of Canadian Federalism." *Canadian Journal of Political Science* 10:4 (1977): 695-725. Capacity of the federal governmental system to make contemporary Canadian society responsive to its demands.

555. Cairns, Alan. "The Other Crisis of Canadian Federalism." *Canadian Public Administration* 22:2 (1979): 175-195.

556. Cameron, David. "Equity and Efficiency." *Canadian Public Policy* 8:3 (1983): 299-303.

557. Cameron, N. "The Taxation of Policyholders' Life Insurance Income." Canadian Public Policy 3:2 (Spring, 1977): 129-140.

558. Campbell, A.E.H. "Regulations and the Orwellian State." Canadian Public Administration 28:1 (1985): 150-155.

559. Campbell, C., and Reese, T. "The Energy Crisis and Tax Policy in Canada and the United States: Federal-Provincial Diplomacy vs. Congressional Law Making." Social Science Journal (Fort Collins) 14:1 (1977): 17-32. A comparison of policies Canada and the U.S. use to deal with the energy crisis.

560. Campbell, H.F. "A Benefit/Cost Rule for Evaluating Public Projects in Canada." Canadian Public Policy 1:2 (Spring, 1975): 171-175.

561. Caplan, Neil. "Anatomy of a Federal-Provincial Conflict." Journal of Canadian Studies 5:1 (1970): 50-61.

562. Carmichael, Edward, Dobson, Wendy, and Lipsey, Richard. "The MacDonald Report: Signpost or Shopping Basket?" Canadian Public Policy 12 (1986): 23-39. Review of the Report of the Royal Commssion on the Economic Union and the Development Prospects for Canada, 1985, known as the MacDonald Report.

563. Carroll, John E. "Water Resources Management as an Issue in Environmental Diplomacy." Natural Resources Journal 26:2 (1986): 207-220.

564. Carter, Richard. "Causes and Remedies of the `Crisis' of Public Finance in Quebec." Politique 3 (1983): 91-116.

565. Cartwright, D. "An Official-Languages Policy for Ontario." Canadian Public Policy 11:3 (September, 1985): 561-577.

566. Castonguay, Charles. "Why Hide the Facts? The Federalist Approach to the Language Crisis in Canada." Canadian Public Policy 5:1 (Winter, 1979): 4-15.

567. Chambers, E.J., et al. "Bill C-20: An Evaluation from the Perspective of Current Transportation Policy and Regulatory Performance." Canadian Public Policy 6:1 (Winter, 1980): 47-62.

568. Chandler, Marsha. "Constitutional Change and Public Policy: The Impact of Resource Amendment (Section 92A)." Canadian Journal of Political Science 19:1 (1986): 103-126. The expansion of provincial jurisdiction given by the Amendment gives the provinces more legitimacy and power in relation to Ottawa at the Federal-Provincial bargaining table.

569. Chapman, Brian. "The Canadian Police Force: A Survey." *Government and Opposition* 12:4 (1977): 496-516.

570. Christofides, L.N. "The Federal Government's Budget Constraint, 1955-1975." *Canadian Public Policy* 3:3 (Summer, 1977): 291-298.

571. Chung, Daniel Cayley. "Internal Security: Establishment of Canadian Security Intelligence Service." *Harvard International Law Journal* 26:1 (1985): 234-248.

572. Clayton, F.A. "Real Property Tax Assessment Practices in Canada." *Canadian Public Policy* (Special Issue, 1976): 347-355.

573. Cohen, J., and Krashinsky, M. "Capturing the Rents on Resource Land for the Public Landowner: The Case for a Crown Corporation." *Canadian Public Policy* 2:3 (Summer, 1976): 411-423.

574. Cole, R. Taylor. "The Universities and Governments Under Canadian Federalism." *The Journal of Politics* 34:2 (1972): 524-553.

575. Coleman, William D. "Analyzing the Associative Action of Business: Policy Advocacy and Policy Participation." *Canadian Public Administration* 28:3 (1985): 413-433.

576. Comeau, Robert. "Money, Inflation, and the Bank of Canada: A Review." *Canadian Public Policy* 2:4 (Autumn, 1976): 626-630.

577. Conklin, David, and Courchene, Thomas. "New Institutions for a Market Economy." *Canadian Public Policy* 12 (1986): 40-50. Review of the Report of the Royal Commssion on the Economic Union and the Development Prospects for Canada, 1985, otherwise known as the MacDonald Report.

578. Copes, Parzival. "Canada's Atlantic Coast Fisheries: Policy Development and the Impact of Extended Jurisdiction." *Canadian Public Policy* 4:2 (Spring, 1978): 155-171.

579. Copes, Parzival. "The Economics of Marine Fisheries Management in the Era of Extended Jurisdiction: The Canadian Perspective." *American Economic Review* 69:2 (1979): 256-260. Effects of the 200-mile limit of jurisdiction over marine rights upon fisheries.

580. Courchene, Thomas. "Canada's New Equalization Program: Description and Evaluation." *Canadian Public Policy* 9:4 (1983): 458-475. Describes and evaluates aspects of the new formula for insuring that provinces have appropriate per capita revenues.

581. Courchene, Thomas. "The Poverty Reports, Negative Income Taxation, and the Constitution: An Analysis and a Compromise Proposal." Canadian Public Administration 16:3 (1973): 349-369.

582. Courchene, Thomas, and Melvin, J. "Energy Revenues: Consequences for the Rest of Canada." Canadian Public Policy (Special Issue, 1980): 192-204.

583. Courville, L., and Dagenais, M.G. "On New Approaches to the Regulation of Bell Canada." Canadian Public Policy 3:1 (Winter, 1977): 76-89.

584. Cousineau, J.-M., and LaCroix, R. "L'Indexation des salaires et le retour à la stabilité des prix." ["Indexation of Salaries and the Return to Price Stability."] Canadian Public Policy 3:2 (Spring, 1977): 155-163.

585. Crowley, R.W. "The Property Tax and Public Policy: A Conference Overview." Canadian Public Policy (Special Issue, 1976): 299-303.

586. Crozier, R.B. "Deficit Financing and Inflation: A Review of the Evidence: Canadian Public Policy 3:3 (Summer, 1977): 270-277.

587. Cutt, James. "Efficiency and Effectiveness in Public Sector Spending: The Programme Budgeting Approach." Canadian Public Administration 13:4 (1970): 396-404.

588. Daly, Michael. "The Swedish Approach to Investing Public Pension Funds: Some Lessons for Canada?" Canadian Public Administration 24:2 (Summer, 1981): 257-271.

589. Darling, Howard. "What Belongs in Transport Policy?" Canadian Public Administration 18:4 (Winter, 1975): 659-669.

590. Davies, D.G. "Tri-Level Task Force on Public Finance in Canada: A Review." Canadian Public Policy 3:1 (Winter, 1977): 114-117.

591. Davies, G.W. "General Income Averaging." Canadian Public Policy 3:2 (Spring, 1977): 164-170.

592. Deans, Tom, and Ware, Alan. "Charity-State Relations: A Conceptual Analysis." Journal of Public Policy 6:2 (1986): 121-135. Compares charity-state relations in England, Canada, and the U.S.

593. Dennis, F.R. "Alleviating the Tax Burden: A Search for Solutions." Governmental Finance 4:2 (1975): 20-24. History of tax rebate and tax reduction programs in Manitoba.

594. DesRochers, Gilles. "Le financement des établissements de santé et de services sociaux." ["The Financing of Health Establishments and Social Services."] Canadian Public Administration 22:3 (1979): 366-379.

595. Dewees, D.N., and Waverman, L. "Energy Conservation: Policies for the Transport Sector." Canadian Public Policy 3:2 (Spring, 1977): 171-185.

596. Dirks, Gerald E. "A Policy Within a Policy: The Identification and Admission of Refugees to Canada." Canadian Journal of Political Science 17:2 (1984): 279-308.

597. Dobell, Peter C. "Quebec Separatism as a Provocation for the Canadian Federal State." Europa-Archiv 32:7 (1977): 215-226.

598. Doern, G. Bruce. "The Mega-Project Episode and the Formulation of Canadian Economic Development Policy." Canadian Public Administration 26:2 (1983): 219-238.

599. Doern, G. Bruce. "The National Research Council: The Causes of Goal Displacement." Canadian Public Administration 13:2 (Summer, 1970): 140-184.

600. Doern, G. Bruce. "The Political Economy of Regulating Occupational Health: The Ham and Beaudry Reports." Canadian Public Administration 20:1 (Spring, 1977): 1-35.

601. Doern, G. Bruce. "Recent Changes in the Philosophy of Policy-Making in Canada." Canadian Journal of Political Science 4:2 (1971): 243-264.

602. Doern, G. Bruce. "Science and Technology in the Nuclear Regulatory Process: The Case of Canadian Uranium Miners." Canadian Public Administration 21:1 (1978): 51-82.

603. Doern, G. Bruce, Hunter, Ian, Swartz, Donald, and Wilson, V. Seymour. "The Structure and Behaviour of Canadian Regulatory Boards and Commissions: Multidisciplinary Perspectives." Canadian Public Administration 18:2 (1975): 189-215.

604. Doerr, Audrey. "Public Administration: Federalism and Intergovernmental Relations." Canadian Public Administration 25:4 (1982): 564-579.

605. Doerr, Audrey. "The Role of Coloured Papers." Canadian Public Administration 25:3 (Fall, 1982): 366-379.

606. Dohle, Gordon. "Government Secrecy in Canada." *Indian Journal of Public Administration* 25:4 (1979): 1025-1035. Examines the concept of governmental secrecy and the Public Service Employment Act and the Federal Court Act as tools of the Government to enforce secrecy.

607. Drache, Daniel. "Rediscovering Canadian Political Economy." *Journal of Canadian Studies* 11:3 (1976): 3-17.

608. Drewry, G. "Parliament and Hanging: Further Episodes in an Undying Saga." *Parliamentary Affairs* 27:3 (1974): 251-261.

609. Drury, C.M. "Quantitative Analysis and Public Policy Making." *Canadian Public Policy* 1:1 (Winter, 1975): 89-96.

610. Duckett, Stephen. "Recent Developments in Canadian Health Services: Lessons for Australia." *Australian Quarterly* 55:1 (1983): 54-65. Reviews Canadian experience, and traces recent Canadian developments including topics of national health policy, extra billing, "opting out," single source funding, and incrementalism.

611. Dunn, Robert, Jr. "Canada and Its Economic Discontents." *Foreign Affairs* 52:1 (1973): 119-140.

612. Dunn, Sheilagh M. "Federalism, Constitutional Reform, and the Economy: The Canadian Experience." *Publius* 13:2 (1983): 129-142. Discusses the new Constitution and its implications for fiscal arrangements, specifically covering the new policies of the federal government providing payments to provinces whether or not they participate in federal-provincial programs.

613. Dupré, J. Stefan. "Reflections on the Fiscal and Economic Aspects of Government by Conference." *Canadian Public Administration* 23:1 (1980): 54-59.

614. Dwivedi, O.P. "The Canadian Government Response to Environmental Concern," *International Journal* 28:1 (1973): 134-152.

615. Dwivedi, O.P. "Environmental Administration in Canada." *International Review of Administrative Sciences* 39:2 (1973): 149-157. Examines the background which led to the establishment of the Federal Department of the Environment in Canada, with focus on environmental pollution issues.

616. Dyck, Rand. "The Canada Assistance Plan: The Ultimate in Cooperative Federalism." *Canadian Public Administration* 19:4 (1976): 587-602.

617. Edwards, Miriam. "Public Choice Theory and Petroleum Policies in Canada, Britain, and Norway." European Journal of Political Research 15:3 (1987): 363-380.

618. Efrat, E.S. "Federations in Crisis -- The Failure of the Old Order." Western Political Quarterly 25:4 (1972): 589-599.

619. Ehrensaft, Philip. "L'Agriculture, l'État, et la stagflation mondiale: la politique canadienne depuis 1970." ["Agriculture, Government, and World Stagflation: Canadian Policy Since 1970."] Études internationales 12:1 (1981): 103-116. Describes general characteristics of the Canadian agricultural economy, and coonsiders changes in system since 1970 based upon energy costs, government regulation, and foreign trade.

620. Empey, W. "The Impact of Higher Energy Prices in Canada." Canadian Public Policy 7:1 (Winter, 1981): 28-34.

621. Esman, Milton J. "The Politics of Official Bilingualism in Canada." Political Science Quarterly 97:2 (1982): 233-254.

622. Esman, Milton J. "Federalism and Modernization: Canada and the United States." Publius 14:1 (1984): 21-38. Since World War II the American model of federalism has become more centralized, while the Canadian model has become less centralized. This essay explains why this is so.

623. Evans, R.G. "Health Services in Nova Scotia." Canadian Public Policy 1:3 (Summer, 1975): 355-366.

624. Feldman, Elliot J., and Feldman, Lily Gardner. "The Impact of Federalism on the Organization of Canadian Foreign Policy." Publius 14:4 (1984): 33-60. Several Canadian provinces have become more active in foreign policy areas in recent years, challenging traditional notions about a federal monopoly in this area. This article explains this phenomenon.

625. Finlayson, Jock. "Canada and Strategic Minerals." International Perspectives (September-October, 1982): 18-21. Government needs to take a position on stockpiling strategic minerals.

626. Foot, D.K. "The Demographic Future of Fiscal Federalism in Canada." Canadian Public Policy 10:4 (December, 1984): 406-414.

627. Fortin, Pierre. "La dimension économique de la crise politique canadienne." ["The Economic Dimension of the Canadian Political Crisis."] Canadian Public Policy 4:3 (Summer, 1978): 309-324.

628. Fortin, Pierre, Paquet, Gilles, and Rabeau, Yves. "Quebec in the Canadian Federation: A Provisional Evaluative Framework." Canadian Public Administration 21:4 (1978): 558-578.

629. Franks, C.E.S. "The Political Control of Security Activities." Queen's Quarterly 91:3 (1984): 565-577.

630. Frenette, Claude C. "Le rôle de l'état dans une société technologique." ["The Role of the State in a Technological Society."] Canadian Public Administration 15:3 (Fall, 1972): 441-448.

631. Friedland, Martin L. "National Security: Some Canadian Legal Perspectives." Israel Yearbook on Human Rights 10 (1980): 257-288. Study of the conflict between individual rights and state authority in three areas: the Official Secrets Act, wiretapping, and emergency legislation.

632. Friedmann, K.A., and Milne, A.G. "The Federal Ombudsman Legislaion: A Critique of Bill C-43." Canadian Public Policy 6:1 (1980): 63-77. A discussion of Bill C-43 and its effect on the federal Ombudsman's power.

633. Friedrich, Carl. "Political Decision-Making, Public Policy, and Planning," Canadian Public Administration 14 (1971): 1-16.

634. Fulton, M. Jane, and Stanbury, W. T. "Comparative Lobbying Strategies in Influencing Health Care Policy." Canadian Public Administration 28:2 (1985): 269-300.

635. Gainer, Walter D., and Powrie, T.L. "Public Revenue from Canadian Crude Petroleum Production." Canadian Public Policy 1:1 (Winter, 1975): 1-12.

636. Gainer, Walter D. "Western Disenchantment and the Canadian Federation." Proceedings of the Academy of Political Science 32:2 (1976): 40-52.

637. Galbraith, J., and Guthrie, A. "Canadian Banking Legislation Ottawa Style: Principles or Pragmatism." Canadian Public Policy 3:1 (Winter, 1977): 101-105.

638. Galligan, Brian. "Federalism and Resource Development in Australia and Canada." Australian Quarterly 54:3 (1982): 236-251. Discusses the Canadian version of "state entrepreneurship in a federal system."

639. Galvin, Charles O. "Tax Reform in the United States and Canada." Law and Contemporary Problems 44:3 (1981): 131-142.

640. Garant, Patrice, et al. "Le côntrole politique des organismes autonomes à fonctions regulatrices et quasi-judiciares." ["The Political Control of Autonomous Organisms in Regulatory and Quasi-Judicial Functions."] Canadian Public Administration 20:3 (Fall, 1977): 444-468.

641. Gay, D. "Réflexions critiques sur les politiques ethniques du gouvernement fédéral canadien 1971-1985 et du gouvernement du Québec." ["Critical Reflections on Ethnc Policy: Canada 1971-1985 and Quebec."] Revue internationale d'Action communautaire 54 (1985): 79-92. Study of Canadian and Quebec multicultural policy during this period.

642. Gibbins, Roger, et al. "Canadian Federalism, the Charter of Rights, and the 1984 Election." Publius 15:3 (1985): 155-169. The 1984 federal election could be significant for the Charter of Rights. Many see a general lessening of federal-provincial tensions creating an era of "national politics," not "territorial politics."

643. Giller, Thomas. "Decommissioning Nuclear Power Plants: The United States, West Germany, and Canada." Hastings International and Comparative Law Review 6:2 (1983): 433-516.

644. Gillespie, W. Irwin. "The June 1975 Budget: Stabilization and Distribution Effects." Canadian Public Policy 1:4 (Autumn, 1975): 546-556.

645. Gillespie, W. Irwin. "Tax Reform: The Battlefield, the Strategies, the Spoils." Canadian Public Administration 26:2 (Summer, 1983): 182-202.

646. Gillespie, W. Irwin, and Johnson, J.A. "Sales Tax Reform: A Critique of the Federal Government's Proposals." Canadian Public Policy 2:4 (Autumn, 1976):638-644.

647. Gilligan, Brian. "Federalism and Resource Development in Australia and Canada." Australian Quarterly 54:3 (1982): 236-251.

648. Globerman, S. "Canadian Science Policy and Technological Sovereignty." Canadian Public Policy 4:1 (Winter, 1978): 34-45.

649. Globerman, S., and Book, S.H. "Formulating Cost and Output Policies in the Performing Arts." Canadian Public Policy 2:1 (Winter, 1976): 33-41.

650. Godbout, J. "Les relations central-local ou le rendez-vous manqué." ["Central Versus Local Power: A Lost Chance."] Revue internationale d'Action communautaire 53 (1985): 125-130. Study of association between local and central power in Quebec.

651. Godsalve, William H.L. "The Goal: Equal Partnership in the Canadian Federation." *Public Management* 52:10 (1970): 2-5. Canadian intergovernmental relationships are characterized by a greater degree of decentralization than those in the United States.

652. Goldberg, Michael A., and Mark, Jonathan. "The Roles of Government in Housing Policy: A Canadian Perspective and Overview." *Journal of the American Planning Association* 51:1 (1985): 34-42. Describes federal, provincial, metropolitan regional, and city government roles in housing policy.

653. Goldsmith, Andrew. "Political Policing in Canada: The Report of the McDonald Commission and the Security Intelligence Services Act, 1984." *Public Law* (1985): 39-50.

654. Goldstein, Jonah. "Public Interest Groups and Public Policy: The Case of the Consumers' Association of Canada." *Canadian Journal of Political Science* 12:1 (1979): 137-156. Illustrates problems and tactics of public advocacy groups in Canada.

655. Gordon, S. "The Political Economy of Big Questions and Small Ones." *Canadian Public Policy* 1:1 (Winter, 1975): 97-106.

656. Gould, Stephen L, Aldall, Alan, and Thompson, Fred. "Zero Base Budgeting: Some Lessons From an Inconclusive Experiment." *Canadian Public Administration* 22:2 (1979): 251-260.

657. Grant, John. "The Environment for Canadian Fiscal Policy." *Canadian Public Policy* 2:4 (Autumn, 1976): 616-619.

658. Grant, John. "The MacDonald Commission on Stabilization Policy." *Canadian Public Policy* 12 (1986): 76-83. Review of the Report of the Royal Commssion on the Economic Union and the Development Prospects for Canada, 1985, otherwise known as the MacDonald Report.

659. Grant, Wyn, and Coleman, William. "Business Associations and Public Policy: A Comparison of Organizational Development in Britain and Canada." *Journal of Public Policy* 4:3 (1984): 209-236.

660. Green, C. "Recent Inflation: Its Causes and Implications for Public Policy." *Canadian Public Policy* 2:1 (Winter, 1976): 42-53.

661. Grubel, H.G., and Smith, S. Sydney. "The Taxation of Windfall Gains on Stocks of Natural Resources." *Canadian Public Policy* 1:1 (Winter, 1975): 13-29.

662. Guruprasad, C. "Planning for Tax Administration in Canada: The PPB System in National Revenue, Taxation." *Canadian Public Administration* 16:3 (Fall, 1973): 399-421.

663. Haglund, D. G. "Unbridled Constraint: The MacDonald Commission Volumes on Canada and the International Political Economy." *Canadian Journal of Political Science* 20:3 (1987): 599-624.

664. Ham, Chris, and Towell, David. "Policy Theory and Policy Practice: An Encounter in the Field of Health Service Management Development." *Policy and Politics* 13:4 (1985): 431-444.

665. Hamilton, Richard E. "A Marketing Board to Regulate Exports of Natural Gas?" *Canadian Public Administration* 16:1 (1973): 83-95.

666. Hartle, Douglas G. "A Proposed System of Program and Policy Evaluation." *Canadian Public Administration* 16:2 (1973): 243-266.

667. Harvey, W.H. "Inflation: A Powerful Tool in Government Science Policy." *Canadian Public Policy* 2:3 (Summer, 1976): 439-450.

668. Hawkes, David C., and Pollard, Bruce G. "The Medicare Debate in Canada: The Politics of New Federalism." *Publius* 14:3 (1984): 183-200. How Canadian federalism has modified federal-provincial jurisdictions to allow for a more efficient and less expensive medicare policy.

669. Hawkins, Freda. "Canadian Immigration: Present Policies, Future Options." *Round Table* 265 (1977): 50-63. Discussion of recent modifications of Canadian immigration policy and new Immigration Act to replace the Immigration Act of 1952. Includes figures on numbers of immigrants to Canada in recent years and where immigrants have come from.

670. Hawkins, Freda. "Great Immigration Debate: Need for Demographic Studies." *International Perspectives* (September/October, 1975): 3-8.

671. Hawkins, Freda. "Immigration and Population: The Canadian Approach." *Canadian Public Policy* 1:3 (Summer, 1975): 285-295.

672. Helliwell, John. "Energy in Canada." *Current History* 79:460 (1980): 125-128.

673. Helliwell, John. "The National Energy Board's 1974-1975 Natural Gas Supply Hearings." *Canadian Public Policy* 1:3 (Summer, 1975): 415-425.

674. Helliwell, John, MacGregor, M., and Plourde, A. "The National Energy Program Meets Falling World Oil Prices." Canadian Public Policy 9:3 (September, 1983): 284-296.

675. Helliwell, John, and McRae, R. "The National Energy Conflict." Canadian Public Policy 7:1 (Winter, 1981): 15-23.

676. Helliwell, John, et al. "Changes in Canadian Energy Demand, Supply, and Policies, 1974-1986." Natural Resources Journal 24:2 (1984): 297-324.

677. Helliwell, John, et al. "Equations Across the Border: RDX2 Meets MPs." International Journal 27:2 (1972): 236-249.

678. Henkin, Louis. "Arctic Anti-Pollution: Does Canada Make -- or Break -- International law?" American Journal of International Law 65:1 (1971): 131-136. Discussion of tensions resulting from Canada passing its own legislation regulating pollution of the seas, and what the relationship should be between the Canadian law and international law.

679. Hinch, Ronald. "Canada's New Sexual Assault Laws: A Step Forward for Women?" Contemporary Crises: Crime, Law, and Social Policy 9:1 (1985): 33-44.

680. Hodgetts, J.E. "Intergovernmental Relations in Canada." Annals of the American Academy of Political and Social Sciences 416 (1974): 170-180.

681. Hogan, James B. "Social Structure and Public Policy: A Longitudinal Study of Mexico and Canada." Comparative Politics 4:4 (1972): 477-510.

682. Holmes, Jean. "A Note on Some Aspects of Contemporary Canadian and Australian Federalism." Journal of Commonwealth and Comparative Politics 12:3 (1974): 313-322. Compares and contrasts federal structures, leadership patterns, and fiscal policy in Canadian and Australian federal systems.

683. Horsey, Michael. "Taking Care of Business: The Public Official as Entrepreneur." Canadian Public Administration 29:4 (1986): 681-685.

684. Hudon, Raymont. "La Commission Macdonald: principes et préceptes." ["The Macdonald Commission: Principles and Precepts."] Politique 9 (1986): 111-145. Examination of the Royal Commission on the Economic Union and the Perspectives of Canadian Development which submitted its report in September, 1985.

685. Hudon, Raymond. "Intégration et Diversité: Les Dilemmes du Fédéralisme Canadien." ["Integration and Diversity: The Dilemmas of Canadian Federalism."] International Political Science Review 5:4 (1984): 455-472. The new Canadian Constitution does not constitute a "peace treaty" between the linguistic groups in Canada.

686. Hum, Derek. "UISP and the MacDonald Commission: Reform and Restraint." Canadian Public Policy 12 (1986): 92-100. Review of the Report of the Royal Commssion on the Economic Union and the Development Prospects for Canada, 1985.

687. Hunter, Roger. "The Private Sector, The Public Sector, and the Laws of Nature." Canadian Public Administration 29:2 (1986): 197-217.

688. Huon De Kermadec, Jean-Michel. "The Persistent Crisis of Canadian Federalism." Revue du Droit public et de la Science politique 6 (1982): 1601-1626.

689. Irwin, Neal A. "Canadian Transportation Infrastructure." Canadian Public Administration 18:4 (1975): 601-629.

690. Isbister, John. "Agriculture, Balanced Growth, and Social Change in Central Canada Since 1850: An Interpretation." Economic Development and Cultural Change 25:4 (1977): 673-698.

691. Islam, Nasir, and Ahmed, Sadrudin. "Business Influence on Government: A Comparison of Public and Private Sector Perceptions." Canadian Public Administration 27:1 (Spring, 1984): 87-101.

692. No entry

693. Jain, Prakash C. "Racism in Canada: Some Recent Surveys." India Quarterly 39:2 (1983): 193-198. Survey results from 1981 public opinion study.

694. Jenkins, Barbara. "Reexamining the `Obsolescing Bargain': A Study of Canada's National Energy Program." International Organization 40:1 (1986): 139-165. The power of the Multinational Corporations in Canada may not diminish as fast as some have suggested, and this places the National Energy Program in a very important position.

695. Johannson, P., and Thomas, J. "A Dilemma of Nuclear Regulation in Canada: Political Control and Public Confidence." Canadian Public Policy 7:3 (Summer, 1981): 433-443.

696. Johnson, A. W. "Canada's Social Security Review, 1973-75: The Central Issues." Canadian Public Policy 1:4 (Autumn, 1975): 456-472.

697. Johnson, A.W. "Planning, Programming, and Budgeting in Canada." *Public Administration Review* 33:1 (1973): 23-30. Analysis of the institutional framework of the budgetary process, how planning works, and other aspects of the budgetary system.

698. Johnson, A.W. "Public Policy: Creativity and Bureaucracy." *Canadian Public Administration* 21:1 (Spring, 1978): 1-15.

699. Johnson, A.W. "The Treasury Board of Canada and the Machinery of Government of the 1970's." *Canadian Journal of Political Science* 4:3 (1971): 346-366.

700. Johnson, Andrew. "A Minister as an Agent of Policy Change: The Case of Unemployment Insurance in the Seventies." *Canadian Public Administration* 24:4 (1981): 612-632.

701. Johnson, Barbara. "Governing Canada's Economic Zone." *Canadian Public Administration* 20:1 (1977): 152-173.

702. Johnson, H.G. "Inflation, Unemployment, and the Floating Rate." *Canadian Public Policy* 1:2 (Spring, 1975): 176-184.

703. Johnson, J.A. "Municipal Tax Reform -- Alternatives to the Real Property Tax." *Canadian Public Policy* (Special Issue, 1976): 335-346.

704. Jones, L.R. "Phases of Recognition and Management of Financial Crisis in Public Organizations." *Canadian Public Administration* 27:1 (Spring, 1984): 48-65.

705. Jones, Nate. "Trans-Canada Highway Revisited." *Canadian Journal of Political and Social Theory* 10:3 (1986): 5-23.

706. Jordan, J.M., and Sutherland, S.L. "Assessing the Results of Public Expenditure: Program Evaluation in the Canadian Federal Government." *Canadian Public Administration* 22:4 (1979): 581-609.

707. Jump, G.V., and Wilson, T.A. "Macro-Economic Effects of the Energy Crisis, 1974-1975." *Canadian Public Policy* 1:1 (Winter, 1975): 30-39.

708. Kalbach, W.E. "Demographic Concerns and the Control of Immigration." *Canadian Public Policy* 1:3 (Summer, 1975): 302-310.

709. Keith, Robert F., and Fischer, David W. "Assessing the Development Decision-Making Process: A Case Study of Canadian Frontier Petroleum Development." *American Journal of Economics and Sociology* 36:2 (1977): 147-164.

710. Kellas, J.G. "Oil, Federalism, and Devolution. A Canadian-British Comparison." Round Table 259 (1975): 273-280. Compares the situation of Alberta with that of Scotland in the era of the energy crisis, and the tendency for national governments to want more control over energy resources.

711. Kernaghan, Kenneth. "Politics, Policy, and Public Servants: Political Neutrality Revisited." Canadian Public Administration 19:3 (1976): 432-456.

712. Kesselman, Jonathan. "The Royal Commission's Proposals for Income Security Reform." Canadian Public Policy 12 (1986): 101-112. Review of the Report of the Royal Commssion on the Economic Union and the Development Prospects for Canada, 1985, otherwise known as the MacDonald Report.

713. Kierans, E. "Notes on the Energy Aspects of the 1974 Budget." Canadian Public Policy 1:3 (Summer, 1975): 426-432.

714. Kirby, M.J.L., Koreker, H.V., and Teschke, W.R. "The Impact of Public Policy-Making Structures and Processes in Canada." Canadian Public Administration 21:3 (1978): 407-417.

715. Kliman, M.L. "The Setting of Domestic Air Fares: A Review of the 1975 Hearings." Canadian Public Policy 3:2 (Spring, 1977): 186-198.

716. Kornberg, Allan, Clarke, Harold, and Stewart, Marianne. "Federalism and Fragmentation: Political Support in Canada." Journal of Politics 41:3 (1979): 889-906. Study indicates that Canada's "Crisis of Confederation" will be resolved only by fundamental alterations in the present system.

717. Kruger, Arthur M. "Canadian Legislation and Experience." Labor Law Journal 21:8 (1970): 455-463.

718. LaCroix, R., and Montmarquette, C. "Inflation et indexation: Perspective canadienne et considérations théoretiques." ["Inflation and Indexation: A Canadian Perspective and Theoretical Considerations."] Canadian Public Policy 1:2 (Spring, 1975): 185-195.

719. Laflamme, Simon. "La politique fédérale canadienne au singulier et au pluriel." ["Canadian Federal Politics in the Singular and in the Plural."] Canadian Journal of Political Science 18:4 (1985): 697-714.

720. LaFramboise, H.L. "Government Spending: Grappling with the Evaluation Octopus." Optimum 9:4 (1978): 39-54. Many Canadians believe that the whole system of representative government and a free press, as spending controls, are failing the public.

721. Lamontagne, Maurice. "Fédéralisme ou association d'Etats indépendants." ["Federalism or Association of Independent States."] Études internationales 8:2 (1977): 208-230. Discusses the idea of a referendum and the discussion of the advisability of a referendum in a historical context. Also discusses both the advantages of an association of independent states and a federal solution to the conflict in Canada at the time.

722. Landry, Réjean, and Lemieux, Vincent . "L'analyse cybernétique des politiques gouvernementales." ["The Cybernetic Analysis of Governmental Policies."] Canadian Journal of Political Science 11:3 (1978): 529-544. Different subsystems of the cybernetic model are examined and regulation of feedback in energy and social affairs policy is studied.

723. Langford, John W. "Summary of the Transportation Seminar Discussion: Boundaries, Premises, and Moods of the Discussion." Canadian Public Administration 18:4 (Winter, 1975): 571-586.

724. LaSelva, Samuel. "Federalism and Unanimity: The Supreme Court and Constitutional Amendment." Canadian Journal of Political Science 16:4 (1983): 757-770. Argues in favor of a rule of unanimity for amending the Canadian Constitution.

725. Laux, Jeanne. "Expanding the State: The International Relations of State-Owned Enterprises in Canada." Polity 15:3 (1983): 329-350. Analysis of the performance of three Canadian state enterprises.

726. Lawson, Robert F., and Ghosh, Ratna. "Canada. [Policy Issues in the Education of Minorities]" Education and Urban Society 18:4 (1986): 449-461.

727. Lea, Sperry, and Volve, John . "Conflict Over Industrial Incentive Policies." Proceedings of the Academy of Political Science 32:2 (1976): 137-148.

728. Leach, Richard H. "Canadian Federalism Revisited." Publius 14:1 (1984): 9-20. Historical analysis of the "crisis in Canadian federalism." Places emphasis on intergovernmental negotiation and regionalism, and pays attention to the effects of the new Constitution on Canadian federalism.

729. Leach, Richard H. "Implications for Federalism of the Reformed Constitution of Canada." Law and Contemporary Problems 45:4 (1982): 149-164.

730. Lederman, W.R. "Cooperative Federalism: Constitutional Revision and Parliamentary Government in Canada." Queen's Quarterly 78:1 (1971): 7-17.

731. Lee, J.M. "Developing a Taste for Canadian Studies." Journal of Commonwealth and Comparative Politics 14:2 (1976): 204-208. Review essay of four books dealing with Canadian politics, and discussion of how hard it is to stimulate academic interest in Canadian politics outside of Canada (in this case in Britain).

732. Leman, Christopher. "Patterns of Policy Development: Social Security in the United States and Canada." Public Policy 25:2 (1977): 261-291. Exploration of the differences in the political context between the U.S. and Canada, and the effect of these differences on Social Security policy.

733. Lemco, Jonathan, and Regenstreif, Peter. "The Fusion of Powers and the Crisis of Canadian Federalism." Publius 14:1 (1984): 109-120. Suggests that reform of Canada's parliamentary system is necessary for resolution of Canadian political and constitutional problems.

734. LeMieux, Vincent. "La représentation et la gouverne." ["Representation and Government."] Canadian Public Policy 12 (1986): 122-126. Review of the Report of the Royal Commssion on the Economic Union and the Development Prospects for Canada, 1985, known as the MacDonald Report.

735. Lemieux, Vincent, Renaud, François, and von Schoenberg, Brigitte. "La régulation des affaires sociales: une analyse politique." ["The Regulation of Social Affairs: A Political Analysis."] Canadian Public Administration 17:1 (1974): 37-54.

736. LeSage, E.C. "A Hitch-Hiker's Guide to Ottawa Public Policy." Canadian Public Administration 28:3 (1985): 463-476.

737. Levy, Gary. "Scrutiny of Science Policy in Canada." Parliamentarian 62:2 (1981): 113-118. How Canadian science policy could be improved.

738. Lipsey, R.G. "Wage Price Controls: How to do a Lot of Harm by Trying to do a Little Good." Canadian Public Policy 3:1 (Winter, 1977): 1-13.

739. Litvak, I.A., and Maule, C. J. "Government-Business Interface: The Case of the Small Technology-Based Firm." Canadian Public Administration 16:1 (Spring, 1973): 96-109.

740. Loo, Robert. "Strategic Planning for Mental Health Services in Canada's Federal Police Force." Canadian Public Administration 29:3 (1986): 469-473.

741. Lubin, Martin. "Public Policy: Canada and the United States: Introduction." *Policy Studies Journal* 14:4 (1986): 555-656.

742. Lukasiewicz, J. "Public Policy and Technology: Passenger Rail in Canada as an Issue in Modernization." *Canadian Public Policy* 5:4 (Autumn, 1979): 518-532.

743. Lundqvist, Lennart. "Do Political Structures Matter in Environmental Politics? The Case of Air Pollution Control in Canada, Sweden, and the United States." *American Behavioral Scientist* 17:5 (1974): 731-750. Suggests that political structures can make a difference in the degree to which governments can or are willing to act in policy areas. Examines the federal-unitary distinction, and the presidential-parliamentary distinctions, and concludes that "structures do indeed matter."

744. Lussier, Gaétan. "Planning and Accountability in Employment and Immigration, Canada." *Canadian Public Administration* 28:1 (1985): 134-142.

745. McAllister, James A. "The Fiscal Analysis of Policy Outputs." *Canadian Public Administration* 23:3 (1980): 458-486.

746. McCaffery, Jerry. "Canada's Envelope Budget: A Strategic Management System." *Public Administration Review* 44:4 (1984): 316-323. Describes Canada's "envelope budget system" which is designed to manage both the process and outcome of the federal budget process in Canada.

747. McCready, Doughas J., and Winn, Conrad. "Health Care Usage in Ontario." *Growth and Change* 9:4 (1978): 8-14.

748. MacDonald, H.I. "Economic Policy: Can We Manage the Economy Any More?" *Canadian Public Policy* 2:4 (Autumn, 1976): 553-560.

749. MacDonald, W.A. "Government Growth and the Limits of Intervention." *Canadian Public Policy* 2:4 (Autumn, 1976): 577-584.

750. McDougall, I. "Canada's Oil and Gas: An `Eleventh Hour' Option That Must Not Be Ignored." *Canadian Public Policy* 1:1 (Winter, 1975): 47-57.

751. MacKinnon, Victor S. "Recent Developments in Canadian Fiscal Administration." *Saipa* 20:4 (1985): 135-150.

752. McRae, J.J. "Economic Theory and Non-Replenishable Resources." *Canadian Public Policy* 1:1 (Winter, 1975): 58-65.

753. McRae, Robert N. "A Major Shift in Canada's Energy Policy: Impact of the National Energy Program." *Journal of Energy and Development* 7:2 (1982): 173-198. Analysis of principles behind the 1980 National Energy Program, and its likely effects in Canada.

754. McRoberts, K. "Bill 22 and Language Policy in Canada." *Queen's Quarterly* 83:3 (1976): 464-477. The passage of Bill 22 in 1974, despite its defects, constituted a first step in giving French primacy in Quebec and redressing the linguistic inequality in the province.

755. Madar, Daniel. "Songs of the Open Road: The Politics of Trucking de-Regulation in the United States and Canada." *Policy Studies Journal* 14:4 (1986): 621-640.

756. Mahler, Gregory. S. "Canadian Federalism and Constitutional Reform." *Journal of Commonwealth and Comparative Politics* 25:2 (1987): 107-125. Study of the 1980-1982 period and the aspects of Canadian federalism which affected the constitutional reform process in Canada.

757. Mahon, Rianne, and Mytelka, Lynn. "Industry, the State, and the New Protectionism: Textiles in Canada and France." *International Organization* 37:4 (1983): 551-581. Studies two questions related to debate on protectionism: First, do trade barriers indicate an attempt to keep traditional advantages by capitalist states? Second, are all advanced capitalist states equally susceptible to protectionism?

758. Mallory, J.R. "Canadian Federalism in Transition." *Political Quarterly* 48:2 (1977): 149-163.

759. Mallory, J.R. "Commentary: The Political Economy Tradition in Canada." *Journal of Canadian Studies* 11:3 (1976): 18-20.

760. Mallory, J.R. "Conflict Management in the Canadian Federal System." *Law and Contemporary Problems* 44:3 (1981): 231-246.

761. Mallory, J.R. "The Macdonald Commission." *Canadian Journal of Political Science* 19:3 (1986): 597-617.

762. Mansell, Robin. "Is Policy Research an Irrelevant Exercise? The Case of Canadian DBS Planning." *Journal of Communication* 35:2 (1985): 154-166. Analysis of government research designed to assess the need for a direct broadcast satellite system.

763. Manzer, Ronald. "Social Policy and Political Paradigms." *Canadian Public Administration* 24:4 (1981): 641-648.

764. Marchak, Patricia. "Canadian Political Economy." *The Canadian Review of Sociology and Anthropology* 22:5 (1985): 673-709. Discusses the issues and literature involved in the study of the political economy up to the mid-1980s.

765. Marmor, Theodore R., Hoffman, Wayne, and Heagy, Thomas. "National Health Insurance: Some Lessons From the Canadian Experience." *Policy Sciences* 6:4 (1975): 447-460. The Canadian experience with health insurance can predict the impact in the U.S. of proposed national health insurance plans.

766. Marr, W.L. "Canadian Immigration Policies Since 1962." *Canadian Public Policy* 1:2 (Spring, 1975): 196-203.

767. Maslove, Allan. "Indicators and Policy Formation." *Canadian Public Administration* 18:3 (Fall, 1975): 474-485.

768. Matkin, James. "The Future of Industrial Relations in Canada." *Canadian Public Policy* 12 (1986): 127-132. Review of the Report of the Royal Commssion on the Economic Union and the Development Prospects for Canada, 1985, known as the MacDonald Report.

769. Maxwell, Judity. "The 1976 Budgets: A Shift Toward Restraint." *Canadian Public Policy* 2:4 (Autumn, 1976): 620-625.

770. Meekison, J.Peter. "Federalism's New Dimension." *International Perspectives* (March, 1977): 8-12.

771. Meisel, John. "Communications in the Space Age: Some Canadian and International Implications." *International Political Science Review* 7:3 (1986): 299-331.

772. Mercier, Jean, and Parent, Richar. "Conflit entre marché et État dans la société technicienne." ["Conflict Between the Market and the State in the Technical Society."] *Politique* 8 (1985): 5-21.

773. Meyboom, Peter. "In-House vs. Contractual Research: The Federal Make-or-Buy Policy." *Canadian Public Administration* 17:4 (Winter, 1974): 563-585.

774. Michelmann, Hans. "Federalism and International Relations in Canada and the Federal Republic of Germany." *International Journal* 41:3 ((1986): 539-571.

775. Migué, Jean-Luc. "Le prix de la santé et le prix des réformes des services de santé." ["The Price of Health and the Price of Reforms of Health Services."] *Journal of Canadian Studies* 8:3 (1973): 26-31.

776. Migue, Jean-Luc. "Le marché politique au Canada." ["The Political Market in Canada."] Canadian Public Policy 2:1 (Winter, 1976): 78-90.

777. Miller, F.C., and Miller, M.B. "The Macro-Economic Effects of Federal Wage and Price Controls." Canadian Public Policy 2:4 (Autumn, 1976): 607-615.

778. Milligan, Frank. "Program Planning and Control in the Canada Council, 1957-78." Canadian Public Administration 23:4 (Winter, 1980): 577-597.

779. Milling, G.B. "Immigration and Labour -- Critic or Catalyst?" Canadian Public Policy 1:3 (Summer, 1975): 311-316.

780. Mishler, William, and Campbell, David . "The Healthy State: Legislative Responsiveness to Public Health Care Needs in Canada, 1920-1970." Comparative Politics 10:4 (1978): 479-498.

781. Moore, A.M. "Income Security and Federal Finance." Canadian Public Policy 1:4 (Autumn, 1975): 473-479.

782. Moore, Milton. "Some Proposals for Adapting Federal-Provincial Financial Agreements to Current Conditions." Canadian Public Administration 24:2 (1981): 232-256.

783. Morrow, Jule. "Employment Equity Planning." Canadian Public Administration 29:4 (1986): 630-632.

784. Muller, R.A. "A Simulation of the Effect of Pollution Control on the Pulp and Paper Industry." Canadian Public Policy 2:1 (Winter, 1976): 91-102.

785. Munro, John A. "British Columbia and the `Chinese Evil': Canada's First Anti-Asiatic Immigration Law." Journal of Canadian Studies 6:4 (1971): 42-53.

786. Munton, Donald. "Acid Rain -- Silver Clouds Can Have Black Linings." International Perspectives (January-February, 1981): 6-9. Canada needs to exert more pressure on the United States to do something about Acid Rain.

787. Munton, Donald J. and Page, Don . "Planning in the East Block: The Post-Hostilities Problems Committees in Canada, 1943-5." International Journal 32:4 (1977): 687-726.

788. Murray, J.A., and Gerace, M.C. "Multinational Business and Canadian Government Affairs." Queen's Quarterly 80:2 (1973): 222-232.

789. Murray, V.V., and McMillan, C.J. "Business-Government Relations in Canada: A Conceptual Map." *Canadian Public Administration* 26:4 (1983): 591-609. Study of the literature which analyses the relations between contemporary business and government.

790. Neill, Robin F. "National Policy and Regional Development: A Footnote to the Deutsch Report on Maritime Union." *Journal of Canadian Studies* 9:2 (1974): 12-20.

791. Neill, Robin F. "Nationalism, Nationalization, and Social Communications: An Economic Perspective on the Canadian Case." *Canadian Review of Studies in Nationalism* 7:1 (1980): 72-87.

792. Nemetz, Peter. "Federal Environmental Regulation in Canada." *Natural Resources Journal* 26:3 (1986): 551-578.

793. Nemetz, Peter. "The Fisheries Act and Federal-Provincial Environmental Regulation: Duplication or Complementarity?" *Canadian Public Administration* 29:3 (1986): 401-424.

794. Nemetz, Peter, Stanbury, W. T., and Thompson, Fred. "Social Regulation in Canada: An Overview and Comparison with the American Model." *Policy Studies Journal* 14:4 (1986): 580-603.

795. Nemetz, Peter, et al. "Toxic Chemical Regulation in Canada: Preliminary Estimates of Costs and Benefits." *Canadian Public Administration* 25:3 (1982): 405-419.

796. Niosi, Jorge, and Duquette, Michel. "La loi et les nombres: le Programme énergétique national et la canadianisation de l'industrie pétrolière." ["Law and the Numbers: The National Energy Program and the Canadianiation of the Oil and Gas Industry."] *Canadian Journal of Political Science* 20:2 (19987): 317-336.

797. Noel, S.J.R. "Consociational Democracy and Canadian Federalism." *Canadian Journal of Political Science* 4:1 (1971): 15-17. One must study the political culture of the Canadian federation to appreciate how it has been able to survive and function effectively despite a minimal harmony among various regions.

798. Norrie, Kenneth H. "Energy, Canadian Federalism, and the West." *Publius* 14:1 (1984): 79-92. Examines whether Western regionalism threatens Canada, or Canadian federalism threatens the West, with particular attention given to the energy debate.

799. Norrie, Kenneth H., Percy, M.B., and Wilson, L.S. "Principles and Practices of Equalization." Canadian Public Policy 8:3 (1983): 290-293.

800. Nuechterlein, Donald E. "The Demise of Canada's Confederation." Political Science Quarterly 96:2 (1981): 225-240. Discussioin of Trudeau's constitutional reform legislation and its effects on Canada.

801. Pal, Leslie A. "Relative Autonomy Revisited: The Origins of Canadian Unemployment Insurance." Canadian Journal of Political Science 19:1 (1986): 71-92. Argues that earlier work on Canadian unemployment insurance focused too narrowly on class struggle and should be reinterpreted.

802. Palley, H. A. "Canadian Federalism and the Canadian Health Care Program: A Comparison of Ontario and Quebec." International Journal of Health Services 17:4 (1987): 595-616.

803. Passaris, Constantine. "Great Immigration Debate: Economic Impact of Immigration." International Perspectives (September/October, 1975): 9-12.

804. Passaris, Constantine. "Canada's Record in Assisting Refugee Movements." International Perspectives (September-October, 1981): 6-9. Discussion of Canada's role in assisting refugee movements, with special attention paid to several individual incidents.

805. Pattison, J.C. "Government Deficits and Inflation: The Evidence Reconsidered." Canadian Public Policy 3:3 (Summer, 1977): 285-290.

806. Paus-Jenssen, Arne. "Resource Taxation and the Supreme Court of Canada: The Cigol Case." Canadian Public Policy 5:1 (Winter, 1979): 45-58.

807. Pelletier, M. "Le revenu minimum garanti: une stratégie de bien-être social ou un instrument de politique économique?" ["A Minimum Guaranteed Income: A Strategie of Social Well-Being, or an Instrument of Political Economics?"] Canadian Public Policy 1:4 (Autumn, 1975): 503-519.

808. Peterson, James S. "Canadian Taxation of Nonresidents." The Columbia Journal of Transnational Law 12:2 (1973): 213-259. Canadian tax reform and tax structures, with particular emphasis on policy toward nonresidents.

809. Phidd, R.W. "The Economic Council of Canada: Its Establishment, Structure, and Role in the Canadian Policy-Making System, 1963-1974. Canadian Public Administration 18:3 (1975): 428-473.

810. Piche, Louise. "Employment Equity: Managing in a Rights-Seeking Environment." Canadian Public Administration 29:4 (1986): 624-630.

811. Pitfield, Michael. "The Shape of Governments in the 1980s: Techniques and Instruments for Policy Formulation at the Federal Level." Canadian Public Administration 19:1 (1976): 8-20.

812. Plunkett, T.J. "The Property Tax and the Municipal Case for Fiscal Reform." Canadian Public Policy (Special Issue, 1976): 313-322.

813. Pollard, Bruce. "Canadian Energy Policy in 1985: Toward a Renewed Federalism?" Publius 16:3 (1986): 163-174.

814. Pomfret, Richard. The Economic Development of Canada. Toronto: Methuen, 1981. After providing a brief historical background, studies patterns of Canadian economic growth and government policy to encourage growth.

815. Porter, John. "Post-Industrialism, Post-Nationalism, and Post-Secondary Education." Canadian Public Administration 14:1 (Spring, 1971): 32-50.

816. Pratt, Henry. "Aging Policy and Process in the Canadian Federal Government." anadian Public Administration 30:1 (1987): 57-75.

817. Préfontaine, Norbert. "What I Think I See: Reflections on the Foundations of Social Policy." Canadian Public Administration 16:2 (1973): 298-348.

818. Prince, Michael, and Chenier, John. "The Rise and Fall of Policy Planning and Research Units: An Organizational Perspective." Canadian Public Administration 23:4 (1980): 519-541.

819. Pross, A. Paul. "From System to Serendipity: The Practice and Study of Public Policy in the Trudeau Years." Canadian Public Administration 25:4 (1982): 520-544.

820. Purvis, D.D. "Exchange Rates and Economic Policy in Theory and Practice." Canadian Public Policy 3:2 (Spring, 1977): 205-218.

821. Rabeau, Yves. "Bien-être ou bien-être provincial: Vers une réfonte du programme de péréquation." ["Well-Being or Provincial Well-Being: Toward a Recasting of a Program of Equalization."] Canadian Public Administration 29:2 (1986): 237-258.

822. Rabeau, Yves. "Un analyse du processus de détermination des salaires dans le monde des conventions collectives des secteurs de la santé et de l'éducation au Canada." ["The Analysis of the Process of Salary Determination in Collective Conventions of the Health and Education Sectors in Canada."] Canadian Public Administration 25:1 (Spring, 1982): 34-62.

823. Rabkin, Yakov. "Transnational Invariables in Science Policies: Canadian and Soviet Experiences." Canadian Public Administration 24:1 (Spring, 1981): 18-43.

824. Ramesh, M. "The Growth and Proliferation of the Machinery of Intergovernmental Relations in Canada." Indian Journal of Public Administration 29:2 (1983): 334-350. Discusses the need to create formal political institutions to promote intergovernmental negotiations in Canada.

825. Ratushny, Ed. "Security in the Multi-Ethnic State: The Canadian Experience." Ethnic Studies Report 2:2 (1984): 1-20.

826. Raynauld, André. "Les politiques de croissance." ["The Politics of Awareness."] Canadian Public Policy 12 (1986): 68-75. Review of the Report of the Royal Commssion on the Economic Union and the Development Prospects for Canada, 1985, otherwise known as the MacDonald Report.

827. Raynauld, André. "Protection of the Environment: Economic Perspectives." Canadian Public Administration 15:4 (Winter, 1972): 558-571.

828. Redding, Forest W. "Fisheries Policy Analysis: A Scheme for Open Polities." Political Science 38:1 (1986): 44-60. Study of policy-making processes in Canada, New Zealand, and the U.S. in this area.

829. Reeves, M. A., and Kerr, W. A. "Implications of the Increasing Emphasis on Monetary Policy for the Federal State: The Case of Canada." Journal of Commonwealth and Comparative Politics 24:3 (1986): 254-268.

830. Reid, F.J. "Canadian Wage and Price Controls." Canadian Public Policy 2:1 (Winter, 1976): 103-112.

831. Reid, Timothy. "Federal Government Experience with Measuring Program Performance." Optimum 9:4 (1978): 17-28.

832. Renaud, François, and Von Schoenberg, Brigitte. "L'implanatation des conseils régionaux de la santé et des services sociaux: analyse d'un processus politique." ["The Establishment of Regional Councils of Health and Social Services: Analysis of a Political Process."] *Canadian Journal of Political Science* 7:1 (1974): 52-69. Analysis of process by which people have been appointed to the regional councils of health and social services.

833. Reschenthaler, G. B. "Regulatory Failure and Competition." *Canadian Public Administration* 19:3 (Fall, 1976): 466-486.

834. Resnick, Philip. "State and Civil Society: The Limits of a Royal Commission." *Canadian Journal of Political Science* 20:2 (1987): 379-401.

835. Reuber, Grant. "The Impact of Government Policies on the Distribution of Income in Canada: A Review." *Canadian Public Policy* 4:4 (Autumn, 1978): 505-529.

836. Richardson, R.M. "Deficit Financing and Inflation: A Reply to the Crozier Report and the Department of Finance." *Canadian Public Policy* 3:3 (Summer, 1977): 278-284.

837. Richmond, Anthony H. "Immigrant Adaptation: A Critical Review of `Three Years in Canada'." *Canadian Public Policy* 1:3 (Summer, 1975): 317-327.

838. Richmond, Anthony H., and Rao, G. Lakshmana. "Recent Developments in Immigration to Canada and Australia: A Comparative Analysis." *International Journal of Comparative Sociology* 17:3-4 (1976): 183-205.

839. Ritchie, Gordon. "Government Aid to Industry: A Public Sector Perspective." *Canadian Public Administration* 26:1 (1983): 36-46.

840. Ritchie, Ronald. "Assessing the Energy Issues from a Canadian Perspective." *International Perspectives* (1981): 19-21.

841. Ritchie, Ronald. "Policy-Making for the Long-Term: The Need to do More," *Canadian Public Administration* 16 (1973): 73-83.

842. Ritchie, Ronald. "Public Policies Affecting Petroleum Development in Canada." *Canadian Public Policy* 1:1 (Winter, 1975): 66-75.

843. Rivest, François. "L'assurance-maladie au Canada: Les raisons de l'implication de l'Etat." ["Sickness Insurance in Canada: Reasons for the Participation of the State."] *Canadian Public Administration* 27:1 (1984): 24-47.

844. Rivest, François. "Les Politiques de régulation et le modèle d'Edelman: une analyse en fonction de la santé dans l'industrie de l'amiante." ["The Politics of Regulation and the Edelman Model: An Analysis of the Health Function in the Asbestos Industry."] Canadian Public Administration 22:2 (1979): 290-311.

845. Robinson, Ivan. "Managing Retrenchment in a Public Service Organization." Canadian Public Administration 28:4 (1985): 513-530.

846. Robinson, John B. "Pendulum Policy: Natural Gas Forecasts and Canadian Energy Policy, 1969-1981." Canadian Journal of Political Science 16:2 (1983): 299-320.

847. Rogers, Forrest. "Recent Monetary Policy." Canadian Public Policy 2:4 (Autumn, 1976): 631-637.

848. Rogge, John. "African Refugees and Canada." International Perspectives (September-October, 1984): 23-26. Discussion of Canadian policies of refugee assistance and how these have been applied to African refugees in recent years.

849. Rosenbluth, G. "Economists and the Growth Controversy." Canadian Public Policy 2:2 (Spring, 1976): 225-239.

850. Rowan, Malcolm. "A Conceptual Framework for Government Policy-Making." Canadian Public Administration 13:3 (1970): 277-296.

851. Rowat, Donald C. "The Commission on the Relations Between Universities and Governments: Summary Report." Canadian Public Administration 14:4 (Winter, 1971): 608-620.

852. Rowat, Donald C. "Laws on Access to Official Documents." Indian Journal of Public Administration 25:4 (1979): 987-1015. Broad analysis of laws relating to exposure of government documents, examining many other countries as well as Canada.

853. Rowat, Donald C. "Relations Between Universities and Governments in Canada." Journal of Constitutional and Parliamentary Studies 5:1 (1971): 8-21. Character and significance of federal financial support of universities.

854. Ruggeri, G.C. "A Note on the Energy-GNP Relationship in Canada, 1961-1980." Journal of Energy and Development 8:2 (1983): 341-346. Analysis of output and energy use in Canada during this period.

855. Ruppenthal, Karl M. "Transport in Canada: Needs, Trends, and Problems." Canadian Public Administration 18:4 (1975): 587-600.

856. Sabetti, Filippo, and Waller, Harold M. "Introduction: Crisis and Continuity in Canadian Federalism." *Publius* 14:1 (1984): 1-8. Discusses historical development of the major themes of tension in Canadian federalism as well as contempoary themes in the study of federalism.

857. Savoie, Donald. "Le programme fédéral de décentralisation: un réexamen." ["The Federal Program of Decentralization: A Re-Examination."] *Canadian Public Policy* 12:3 1986): 413-423.

858. Sayeed, K.B. "Public Policy Analysis in Washington and Ottawa." *Political Science* 4:1 (1973): 85-101.

859. Scarfe, B. "The Federal Budget and Energy Program, October 28th, 1980: A Review." *Canadian Public Policy* 7:1 (Winter, 1981): 1-14.

860. Schlegal, John P. "Federalism and Canadian Foreign Policy." *Round Table* 282 (1981): 179-191. How domestic values and structures, especially the fact that Canada is federal, affect foreign policy. Uses three case studies to show that the federal structure affected Canadian foreign policy formation.

861. Schultz, Richard. "Intergovernmental Cooperation, Regulatory Agencies, and Transportation Regulation in Canada: the Case of Part III of the National Transportation Act." *Canadian Public Administration* 19:2 (1976): 183-207.

862. Schultz, Richard. "Regulation as Maginot Line: Confronting the Technological Revolution in Telecommunications." *Canadian Public Administration* 26:2 (Summer, 1983): 203-218.

863. Schwartz, Mildred. "Comparing United States and Canadian Public Policy: A Review of Strategies." *Policy Studies Journal* 14:4 (1986): 566-579.

864. Scott, Anthony. "Financing Confederation." *Canadian Public Policy* 8:3 (1983): 283-286.

865. Scott, Anthony. "The MacDonald Report: The Reviews in Review." *Canadian Public Policy* 12 (1986): 1-10. Review of the Report of the Royal Commssion on the Economic Union and the Development Prospects for Canada, otherwise known as the MacDonald Report.

866. Sedjo, Roger A. "Price Trends, Economic Growth, and the Canadian Balance of Trade: A Three-Country Model." *Journal of Political Economy* 79:3 (1971): 596-613.

867. Sharma, J.P. "Federal Financial Relations in Canada." *Journal of Constitutional and Parliamentary Studies* 8:4 (1974): 587-599. Review of taxing powers of federal and provincial governments, tax-sharing agreements, transfer payments, and other intergovernmental fiscal arrangements.

868. Shearer, Ronald. "The New Face of Canadian Mercantilism: The MacDonald Commission and the Case for Free Trade." *Canadian Public Policy* 12 (1986): 51-58. Review of the Report of the Royal Commssion on the Economic Union and the Development Prospects for Canada, 1985, otherwise known as the MacDonald Report.

869. Sheeman, B.S. "Federal Funds and University Research." *Canadian Journal of Political Science* 6:1 (1973): 121-130.

870. Shepherd, John J. "Government Aid to Industry: A Private Sector Perspective." *Canadian Public Administration* 26:1 (1983): 47-56.

871. Sherbaniuk, D.J. "Is the Property Tax a Good Tax?" *Canadian Public Policy* (Special Issue, 1976): 310-312.

872. Silverstein, Harvey B. "Canada and Hydrogen Systems: An Energy Policy for a Nation." *International Journal* 36:2 (1981): 294-310.

873. Simeon, Richard. "Considerations on Centraliation and Decentralization." *Canadian Public Administration* 29:3 (1986): 445-461.

874. Simeon, Richard. "Intergovernmental Relations and the Challenges to Canadian Federalism." *Canadian Public Administration* 23:1 (1980): 14-32.

875. Simeon, Richard. "Natural Resource Revenues and Canadian Federalism: A Survey of the Issues." *Canadian Public Policy* (Special Issue, 1980): 182-191.

876. Simeon, Richard. "The `Overload Thesis' and Canadian Government." *Canadian Public Policy* 2:4 (Autumn, 1976): 541-552.

877. Skogstad, G. "The Farm Products Marketing Agencies Act: A Case Study of Agricultural Policy." *Canadian Public Policy* 6:1 (Winter, 1980): 89-100.

878. Skogstad, G., and Davey, B. "The Politics of Agricultural Policy-Making in Canada." *Canadian Journal of Agricultural Economics* 35:3 (1987): 663-665.

879. Smiley, Donald. "The Canadian Federation and the Challenge of Quebec Independence." Publius 8:1 (1978): 199-224. Discusses the uncertainty caused by the election of Rene Levesque in 1976, and responses to Quebec nationalism at the time and since then.

880. Smiley, Donald. "The Challenge of Canadian Ambivalence." Queen's Quarterly 88:1 (1981): 1-12. Study of Canadian national and provincial loyalties and their effect on national unity.

881. Smiley, Donald. "The Dominance of Withinputs?: Canadian Politics." Polity 6:2 (1973): 276-281.

882. Smiley, Donald. "Federal States and Federal Societies with Special Reference to Canada." International Political Science Review 5:4 (1984): 443-454.

883. Smiley, Donald. "Federal-Provincial Conflict in Canada." Publius 4:3 (1974): 7-24. Historical discussion of the weakening of centralized federalism in Canada since World War Two, and how federal-provincial conflict has been managed in recent years.

884. Smiley, Donald. "Public Sector Politics, Modernization, and Federalism: The Canadian and American Experiences." Publius 14:1 (1984): 39-60. Compares Canadian and American federalism in terms of modernization theory, and explains why the two systems behave differently.

885. Smiley, Donald. "The Structural Problem of Canadian Federalism," Canadian Public Administration 14:3 (1971): 326-344.

886. Smiley, Donald. "Update: The Canadian Federation in 1978." Publius 9:1 (1979): 237-241. Describes proposed changes in the Constitutional reform movement.

887. Smith, Lawrence B. "Myths and Realities in Mortgage Finance and the Housing Crisis." Canadian Public Policy 2:2 (Spring, 1976): 240-248.

888. Smith, Lawrence B. "The Crisis in Rental Housing: A Canadian Perspective." Annals of the American Academy of Political and Social Science 465 (1983): 58-75.

889. Smith, L. Graham. "Electric Power Planning in Ontario: Public Participation at a Normative Level." Canadian Public Administration 26:3 (1983): 360-377. Study of public participation in the planning process of the Royal Commission on Electric Power Planning in Ontario, 1974-1980.

890. Smith, Patrick. "Planning and Open Government: Recent Policy Options and Applications in Canada." Planning and Administration 11:2 (1984): 54-62.

891. Smith, Stuart. "Canadian Minerals under Siege." International Perspectives 1987 (January-February): 9-11.

892. Solomon, Peter. "Government Officials and the Study of Policy Making." Canadian Public Administration 26:3 (Fall, 1983): 420-440.

893. Spragge, Godfrey. "Canadian Planners' Goals: Deep Roots and Fuzzy Thinking." Canadian Public Administration 18:2 (1975): 216-234.

894. Sproule-Jones, Mark. "An Analysis of Canadian Federalism." Publius 4:4 (1974): 109-136. Uses public choice theory to explain the organization and operation of Canadian federalism.

895. Sproule-Jones, Mark. "A Fresh Look at an Old Problem: Coordinating Canada's Shore Management Agencies." Western Political Quarterly 32:3 (1979): 278-285. There is a new theory that accounts for substantial coordination between resource agencies and the lack of coordination of shoreline uses.

896. Sproule-Jones, Mark. "The Social Appropriateness of Water Quality Management for the Lower Fraser River." Canadian Public Administration 21:2 (Summer, 1978): 176-194.

897. Stack, Steven. "The Political Economy of Income Inequality: A Comparative Analysis." Canadian Journal of Political Science 13:2 (1980): 273-286.

898. Stanbury, W.T., and Lermer, George. "Regulation and the Redistribution of Income and Wealth." Canadian Public Administration 26:3 (1983): 378-401. Discusses various ways in which Canada has made use of regulation as a technique to redistribute income.

899. Star, S. "In Search of a Rational Immigration Policy." Canadian Public Policy 1:3 (Summer, 1975): 328-342.

900. Starnes, John. "Canadian Security." International Perspectives (September-October, 1984): 23 -26. Description of the Security Intelligence Service and an explanation of why it is important.

901. Steele, G.G.E. "`Needed -- A Sense of Proportion!' Notes on the History of Expenditure Control." Canadian Public Administration 20:3 (Fall, 1977): 433-443.

902. Stein, S.B. "Environmental Control and Different Levels of Government." Canadian Public Administration 14:1 (1971): 129-144.

903. Stewart, Larry. "Canada and the Uranium Cartel." International Perspectives (July-August, 1980): 21-25. What steps should be taken by the Canadian government to regulate and/or control the uranium industry in Canada.

904. Stewart, W.B. "The C.B.C.: Canadian? Regional? Popular? An Examination of Program Objectives for English Television." Canadian Public Administration 16:3 (1973): 447-467.

905. Strick, J.C. "Conditional Grants and Provincial Government Budgeting," Canadian Public Administration 14 (1971): 217-236.

906. Studnicki-Gizbert, K.W. "The Administration of Transport Policy: The Regulatory Problems." Canadian Public Administration 18:4 (Winter, 1975): 642-658.

907. Sultan, R.G.M. "Papers on the 1977 Bank Act Revision: A Comment." Canadian Public Policy 3:1 (Winter, 1977): 90-94.

908. Svoboda, C.V. "Federal-Provincial Co-operation in Development Assistance." International Perspectives (May-June-July-August, 1979): 25-28. How the federal government and the provincial governments coordinate foreign development programs.

909. Tanny, Stephen M. "Post-Industrial Canada: An Econometric Modelling approach." Futures 10:1 (1978): 44-53.

910. Tarnopolsky, Walter. "Race Relations Commissions in Canada, Australia, New Zealand, the United Kingdom, and the United States." Human Rights Law Journal 6 (1985): 145-178. Studies the efforts to prohibit racial discrimination in these countries, and how courts and special commissions have been used when the legislatures have not acted.

911. Taylor, Malcolm G. "The Canadian Health Insurance Program." Public Administration Review 33:1 (1973): 31-39. Brief description of historical background of federal involvement in the Canadian Health Insurance Program, with discussion of costs and effects on resources.

912. Taylor, Malcolm G. "Quebec Medicare: Policy Formulation in Conflict and Crisis." Canadian Public Administration 15:2 (1972): 211-250.

913. Teichman, Judith. "Argentine and Canadian Divergencies: The Contributions of Dependency and World-System Analyses." Canadian Journal of Political Science 15:3 (1982): 597-601.

914. Teichman, Judith. "Businessmen and Politics in the Process of Economic Development: Argentina and Canada." Canadian Journal of Political Science 15:1 (1982): 47-66.

915. Thomas, Brownlee. "Teleglobe Canada: Outside the (CRTC)) Regulatory Camp." Canadian Public Administration 29:3 (1986): 424-444.

916. Thompson, Donald N. "Canada's New Competition Policy: Status and Outlook." California Management Review 16:4 (1974): 93-103. Analysis of 1973 Combines Investigation Act and Foreign Investment Review Act to explain current Canadian policy to investment.

917. Thorburn, Hugh. "The Politics of Economic Development in Canada." Queen's Quarterly 90:1 (1983): 138-150. Focuses upon the often strained relationship which exists within Canada's federal system between business, labor, and the government. Suggestions are made for modifications in public policy to encourage economic growth.

918. Tobin, Richard, and Fitzgeald, Roy. "Assessing the Consequences of Corporate Discretion on Regulatory Compliance: The Case of Motor Vehicle Safety in Canada." Law and Policy 8:1 (1986): 59-76.

919. Todd, Daniel, and Simpson, Jamie. "Aerospace, The State, and the Regions: A Canadian Perspective." Political Geography Quarterly 4:2 (1985): 111-130. Studies the relationship of the aerospace industry and the state, and examines what the role of the Canadian government should be in promoting and protecting a Canadian aerospace industry.

920. Toner, Glen, and Doern, G. Bruce. "The Two Energy Crises and Canadian Oil and Gas Interest Groups: A Re-Examination of Berry's Propositions." Canadian Journal of Political Science 19:3 (1986): 467-494.

921. Tovell, F.M. "Cultural Affairs: The Canadian Experience." International Perspectives (September-October, 1976): 32-38.

922. Trent, John. "Reform of the Canadian Federal System: A Note." Political Science Review 17:1-2 (1978): 62-90. How Canada arrived at the situation of great federal-provincial tension in the late 1970's, and some of the proposals for reform that were put forward.

923. Trent, John. "Terrain d'entente et territoires contestés: les positions fédérales et provinciales à l'égard de l'avenir constitutionnel du Canada." ["Area of Agreement and Contested Territories: Federal and Provincial Positions Regarding the Constitutional Future of Canada."] Études internationales 8:2 (1977): 172-196. Discusses sources of federal-provincial conflict, including theories of statehood and nationhood, and the development of a constitutional debate describing federal and provincial positions articulated in the course of the debate.

924. Trezise, P.H. "The Energy Challenge." Proceedings of the Academy of Political Science 32:2 (1976): 113-123. Canada and the US have had trans-border irritations about energy conservation policy, but inroads have been made for a treaty that could help energy relations and Canadian-American relations in general.

925. Tuohy, C.J. "Medical Politics after Medicare: The Ontario Case." Canadian Public Policy 2:2 (Spring, 1976): 192-210.

926. Tupper, Allan. "Planning, Politics, and Accountability." Canadian Public Administration 28:1 (1985): 156-169.

927. Tupper, Allan. "Public Enterprise as Social Welfare: The Case of the Cape Breton Development Corporation." Canadian Public Policy 4:4 (Autumn, 1978): 530-546.

928. Ulrich, Alvin, Furtan, William, and Schmitz, Andrew. "The Cost of a Licensing System Regulation: An Example from Canadian Prairie Agriculture." Journal of Political Economy 95:1 (1987): 160-178.

929. Upton, L.F.S. "The Origins of Canadian Indian Policy." Journal of Canadian Studies 8:4 (1973): 51-61.

930. Usher, D. "How Should the Redistributive Power of the State Be Divided Between Federal and Provincial Governments?" Canadian Public Policy 6:1 (Winter, 1980): 16-29.

931. Uslaner, E. M. "Energy Politics in the U.S.A. and Canada." Energy Policy 15:5 (1987): 432-440.

932. Vanderkamp, John. "Transfers and Migration." Canadian Public Policy 8:3 (1983): 293-297.

933. Van Loon, Richard. "The Policy and Expenditure Management System in the Federal Government: The First Three Years." Canadian Public Administration 26:2 (Summer, 1983): 255-285.

934. Van Loon, Richard. "Reforming Welfare in Canada: The Case of the Social Security Review." *Public Policy* 27:4 (1979): 469-504. Study of 1973 to 1978 period in which a review of welfare policy in Canada was undertaken to improve operation and benefits of the system.

935. Van Loon, Richard. "Stop the Music: The Current Policy and Expenditure Management System in Ottawa." *Canadian Public Administration* 24:2 (1981): 175-199.

936. Veilleux, Gérard. "Intergovernmental Canada: Government by Conference? A Fiscal and Economic Perspective." *Canadian Public Administration* 23:1 (1980): 33-53.

937. Verney, Douglas. "The Role of the Private Social Science Research Council of Canada in the Formation of Public Science Policy, 1968-1974." *Canadian Public Policy* 1:1 (Winter, 1975): 107-117.

938. Verney, Douglas, and Verney, Diana M. "A Canadian Political Community? The Case for Tripartite Confederalism." *Journal of Commonwealth and Comparative Politics* 12:1 (1974): 1-19. The fundamental nature of Canada, and whether it is possible to avoid future tensions between the federalists and primarily the population of Quebec through a "new deal" with Quebec.

939. Villanueva, A.B. "Nuclear Power, Private Attorneys General, and the Regulatory Process." *Canadian Public Administration* 18:3 (Fall, 1975): 399-408.

940. Vineberg, R.A. "Federal-Provincial Relations in Canadian Immigration." *Canadian Public Administration* 30:2 (1987): 299-317.

941. Walters, Vivienne. "State, Capital, and Labour: The Introduction of Federal-Provincial Insurance for Physician Care in Canada." *Canadian Review of Sociology and Anthropology* 19:2 (1982): 157-172. Examination of the origins of federal-provincial insurance programs for physician care.

942. Wan, Thomas T.H., and Broida, Joel H. "Factors Affecting Variations in Health Services Utilization in Quebec, Canada." *Socio-Economic Planning Sciences* 15:5 (1981): 231-242. Impact on Quebec health services of the change in utilization of health services in a large number of areas in the province.

943. Warhurst, John. "Canada's Intergovernmental Relations Specialists." *Australian Journal of Public Administration* 42:4 (1983): 459-485. Study of the civil servants on both the federal and provincial levels of government whose task it is to specialize in intergovernmental relations.

944. Waters, W.G. "Investment Criteria and the Expansion of Major Airports in Canada." <u>Canadian Public Policy</u> 3:1 (Winter, 1977): 23-35.

945. Watts, Rob. "Family Allowances in Canada and Australia, 1940-1945: A Comparative Critical Case Study." <u>Journal of Social Policy</u> 16:1 (1987): 19-48.

946. Watts, Ronald. "The MacDonald Commission Report and Canadian Federalism." <u>Publius</u> 16:3 (1986): 175-187.

947. Waverman, L. "The Two Price System in Energy: Subsidies Forgotten." <u>Canadian Public Policy</u> 1:1 (Winter, 1975): 76-88.

948. Weaver, Sally M. "The Joint Cabinet/National Indian Brotherhood Committee: A Unique Experiment in Pressure Group Relations." <u>Canadian Public Administration</u> 25:2 (1982): 211-239.

949. Weller, Geoffrey. "Common Problems, Alternative Solutions: A Comparison of the Canadian and American Health Systems." <u>Policy Studies Journal</u> 14:4 (1986): 604-620.

950. Westmacott, Martin. "The National Transportation Act and Western Canada: A Case Study in Co-Operative Federalism." <u>Canadian Public Administration</u> 16:3 (1973): 447-468.

951. Wier, Richard A. "Federalism, Interest Groups, and Parliamentary Government: The Canadian Medical Association." <u>Journal of Commonwealth Political Studies</u> 11:2 (1973): 159-175. Study of the role of interest groups in the formulation of public policy in parliamentary systems of government.

952. Wildavsky, Aaron. "From Chaos Comes Opportunity: The Movement Toward Spending Limits in American and Canadian Budgeting." <u>Canadian Public Administration</u> 26:2 (1983): 163-181.

953. Wiltshire, Kenneth. "Working with Intergovernmental Agreements: The Canadian and Australian Experience." <u>Canadian Public Administration</u> 23:3 (1980): 353-379.

954. Winham, G. "Attitudes on Pollution and Growth in Hamilton, or `There's an Awful Lot of Talk These Days About Ecology.'" <u>Canadian Journal of Political Science</u> 5:3 (1972): 389-401.

955. Woodcock, George. <u>Confederation Betrayed</u>. Madeira Park, B.C.: Harbour Publications, 1981. How federal governments have usurped provincial powers over the years since Confederation, and suggestions for change of the power imbalance found in Canada today.

956. Woodside, Kenneth. "Policy Instruments and the Study of Public Policy." *Canadian Journal of Political Science* 19:4 (1986): 775-793.

957. Wright, Douglas T. "The Financing of Post-Secondary Education: Basic Issues and Distribution of Costs." *Canadian Public Administration* 14:4 (Winter, 1971): 595-607.

958. Wright, Gerald, and Maureen Appel Molot. "Capital Movements and Government Control." *International Organization* 28:4 (1974): 671-688.

4
Regionalism and Local Politics

Books

959. Andrew, J. V. *Backdoor Bilingualism: Davis's Sell-Out of Ontario and Its National Consequences*. Richmond Hill, Ont.: BMG Publications, 1979.

960. Antoft, K., ed. *A Guide to Local Government in Nova Scotia*. Halifax: Institute of Public Affairs, Dalhousie University, 1977.

961. Artibise, Alan F.J., and Stelter, Gilbert Arthur, eds. *The Usable Urban Past: Planning and Politics in the Modern Canadian City*. Toronto: Macmillan of Canada, 1979. Essays on municipal government and politics, and urban planning.

962. Aubin, H. *City for Sale*. Toronto: Lorimer, 1977.

963. Aucoin, Peter. *Party Government and Regional Representation in Canada*. Toronto: University of Toronto Press, 1985.

964. Axworthy, Lloyd, and Gillies, J.M., eds. *The City: Canada's Prosects and Canada's Problems*. Toronto: Butterworths, 1973.

965. Baine, R. P., and McMurray, A.L. *Toronto: An Urban Study*. Toronto: Clarke, Irwin, 1970.

966. Baine, R.P. *Calgary: An Urban Study*. Toronto: Clarke, Irwin, 1973.

967. Bartlett, Richard H. Subjugation, *Self-Management, and Self- Government of Aboriginal Lands and Resources in Canada*. Kingston, Ont.: Institute of Intergovernmental Relations, 1986.

968. Beck, J.M. The Evolution of Municipal Government in Nova Scotia, 1749 - 1973. Halifax: Queen's Printer, 1973.

969. Bellamy, David J., Pammett, Jon H., and Rowat, Donald C., eds. The Provincial Political Systems: Comparative Essays. Toronto: Methuen, 1976. Essays dealing with provincial political cultures, provincial political party and electoral systems, leadership, and parliamentary behavior in the provinces, and the structures and processes of provincial governmental organization.

970. Bercuson, David, and Buckner, Phillip A., eds. Eastern and Western Perspectives: Papers from the Joint Atlantic Canada/ Western Canadian Studies Conference. Toronto: University of Toronto Press, 1981. Essays on regionalism, history, and development contributed from different parts of Canada.

971. Bettison, David George. The Politics of Canadian Urban Development. Edmonton, Alta.: University of Alberta Press, 1975. Review of federal government policy to encourage the development of urban areas and also to alleviate the problems of urban growth.

972. Bettison, David George, Kenward, John K., and Taylor, Larrie. Urban Affairs in Alberta. Edmonton: University of Alberta Press, 1975. Analysis of the development of urban areas and provincial governmental urban policy in Alberta.

973. Bishop, O.B., et al., eds. Bibliography of Ontario History, 1867- 1976: Cultural, Economic, Political, Social. Toronto: University of Toronto Press, 1982.

974. Black, A., and Powell, M. Municipal Government and Finance: An Annotated Bibliography. Ottawa: Central Mortgage and Housing Corporation, 1971.

975. Blake, Donald. Two Political Worlds: Parties and Voting in British Columbia. Vancouver: University of British Columbia Press, 1985. Study of British Columbia election in 1979 covering the party system, social class, and the link for B.C. voters between provincial politics and federal politics.

976. Boldt, Menno, and Long, J. Anthony, eds. The Quest for Justice: Aboriginal Peoples and Aboriginal Rights. Toronto: University of Toronto Press, 1985.

977. Boldt, Menno, and Long, J. Anthony. Pathways to Self-Determination: Canadian Indians and the Canadian State. Toronto: University of Toronto Press, 1983. Various options of self-government which would allow Indian groups greater degrees of self-government.

978. Bourne, L.S., et al., eds. *Urban Futures for Central Canada*. Toronto: University of Toronto Press, 1974.

979. Breton, Albert, and Breton, Raymond. *Why Disunity? An Analysis of Linguistic and Regional Cleavages in Canada*. Montreal: Institute for Research on Public Policy, 1980.

980. Brown, M.P. Sharon. *Eastern Arctic Study Annotated Bibliography*. Kingston, Ontario: Center for Resource Studies, 1984.

981. Buchanan, Jim. *Canadian Indian Policy: A Bibliography*. Monticello, Ill.: Vance Bibliographies, 1979.

982. Buchanan, Jim. *Canadian Indian Policy: A Bibliography Supplement, 1979-1986*. Monticello, Ill.: Vance Bibliographies, 1986.

983. Caldarola, Carlo, ed. *Society and Politics in Alberta*. Toronto: Methuen, 1979. Essays on party politics, political culture, party support, and class, status, and power in Alberta.

984. Cameron, David M., ed. *Regionalism and Supernationalism: Challenges and Alternatives to the Nation-State in Canada and Europe*. Montreal, Quebec: Institute for Research on Public Policy, 1981.

985. Caulfield, J. *The Tiny Perfect Mayor: David Crombie and Toronto's Reform Aldermen*. Toronto: Lorimer, 1974.

986. Chandler, Marsha A., and Chandler, William M. *Public Policy and Provincial Politics*. Toronto: McGraw-Hill Ryerson, 1979. Study of the context in which provincial policy is made, the social, economic, and political structures which influence policy, the federal system, and specific policy areas including social policy and resource development policy.

987. Clarkson, S. *City Lib: Parties and Reform*. Toronto: Hakkert, 1972.

988. Colton, T.J. *Big Daddy: Frederick G. Gardiner and the Building of Metropolitan Toronto*. Toronto: University of Toronto Press, 1980.

989. Conway, J.F. *The West: The History of a Region in Confederation*. Toronto: Lorimer, 1983.

990. Dacks, Gurston. A Choice of Futures: Politics in the Canadian North. Toronto: Methuen, 1981. Study of natives and native rights, the political evolution of the North, and Northern issues in the 1980's.

991. Data Laboratories Research Consultants. Report of a Special Survey of Newfoundlanders' Attitudes Towards Confederation with Canada. Montreal: Data Laboratories Research Consultants, 1979.

992. Dennis, M., and Fish, S. Programs in Search of a Policy. Toronto: Hakkert, 1972.

993. Dickerson, M.O., et al., eds. Problems of Change in Urban Government. Waterloo: Wilfrid Laurier University Press, 1980.

994. Doern, R. Wednesdays Are Cabinet Days. Winnipeg: Queenston House, 1981. Study of the Schreyer Government in Manitoba and the way the government functioned and made policy.

995. Dunn, Martin. Access to Survival: A Perspective on Aboriginal Self-Government for the Constituency of the Native Council of Canada. Kingston, Ont.: Institute of Intergovernmental Relations, 1986.

996. Dyck, Noel, ed. Indigenous Peoples and the Nation-State: 'Fourth World' Politics in Canada, Australia, and Norway. St. Johns, Newf.: University of Newfoundland, 1985. Essays on the Canadian Constitution, James Bay issues, and the relationship between Aboriginal peoples and governments.

997. Dyck, Rand. Provincial Politics in Canada. Scarborough, Ont.: Prentice-Hall Canada, 1986. With a different chapter on each province, this text covers an impressive range of discussion of the major political issues in the provinces today.

998. Eager, Evelyn. Saskatchewan Government: Politics and Pragmatism. Saskatoon: Prairie Books, 1980. Study of structures and processes of Saskatchewan politics, including formal governmental institutions, political party organization and behavior, electoral behavior, and the public service.

999. Elkins, David J., and Simeon, Richard, eds. Small Worlds: Provinces and Parties in Canadian Political Life. Toronto: Methuen, 1980. Collection of essays dealing with provincial political culture, voting behavior, electoral coalitions, party systems, and public policy.

1000. Feldman, Lionel, ed. Politics and Government of Urban Canada. Toronto: Methuen, 1981.

1001. Feldman, Lionel D., and Goldrick, Michael D'Arcy, eds. <u>Politics and Government of Urban Canada: Selected Readings</u>. Toronto: Methuen, 1981, 4th ed. Articles including discussion of theories of local government, the Canadian urban phenomenon, urban political forces, urban reform, and the role of cities in intergovernmental relations.

1002. Feldman, Lionel D., and Graham, Katherine A. <u>Bargaining for Cities: Municipalities and Intergovernmental Relations -- An Assessment</u>. Toronto: Butterworths, 1979.

1003. Fraser, G. <u>Fighting Back: Urban Renewal in Trefann Court</u>. Toronto: Hakkert, 1972.

1004. Freeman, B., and Hewitt, M., eds. <u>Their Town: The Mafia, the Media, and the Party Machine</u>. Toronto: Lorimer, 1979. Study of Hamilton, Ontario municipal government.

1005. Gagan, D.P., ed. <u>Prairie Perspectives</u>. Toronto: Holt, Rinehart, Winston, 1970.

1006. Gertler, L., and Crowley, R. <u>Changing Canadian Cities: The Next 25 Years</u>. Toronto: McClelland and Stewart, 1977.

1007. Gibbins, Roger. <u>Regionalism: Territorial Politics in Canada and the United States</u>. Toronto: Butterworths, 1982. Discussion of regional variations across Canada in political party organization and behavior, electoral behavior, political culture, and attitudes, set in the general context of a discussion of Canadian federalism.

1008. Gibbins, Roger. <u>Prairie Politics and Society: Regionalism in Decline</u>. Toronto: Butterworths, 1980. Importance of theme of regionalism in provincial government behavior, 1905 - 1980.

1009. Gordon, D.R. <u>City Limits: Barriers to Change in Urban Government</u>. Don Mills, Ont.: Musson, 1973.

1010. Graham, Katherine A., et al. <u>A Climate for Change: Alternatives for the Central and Eastern Arctic</u>. Institute of Local Government, 1984.

1011. Graham, Katherine A., and McAllister, Anne B. <u>The Inuit Land Claim: Constitutional Development and Local Government Reform in the Northwest Territories: An Overview</u>. Kingston, Ontario: Institute of Local Government, 1981.

1012. Graham, Katherine A., et al. <u>Local and Regional Government in the Northwest Territories</u>. Kingston: Queen's University Press, 1980.

98 Contemporary Canadian Politics

1013. Hanigan, L., et al. Les communautés urbaines de Montréal et de Québec, premier bilan. [The Urban Communities of Montreal and Quebec, First Edition] Montréal: Presses de l'Université de Montréal, 1975.

1014. Harvey, E.R. Sydney, Nova Scotia: An Urban Study. Toronto: Clarke, Irwin, 1971.

1015. Hawkes, David C. Aboriginal Self-Government: What Does It Mean? Kingston, Ont.: Institute of Intergovernmental Relations, 1985.

1016. Higgins, Donald J. H. Urban Canada: Its Government and Politics. Toronto: Macmillan of Canada, 1977. Study of governmental structures at all levels of government, but especially cities, that make policy affecting urban areas, as well as the political processes involved in the development of urban areas.

1017. Hodgins, B.W., et al. The Canadian North. Scarborough, Ont.: Prentice-Hall of Canada, 1977.

1018. Innis, Hugh R., ed. Regional Disparities. Toronto: McGraw-Hill Ryerson, 1972.

1019. Jackson, F.L. Newfoundland in Canada: A People in Search of a Polity. St. John's, Nfld.: H. Cuff Publications, 1984.

1020. Joyce, J.C., ed. Challenging Tomorrow Today: Insights Into Municipal Administration. Montreal and Toronto: Renouf, 1979.

1021. Kaplan, Harold. Reform, Planning, and City Politics: Montreal, Winnipeg, Toronto. Toronto: University of Toronto Press, 1982. Massive study of how three Canadian cities initiated and developed a number of programs related to urban planning and reform.

1022. Kerr, Donald, ed. Western Canadian Politics: The Radical Tradition. Edmonton, Alberta: NeWest Institute, 1981. Essays on the growth of the CCF in the Canadian west, its development in Saskatchewan, and its role in western politics in the 1970's.

1023. Lacroix, Robert, and Rabeau, Yves. Politiques nationales, conjonctures régionales: la stabilisation économique. [National Politics and Regions: Economic Stabilization] Montreal: Les Presses de l'Université de Montréal, 1981. Analysis of taxation policies and other tools of the national government to stabilize the Canadian economy and to minimize regional disparities.

1024. Lakos, Amos. *Comparative Provincial Politics of Canada: A Bibliography of Select Periodical Articles, 1970-1977*. Waterloo, Ont.: University of Waterloo Library, 1979.

1025. Leadbeater, D., ed. *The Political Economy of Alberta*. Toronto: Lorimer, 1981.

1026. Leo, Christopher. *The Politics of Urban Development: Canadian Urban Expressway Disputes*. Toronto: Institute of Public Administration of Canada, 1977.

1027. Lithwick, N.H. *Urban Canada: Problems and Prospects*. Ottawa: Central Mortgage and Housing Corporation, 1970.

1028. Lorimer, James. *A Citizen's Guide to City Politics*. Toronto: James, Lewis, and Samuel, 1972.

1029. Lorimer, James. *The Real World of City Politics*. Toronto: James, Lewis, and Samuel, 1972.

1030. Lorimer, James. *The Developers*. Toronto: Lorimer, 1978.

1031. Lorimer, James, and MacGregor, C., eds. *After the Developers*. Toronto: Lorimer, 1981.

1032. Lorimer, James, and Ross, Evelyn, eds. *The Second City Book: Studies of Urban and Suburban Life*. Toronto: Lorimer, 1977.

1033. Lorimer, James., and Ross, Evelyn, eds. *The City Book: The Politics and Planning of Canada's Cities*. Toronto: J. Lorimer, 1976.

1034. McAllister, James A. *The Government of Edward Schreyer: Democratic Socialism in Manitoba*. Montreal: McGill-Queen's University Press, 1984. Evaluation of the New Democratic Party government of Manitoba and explanation of why it was unable to fulfill all of the goals of its supporters.

1035. MacDonald, Donald, ed. *The Government and Politics of Ontario*. Toronto: Van Nostrand Reinhold, 1980. Essays dealing with basic structures of Ontario government, the government policy-making process, voting behavior and political parties, and some specific policy fields of importance.

1036. McDonald, Donald S. *Government and Politics of Ontario*. Toronto: Macmillan of Canada, 1975.

1037. Magnusson, Warren, and Sancton, Andrew, eds. *City Politics in Canada*. Toronto: University of Toronto Press, 1983. Collection of essays dealing with municipal politics in Montreal, Ottawa, Toronto, Halifax, Vancouver, Winnipeg, and Edmonton.

1038. Malone, Marc. *Financing Aboriginal Self-Government in Canada*. Kingston, Ont.: Institute of Intergovernmental Relations, 1986.

1039. Manthorpe, J. *The Power and the Tories: Ontario's Politics -- 1943 to the Present*. Toronto: Macmillan, 1975.

1040. Médam, A. *Montréal interdite*. Paris: Presses Universitaires de France, 1978.

1041. Meynaud, J., and Léveillée, J. *La régionalisation municipale au Québec*. [Municipal Regionalization in Quebec] Montréal: Nouvelle Frontière, 1973.

1042. Miles, S.R., et al. *Developing a Canadian Urban Policy: Some Problems and Proposals*. Toronto: Intermet, 1973.

1043. Neary, P., ed. *The Political Economy of Newfoundland, 1929 - 1972.* Toronto: Copp Clark, 1973.

1044. Noel, S.J.R. *Politics in Newfoundland*. Toronto: University of Toronto Press, 1971.

1045. Nowlan, D., and Nowlan, N. *The Bad Trip -- The Untold Story of the Spadina Expressway*. Toronto: House of Anansi, 1970.

1046. Oervik, Nils. *Northern Development, Northern Security*. Kingston, Ont.: Centre for International Relations, 1983.

1047. Paine, R. *Political Rhetoric in the New Newfoundland*. St. John's: Breakwater Books, 1981.

1048. Paquette, Jerald E. *Aboriginal Self-Government and Education in Canada*. Kingston, Ont.: Institute of Intergovernmental Relations, 1986.

1049. Perks, W.T., and Robertson, I.M., eds. *Urban and Regional Planning in a Federal State: The Canadian Experience*. Toronto: McGraw-Hill Ryerson, 1979.

1050. Peters, Evelyn J. *Aboriginal Self-Government in Canada: A Bibliography, 1986.* Kingston, Ontario: Queen's University, 1986.

1051. Peterson, Everett B., and Wright, Janet B., eds. *Northern Resource and Land Use Policy Study*. Ottawa, Ont.: Canadian Arctic Resources Committee, 1978.

1052. Phillips, Paul. *Regional Disparities*. Toronto: Lorimer, 1978. The nature of regional disparities, the significance of confederation in the effort to minimize disparities, and a proposal for a new national policy to alleviate disparities.

1053. Plunkett, Thomas J., and Betts, George M. _The Management of Canadian Urban Government: A Basic Text For A Course In Urban Management_. Kingston, Ont.: Institute of Local Government, Queen's University, 1978.

1054. Plunkett, T.J. _The Financial Structure and the Decision-Making Process of Canadian Municipal Government_. Ottawa: Central Mortgage and Housing Corporation, 1972.

1055. Ponting, J. Rick, ed. _Arduous Journey: Canadian Indians and Decolonization_. Toronto: McClelland and Stewart, 1986.

1056. Powell, A., ed. _The City: Attacking Modern Myths_. Toronto: McClelland and Stewart, 1972.

1057. Purich, Donald J. _Our Land: Native Rights in Canada_. Toronto: J. Lorimer, 1986.

1058. Rawlyk, George et al. _Regionalism in Canada: Flexible Federalism or Fractured Nation?_ Scarborough, Ont.: Prentice Hall of Canada, 1979.

1059. Rawlyk, George A., ed. _The Atlantic Provinces and the Problems of Confederation._ St. John's, Nfld.: Breakwater, 1979. Collection of articles dealing with general historical framework, role of newspapers in the Atlantic provinces, and the political elite in the Atlantic provinces.

1060. Rea, K.J. _The Political Economy of Northern Development_. Science Council of Canada, 1976.

1061. Richards, J., and Pratt, L. _Prairie Capitalism: Power and Influence in the New West_. Toronto: McClelland and Stewart, 1979.

1062. Richardson, B. _The Future of Canadian Cities_. Toronto: New Press, 1972.

1063. Riddell, Barry, and Lynch, John. _Urban Politics_. Toronto: Maclean-Hunter Learning Materials Co., 1972.

1064. Robin, Martin, ed. _Canadian Provincial Politics: The Party Systems of the Ten Provinces_. Scarborough, Ont.: Prentice-Hall of Canada, 1978. Collection of articles about the state of political party competition within each of the provinces.

1065. Robin, Martin. _Pillars of Profit: The Company Province, 1934-1972_. Toronto: McClelland and Stewart, 1973. Study of provincial politics in British Columbia.

1066. Robin, Martin. The Rush for Spoils: The Company Province, 1871-1933. Toronto: McClelland and Stewart, 1972. Study of provincial politics in British Columbia.

1067. Robinson, I.M. Canadian Urban Growth Trends. Vancouver: University of British Columbia Press, 1981.

1068. Rose, A. Governing Metropolitan Toronto: A Social and Political Analysis, 1953 - 1971. Los Angeles: University of California Press, 1972.

1069. Roussopoulos, D., ed. The City and Radical Social Change. Montreal: Black Rose, 1979.

1070. Rowat, D.C., ed. Provincial Policy-Making: Comparative Essays. Ottawa: Carleton University Press, 1981.

1071. Rowat, Donald C. Your Local Government: A Sketch of the Municipal System in Canada. Toronto: Macmillan of Canada, 1975. Background for a study of local government, how local governments are organized, what they do, and their structures.

1072. Rowat, Donald C. The Government of Federal Capitals. Toronto: University of Toronto Press, 1973.

1073. Rowat, Donald C., ed. Provincial Government and Politics: Comparative Essays. 2nd ed. Ottawa: Carleton University Press, 1973.

1074. Sager, Eric W., Fischer, Lewis R., and Pierson, Stuart O. Atlantic Canada and Confederation: Essays in Canadian Political Economy. Toronto: University of Toronto Press, 1983.

1075. Schwartz, M. Politics and Territory: The Sociology of Regional Persistence in Canada. Montreal: McGill-Queen's University Press, 1974.

1076. Sewell, J. Up Against City Hall. Toronto: James, Lewis, and Samuel, 1972.

1077. Sewell, J. Inside City Hall. Toronto: Hakkert, 1971.

1078. Shaw, Timothy, and Yash, Tandon, eds. Regional Development at the National Level: Volume I: Canadian and African Perspectives. Lanham, Md.: University Press of America, 1985. Essays focusing upon regional political issues, including language and technology, and analysis of regional policies in specific policy areas.

1079. Spurr, P. Land and Urban Development. Toronto: Lorimer, 1976.

1080. Stein, D.L. *Toronto for Sale*. Toronto: New Press, 1972.

1081. Stelter, Gilbert Arthur, and Artibise, Alan F. J., eds. *Power and Place: Canadian Urban Development in the North American Context*. Vancouver: University of British Columbia Press, 1986.

1082. Stevenson, Garth, and Pratt, L., ed. *Western Separatism: Myths, Realities, and Dangers*. Edmonton: Hurtig, 1981.

1083. Swainson, D., ed. *Historical Essays on the Prairie Provinces*. Toronto: McClelland and Stewart, 1970.

1084. Tindal, C. R., and Tindal, S. Nobes. *Local Government in Canada: An Introduction*. Toronto: McGraw-Hill Ryerson, 1979. Introductory textbook, includes discussion of history and effects of urbanization, local government reform, machinery of municipal government, and municipal management.

1085. Tindal, C. R. *Structural Changes in Local Government: Government for Urban Regions*. Toronto: Institute of Public Administration of Canada, 1977.

1086. Waddell, K. Bruce, *A Survey of Public Review Hearings in Northern Canada*. Ottawa: Indian and Northern Affairs, Canada, 1981.

1087. Walsh, Bren. *More than a Poor Majority: The Story of Newfoundland's Confederation with Canada*. St. John's, Nfld.: Breakwater, 1985.

1088. Ward, W. Peter. *White Canada Forever: Popular Attitudes and Public Policy Toward Orientals in British Columbia*. Montreal: McGill-Queen's University Press, 1978. Political-history of the role of Asians in British Columbia and race relations in British Columbia history.

1089. Whittington, Michael S., ed. *The North*. Toronto: University of Toronto Press, 1985. Constitutional development of the North, economic issues, problems of development, and the topic of sovereignty.

1090. Wolforth, J.R. *Urban Prospects*. Toronto: McClelland and Stewart, 1971.

Articles

1091. Abele, Francis, and Dickerson, M. "The 1982 Plebiscite on Division of the Northwest Territories: Regional Government and Federal Policy." *Canadian Public Policy* 11:1 (March, 1985): 1-16.

1092. Abele, Frances, and Dosman, E.J. "Interdepartmental Coordination and Northern Development." Canadian Public Administration 24:3 (1981): 428-451.

1093. Andrew, Caroline. "Espace et politique: le cas de Montréal." ["Territory and Politics: The Case of Montreal."] Canadian Journal of Political Science 12:2 (1979): 369-384. Bibliographic review article dealing with five books on Montreal's urban development.

1094. Andrew, Caroline, Blais, André, and Des Rosiers, Rachel. "Les échevins et la formulation des politiques: note méthodologique." ["The Aldermen and the Formulation of Politics: A Methodological Note."] Canadian Public Administration 20:2 (1977): 231-241.

1095. Andrew, Caroline, et al. "Le logement public à Hull." ["Public Housing in Hull."] Canadian Journal of Political Science 8:3 (1975): 403-430.

1096. Angers, Bernard. "Considérations sur le financement des municipalités du Québec." ["Considerations on the Financing of Municipalities of Quebec."] Canadian Public Policy 2:4 (Autumn, 1976): 599-606.

1097. Angers, Bernard. "Certaines considerations relatives à la question municipale." ["Some Considerations on the Municipal Question."] Canadian Public Administration 20:2 (1977): 380-388.

1098. Armstrong, J.L. "Retrenchment at City Hall." Canadian Public Administration 29:4 (1986): 542-544.

1099. Atkinson, Michael, and Mancuso, Maureen. "Do We Need a Code of Conduct for Politicians? The Search for an Elite Political Culture of Corruption in Canada." Canadian Journal of Political Science 18:3 (1985): 459-480. Attempt to develop a theory of local public rule in Canada which is "sensitive to" regional variation and historical events.

1100. Aucoin, Peter, and Bakvis, Herman. "Organizational Differentiation and Integration: The Case of Regional Economic Development Policy in Canada." Canadian Public Administration 27:3 (1984): 348-371.

1101. Beecroft, Eric. "Local Government in Canada." Studies in Comparative Local Government 5:1 (1971): 5-27. Covers structural and fiscal reform, federal-provincial-municipal relationships, multi-level consultation, provincial-municipal relationships, and community development issues primarily in Ontario, Manitoba, New Brunswick, and British Columbia.

1102. Bélanger, Gérard. "Questions de base à toute réforme du financement municipal." ["Questions Underlying All Municipal Financial Reform."] Canadian Public Administration 20:2 (Summer, 1977): 370-379.

1103. Bellavance, Michel. "Le ministère de l'Education du Québec et la gestion de l'enseignement supérieur." ["The Minister of Education of Quebec and the Management of Higher Education."] Canadian Public Administration 24:1 (Spring, 1981): 73-91.

1104. Bissonette, Lise. "Orthodoxie fédéraliste et rélations régionales trans-frontières -- une menace illusoire." ["The Federalist Orthodoxy and Regional Transboundary Relations, a Deceptive Threat."] Études internationales 12:4 (1981): 635-656. Examines relations between some Canadian provinces and American states to assess their effect upon the relations between the two federal governments.

1105. Blackman, W.J. "A Western Canadian Perspective on the Economics of Confederation." Canadian Public Policy 3:4 (Autumn, 1977): 414-430.

1106. Blais, André. "Third Parties in Canadian Provincial Politics." Canadian Journal of Political Science 6:3 (1973): 422-438. Tests Pinard's notion that one-party dominance is a necessary condition for the rise of third parties.

1107. Blake, D.E. "LIP and Partisanship: An Analysis of Local Initiatives Program." Canadian Public Policy 2:1 (Winter, 1976): 17-32.

1108. Blakeney, Allan. "The Relationship Between Provincial Ministers and Their Deputy Ministers." Canadian Public Administration 15 (Spring, 1972): 42-45.

1109. Boldt, Menno. "Enlightenment Values, Romanticism, and Attitudes Toward Political Status: A Study of Native Leaders in Canada." Canadian Review of Sociology and Anthropology 18:4 (1981): 545-565. Analysis of Enlightenment and Romanticism philosophies and the impact on increased self-determination.

1110. Boldt, Menno. "Philosophy, Politics, and Extralegal Action: Native Indian Leaders in Canada." Ethnic and Racial Studies 4:2 (1981): 205-221. Study of Indian leaders concerning the relationship between extralegal actions and philosophy.

1111. Boldt, Menno. "Social Correlates of Nationalism: A Study of Native Indian Leaders in a Canadian Internal Colony." Comparative Political Studies 14:2 (1981): 205-232. Selection of social background data and political goals of native Indian leaders.

1112. Boldt, Menno, and Long, J. Anthony. "Tribal Traditions and European-Western Political Ideologies: The Dilemma of Canada's Native Indians." *Canadian Journal of Political Science* 17:3 (1984): 537-554.

1113. Boldt, Menno, and Long, J. Anthony. "Political Attitudes of Members of an Internal Colony: A Study of Native Indian University Students in Canada." *Plural Societies* 14:3-4 (1983): 85-107.

1114. Bone, Robert M. "Canada's Last Frontier: The North." *Current History* 66:392 (1974): 161-164.

1115. Bone, Robert, and Green, M. "Housing Assistance and Maintenance for the Métis in Northern Saskatchewan." *Canadian Public Policy* 9:4 (December, 1983): 476-485.

1116. Brody, Hugh. "Ecology, Politics, and Change: The Case of the Eskimo." *Development and Change* 9:1 (1978): 21-40. The search for raw materials will destroy traditional life and culture of the Eskimo.

1117. Brody, Hugh. "Eskimo Politics: The Threat from the South." *New Left Review* 79 (1973): 60-68.

1118. Bryden, Kenneth. "Executive and Legislature in Ontario: A Case Study on Governmental Reform." *Canadian Public Administration* 18:2 (1975): 235-252.

1119. Burns, Ronald M. "Government in an Urban Society," *Canadian Public Administration* 14 (1971): 415-426.

1120. Busey, J.L. "Books on Canadian Provincial Government." *Social Science Journal* (Fort Collins) 14:1 (1977): 149-155. There is a lack of studies on Canadian provincial politics, but it is hoped this gap will be filled with the maturation of Canadian political studies.

1121. Cameron, David. "Regional Economic Disparities: The Challenge to Federalism and Public Policy." *Canadian Public Policy* 7:4 (Autumn, 1981): 500-518.

1122. Cameron, David. "Provincial Responsibilities for Municipal Government." *Canadian Public Administration* 23:2 (1980): 222-235.

1123. Cameron, David. "Regional Integration in the Maritime Provinces." *Canadian Journal of Political Science* 4:1 (1971): 24-25. Suggests that the regional label "Maritime Provinces" is of geographic use only, and is not a meaningful tool for analysis.

1124. Campbell, Alexander, Regan, Gerald, and Hatfield, Richard. "The Move Toward Maritime Integration and the Role of the Council of Maritime Premiers." *Canadian Public Administration* 15:4 (1972): 591-609.

Regionalism and Local Politics   107

1125. Careless, Anthony. "The Struggle for Jurisdiction: Regionalism versus Rationalism." Publius 14:1 (1984): 61-78. Regional ties and sectional jealousies over jurisdictional boundaries have often gotten in the way of an "economically rational" policy making process.

1126. Cartwright, Don. "An Official Languages Policy for Ontario." Canadian Public Policy 11:3 (1985): 561-77. The Government of Ontario has resisted requests that French be made an official language of the Province.

1127. Chandler, Marsha. "State Enterprise and Partisanship in Provincial Politics." Canadian Journal of Political Science 15:4 (1982): 711-740.

1128. Chekki, Dan. "Planning and Citizen Participation in a Canadian City." Community Development Journal 14:1 (1979): 34-40. Structure, functions, and problems of the "Unicity" government of Winnipeg.

1129. Chi, N.H. "The Regression Model of Regionalism: A Critique." Canadian Journal of Political Science 5:2 (1972): 291-297. A mathematical analysis of the value of the concept of "regionalism" for explanation of social and political phenomena. Critique of William P. Irvine's 1971 study of regional effects in data analysis.

1130. Chorney, Harold, and Hansen, Phillip. "Neo-Conservatism, Social Democracy, and `Province-Building': The Experience of Manitoba." Canadian Review of Sociology and Anthropology 22:1 (1985): 1-29.

1131. Clarkson, Stephen. "Barriers to Entry of Parties into Toronto's Civic Politics: Towards a Theory of Party Penetration." Canadian Journal of Political Science 4:2 (1971): 206-223.

1132. Cohen, Maxwell. "The Arctic and the National Interest." International Journal 26:1 (1971): 52-81.

1133. Coleman, William, and Grant, Wyn. "Regional Differentiation of Business Interest Associations: A Comparison of Canada and the United Kingdom." Canadian Journal of Political Science 18:1 (1985): 3-30.

1134. Collin, Jean-Pierre. "Le Partage Fiscal Banlieue-Ville Centrale: Les Montrealais Subventionnent-ils Les Banlieusards?" ["The Fiscal Distribution Between Suburbs And Central City: Are the Inhabitants of Montreal Subsidizing Those of the Suburbs?"] Canadian Journal of Political Science 17:1 (1984): 109-132. Data from 1969-1980 are analyzed to examine the question of whether Montreal citizens are subsidizing the social expenses of the suburbs.

1135. Copithorne, L. "Natural Resources and Regional Disparities: A Skeptical View." Canadian Public Policy 5:2 (Spring, 1979): 181-194.

1136. Corbett, John G. "Canadian Cities: How `American' Are They?" Urban Affairs Quarterly 13:3 (1978): 383-397.

1137. Cotterill, E.M.R. "The Territorial North." Canadian Public Administration 27:2 (1984): 188-196.

1138. Courchene, T. "A Market Perspective on Regional Disparities." Canadian Public Policy 7:4 (Autumn, 1981): 506-518.

1139. Dacks, Gurston. "The Case Against Dividing the Northwest Territories." Canadian Public Policy 12:1 (1986): 163-174. Although the Inuit are seeking the division of the Territories, there are many reasons for not going through with the division that has been proposed.

1140. Dacks, Gurston. "The Politics of Development in Canada's North." Current History 83:493 (1984): 220-234.

1141. Dacks, Gurston. "Politics on the Last Frontier: Consociationalism in the Northwest Territories." Canadian Journal of Political Science 19:2 (1986): 345-362.

1142. Dahms, F.A. "The Evolution of Settlement Systems: A Canadian Example, 1851 - 1970." Journal of Urban History 7:2 (1981): 169-204. Settlements in Wellington County, Ontario, are examined to understand patterns of urban government and centralization.

1143. D'Entremont, H., and Robardet, Patrick. "More Reform in New Brunswick: Rural Municipalities." Canadian Public Administration 20:3 (Fall, 1977): 469-480.

1144. Divay, Gérard, and Léveillée, Jacques. "The Process of Municipal Reform Within the Framework of the Development of the State of Quebec." Revue français d'Administration publique 17 (1981): 67-83.

1145. Divay, Gérard. "Le développment d'initiative locale." ["The Development of Local Initiative."] Canadian Public Administration 23:2 (1980): 236-251.

1146. Doré, Philippe. "Saskatchewan: Lieutenant-Governor's Death Causes Constitutional Problems." Parliamentarian 59:3 (1978): 176-177.

Regionalism and Local Politics   109

1147.   Eagles, Paul F.J. "Environmentally Sensitive Area
        Planning in Ontario, Canada." Journal of American
        Planning Association 47:3 (1981): 313-323. Role of
        municipal governments in protecting natural area
        from damage when development takes place.

1148.   Entremont, Harley, and Robardet, Patrick . "More
        Reform in New Brunswick: Rural Municipalities."
        Canadian Public Administration 20:3 (1977): 469-480.

1149.   Farrow, R.M. "The Role of the Municipality in the
        Three-Level System of Government." Governmental
        Finance 2:2 (1973): 2-5. The idea of decentralizing
        public decision-making is being studied in the con-
        text of Canadian municipal government.

1150.   Fernandes, Peter P., and Laberge, Myriam. "Setting
        Local Government Priorities through the Budget Pro-
        cess." Government Finance Review 2:2 (1986): 21-28.

1151.   Filion, Pierre. "Core Redevelopment, Neighbourhood
        Revitalization, and Municipal Government Motivation:
        Twenty Years of Urban Renewal in Quebec City."
        Canadian Journal of Political Science 20:1 (1987):
        131-148.

1152.   Fleck, James D. "Reorganization of the Ontario
        Government." Canadian Public Administration 15:2
        (Summer, 1972): 383-385.

1153.   Fleck, James D. "Restructuring the Ontario Govern-
        ment." Canadian Public Administration 16:1 (1973):
        55-68.

1154.   Freeman, M.M.R., and Hackman, L.M. "Bathurst Island
        NWT: A Test Case of Canada's Northern Policy."
        Canadian Public Policy 1:3 (Summer, 1975): 402-414.

1155.   Frisken, Frances. "Canadian Cities and the American
        Example: A Prologue to Urban Policy Analysis."
        Canadian Public Administration 29:3 (1986): 345-376.

1156.   Fuga, Olga. "New Winnipeg Government is Unique
        Urban Experiment." National Civic Review 62:4
        (1973): 189-196.

1157.   Gallant, E. "L'Aménagement de la Capitale Nation-
        ale." ["The Preparation of the National Capital."]
        Canadian Public Policy 1:2 (Spring, 1975): 158-161.

1158.   Gartner, Gerry J. "A Review of Cooperation Among
        the Western Provinces." Canadian Public Administra-
        tion 20:1 (1977): 174-187.

1159.   Garven, Garnet, and Long, Richard J. "Capital
        Budget Decision-Making Processes in Canadian Urban
        Municipalities." Canadian Public Administration
        24:4 (1981): 634-640.

110 Contemporary Canadian Politics

1160. Gibbins, Roger. "Regional Politics in the Wake of the Canada Act." Canadian Issues 5 (1983): 131-137.

1161. Gibbins, Roger. "Models of Nationalism: A Case Study of Political Ideologies in the Canadian West." Canadian Journal of Political Science 10:2 (1977): 341-373. The utility of the nationalism concept for the study of political beliefs in Alberta, using sample survey data.

1162. Godbout, J. "La formation de la communauté urbaine de Québec et le rôle de l'Etat dans la restructuration des pouvoirs locaux." ["The Creation of the Urban Community of Quebec, and the Role of the State in the Restructuring of Local Powers."] Recherches sociographiques 12:2 (1971): 185-225.

1163. Goldrick, M.D. "Present Issues in the Growth of Cities." Canadian Public Administration 14:3 (Fall, 1971): 452-461.

1164. Graham, J.F. "An Introduction to the Nova Scotia Royal Commission." Canadian Public Policy 1:3 (Summer, 1975): 349-354.

1165. Gray, J.A. "Royal Commission and Forest Policy in British Columbia: A Review of the Pearse Report." Canadian Public Policy 3:2 (Spring, 1977): 219-223.

1166. Guillemin, Jeanne. "The Politics of National Integration: A Comparison of United States and Canadian Indian Administrations." Social Problems 25:3 (1978): 319-332. A comparison of North American Indian administrations and their problems.

1167. Hahn, Harlan. "Ethos and Social Class: Referenda in Canadian Cities." Polity 2:3 (1970): 295-315.

1168. Hanson, Bill. "Special Problems of Indian/Native People." Canadian Public Administration 29:4 (1986): 632-634.

1169. Hanson, Eric J. "The Future of Western Canada: Economic, Social, and Political." Canadian Public Administration 18:1 (1975): 104-120.

1170. Harris, Richard. "The New Left in Urban Politics." Queen's Quarterly 92:3 (1985): 572-589. Study of the impact of the New Left upon community politics indicates that the contributions of the movement were few and quite small.

1171. Harris, Richard. "A Social Movement in Urban Politics: A Reinterpretation of Urban Reform in Canada." International Journal of Urban and Regional Research 11:3 (1987): 363-381.

1172. Hautecoeur, J.P. "Variations et invariance de l'Acadie dans le néo-nationalisme acadien." ["Variations and Uniformity of Acadia in Acadian Neo-Nationalism."] Recherches sociographiques 12:3 (1971): 259-270.

1173. Heck, James D. "Restructuring the Ontario Government." Canadian Public Administration 16:1 (1973): 55-68.

1174. Hedlin, Ralph. "Economics of One Prairie Province." Canadian Public Administration 13:4 (Winter, 1970): 354-359.

1175. Higgins, Donald J.H. "Municipal Politics and Government: Development of the Field in Canadian Political Science." Canadian Public Administration 22:3 (1979): 380-401.

1176. Higgins, Donald. "The Processes of Reorganizing Local Government in Canada." Canadian Journal of Political Science 19:2 (1986): 219-242. Studies the processes by which change either occurs or is avoided or delayed. Examines 81 instances between 1953 and 1983 of change in local government in Canada.

1177. Husband, D.D. "National Versus Regional Growth: Some Issues." Canadian Public Administration 14:4 (1971): 538-555.

1178. Ircha, M.C. "Urban Economic Development and Regulation by Municipal Licensing." Canadian Public Administration 28:3 (1985): 477-482.

1179. Irvine, William. "Assessing Regional Effects in Data Analysis." Canadian Journal of Political Science 4:1 (1971): 21-24. How to analyze data measuring the effects of regions on dependent variables.

1180. Jackson, Michael. "Une minorité ignorée: Les Franco-Canadiens de la Saskatchewan." ["An Ignored Minority: The French-Canadians of Saskatchewan."] Journal of Canadian Studies 7:3 (1972): 3-22.

1181. Jessop, J., and Weaver, C. "La coopération communautaire: une stratégie pour le développement local." ["Community Cooperation: A Strategy for Local Development."] Revue internationale d'Action communautaire 53 (1985): 149-160. Study of different models of development focusing upon British Columbia.

1182. Jones, L.R. "Coping with Revenue and Expenditure Constraints in the Provincial Government Context." Canadian Public Administration 29:4 (1986): 528-541.

1183.   Jones, L. R. "Financial Restriant Management and Budget Control in Canadian Provincial Governments." Canadian Public Administration 29:2 (1986): 259-281.

1184.   Kay, Barry J. "Urban Decision-Making and the Legislative Environment: Toronto Council Re-examined." Canadian Journal of Political Science 15:3 (1982): 553-574.

1185.   Kerr, Anthony G. "The Principles of a Financial Information System for Municipalities." Governmental Finance 2:2 (1973): 7-11. How to resolve problems in classifying and reporting municipal accounting information.

1186.   Kierans, Eric. "The Corporate Impact on Political Authority in Regional Systems." Revue d'Integration européenne 3:3 (1980): 381-392.

1187.   Kitchen, Harry M. "Some Organizational Implications of Providing an Urban Service: The Case of Water." Canadian Public Administration 18:2 (Summer, 1975): 297-308.

1188.   Koch, Agnes, and Labovitz, Sanford. "Interorganizational Power in a Canadian Community: A Replication." Sociological Quarterly 17:1 (1976): 3-15.

1189.   Kopinac, Kathryn. "Women in Canadian Municipal Politics: Two SASGs Forward, One Step Back." Canadian Review of Sociology and Anthropology 22:3 (1985): 394-410. Studies patterns of women's increasingly frequent elections to municipal office.

1190.   Krause, Robert, and Price, Trevor. "The Impact of Financial Restraint on the Provision of Municipal Services in Canada." Planning and Administration 13:1 (1986): 58-63.

1191.   Krueger, Ralph R. "The Provincial-Municipal Government Revolution in New Brunswick." Canadian Public Administration 13:1 (1970): 51-99.

1192.   Lang, A.H. "G. M. Dawson and the Economic Development of Western Canada." Canadian Public Administration 14:2 (Summer, 1971): 236-255.

1193.   Lapointe, Jean-Louis. "La réforme de la fiscalité municipale au Québec." ["The Reform of Municipal Fiscal Relations in Quebec."] Canadian Public Administration 23:2 (1980): 269-280.

1194.   Leith, J.C. "What is Ontario's Mineral Resource Policy?" Canadian Public Policy 4:3 (Summer, 1978): 352-363.

1195. Lemieux, Vincent. "Le pouvoir des coordinateurs régionaux." ["The Power of Regional Coordinators."] Canadian Public Administration 21:2 (Summer, 1978): 161-175.

1196. Levy, Thomas Allen. "Developing Regionalism in the Maritimes and Western Canada." Current History 66:392 (1974): 167-172.

1197. Lightbody, James. "The Reform of a Metropolitan Government: The Case of Winnipeg, 1971." Canadian Public Policy 4:4 (Autumn, 1978): 489-504.

1198. Lithwick, N.H. "Urban Policy-Making: Shortcomings in Political Technology." Canadian Public Administration 15:4 (1972): 571-584.

1199. Lomas, A.A. "The Council of Maritime Premiers: Report and Evaluation after 5 Years." Canadian Public Administration 20:1 (1977) 188-200.

1200. Lyon, Vaughan. "Minority Government in Ontario, 1975-1981: An Assessment." Canadian Journal of Political Science 17:4 (1984): 685-706.

1201. McDavid, James C. "The Canadian Experience with Privatizing Residential Solid Waste Collection Services." Public Administration Review 45:5 (1985): 602-608.

1202. McDavid, James C. "Part-Time Firefighters in Canadian Municipalities: Cost and Effectiveness Comparisons." Canadian Public Administration 29:3 (1986): 377-387.

1203. McLarty, R.A. "Tracking Down the Saskatchewan Budget Bureau and Planning Board of 1964." Canadian Public Administration 22:1 (1979): 115-123.

1204. McMillan, H. Stewart. "Long-Term Municipal Financing." Government Financing 4:2 (1975): 16-19. Studies Saskatchewan's program to help local governments avoid the inflationary costs of municipal bonds.

1205. MacMillan, James A, and Nickel, Edith . "An Economic Appraisal of Urban Housing Assistance: Rental Supplements Versus Public Housing." Canadian Public Administration 17:3 (1974): 443-460.

1206. Magnusson, Warren. The Local State in Canada: Theoretical Perspectives." Canadian Public Administration 28:4 (1985): 575-599.

1207. Mahoney, Patrick. "In Ottawa: The Role of the Canadian Government in Municipal Finance." Governmental Finance 1:3 (1972): 18-22. The role of municipalities under the Canadian Constitution, federal policy, and the federal role in municipal finance.

1208. Mallory, J.R. "Restructuring the Government of Ontario: A Comment." Canadian Public Administration 16:1 (1973): 69-72.

1209. Mansbridge, Stanley H. "Of Social Policy in Alberta: Its Management, Its Modification, Its Evaluation, and Its Meaning." Canadian Public Administration 21:3 (1978): 311-323.

1210. Martin, F. "Incidence de la crise de l'énergie sur le développement régional canadien." ["The Effect of the Energy Crisis on Canadian Regional Development."] Canadian Public Policy 1:1 (Winter, 1975): 39-46.

1211. Massam, Bryan H. "Forms of Local Government in the Montreal Area, 1911-1971: A Discriminant Approach." Canadian Journal of Political Science 6:2 (1973): 243-253. Study of the relationship between socio-economic variables and characteristics of local government in the Montreal area.

1212. Masson, Jack K. "Decision-Making Patterns and Floating Coalitions in an Urban City Council." Canadian Journal of Political Science 8:1 (1975): 128-137. Voting behavior of the Edmonton city council from 1966 to 1972, and the roll of party organization on that level of government.

1213. Matthews, R. "Two Alternative Explanations of the Problem of Regional Dependency in Canada." Canadian Public Policy 7:2 (Spring, 1981): 268-283.

1214. Matthews, Ralph. "Perspectives on Recent Newfoundland Politics." Journal of Canadian Studies 9:2 (1974): 20-35.

1215. Matthews, R. "Ethical Issues in Policy Research: The Investigation of Community Resettlement in Newfoundland." Canadian Public Policy 1:2 (Spring, 1975): 204-218.

1216. Michelmann, Hans J., and Steeves, Jeffrey. "The 1982 Transition in Power in Saskatchewan: The Progressive Conservatives and the Public Service." Canadian Public Administration 28:1 (1985): 1-23.

1217. Migué, Jean-Luc. "Politiques régionales: traitement du malade ou maladie gu guérisseur?" ["Regional Politics: Treatment of an Illness or Illness of a Recovery?"] Canadian Public Administration 21:2 (Summer, 1978): 195-211.

1218. Millerd, Frank W. "Canadian Urban Industrial Growth from 1961 to 1971." Growth and Change 14:1 (1983): 20-26.

1219. Molot, Maureen Appel, and Laux, Jeanne Kirk. "The Politics of Nationalization." Canadian Journal of Political Science 12:2 (1979): 227-258. The 1975 decision of the New Democratic Party Government in Saskatchewan to take over Saskatchewan's potash industry.

1220. Moore, Mike, and Vanderhaden, Gary. "Northern Problems or Canadian Opportunities." Canadian Public Administration 27:2 (1984): 182-187.

1221. Morin, Serge J. "New Brunswick's Francophones: A Structural Injustice." Peace Research Reviews 6:2 (1974): 49-52. Francophones of New Brunswick are victims of a variety of injustices, legal, social, and cultural.

1222. Morisset, Jean. "The Demand for Ethnic Autonomy in the Canadian Northwest." Journal of Social and Political Studies 4:4 (1979): 345-358. A historical examination of the demands by the Dene nation for ethnic autonomy.

1223. Morley, T. "Labour in British Columbia Politics." Queen's Quarterly 83:2 (1976): 291-298.

1224. Neary, Peter. "Party Politics in Newfoundland, 1949-1971: A Survey and Analysis." Journal of Canadian Studies 6:4 (1971): 3-14.

1225. Neary, Peter. "Politics in Newfoundland: The End of the Smallwood Era." Journal of Canadian Studies 7:1 (1972): 3-21.

1226. Norrie, K.H. "Some Comments on Prairie Economic Alienation." Canadian Public Policy 2:2 (Spring, 1976): 211-224.

1227. O'Brien, Allan. "Local Government Priorities for the Eighties." Canadian Public Administration 19:1 (1976): 102-111.

1228. Ornstein, Michael D., Stevenon, H. Michael, and Williams, A. Paul. "Region, Class, and Political Culture in Canada." Canadian Journal of Political Science 13:2 (1980): 227-272.

1229. Overton, James. "Living Patriotism: Songs, Politics, and Resources in Newfoundland." Canadian Review of Studies in Nationalism 12 (1985): 239-259. Role of "popular culture" in the success of the Conservative Party's success is analyzed.

1230. Pell, David, and Wismer, Susan. "We'll Do It Ourselves: Community Development Canadian Style." Development 3 (1982): 40-46.

1231. Pharand, Donat. "The Legal Régime of the Arctic: Some Outstanding Issues." International Journal 39:4 (1984): 742-799. Discusses Canada's claim to jurisdiction over the waters of its Arctic archipelago.

1232. Plunkett, Thomas J. "Structural Reform of Local Government in Canada." Public Administration Review 33:1 (1973): 40-51. Focus upon structural reform in metropolitan Toronto, Winnipeg, and Montreal areas, and in British Columbia and New Brunswick on the provincial level.

1233. Plunkett, T.J., and Hooson, W. "Municipal Structure and Services." Canadian Public Policy 1:3 (Summer, 1975): 367-375.

1234. Plunkett, T.J., and Graham, Katherine. "Whither Municipal Government?" Canadian Public Administration 25:4 (1982): 603-618.

1235. Poel, Dale H. "The Diffusion of Legislation Among the Canadian Provinces: A Statistical Analysis." Canadian Journal of Political Science 9:4 (1976): 605-626. Measures the relative speed by which Canadian provinces adopted acts related to various legislative topics relative to socio-economic and other political characteristics of the provinces.

1236. Proudfoot, S. "The Politics of Approval: Regulating Land Use on the Urban Fringe." Canadian Public Policy 7:2 (Spring, 1981): 284-296.

1237. Quesnel, Louise. "La démocratie municipale au Québec." ["Municipal Democracy in Quebec."] Politique 9 (1986): 61-97.

1238. Quesnel-Ouellet, Louise. "La coopération à l'intérieur d'une région métropolitaine: éléments d'analyse." ["The Cooperation Inside a Metropolitan Region: Elements of Analysis."] Canadian Public Administration 16:3 (1973): 432-446.

1239. Quesnel-Ouellet, Louise. "Situations et attitudes face au changement dans les structures municipales." ["Situations and Attitudes Toward Municipal Reorganization."] Canadian Journal of Political Science 6:2 (1973): 195-218. Influence of popular characteristics upon attitudes toward local government and annexation in Quebec.

1240. Quesnel-Ouellet, Louise. "Régionalisation et conscience politique régional: la communauté urbaine de Québec." ["Regionalization and Regional Political Conscience: The Urban Community of Quebec."] Canadian Journal of Political Science 4:2 (1971): 191-205.

1241. Raboy, Marc. "Urban Struggles and Municipal Politics: The Montreal Citizens' Movement." International Review of Community Development 39-40 (1978): 145-164. Study of the Montreal Citizen's Movement, its proposed reforms, and its effects on the nature of social struggle in Quebec.

1242. Raynauld, André. "Pour une politique de stabilisation régionale." ["For a Politics of Regional Stabilization."] Canadian Public Administration 14:3 (1971): 344-353.

1243. Redcliffe-Maud, Lord. "The Politics of Local Government Progress." Canadian Public Administration 17:3 (1974): 389-405.

1244. Reeve, A.W. "Local Government Revenue Sources in Canada." Governmental Finance 2:2 (1973): 12-17. How the British North America Act limitations on fundraising have affected municipal and provincial spending patterns. Describes sources of local government revenue.

1245. Reeves, W., and Frideres, J. "Government Policy and Indian Urbanization: The Alberta Case." Canadian Public Policy 7:4 (Autumn, 1981): 584-595.

1246. Richardson, N.H. "Insubstantial Pageant: The Rise and Fall of Provincial Planning in Ontario." Canadian Public Administration 24:4 (1981): 563-586.

1247. Richmond, Dale E. "Some Common Issues in Provincial-Municipal Transfer Systems." Canadian Public Administration 23:2 (1980): 252-268.

1248. Ridler, Neil B. "Fiscal Constraints and the Growth of User Fees Among Canadian Municipalities." Canadian Public Administration 28:1 (1985): 124-137.

1249. Ridler, Neil. "PPB -- Its Relevance to Financially Constrained Municipalities." Canadian Public Administration 19:2 (Summer, 1976): 238-253.

1250. Robinson, Ira, and Webster, Douglas R. "Regional Planning in Canada: History, Practice, Issues, and Prospects." Journal of the American Planning Association 51:1 (1985): 23-33. History and practice of regional planning in Canada, with a description of many of the major issues involved and prospects for future planning effectiveness.

1251. Rowat, Donald C. "A Note on the Uniqueness of the Study of Local Government." Canadian Public Administration 26:3 (1983): 441-446. Study of the ways in which local governments in Canada vary from the higher levels of government.

118   Contemporary Canadian Politics

1252.   Rowat, Donald C. "Current Trends in the Structure and Power of Local Government in Canada." <u>Polish Round Table</u> 7 (1976-1977): 165-187. Differences between local governments, and proposals for reorganization are discussed.

1253.   Rowat, Donald C. "The Role of Canada's Urban Municipalities in Governmental Decision-Making." <u>Studies in Comparative Local Government</u> 8:1 (1974): 43-49. Examines actual share of total decision-making power held by city governments and the degree to which cities can influence decisions of higher levels of government. Also compares Canadian cities with cities in other federal governments.

1254.   Rowat, Donald C. "Comparing the Governance of Federal Capitals." <u>Journal of Constitutional and Parliamentary Studies</u> 7:3 (1973): 24-32. How Ottawa is governed, with specific references to comparable cases in the United States, Australia, and West Germany.

1255.   Salyzyn, Vladimir. "Solving Local Intergovernmental Fiscal Problems." <u>Governmental Finance</u> 4:2 (1975): 5-10. Municipal governments cannot be left completely dependent upon property tax as their sole or primary course of income, but successful alternatives have yet to be found.

1256.   Sancton, Andrew. "The Impact of Language Differences on Metropolitan Reform in Montreal." <u>Canadian Public Administration</u> 22:2 (1979): 227-250.

1257.   Savoie, D.J. "The Toppling of DREE and Prospects for Regional Economic Development." <u>Canadian Public Policy</u> 10:3 (September, 1984): 328-337.

1258.   Sharman, Campbell. "The Strange Case of a Provincial Constitution: The British Columbia Constitution Act." <u>Canadian Journal of Political Science</u> 17:1 (1984): 87-108. Case study of the British Columbia Constitution Act which shows that provincial constitutions do not always follow the outlines of the British North America Act as closely as some might think.

1259.   Shoyama, T.K. "Some Financial and Economic Implications of One Prairie Province." <u>Canadian Public Administration</u> 13:4 (1970): 344-353.

1260.   Siegel, David. "Provincial-Municipal Relations in Canada: An Overview." <u>Canadian Public Administration</u> 23:2 (1980): 281-317.

1261.   Simeon, Richard. "Regionalism and Canadian Political Institutions." <u>Queen's Quarterly</u> 82:4 (1975): 499-511.

1262. Simeon, Richard, and Elkins, David J. "Regional Political Cultures in Canada." *Canadian Journal of Political Science* 7:3 (1974): 397-437. Canadian politics is regional in nature; studies the extent to which populations in Canada differ in basic political orientations and the sources of "regional cultures."

1263. Smallwood, Frank. "Reshaping Local Government Abroad: Anglo-Canadian Experiments." *Public Administration Review* 30:5 (1970): 521-530. Examination of metropolitan-level governments in Canada, and how Canadians, and the English, have been able to effectively establish metropolitan-level governments.

1264. Smiley, D.V. "Territorialism and Canadian Political Institutions." *Canadian Public Policy* 3:4 (Autumn, 1977): 449-457.

1265. Smith, David E. "Interpreting Prairie Politics." *Journal of Canadian Studies* 7:4 (1972): 18-32.

1266. Smith, Patrick. "Regional Governance in British Columbia." *Planning and Administration* 13:2 (1986): 7-21.

1267. Sproule-Jones, M. "A Description and Explanation of Citizen Participation in a Canadian Municipality." *Public Choice* 17 (1974): 73-83.

1268. Stabler, Jack. "Fiscal Viability and the Constitutional Development of Canada's Northern Territories." *Polar Record* 146 (1987): 551-568.

1269. Stein, L.A. "Municipal Controls Over Freedom of Assembly in Canada and the United States." *Public Law* (London) (1971): 115-140.

1270. Stevenson, G. "Political Constraints and the Province-Building Objective." *Canadian Public Policy* (Special Issue, 1980): 265-274.

1271. Taylor, Charles. "The Politics of the Steady State." *New Universities Quarterly* 32:2 (1978): 157-184. Discussion of consequences for Western society of an enforced slowdown in economic growth.

1272. Tennant, Paul. "The NDP Government of British Columbia: Unaided Politicians in an Unaided Cabinet." *Canadian Public Policy* 3:4 (Autumn, 1977): 489-503.

1273. Tennant, Paul, and Zirnhelt, David. "Metropolitan Government in Vancouver: The Strategy of Gentle Imposition." *Canadian Public Administration* 16:1 (Spring, 1973): 124-138.

1274. Thayer, F.C. "Regional Administration: The Failure of Traditional Theory in the United States and Canada." Canadian Public Administration 15:3 (1972): 449-464.

1275. Thériault, J. Yvon. "État, ethnie, et démocratie: Réflections sur la question politique en Acadie." ["State, Ethnic Group, and Democracy: Relfections on Politics in Acadia."] Canadian Review of Studies in Nationalism 11:2 (1984): 201-218.

1276. Tindal, C.R. "Regional Development in Ontario." Canadian Public Administration 16:1 (1973): 110-123.

1277. Todd, Daniel. "Regional Intervention in Canada and the Evolution of Growth Center Strategies." Growth and Change 8:1 (1977): 29-34.

1278. Usher, D. "Some Questions About the Regional Development Incentives Act." Canadian Public Policy 1:4 (Autumn, 1975): 557-575.

1279. Wagdin, George A. "The Municipal Revenue-Expenditure Gap in Canada." Municipal Finance 43:3 (1971): 122-126. Some steps taken to close the "municipal revenue-expenditure" gap.

1280. Wallace, D.M. "Budget Reform in Saskatchewan: A New Approach to Program-Based Management." Canadian Public Administration 17:4 (1974): 586-599.

1281. Weller, Geoffrey R. "Managing Canada's North: The Case of the Provincial North." Canadian Public Administration 27:2 (1984): 197-209.

1282. Weller, Geoffrey R. "Local Government in the Canadian Provincial North." Canadian Public Administration 24:1 (1981): 44-72.

1283. Weller, Geoffrey R. "Hinterland Politics: The Case of Northwestern Ontario." Canadian Journal of Political Science 10:4 (1977): 727-754. Internal politics of one subprovincial region, northwestern Ontario.

1284. Wilson, W.A. "Foreign Affairs Survey Reflects Canadian Regionalism." International Perspectives (May-June, 1980): 11-14. There are regional differences in the Canadian population as to the issues which are perceived as most important and which areas of the world are perceived with most interest.

1285. Winn, Conrad, and John McMenemy. "Political Alignment in a Polarized City: Electoral Cleavages in Kitchener, Ontario." Canadian Journal of Political Science 6:2 (1973): 230-242. Development of electoral cleavages and their similarity between the municipal and provincial levels of voting.

1286. Wood, John. "East Indians and Canada's New Immigration Policy." Canadian Public Policy 4:4 (Autumn, 1978): 547-567.

1287. Woodcock, George. "Callaghan's Toronto: the Persona of a City." Journal of Canadian Studies 7:3 (1972): 23-26.

1288. Woodward, R.S. "The Effectiveness of DREE's New Location Subsidies." Canadian Public Policy 1:2 (Spring, 1975): 219-229.

1289. Young, Dennis A. "Case Study/British Columbia: Governing for Economic Development." Public Management 52:10 (1970): 8-9. Economic problems of British Columbia, and challenges for effective public management there.

1290. Young, R.A., Faucher, Philippe, and Blais, André. "The Concept of Province-Building: A Critique." Canadian Journal of Political Science 17:4 (1984): 783-818.

1291. Young, W.D. "A Profile of Activities in the British Columbia NDP." Journal of Canadian Studies 6:1 (1971): 19-26.

1292. Young, R.A. "Remembering Equal Opportunity: Clearing the Undergrowth in New Brunswick." Canadian Public Administration 30:1 (1987): 88-102.

1293. Zimmerman, Joseph F. "The Metropolitan Area Problem." Annals of the American Academy of Political and Social Science 416 (1974): 133-147.

5
English Canada and Political Culture

Books

1294. Banting, Keith. State and Society: Canada in Comparative Perspective. Toronto: University of Toronto Press, 1986.

1295. Bell, David, and Tepperman, Lorne. The Roots of Disunity: A Look at Canadian Political Culture. Toronto: McClelland and Stewart, 1979. Goes beyond the question of Quebec separatism to study Canadian political culture and political diversity. Suggests that the question of disunity is not new, and that precedents for tension in Canadian nationalism are readily apparent in Canadian history.

1296. Bell, David, and Tepperman, Lorne. First Principles: A Study of Canadian Political Culture. Toronto: McClelland and Stewart, 1979.

1297. Berkowitz, Stephen D., and Logan, Robert K., eds. Canada's Third Option. Toronto: Macmillan of Canada, 1978. Essays dealing with Canadian nationalism in the 1970's, and the implications of this nationalism both for domestic Canadian politics and for Canadian-American relations.

1298. Brimelow, Peter. The Patriot Game: Canada and the Canadian Question Revisited. Stanford, Calif.: Hoover Institution Press, 1986.

1299. Brown, Brian A. The Canadian Challenge. Saanichton, B.C.: Hancock House, 1978.

1300. Canada. Multiculturalism Programme. Multiculturalism and the Government of Canada. Ottawa: Minister of State, Multiculturalism, 1978.

1301. Canada. Privy Council Office. *A National Understanding: Statement of the Government of Canada on the Official Languages Policy: The Official Languages of Canada.* Ottawa: Privy Council, 1977.

1302. Carty, R. Kenneth, and Ward, W. Peter, eds. *Entering the Eighties: Canada in Crisis.* Toronto: Oxford University Press, 1980. Essays on ideas of nationalism, the status of Quebec, the economy, and parliament and party politics.

1303. Carty, R. Kenneth, and Ward, W. Peter, eds. *National Politics and Community in Canada.* Vancouver: University of British Columbia Press, 1986.

1304. Clarke, Harold, et al. *Absent Mandate: The Politics of Discontent in Canada.* Toronto: Gage, 1984.

1305. Cook, R. *The Maple Leaf Forever: Essays in Nationalism and Politics in Canada.* Toronto: Macmillan of Canada, 1971.

1306. Cooper, Barry, Kornberg, Allan, and Mishler, William. *The Resurgence of Conservatism in Anglo-American Democracies.* Durham: Duke University Press, 1988.

1307. Crispo, J.H.G. *Mandate for Canada.* Don Mills, Ont.: General Publishing, 1979.

1308. Dahlie, J., and Fernando, T., eds. *Ethnicity, Power, and Politics in Canada.* Toronto: Methuen, 1980.

1309. Desbarats, Peter. *Canada Lost, Canada Found: The Search for a New Nation.* Toronto: McClelland and Stewart, 1981. Subtitled "A Polemic," this is a collection of essays on nationalism, confederation, political leadership, the status of Quebec, the status of the West, and Pierre Trudeau.

1310. Gagne, Wallace, ed. *Nationalism, Technology and the Future of Canada.* Toronto: Macmillan of Canada, 1976. Collection of six essays discussing the effect of technology on Canadian politics. Includes discussion of Canadian-American relations, labor, and French-Canadian nationalism.

1311. Geddes, G., ed. *Divided We Stand.* Toronto: Peter Partin, 1977.

1312. Gibbins, Roger. *Conflict and Unity: An Introduction to Canadian Political Life.* Toronto: Methuen, 1985.

1313. Godfrey, W.G. *Canadian Political Cultures.* Toronto: Butterworths, 1981.

1314. Gordon, W. What is Happening to Canada? Toronto: McClelland and Stewart, 1978.

1315. Graham, Ron. One-Eyed Kings: Promise & Illusion in Canadian Politics. Toronto: Collins, 1986.

1316. Granatstein, J.L., et al. Twentieth Century Canada. Toronto: McGraw-Hill Ryerson, 1983.

1317. Grant, George. Lament for a Nation: The Defeat of Canadian Nationalism. Toronto: McClelland and Stewart, 1970.

1318. Groenewold, H. J. Multiculturalism: Can Trudeau's Liberalism Tolerate It? St. Catharines, Ont.: Paideia Press, 1978. Deals with the effect of multiculturalism and ethnic minorities on liberal politics.

1319. Harvey, T.G., and Harvey, S. Politial Culture in a Canadian Community. Toronto: Copp Clark, 1973.

1320. Heisey, A. The Great Canadian Stampede: The Rush to Economic Nationalism. Toronto: Griffin House, 1973.

1321. Hutchison, Bruce. The Unfinished Country: To Canada with Love and Some Misgivings. Vancouver: Douglas and McIntyre, 1985.

1322. Laxer, Robert M., ed. Bilingual Tensions in Canada. Toronto: Ontario Institute for Studies in Education, 1979. Starting with the Pepin-Robarts Task Force on Canadian Unity, studies the importance of bilingualism and language, and focuses upon several points of tension including the 1976 Air Traffic controllers dispute, Quebec's Bill 101, and the question of language and education policy.

1323. Manzer, Ronald. Canada: A Socio-Political Report. Toronto: McGraw Hill Ryerson, 1974.

1324. Menzies, Heather. The Railroad's Not Enough: Canada Now. Toronto: Clarke, Irwin, and Co., Ltd., 1978. Study of Canadian nationalism, the nature of Canadian political culture, and the impact of regionalism upon the development of nationalism.

1325. Morton, William Lewis. The Canadian Crisis: Its Causes and Its Outcome. Winnipeg: Great-West Life Assurance, 1978.

1326. Murray, Janice, ed. Canadian Cultural Nationalism. New York: New York University Press, 1977. Essays on Canadian cultural nationalism, and how it affects the United States and U.S.-Canadian relations.

126 Contemporary Canadian Politics

1327. Newman, P.C. *Home Country*. Toronto: McClelland and Stewart, 1973.

1328. Palmer, B.D. *Working Class Culture in Canada*. Toronto: Butterworths, 1981.

1329. Presthus, R., ed. *Cross-National Perspectives: United States and Canada*. Leiden: Brill, 1977.

1330. Resnick, Philip. *Parliament vs. People: An Essay on Democracy and Canadian Political Culture*. Vancouver: New Star Books, 1984.

1331. Resnick, Phillip. *The Land of Cain: Class and Nationalism in English Canada, 1945-1975*. Vancouver: New Star Books, 1977.

1332. Richmond, Anthony, ed. *After the Referenda: The Future of Ethnic Nationalism in Britain and Canada*. Downsview, Ont.: York University Institute for Behavioral Research, 1981.

1333. Roche, Douglas J. *The Human Side of Politics*. Toronto: Clarke, Irwin, 1976. Memoirs of a Conservative MP, discussing changes needing to be made in Canadian politics, economics, and society.

1334. Royal Commission on the Status of Women in Canada. *Cultural Tradition and Political History of Women in Canada.* Ottawa: Information Canada, 1971.

1335. Sheer, Alain. *North America -- Law, Politics, and Economics*. Durham, N.C.: Duke University, 1981.

1336. Shiels, Frederick L., ed. *Ethnic Separatism and World Politics*. Lanham, Md.: University Press of Amertica, 1984.

1337. Thorson, J.T. *Wanted: A Single Canada*. Toronto: McClelland and Stewart, 1973. Criticism of bilingualism-biculturalism policy. Argues for less regulation and a greater degree of cooperation.

1338. Verney, Douglas V. *Three Civilizations, Two Cultures, One State: Canada's Political Traditions*. Durham: Duke University Press, 1986.

Articles

1339. Adamson, Christopher, Findlay, Peter, Oliver, Michael, and Solberg, Janet. "The Unpublished Research of the Royal Commission on Bilingualism and Biculturalism." *Canadian Journal of Political Science* 7:4 (1974): 709-720. Bibliographic review of unpublished research of the Royal Commission on Bilingualism and Biculturalism.

1340. Andrew, C. "Le Rapport Fullerton: Perspective de la science politique." ["The Fullerton Report: Perspective of Political Science."] Canadian Public Policy 1:2 (Spring, 1975): 162-170.

1341. Beaujot, Roderic. "A Demographic View on Canadian Language Policy." Canadian Public Policy 5:1 (Winter, 1979): 16-29.

1342. Bergeron, Gérard. "Lecture du Livre blanc et du Livre beige selon une perspective `super-fédéraliste'." ["Reading of the White Paper and the Beige Paper According to a `Super-Federalist' Perspective."] Canadian Public Policy 6:3 (Summer, 1980): 506-520.

1343. Bergeron, Gérard. "Projet d'un nouveau Commonwealth canadien." ["Project of a New Canadian Commonwealth."] Études internationales 8:2 (1977): 240-253. Suggests that a rethinking of Canadian federalism is in order, and a new association -- he uses the term Commonwealth -- should be created which would more realistically describe the relationship among the political actors.

1344. Bibby, Reginal W. "Consensus in Diversity: An Examination of Canadian Problem Perception." International Journal of Comparative Sociology 20:3 (1979): 274-281.

1345. Black, J. H., Niemi, R. G., and Powell, G. B. "Age, Resistance, and Political Learning in a New Environment: The Case of Canadian Immigrants." Comparative Politics 20:1 (1987): 73-84.

1346. Bonenfant, Jean-Charles. "Les études de la Commission royale d'enquête sur le bilinguisme et le biculturalisme." ["Studies of the Royal Commission of Inquiry on Bilingualism and Biculturalism."] Canadian Journal of Political Science 4:3 (1971): 406-416; 5:2 (1972): 304-309; 5:3 (1972): 444-450; 6:1 (1973): 144-148. Review article discussing several different analyses of the Royal Commission on Bilingualism and Biculturalism.

1347. Brotz, H. "Multiculturalism in Canada: A Muddle." Canadian Public Policy 6:1 (Winter, 1980): 41-46.

1348. Bullivant, Brian M. "Searching for an Ideology of Pluralism: Some Results of a Cross-National Survey." Ethnic and Racial Studies 3:4 (1980): 465-474.

1349. Cairns, Alan. "Political Science in Canada and the Americanization Issue." Canadian Journal of Political Science 8:2 (1975): 191-234. Discussion of the discipline of political science in Canada and its relation to American political science.

1350. Cannon, Gordon. "Consociationalism versus Control: Canada as a Case Study." Western Political Quarterly 35:1 (1982): 50-64. An attempt to explain why Canada has had stability with the English/French cultural split.

1351. Carty, R.K., Ward, W.P., and Simeon, R. "National Politics and Community in Canada." American Political Science Review 81:4 (1987): 1383-1384.

1352. Chandrasekhar, S. "A History of Canadian Legislation with respect to Immigration from India." Plural Societies 16:3 (1986): 254-271.

1353. Charland, Maurice. "Technological Nationalism." Canadian Journal of Political and Social Theory 10:1-2 (1986): 196-220.

1354. Chrétien, Jean. "Le profil du gouvernement des années 80." ["A Profile of Government in the 80's."] Canadian Public Administration 19:1 (Spring, 1976): 112-120.

1355. Clark, Ian Christie. "The Cultural Property Export and Import Act of Canada: Legislation to Encourage National Cooperation." New York University Journal of International Law and Politics 15:4 (1983): 771-788.

1356. Clarkson, Stephen. "Anti-Nationalism in Canada: The Ideology of Mainstream Economics." Canadian Review of Studies in Nationalism 5:1 (1978): 45-65.

1357. Clarkson, Stephen. "Lament for a Non-Subject: Reflections on Teaching Canadian-American Relations." International Journal 27:2 (1972): 265-275.

1358. Classen, H.G. "The Chimera of the Homogeneous State." Queen's Quarterly 79:4 (1972): 458-469.

1359. Cole, Douglas. "The Integration of Canada: An Overview." Canadian Review of Studies in Nationalism 7:1 (1980): 4-14.

1360. Crawford, Craig, and Curtis, James. "English Canadian - American Differences in Value Orientations: Survey Comparisons Bearing on Lipset's Thesis." Studies in Comparative International Development. 14:3 (1979): 23-44. Americans are more achievement-, tradition-, and equality-oriented in decision-making than are Canadians.

1361. Cullen, Dallas, Jobson, J.D., and Schneck, Rodney. "Towards the Development of a Canadian-American Scale: A Research Note." Canadian Journal of Political Science 11:2 (1978): 409-418. Development of a scale to measure Canadian attitudes towards Americans.

1362. Cuneo, Carl J. "The Social Bases of Political Continentalism in Canada." *Canadian Review of Sociology and Anthropology*. 13:1 (1976): 55-70. Analysis of degree of mass support for the political union of Canada and the United States.

1363. Cuneo, Carl J. "Education, Language, and Multidimensional Continentalism." *Canadian Journal of Political Science* 7:3 (1974): 536-549. Willingness of Canadians and Americans to support the annexation of Canada to the United States in political, economic, sociocultural, and military terms.

1364. Drummond, R. "Nationalism and Ethnic Demands: Some Speculations on a Congenial Note." *Canadian Journal of Political Science* 10:2 (1977): 375-389. Discussion and modification of J. Lightbody's model of nationalism.

1365. Elliott, Jean Leonard. "Emerging Ethnic Nationalism in the Canadian Northwest Territories." *Canadian Review of Studies in Nationalism* 11:2 (1984): 231-244.

1366. Gagan, David P. "The Relevance of `Canada First'." *Journal of Canadian Studies* 5:4 (1970): 36-43.

1367. Glazier, Kenneth M. "The Surge of Nationalism in Canada Today." *Current History* 66:392 (1974): 150-154.

1368. Glickman, Yaacov. "Ethnicity and National Allegiance in the Canadian Jewish Body Politic." *Canadian Review of Studies in Nationalism* 11:2 (1984): 219-230.

1369. Guidon, Hubert. "Societal Changes and Their Impact." *Canadian Public Administration* 21:3 (Fall, 1978): 441-448.

1370. Handler, Richard. "Canadian Content and the Nationalism of Applebaum-Hébert." *Canadian Public Policy* 11:4 (1985): 677-684. Focuses upon the question of Canadian cultural content and the idea of a single national culture.

1371. Hutchison, Bruce. "Canada's Time of Troubles." *Foreign Affairs* 56:1 (1977): 175-189.

1372. Hyndman, James E. "National Interest and the New Look." *International Journal* 26:1 (1971): 5-18.

1373. Jabbra, Nancy W. "Community Politics and Ethnicity Among Lebanese in Nova Scotia." *Canadian Review of Sociology and Anthropology* 21:4 (1984): 449-465.

1374. Juteau-Lee, Danielle. "Ethnic Nationalism: Ethnicity and Politics." *Canadian Review of Sociology and Anthropology* 21:4 (1984): 189-200.

1375. Knopff, Rainer. "Liberal Democracy and the Challenge of Nationalism in Canadian Politics." *Canadian Review of Studies in Nationalism* 9:1 (1982): 23-42.

1376. Knopff, Rainer. "Language and Culture in the Canadian Debate: the Battle of the White Papers." *Canadian Review of Studies in Nationalism* 6:1 (1979): 66-82.

1377. Labovitz, Sanford, and Purdy, Ross. "Territorial Differentiation and Social Change in the United States and Canada." *American Journal of Economics and Sociology* 29:2 (1970): 127-147. Tests a theory linking territorial differentiation to societal change. Data strongly support the theory of differentiation.

1378. Laponce, J.A. "The French Language in Canada: Tensions Between Geography and Politics." *Political Geography Quarterly* 3:2 (1985): 91-104.

1379. Laponce, J.A. "Nation-Building as Body-Building: A Comparative Study of the Personalization of City, Province, and State by Anglophone and Francophone Canadians." *Social Science Information* 23:6 (1984): 977-991. Study of whether there was a difference between English-speaking (British Columbia) and French-speaking (Quebec) Canadians in terms of their perceptions of governmental units in animate or inanimate terms.

1380. Laundy, Philip. "Report of the Task Force on Canadian Unity." *Parliamentarian* 60:3 (1979): 133-140.

1381. LaViolette, Forrest. "The Canadian Japanese: A New Look." *Pacific Affairs* 50:1 (1977): 107-123.

1382. Layton, Jack. "Nationalism and the Canadian Bourgeoisie: Contradictions of Dependence." *Canadian Review of Studies in Nationalism* 3:2 (1976): 146-171.

1383. LeDuc, Lawrence, "Canadian Attitudes Toward Quebec Independence." *Public Opinion Quarterly* 41:3 (1977): 347-355.

1384. Lentner, Howard H. "Canadian Separatism and Its Implications for the United States." *Orbis* 22:2 (1978): 375-394.

1385. Lester, Normand. "Les conditionnements de la décision politique au Canada." ["Conditions of Political Decisions in Canada."] Politique étrangère 36:3 (1971): 215-249. In an analysis of factors that determine the general political nature of Canada, concludes that there is a major influence by the United States in all aspects of Canadian life. In internal politics, tensions between English and French-speaking Canadians contribute to the image of Canada as an "uncertain country."

1386. Levitt, Joseph. "English Canadian Nationalists and the Canadian Character, 1957-1974." Canadian Review of Studies in Nationalism 12:2 (1985): 223-238.

1387. Lijphart, Arend. "Religious vs. Linguistic vs. Class Voting: the `Crucial Experiment' of Comparing Belgium, Canada, South Africa, and Switzerland." American Political Science Review 73:2 (1979): 442-458. Multivariate analysis examining voting and party choice as functions of religious and linguistic characteristics.

1388. Lijphart, Arend. "Cultural Diversity and Theories of Political Integration." Canadian Journal of Political Science 4:1 (1971): 1-14. Concept of political integration should be defined more broadly than it traditionally has been in order to maximize its analytic value.

1389. Linteau, Paul-André. "Canadian Suburbanization in a North American Context: Does the Border Make a Difference?" Journal of Urban History 13:3 (1987): 252-274.

1390. Lithwick, N.H. "Poverty in Canada: Some Recent Empirical Findings." Journal of Canadian Studies 6:2 (1971): 27-41.

1391. Litvak, Isaiah, and Maule, Christopher. "Bill C-58 and the Regulation of Periodicals in Canada." International Journal 36:1 (1980-1981): 70-90.

1392. LoGalbo, John R. "The Time and Reader's Digest Bill: C-58 and Canadian Cultural Nationalism." New York University Journal of International Law and Politics 9:2 (1976): 237-276. Traces the development of Canadian protectionist measures in the area of publications. Analyzes Bill C-58 and its impact. Resulting political ramifications of the Bill are discussed.

1393. McCormack, Thelma. "The Political Culture and the Press of Canada." Canadian Journal of Political Science 16:3 (1983): 451-472.

1394. McRae, K.D. "Bilingual Language Districts in Finland and Canada: Adventures in Transplanting of an Institution." *Canadian Public Policy* 4:3 (Summer, 1978): 331-351.

1395. Mallory, J.R. "The Canadian Dilemma: French and English." *The Political Quarterly* 41:3 (1970): 281-297.

1396. Marchak, Patricia. "Nationalism and Regionalism in Canada." *Canadian Review of Studies in Nationalism* 7:1 (1980): 15-31.

1397. Mathie, William. "Political Community and the Canadian Experience: Reflections on Nationalism, Federalism, and Unity." *Canadian Journal of Political Science* 12:1 (1979): 3-20. A theoretical defense of the concept of national unity in a Canadian context.

1398. Migué, Jean Luc. "Du gouvernement et des hommes." ["Of Government and Men."] *Canadian Public Administration* 20:4 (1977): 679-683.

1399. Moodley, Kogila. "Canadian Multiculturalism as Ideology." *Ethnic and Racial Studies* 6:3 (1983): 320-331.

1400. Moore, A.M. "Fact and Fantasy in the Unity Debate." *Canadian Public Policy* 5:2 (Spring, 1979): 206-222.

1401. Moore, Marie-France. "Nationalisme et contre-culture au Québec." ["Nationalism and Counter-Culture in Quebec."] *Canadian Review of Studies in Nationalism* 5:2 (1978): 284-306.

1402. Munro, John. "Transportation and Canadian Nationalism," *Canadian Review of Studies in Nationalism* 7:1 (1980): 88-107.

1403. Palmer, Howard. "Mosaic Versus Melting Pot? Immigration and Ethnicity in Canada and the United States." *International Journal* 31:3 (1976): 488-528.

1404. Pereira, Cecil, Adams, Bert, and Bristow, Mike. "Canadian Beliefs and Policy Regarding the Admission of Ugandan Asians to Canada." *Ethnic and Racial Studies* 1:3 (1978): 352-376.

1405. Presthus, Robert. "Introduction: Some Conditions of Comparative Analysis in the United States and Canada." *International Journal of Comparative Sociology* 18:1-2 (1977): 1-6.

1406. Preston, R.A. "Two Centuries in the Shadow of Behemoth: The Effect on the Canadian Psyche." *International Journal* 31:3 (1976): 413-433.

1407. Pullman, D.R., and Loree, D.J. "Conceptions of Class and the Canadian Setting." International Journal of Comparative Sociology 17:3-4 (1976): 164-182.

1408. Randall, Stephen. "Canada's Economic `Bashionalists'." The Atlantic Community Quarterly 9:2 (1971): 229-234. Criticism of economic nationalism.

1409. Raynauld, André. "Social Indicators: The Need for a Broader Socioeconimic Framework." Canadian Public Administration 18:1 (1975): 91-103.

1410. Rayside, David M. "The Impact of the Linguistic Cleavage on the `Governing' Parties of Belgium and Canada." Canadian Journal of Political Science 11:1 (1978): 61-98. Study of the tensions between the English- and French-Canadians in the Liberal Party of Canada, and the Flemish and francophone Belgians in the Social Christian Party in Belgium, when they formed the Government an the ability of the respective Government parties to avoid linguistic conflict.

1411. Rich, Harvey. "The Vertical Mosaic Revisited: Toward a Macro-Sociology of Canada." Journal of Canadian Studies 11:1 (1976): 14-31.

1412. Richert, J.P. "Political Participation and Political Emancipation: The Impact of Cultural Membership." Western Political Quarterly 27:1 (1974): 104-116.

1413. Richert, J.P. "English- and French-Canadian Children's Perception of the October Crisis." Journal of Social Psychology 89:1 (1973): 3-13.

1414. Roberts, William. "Culture, Money, and Canadian Readers." Journal of Canadian Studies 10:2 (1975): 25-29.

1415. Roblin, D. "A New National Policy and Canadian Nationalism." Canadian Public Administration 16:4 (1973): 542-556.

1416. Rotstein, Abraham. "Canada: the New Nationalism." Foreign Affairs 55:1 (1976): 97-118.

1417. Rutan, Gerald F. "Two Views of the Concept of Sovereignty: Canadian-Canadian." Western Political Quarterly 24:3 (1971): 456-466.

1418. Schoner, Bertram, and Schwindt, Richard . "Advertising, Direct Foreign Investment, and Canadian National Identity." Canadian Review of Studies in Nationalism 7:1 (1980): 127-150.

1419. Schreiber, E.M. "Cultural Cleavages Between Occupational Categories: The Case of Canada." Social Forces 55:1 (1976): 16-29.

1420. Schwartz, M.A. "The Social Make-Up of Canada and Strains in Confederation." Canadian Public Policy 3:4 (Autumn, 1977): 458-469.

1421. Sigler, John H., and Goresky, Dennis. "Public Opinion on United States-Canadian Relations." International Organization 28:4 (1974): 637-670.

1422. Sinclair, Peter R. "Political Powerlessness and Sociodemographic Status in Canada." Canadian Review of Sociology and Anthropology 16:2 (1979): 125-135. Analysis of a national election survey showing the limited association between the experience of powerlessness and sociodemographic position.

1423. Smiley, Donald. "Canada and the Quest for a National Policy." Canadian Journal of Political Science 8:1 (1975): 40-62. Economic policy is analyzed with respect to whether national or regional goals are being furthered.

1424. Smith, Allan. "The Continental Dimension in the Evolution of the English-Canadian Mind." International Journal 31:3 (1976): 442-469.

1425. Smith, Burton M. "The United States in Recent Canadian Nationalism." World Affairs 140:3 (1978): 195-205. Treats the role of the United States as an issue in recent Canadian debates focusing upon nationalism.

1426. Smith, David E. "Recent Trends in Canadian Politics." Western Political Quarterly 23:2 (1970): 348-363.

1427. Smith, Michael B. "Sectoral Free Trade with Canada." International Perspectives (1984): 17-18.

1428. Soderstrom, Lee. "The Canadian Experience." Proceedings of the Academy of Political Science 33:4 (1980): 224-233.

1429. Spry, Graham. "Canada: Notes on Two Ideas of Nation in Confrontation." Journal of Contemporary History 6:1 (1971): 173-196. Discussion of two different concepts of "nation" and how they affect discussion and resolution of the debate over the role of Quebec in Canadian federalism.

1430. Tanaka, June K. "Fruit of Diaspora: The Japanese Experience in Canada." Japan Interpreter 12:1 (1978): 110-117.

1431. Thomson, Dale C. "Canada Through Blue- and Pink-Coloured Glasses." International Journal 26:1 (1971): 178-185.

1432. Thorburn, H. "Needed: A New Look at the Two-Nations Theory." Queen's Quarterly 80:2 (1973): 268-273.

1433. Toh, Swee-Hin. "Canada's Gain from Third World Brain Drain, 1962-1974." Studies in Comparative International Development 12:3 (1977): 25-45. Patterns of immigration and areas of professional specialty areas from the Third World to Canada, 1962 to 1974.

1434. Trenton, Thomas. "Canadian Nationalism, Dogmatism, and Internationalism: A Case of Independence?" Canadian Review of Studies in Nationalism 5:1 (1978): 104-113.

1435. Trudeau, Pierre Elliott. "Canada's Dual Loyalty: Francophonie and the Commonwealth." Politique internationale 2 (1978-1979): 33-42.

1436. Usher, D. "The English Response to the Prospect of the Separation of Quebec." Canadian Public Policy 4:1 (Winter, 1978): 57-76.

1437. Verney, Douglas. "Has There Been a Distinctive Canadian Political Tradition?" Journal of Commonwealth and Comparative Politics 16:3 (1978): 231-255. Asks whether there is anything distinctive or unusual in Canada's history and political thought that differentiates it from the United States and Britain.

1438. Watson, Graham. "The Reification of Ethnicity and Its Political Consequences in the North." Canadian Review of Sociology and Anthropology 18:4 (1981): 453-469. Discussion of the management of ethnic identities by native Indians and the constrictions imposed by the government.

1439. White, Graham. "The Life and Times of the Camp Commission," Canadian Journal of Political Science 13 (1980): 357-377.

1440. Wilson, John. "The Canadian Political Cultures: Towards a Redefinition of the Nature of the Canadian Political System." Canadian Journal of Political Science 7:3 (1974): 438-483. It is not sufficient to simply discuss an English- and a French-Canadian political culture. Noteworthy differences appear on the provincial level as well and must be taken into consideration.

1441. Yalden, Maxwell F. "Language and Power in Canada." Society 19:1 (1981): 45-50.

6
French Canada and Quebec

Books

1442. Basham, Richard. _Crisis in Blanc and White: Urbanization and Ethnic Identity in French Canada_. Cambridge, Ma.: Schenkman Publishing Co., 1978. Discussion of French-Canadian history, how the French maintained their identities under an English majority, and the "crisis" of maintaining a French identity in an overwhelmingly English society today.

1443. Behiels, Michael D. _Prelude to Quebec's Quiet Revolution: Liberalism Versus Neo-Nationalism, 1945-1960_. Kingston: McGill-Queen's University Press, 1985. Political-historical account of two competing ideological movements in Quebec between World War II and the fall of the Union Nationale government in June of 1960.

1444. Bellavance, Lionel. _Les Partis Indépendantistes Québecois de 1960 - 1973_. [Quebec Independence Parties From 1960 - 1973] Montréal: Les Anciens Canadiens, 1973. A political history of five different independence movements in Quebec.

1445. Bellavance, Michel, and Gilbert, Marcel. _L'Opinion Publique et La Crise d'Octobre_. [Public Opinion and the October Crisis] Montréal: Éditions du jour, 1971. Study of the political psychology of public opinion and ideology, and the developments of the October Crisis of 1970 and the growth of Quebec nationalist groups at that time.

1446. Bellavance, Michel, Patry, Maurice, and Parenteau, Roland. _L'analyse des politiques gouvernementales_. [The Analysis of Governmental Politics] Laval, Québec: Les Presses de l'Université Laval, 1983. Three case studies of governmental politics and policy-making: Radio Quebec, the Quebec Office of Planning and Development, and industrial development.

1447. Benjamin, J., and O'Neill, P. Les mandarins du pouvoir. [The Mandarins of Power] Montréal: Éditions Québec-Amérique, 1978.

1448. Bergeron, Gerard. Ce jour-la...: Le Referendum. Montréal: Quinze, 1978.

1449. Bergeron, Gerard. Du Duplessisme à Trudeau et Bourassa, 1956 - 1971. [From Duplessism to Trudeau and Bourassa, 1956-1971] Montréal: Parti pris, 1971.

1450. Bergeron, Gerard. Incertitudes d'un certain pays: le Québec et le Canada dans le monde, 1958-1978. [Uncertainties of a Certain Country: Quebec and Canada in the World, 1958-1978] Québec: Les Presses de l'Université Laval, 1979.

1451. Bergeron, Gérard. L'Indépendance: Oui, Mais... [Independence: Yes, But...] Paris: Quinze, 1977. Analysis of the 1976 Quebec election in the context of the post-Quiet Revolution Quebec.

1452. Bergeron, Gerard, and Pelletier, Réjean, eds. L'État du Québec en devenir. [The State of Quebec in the Future] Montréal: Boréal, 1980.

1453. Bernard, Andre. La politique au Canada et au Québec. [Politics in Canada and in Quebec] 2nd Ed. Montréal: Les Presses de l'Université du Québec, 1976. Introductory textbook covering the environment, culture, ideology, public opinion, elections and voting, parties and pressure groups, federalism, intergovernmental relations, and formal governmental structures.

1454. Bernard, André. Québec: Élections, 1976. Montréal: Hurtubise, 1976.

1455. Bernard, André. What Does Québec Want? Toronto: James Lorimer, 1978. Analysis of the goals of the Parti Québécois, and how it intended to achieve those goals after coming to power in Quebec in 1976.

1456. Bernard, André, and Descôteaux, Bernard. Québec: élections 1981. [Quebec: Elections 1981] LaSalle, Quebec: Hurtubise, 1981. Study of the 1981 Quebec provincial election. Includes analysis of the period between 1976 and 1981, and its effect on the outcome of the 1981 election.

1457. Boily, R. Québec, 1940-1969, Bibliographie. Montréal: Les Presses de l'Université de Montréal, 1971.

1458. Boily, R. La réforme électorale au Québec. Montréal: Éditions du Jour, 1970.

1459. Boismenu, Gerard, ed. Espace régional et nation: pour un nouveau débat sur le Québec. [Regional Space and Nation: For a New Debate on Quebec] Montréal: Boréal Express, 1983.

1460. Boisvert, M.A. Les implications économiques de la souveraineté association. [The Economic Implications of Sovereignty-Association] Montréal: Les Presses de l'Université de Montréal, 1980.

1461. Bourassa, Robert. Power From the North. Scarborough, Ontario: Prentice-Hall of Canada, 1985. Claim for development of Quebec's hydroelectric potential and the value of exporting that power to the New England states.

1462. Bourassa, Robert. L'union monetaire et l'union politique sont indissociables. [The Monetary Union and the Political Union are Indivisible] Montréal: Parti Libéral du Québec, 1980.

1463. Bourque, Gilles, and Dostaler, Gilles. Socialisme et indépendance. [Socialism and Independence] Montréal: Boréal Express, 1980. Study of nationalist movement in Quebec, the rise of René Lévesque, and the problems faced by the Parti Québécois in government after it won power in 1976.

1464. Bourque, Gilles, and Legaré, Anne. Le Québec: la question nationale. [Quebec: The National Question] Paris: F. Maspero, 1979. A political history of the French community in what is today Quebec, from approximately 1760 through the 1970's.

1465. Brichant, A. Option Canada: The Economic Implications of Separatism for the Province of Quebec. Montreal: The Canada Committee, 1968.

1466. Brière, M., and Grandmaison, J. Un nouveau contrat social. [A New Social Contract] Ottawa: Leméac, 1980.

1467. Brossard, J. L'accession à la souveraineté et le cas du Québec. [The Approach of Sovereignty and the Case of Quebec] Montréal: Les Presses de l'Université de Montréal, 1976.

1468. Burns, R. M., ed. One Country or Two? Montreal: McGill-Queen's University Press, 1971. Essays on the subject of nationhood and nationalism in Canada, with discussion of the concept of Quebec separatism.

1469. Cameron, David R. Nationalism, Self-Determination and the Quebec Question. Toronto: Macmillan of Canada, 1974. Discussion of the concepts of nationalism and self-determination, how they are affected by the federal political relationship, and what Quebec's rights are in the Canadian federal system.

1470. Canada. Federal-Provincial Relations Office. Interim Report on Relations Between the Government of Canada and the Province of Quebec 1967-1977. Ottawa: Federal-Provincial Relations Office, 1979.

1471. Chaput-Rolland, S. Regards 1970-71: les heures sauvages. [Views of 1970-71: The Savage Hours] Montréal: le Cercle du livre de France, 1972.

1472. Chodos, R., and Auf der Maur, N., eds. Quebec: A Chronicle, 1968-1972. Toronto: James, Lewis, and Samuel, 1972.

1473. Clift, Dominique. Quebec Nationalism in Crisis. Montreal: McGill-Queen's University Press, 1982. Analysis of the Quiet Revolution, political nationalism in Quebec, and French-Canadian cultural nationalism, along with the rise to power of the Parti Québécois and its behavior once in office.

1474. Clift, Dominique, and Arnopoulos, D.M. Le fait anglais au Québec. [The English Fact in Quebec] Montréal: Éditions Libre Expression, 1979.

1475. Cloutier, Edouard. Sondage sur la perception des problèmes constitutionnels Québec-Canada par la population du Québec. [Poll on the Perception of Quebec-Canada Constitutional Problems by the Population of Quebec] Québec: Gouvernement du Québec, Ministère des affaires intergouvernementales, 1979.

1476. Cloutier, Édouard, and Latouche, Daniel, eds. Le système politique Québécois. [The Quebec Political System] Montréal: Hurtubise, 1979. Essays covering a range of subjects related to Quebec politics, including society, federalism, public administration, planning, and political culture.

1477. Coleman, William D. The Independence Movement in Quebec, 1945-1980. Toronto: University of Toronto Press, 1984. Study of the movement which united labor, business, and parts of the middle class of Quebec after the "Quiet Revolution" in support of independence for Quebec.

1478. Cook, Ramsay. Canada, Quebec, and the Uses of Nationalism. Toronto: McClelland and Stewart, 1986.

1479. Cotnam, J. Contemporary Quebec: An Analytical Bibliography. Toronto: McClelland and Stewart, 1973.

1480. Crean, Susan, and Rioux, Marcel. Two Nations: An Essay on the Culture and Politics of Canada and Quebec in a World of American Pre-eminence. Toronto: Lorimer, 1983.

1481. Croisat, Maurice. Le fédéralisme canadien et la question du Québec. [Canadian Federalism and the Question of Quebec] Paris: Éditions Anthropos, 1979. Quebec's role in the Canadian federation, with specific discussion of the federal division of powers in the constitution, the structure of powers and provincial participation, political parties, regionalism, federal-provincial consultation, and the effects of the Quiet Revolution.

1482. Dagenais, Gerard. Pour un Québec français: chronique des années 1970, 1971, 1972. [For a French Quebec: A Chronicle of the Years 1970, 1971, and 1972] Montréal: Éditions du Jour, 1973.

1483. Daniels, Dan, ed. Québec, Canada, and the October Crisis. Montreal: Black Rose Books, 1973. Essays on the October, 1970, crisis in Quebec, explaining what happened and what continued to happen politically for several years thereafter.

1484. Desrosiers, R. Le personnel politique québécois. [Quebec Political Personnel] Montréal: Boréal Express, 1972.

1485. Dion, Léon. La prochaine révolution. [The Next Revolution] Montréal: Leméac, 1973. Discusses national identity in Quebec, Quebec's economic life, its political life in the Bourassa era, and various degrees of political participation there.

1486. Dion, Léon. Le Québec et le Canada: les voies de l'avenir. [Quebec and Canada: Paths of the Future] Montréal: Les Éditions Québecor, 1980.

1487. Dion, Léon. Québec: The Unfinished Revolution. Montreal: McGill-Queen's University Press, 1976. Essays and articles dealing with a wide range of Quebec issues: culture, politics, economics, and the like.

1488. Dixon, M., Jonas, S, and Vaillancourt, P., eds. Québec and the Parti Québecois. San Francisco: Synthesis Publications, 1978.

1489. Dofny, J., and Arnaud, N. Nationalism and the National Question. Montreal: Black Rose, 1978.

1490. Dolment, M., and Barthe, M. La femme au Québec. [Women in Quebec] Montréal: Les Presses Libres, 1973.

1491. Drache, D., ed. Quebec: Only the Beginning. Toronto: New Press, 1972.

1492. Dumont, F. The Vigil of Quebec, October 1970: The Impasse? Toronto: University of Toronto Press, 1974.

1493. Dupont, P. _How Lévesque Won: The Story of the PQ's 1976 Election Victory_. Toronto: Lorimer, 1977.

1494. Feldman, E.J., ed. _The Quebec Referendum: What Happened and What Next? A Dialogue the Day After with Claude Forget and Daniel Latouche, May 21, 1980_. Cambridge University: Consortium for Research on North America, 1980.

1495. Fitzmaurice, John. _Quebec and Canada: Past, Present, and Future_. New York: St. Martin's Press, 1985. Study of Quebec history, economics, society, and politics, focusing upon both the survival of Quebec in Canada and the political structures and patterns of political behavior important to the Quebec political system. Includes analysis of the 1980 Referendum, and the 1982 patriation of the Constitution.

1496. Fournier, P. _The Quebec Establishment: The Ruling Class and the State_. Montreal: Black Rose, 1976.

1497. Fullerton, Douglas. _The Dangerous Delusion: Quebec's Independence Obsession_. Toronto: McClelland and Stewart, 1978. Personal perspective of issues related to Quebec and French-Canadian nationalism from the early 1960's through the late 1970's.

1498. Gagnon, Alain, ed. _Quebec: State and Society_. Toronto: Methuen, 1984. Essays dealing with Quebec nationalism, social class, regionalism, organized interest groups, and language and educational policy.

1499. Gagnon, Henri. _La Confédération: Y'a rien là_. [Confederation: There is Nothing There] Montréal: Parti Pris, 1977. Study of the problem of national identity in Quebec, and the various national liberation movements there. Includes both historical and political analysis.

1500. Gélinas, A. _Organismes autonomes et centraux de l'administration Québécoise_. [Autonomous and Central Organizations of the Quebec Administration] Montréal: Les Presses de l'Université de Québec à Montréal, 1976.

1501. Gellner, J. _Bayonets in the Streets: Urban Guerillas at Home and Abroad_. Don Mills, Ontario: Collier-Macmillan, 1974.

1502. Haggart, Ron, and Golden, Aubrey. _Rumours of War_. Toronto: New Press, 1971. Study of the October, 1970 violence in Quebec, the invocation of the War Measures Act, and the significance of the outcome of the event.

French Canada and Quebec   143

1503. Harbron, John D. Canada Without Quebec. Don Mills, Ont.: Musson Book Co., 1977. Study of Quebec nationalism.

1504. Henault, G.M. Culture et management: le cas de l'enterprise québécoise. [Culture and Management: The Case of Quebec Enterprise] Montréal: McGraw-Hill, 1974.

1505. Herbert, F. Quinn. The Union Nationale: Quebec Nationalism from Duplessis to Levesque. Toronto: University of Toronto Press, 1979.

1506. Jacobs, Jane. The Question of Separatism: Quebec and the Struggle Over Sovereignty. New York: Random House, 1980. The relationship between the Sovereignty-Association movement and city government in Quebec, and economic consequences of federalism.

1507. Jean, M., ed. Québécoises du 20e siècle. [Quebeckers of the 20th Century] Montréal: Presses Libres, 1974.

1508. Krull, Achim, and Shukyn, Murray. Quebec Independence: The Background to a National Crisis. Toronto: Clarke, Irwin, 1978.

1509. Kwavnick, D., ed. The Tremblay Report. Toronto: McClelland and Stewart, 1973.

1510. Lacoursière, J., and Huguet, H.-A. Québec, 72-73: Bilan. [Quebec, 72-73: Balance Sheet] Montréal: Éditions fides, 1974.

1511. Lambert, Ronald. The Sociology of Contemporary Quebec Nationalism: An Annotated Bibliography and Review. New York: Garland Publications, 1981.

1512. Lamontagne, L. Le Canada français d'aujourd'hui. [French Canada of Today] Toronto: University of Toronto Press, 1970.

1513. Lamontagne, Maurice. The Double Deal: A Response to the Parti Quebecois White Paper and Referendum Question. Montreal: Optimum Publishing Company, 1980. Critical response to the Parti Québécois' White Paper on Sovereignty-Association.

1514. Larocque, A. Défis au Parti Québécois. [Challenges to the Parti Québécois] Montréal: Éditions du Jour, 1971.

1515. LaTerreur, Marc. Les tribulations de conservateurs au Québec: de Bennett à Diefenbaker. [The Tribulations of the Conservatives in Quebec: From Bennett to Diefenbaker] Québec: Les Presses de l'Université Laval, 1973. Political history from 1930 through 1963 of the Conservative party in Quebec.

1516. Latouche, Daniel. *Canada and Quebec: Past and Future.* Toronto: University of Toronto Press, 1986.

1517. Latouche, Daniel, Lord, G., and Vaillancourt, J.-G. *Le processus électoral au Québec: les élections provinciales de 1970 et du 1973.* [*The Electoral Process in Quebec: Provincial Elections of 1970 and 1973*] Montréal: Hurtubise, 1976.

1518. Latouche, Daniel, and Poliquin-Bourassa, D., eds. *Le Manuel de la Parole, Manifestes Québécois.* [*The Handbook of the Word: Quebec Manifestos*] Montréal: Éditions du Boréal Express, 1978.

1519. Laurin, C. *Ma traversée du Québec.* [*My Passage Through Quebec*] Montréal: Les éditions du Jour, 1970.

1520. Legendre, Camille. *French Canada in Crisis: A New Society in the Making?* London: Minority Rights Group, 1980.

1521. Lemay, Valere. *Notre choix: souveraineté ou federalisme.* [*Our Choice: Sovereignty or Federalism*] Montréal: Éditions Charmay, 1977.

1522. Lemieux, Vincent. *La fête continue.* [*The Celebration Continues*] Montréal: Boréal Express, 1979. A study of political life and political behavior in Quebec in the period between the Quiet Revolution and the Parti Québécois referendum on Sovereignty-Association.

1523. Lemieux, Vincent. *Le quotient politique vrai -- le vote provincial et fédéral au Québec.* [*The True Political Quotient: The Provincial and Federal Vote in Quebec*] Québec: Les Presses de l'Université Laval, 1974.

1524. Lemieux, Vincent. *Parenté et politique: L'organisation sociale dans l'île d'Orléans.* [*Kinship and Politics: Social Organization on the Isle of Orleans*] Québec: Les Presses de l'Université Laval, 1971.

1525. Lemieux, Vincent, and Hudon, R. *Patronage et politique au Québec, 1944-1972.* [*Patronage and Politics in Quebec, 1944-1972*] Montréal: Boréal Express, 1975.

1526. Léonard, J.-F., ed. *La chance au coureur: Bilan de l'action du gouvernement du Parti Québécois.* [*The Luck of the Runner: Balance-Sheet of the Action of the Government of the Parti Québécois*] Montréal: Éditions Nouvelle Optique, 1978.

1527. Lescop, Renee. Le parti québécois du général de Gaulle. [The Parti Quebecois of General de Gaulle] Montréal: Boréal Express, 1981.

1528. Lévesque, René. My Quebec. [English translation by Gaynor Fitzpatrick] Toronto: Methuen, 1979. Political autobiography of René Lévesque from his early years through 1979, after his election as Premier of Quebec but before the Sovereignty-Association referendum took place.

1529. Lévesque, René. La passion du Québec. [The Passion of Quebec] Montréal: Éditions Québec/Amérique, 1978. Explanation of the goals of the Parti Québécois, its rise to power in Quebec, what the intent of the Sovereignty-Association movement was, and a view to the future.

1530. Lévesque, René. La solution: le programme du Parti Québécois. [The Solution: The Program of the Parti Québécois] Montréal: Les éditions du Jour, 1970.

1531. Lévesque, René. La souveraineté et l'économie. [Sovereignty and the Economy] Montréal: Les éditions du Jour, 1970.

1532. McGraw, D. Le développement des groupes populaires à Montréal (1963-1973). [The Development of Popular Groups in Montreal (1963-1973)] Montréal: Les éditions cooperatives Albert St-Martin, 1978.

1533. McRoberts, Kenneth, and Posgate, Dale. Quebec: Social Change and Political Crisis. Toronto: McClelland and Stewart, 1980. Historical analysis of the evolution of Quebec politics, the concept of Quebec nationalism, and the consequences of Quebec nationalism for the modern state.

1534. Mallea, J., ed. Quebec's Language Policies: Background and Response. Québec: Les Presses de l'Université Laval, 1977.

1535. Malone, Marc. Une place pour le Québec au Canada. [A Place for Quebec in Canada.] Montréal, Québec: Institut de recherches politiques, 1986.

1536. Migué, Jean-Luc, ed. Le Québec d'aujourd'hui. [Quebec of Today] Montréal: Hurbubise, 1971. Essays dealing with a variety of contemporary Québec political issues, including voting behavior, electoral reform, ideology, budgetary debates, political parties, and economic development.

1537. Milner, Henry. Politics in the New Quebec. Toronto: McClelland and Stewart, 1978. Discussion of the evolution of Quebec nationalism, Quebec ideology, the growth of the Parti Québécois, and the idea of Canadian unity.

1538. Milner, S.H., and Milner, Henry. The Decolonization of Quebec. Toronto: McClelland and Stewart, 1973.

1539. Monière, Denis. The Development of Ideologies in Quebec. Toronto: University of Toronto Press, 1981.

1540. Monière, Denis. Les enjeux du référendum. [The Stakes of the Referendum] Montréal: Québec-Amérique, 1979.

1541. Monière, Denis. Pour la suite de l'histoire: essai sur la conjoncture politique au Québec. [For the Following of History: Essay on Political Crossroads in Quebec] Montréal: Québec/Amérique, 1982. Examination of the background of the Quebec nationalist movement, what its goals were, how Canadian federalism causes problems for Quebec, and what the Parti Québécois would do to respond to these problems.

1542. Monière, Denis, and Vachet, A. Les idéologies au Québec (Bibliographie). [Ideologies in Quebec (Bibliography)] Québec: Bibliothèque nationale du Québec, 1976.

1543. Monnet, F.-M. Le défi québécois. [The Quebec Challenge] Montréal: Éditions Quinze, 1977.

1544. Morf, G. Terror in Quebec: Case Studies of the FLQ. Toronto: Clarke, Irwin, 1970.

1545. Morin, Claude. Le combat Québécois. [The Quebec Battle] Montréal: Éditions Boréal Express, 1973.

1546. Morin, Claude. Le pouvoir Québecois...en négotiation. [Quebec's Power...In Negotiation] Montréal: Éditions Boréal Express, 1972.

1547. Morin, Claude. Quebec Versus Ottawa: The Struggle for Self-Government, 1960-72. Toronto: University of Toronto Press, 1976. A political history of the rise of Quebec nationalism through a critical period of political turbulence in Quebec.

1548. Morris, R.N., and Lanphier, C.M. Three Scales of Inequality: Perspectives on French-English Relations. Montreal: Academic Press, 1977.

1549. Murray, V., and Murray, D. De Bourassa à Lévesque. [From Bourassa to Lévesque] Montréal: Éditions Quinze, 1978.

1550. Murray, V. Le parti québécois: de la fondation à la prise du pouvoir. [The Parti Québécois: From the Beginning to the Capture of Power] Montréal: Hurtubise, 1976.

1551. Nardocchio, Elaine F. Theatre and Politics in Modern Quebec. Edmonton, Alta.: University of Alberta Press, 1986.

1552. Niosi, J. La bourgeoisie canadienne: La formation et le développement d'une classe dominante. [The Canadian Bourgeoisie: The Formation and Development of a Dominant Class] Montréal: Éditions Boréal Express, 1980.

1553. Orban, Edmond, et al. La modernisation politique du Québec. [The Political Modernization of Quebec] Sillery, Québec: Boréal Express, 1976. Essays covering a range of Quebec issues, including political parties, federalism, modernization, and public administration.

1554. Orban, Edmond. Un modèle de souveraineté-association? Le conseil nordique. [A Model of Sovereignty-Association? The Northern Council] Montréal: Hurtubise, 1978.

1555. Penner, Norman, et al. Keeping Canada Together Means Changing Our Thinking. Toronto: Amethyst Publications, 1978. Essays written after the 1976 election to power of the Parti Québécois in Quebec. Essays focus on the meaning of the Quiet Revolution, what the PQ ascendancy would mean for Canada and Quebec, and federal-provincial relations in general.

1556. Québec (Province). Conseil exécutif. La nouvelle entente Québec-Canada: proposition du gouvernement du Québec pour une entente d'égal à égal, la souveraineté-association. [The New Quebec-Canada Understanding] Quebec: Conseil executif, 1979. A proposition put forward by the government of Quebec describing the concept of "sovereignty-association" and Quebec's role in a new type of Canadian federation.

1557. Québec (Province). Conseil exécutif. Quebec-Canada, A New Deal: The Quebec Government Proposal for a New Partnership Between Equals, Sovereignty-Association. Quebec: Conseil executif, 1979. Proposal by the P.Q. for a new relationship between the federal government and Quebec, describing the concept of "sovereignty-association" and the idea of a referendum.

1558. Québec (Province). Ministère des Affaires Intergouvernementales. Quebec's Traditional Stands on the Division of Powers 1900-1976. Quebec: Government of Quebec, 1979.

1559. Quebec Liberal Party. Choose Quebec and Canada: A Working Document for the Members of the Quebec Liberal Party. Montreal: Quebec Liberal Party, 1979.

1560. Quinn, Herbert Furlong. The Union Nationale: Quebec Nationalism from Duplessis to Levesque. 2nd Edition. Toronto: University of Toronto Press, 1979. Includes not only historical development of the Union Nationale, but also considerable discussion of Quebec's economic and industrial development into the 1960's.

1561. Reid, M. The Shouting Signpainters: A Literary and Political Account of Quebec Revolutionary Nationalism. Toronto: McClelland and Stewart, 1972.

1562. Rioux, M. Quebec in Question. Toronto: James, Lewis, and Samuel, 1971.

1563. Riverin, Alphonse, et al. L'Administrateur public: un etre "pifometrique". [The Public Administrator: A Simple Man] Sillery, Québec: Presses de l'Université du Québec, 1981.

1564. Rotstein, A., ed. Power Corrupted. Toronto: New Press, 1971.

1565. Roy, Jean-Louis. Le choix d'un pays : le debat constitutionnel, Quebec, Canada, 1960-1976. [The Choice of a Country] Montreal: Leméac, 1978. Study of Quebec's role in the Canadian federation. Includes discussion of the Quiet Revolution through the rise of nationalist elements to power in 1976.

1566. Roy, Jean-Louis. Les programmes electoraux du Québec. [The Electoral Programs of Quebec] 2 vols. Ottawa: Leméac, 1970. Compendium of electoral programs of the major political parties for all elections from 1867 to 1966.

1567. Royal Bank of Canada. Submission to the Parliamentary Committee on Education, Cultural Affairs and Communications, Quebec, Regarding the Charter of the French Language in Quebec, Bill 1. Montreal: Royal Bank of Canada, 1977.

1568. Ruez, Michel. L'idee d'independance au Quebec: Espoirs et desillusions. [The Idea of Independence in Quebec: Hopes and Disillusions] Talence, France: Maison des sciences de l'homme d'Aquitaine, 1986.

1569. Ryan, C. A Stable Society. Montreal: Éditions Heritage, 1978.

1570. Ryerson, Stanley B. French Canada: A Study in Canadian Democracy. Toronto: Progress Books, 1980. Political history of French-Canada, with historical analysis of its democratic traditions, its problem of national equality with English Canada, and a discussion of the impact of the rise of the Parti Québécois.

1571. Shaw, William F., and Albert, Lionel. *Partition: The Price of Quebec's Independence*. Montreal: Thornhill Publishers, 1980. Examination of the consequences of Quebec seceeding from Canada, not only to Canada, but also to Quebec. Also examines the nature of Quebec nationalism, and Quebec's claim to territory and resources.

1572. Shere, Waris, ed. *Miracles of Survival: Canada and French Canada*. Smithtown, N.Y.: Exposition Press, 1981.

1573. Soldatos, Panayotis. *Souveraineté association: l'urgence de réfléchir*. [*Sovereignty-Association: The Need to Deliberate*] Montréal : Éditions France-Amérique, 1979. Discussion of nationalism and sovereignty, and what they mean for Quebec. Also includes analysis of the rise of the P.Q., and how the sovereignty-association movement could be used to reform Canadian federalism.

1574. Soldatos, Panayotis., ed. *Nationalisme et intégration dans le contexte canadien*. [*Nationalism and Integration in the Canadian Context*] Montréal: Les Presses de l'Université de Montréal, 1980.

1575. Spicer, K. *Cher péquiste...et néanmoins ami*. [*Dear PQist...and Nevertheless Friend*] Montréal: Les Éditions la Presse, 1979.

1576. Tellier, L-N. *Le Québec: État nordique*. [*Quebec: Northern State*] Montréal: Éditions Quinze, 1977.

1577. Thompson, D., ed. *Quebec Society and Politics: Views from the Inside*. Toronto: McClelland and Stewart, 1973.

1578. Tremblay, Rodrigue. *La 3e [i.e. troisieme] option*. [*The Third Option*] Montréal: France-Amerique, 1979.

1579. Vadeboncoeur, Pierre. *Chaque jour, l'independance*. [*Each Day, Independence*] Montreal: Leméac, 1978.

1580. Vadeboncoeur, Pierre. *To Be or Not to Be, That is the Question!* Montréal: l'Hexagone, 1980.

1581. Valaskakis, Kimon. *Le Quebec et son destin international: les enjeux geopolitiques*. [*Quebec and Its International Destiny: Geopolitical Stakes*] Montréal: Quinze, 1980.

1582. Valaskakis, Kimon. *Le referendum et les defis du futur*. [*The Referendum and the Challenges of the Future*] Montréal: Parti libéral du Québec, 1980.

1583. Vallières, P. *Choose!* Toronto: New Press, 1972.

1584. Vallières, P. Un Québec impossible. [An Impossible Quebec] Montréal: Québec-Amérique, 1977.

1585. Vallières, P. White Niggers of America. Toronto: McClelland and Stewart, 1971.

1586. Veltman, Calfin, ed. Contemporary Quebec. Montréal: Université de Québec à Montréal, 1981. Essays covering the economic and political setting in Quebec, including treatment of the Canadian constitutional situation, the language question, Quebec's foreign policy, and social issues in Quebec.

1587. Verduyn, Christl, and Plourde, Marc, trans. The Impossible Option: A Post-Referendum Comment. Montréal: Éditions Heritage, 1980.

1588. Verney, Douglas. Three Civilizations, Two Cultures, One State: Canada's Political Traditions. Durham, N.C.: Duke University Press, 1986. Examines 150 years of Canadian debate over a Canadian cultural identity, what culture is, and what its relationship to the state should be.

1589. Wade, M. The French Canadians. 2 vols. Toronto: Macmillan, 1970.

1590. Walsh, Sandra. Quebec and Confederation: Bibliography of Material in the Library of the Ontario Ministry of Treasury, Economics and Intergovernmental Affairs. Monticello, Ill.: Vance Bibliographies, 1979.

Articles

1591. Albinski, Henry S. "Quebec and Canadian Unity." Current History 66:392 (1974): 155-160.

1592. Albrecht-Carrié, René. "The Canadian Dilemma." Journal of Canadian Studies 9:1 (1974): 53-62.

1593. Ali, Mehrunnisa. "The Problem of Quebec." Pakistan Horizon 24:3 (1971): 20-31.

1594. Andrew, C., Blais, A., and Desrosiers, R. "L'information sur le logement public à Hull." ["Information on Public Housing in Hull."] Recherches sociographiques 16:3 (1975): 375-383.

1595. Balthazar, Louis. "Le nationalisme au Québec." ["Nationalism in Quebec."] Études internationales 8:2 (1977): 266-281. Description of factors in Quebec encouraging the development of nationalistic sentiment, and a historical perspective of the development of nationalism.

1596. Balthazar, Louis. "Policy Discussions with Quebec Intellectuals." <u>International Perspectives</u> (July/August, 1975): 55-58.

1597. Baudouin, Jean-Louis. "The New Quebec Charter of Fundamental Freedoms." <u>Revue juridique et politique</u> 31:3 (1977): 979-987.

1598. Bauer, Julien. "Patrons et patronat au Québec." ["Employers and Their Associations in Quebec."] <u>Canadian Journal of Political Science</u> 9:3 (1976): 473-491. Cleavages which exist within employers' associations in relation to labor unions.

1599. Bélanger, Gérard. "Commentaire sur `Quebec in the Canadian Federation: A Provisional Evaluative Framework'." ["Commentary on `Quebec in the Canadian Federation: A Provisional Evaluative Framework.'"] <u>Canadian Public Administration</u> 21:4 (Winter, 1978): 579-583.

1600. Bélanger, P.R., and Maheu, L. "Pratique politique étudiante au Québec." ["Studying Political Practices in Quebec."] <u>Recherches sociographiques</u> 13:3 (1972): 309-342.

1601. Bernier, Ivan. "L'économie québécoise face á la concurrence extérieure: Les fondements scientifiques de la politique d'achat préférentiel du Québec." ["Quebec's Economy in the Face of Foreign Competition: The Scientific Bases of the Preference Trade Policy of the Province."] <u>Études internationales</u> 15:1 (1984): 61-93. Studies the Quebec Government's procurement policy with regard to how big a role scientific studies played in the policy making process. Concludes that studies were not very thorough, and had a very limited role, and that scientific research "as a tool for reaching decisions in the field of international trade, is seen by governments with some degree of suspicion."

1602. Blais, André. "Politique agricole et résultats électoraux en milieu agricole au Québec." ["Agricultural Politics and Electoral Results in Agricultural Settings in Quebec."] <u>Canadian Journal of Political Science</u> 11:2 (1978): 333-382. Studies the degree to which the Quebec government's agricultural policies influence provincial vote in rural areas.

1603. Blais, André, and Crête, Jean. "La clientèle péquiste en 1985: caractéristiques et évolution." ["The Parti Quebecois Clientele in 1985: Characteristics and Evolution."] <u>Politique</u> 10 (1986): 5-29.

1604. Blais, André, and McRoberts, Kenneth. "The Dynamics and Constraints of Public Finance in Quebec." <u>Politique</u> 3 (1983): 27-62.

1605. Bonin, B. "L'Immigration étrangère au Québec."
["Foreign Immigration to Quebec."] Canadian Public
Policy 1:3 (Summer, 1975): 296-301.

1606. Boucher, Michel. "Le référendum de mai 1980:
présentation de quelques résultats statistiques."
["The May 1980 Referendum: Presentation of Some
Statistical Results."] Politique 6 (1984): 102-124.
Statistical analysis of the May, 1980, Quebec
Referendum on Sovereignty-Association election
results.

1607. Bourgault, Jacques. "L'attitude des mass media vis-
à-vis du gouvernement québécois." ["The Attitude of
the Mass Media vis a vis the Government of Quebec."]
Études internationales 8:2 (1977): 320-336. Discusses the role of the media in society, describes
the empirical basis of this study, including which
media are indluded, and the importance of the findings for a stable social system.

1608. Bourgault, Jacques. "Problèmes liés à la nomination
et à l'évaluation des présidents de sociétés d'État
au Québec." ["Problems Related to the Appointment
and the Evaluation of Presidents of the State-Owned
Companies in Quebec."] Politiques et Management
public 3 (1985): 179-196.

1609. Bourgeault, Guy. "Le nationalisme Québécois et
l'Église." ["Quebec Nationalism and the Church."]
Canadian Review of Studies in Nationalism 5:2
(1978): 189-207.

1610. Bourque, G., and Laurin-Frenette, N. "Classes
sociales et idéologies nationalistes au Québec,
1760-1970." ["Social Classes and Nationalist
Ideologies in Quebec, 1760-1970."] Homme et la
Société 24-25 (1972): 221-247.

1611. Bouthillier, G., and Meynaud, J. "Le choix des
langues au Québec: le débat actuel." ["The Choice
of Languages in Quebec: The Actual Debate."] Res
Publica 13:3-4 (1971): 517-532. Weights the tendencies toward French unilingualism in Quebec and the
corresponding pressures to maintain English usage
there.

1612. Breton, R. "The Socio-Political Dynamics of the
October Events." Canadian Review of Sociology and
Anthropology 9:1 (1972): 33-56. Analysis of the
October, 1970 acts of violence of the F.L.Q. in
Quebec.

1613. Brooks, Stephen, and Tanguay, A. Brian. "Quebec's
Caisse de dépôt et placement: Tool of Nationalism?"
Canadian Public Administration 28:1 (1985): 99-119.

1614. Brossard, Jacques. "Le droit du peuple québécois à l'autodétermination et à l'indépendance." ["The Right of the Quebec People to Self Determination and to Independence."] Études internationales 8:2 (1977): 151-171. Describes both the Canadian constitutional basis and a basis under international law for a claim to a right to self-determination by Quebec citizens, including discussion of a right of secession.

1615. Brossard, Jacques. "The Quebec People's Right to Self-Determination in International Law." Canadian Yearbook of International Law 15 (1977): 84-145.

1616. Brunelle, Dorval. "From the 'Quiet Revolution' to Bourassa's Fall." Politique aujourd'hui 1978 (7-8): 5-16.

1617. Caldwell, Gary. "Discovering and Developing English-Canadian Nationalism in Québec." Canadian Review of Studies in Nationalism 11:2 (1984): 245-256.

1618. Cambrosio, Alberto, Davis, Charles, and Keating, Peter. "Le Québec face au biotechnologies." ["Quebec Facing Biotechnologies."] Politique 8 (1985): 77-101.

1619. Cameron, David. "Does Quebec Have a Right to Self-Determination?" Journal of Canadian Studies 7:1 (1972): 1-2.

1620. Carter, Richard. "Vers une plus grande décentralisation du financement gouvernemental au Québec." ["Toward a Greater Decentralization of Governmental Finance in Quebec."] Canadian Public Administration 28:1 (1985): 47-69.

1621. Castonguay, Charles. "Pour une politique des districts bilingues au Québec." ["For a Politics of Bilingual Districts in Quebec."] Journal of Canadian Studies 11:3 (1976): 50-59.

1622. Coleman, William D. "From Bill 22 to Bill 101: The Politics of Language Under the Parti Québécois." Canadian Journal of Political Science 14:3 (1981): 459-485. Examines the differences between the language policies of Quebec's major parties of the 1970's focusing upon the Quebec Liberal Party's Bill 22 in 1974 and the Parti Québécois' Bill 101 in 1977.

1623. Connord-Lajambe, Hélène. "L'autonomie énergétique du Québec dans une perspective écologique." ["The Energetic Autonomy of Quebec in an Ecological Perspective."] Futuribles 45 (1981): 33-56.

1624. Crépeau, Paul. "La réforme du Code civil du Québec." ["The Reform of the Civil Code in Quebec."] Revue Internationale de Droit Comparé. 31:2 (1979): 269-284.

1625. Dion, Léon, and de Sève, Micheline. "Québec ou l'emergence d'une formule politique alternative." ["Quebec and the Emergence of an Alternative Political Formula."] Canadian Review of Studies in Nationalism 5:2 (1978): 258-283.

1626. Dobell, Peter C. "Québec Separatism: Domestic and International Implications." World Today 33:4 (1977): 149-159.

1627. Dobell, Peter C. "The Referendum in Quebec and the Future of Canada." Europa-Archiv 35:9 (1980): 281-288.

1628. DuPrat, J.-P. "Les institutions québécoises." ["Quebec Institutions."] Revue juridique et economique du Sud-Ouest Série juridique 22:1-2 (1971): 3-31.

1629. Falardeau, Jean-Charles. "On Ideologies in Quebec." Recherches sociographiques 17:3 (1976): 393-402.

1630. Fenwick, Rudy. "Ethnic Culture and Economic Structure: Determinants of French-English Earnings Inequality in Quebec." Social Forces 61:1 (1982): 1-20.

1631. Fenwick, Rudy. "Social Change and Ethnic Nationalism: An Historical Analysis of the Separatist Movement in Quebec." Comparative Studies in Society and History 23:2 (1981): 196-216. Examination of the effects of modernization and economic development on the emergence of nationalism in Quebec.

1632. Fernandez, L., and Maublanc, J.P. "Local Government Autonomy and Decentralization in Quebec." Revue du Droit publique et de la Science politique 2 (1984): 379-404.

1633. Fontaine, André. "La France et le Québec." ["France and Quebec."] Études internationales 8:2 (1978): 393-402. Discusses the French role -- both formal and informal -- in the Sovereignty-Association movement in Quebec.

1634. Forget, Claude E. "Développement et implantation de l'idée de régionalisation des services de santé et des services sociaux au Québec." ["Development and Implantation of the Idea of Regionalization of Health Services and Social Services in Quebec."] Canadian Public Administration 17:1 (1974): 26-36.

French Canada and Quebec   155

1635. Fortin, Louise-E. "La politique technologique québécoise." ["Quebec Technological Politics."] Politique 8 (1985): 23-44.

1636. Fournier, Pierre. "The Future of Quebec Nationalism." Journal of Commonwealth and Comparative Politics 21:1 (1983): 3-21.

1637. Fournier, Pierre. "The Parti Québécois and Economic Conditions in Quebec." Politique aujourd'hui 1978 (7-8): 69-81.

1638. Gagnon, A.G. "Ascendance politique et dynamismes régionaux au Québec." ["Political Influence and Regional Dynamics in Quebec."] Revue internationale d'Action communautaire 53 (1985): 87-94.

1639. Gilbert, Marcel. "L'information gouvernementale et les courriéristes parlementaires qu Québec." ["Government Information and Parliamentary Correspondents in Quebec."] Canadian Journal of Political Science 4:1 (1971): 26-51. Role of reporters in covering governmental activities in Quebec, emphasizing sources and evaluation of sources.

1640. Gingras, François-Pierre. "The Independentist Ideology in Quebec: National Demands to Social Project." Cahiers Internationaux de Sociologie 59 (1975): 273-284.

1641. Gingras, François-Pierre, and Nevitte, Neil. "La Révolution en Plan et le Paradigm en Cause." ["Revolution Stopped and the Paradigm Contested".] Canadian Journal of Political Science 16:4 (1983): 691-716. Changes during the 1960s in Quebec.

1642. Glazier, Kenneth. "Separatism and Quebec." Current History 72:426 (1977): 154-157.

1643. Gold, Gerald L. "La revendication de nos droits: The Quebec Referendum and Francophone Minorities in Canada." Ethnic and Racial Studies 7:1 (1984): 106-128.

1644. Gow, J. Ian. "Quebec Nationalism in the 1980's: A Spent Force?" Canadian Public Administration 28:4 (1985): 617-625.

1645. Gow, J. Ian. "One Hundred Years of Quebec Administrative History, 1867-1970." Canadian Public Administration 28:2 (1985): 244-288.

1646. Guidon, Hubert. "The Modernization of Quebec and the Legitimacy of the Canadian State." Canadian Review of Sociology and Anthropology 15:2 (1978): 227-245. The political discontent of Quebec is rooted in and is a consequence of modernization.

1647. Guidon, Hubert. "The Modernization of Quebec and the Legitimacy of the Canadian State." Recherches sociographiques 18:3 (1977): 337-366.

1648. Guimond, Serge, and Dube-Simard, Lise. "Relative Deprivation Theory and the Quebec Nationalist Movement: The Cognition-Emotion Distinction and the Personal-Group Deprivation Issue." Journal of Personality and Social Psychology 44:3 (1983): 526-535. The importance of relative deprivation explains militant sociopolitical attitudes or nationalism.

1649. Hagy, James W. "René Lévesque and the Québec Separatists." The Western Political Quarterly 24:1 (1971): 55-58.

1650. Halary, Charles, and Soucy, Pierre-Yves. "P.Q. -- In Search of an International Status." Politique aujourd'hui 1978 (7-8): 93-102.

1651. Hamel, Jacques, and Thériault, Yvon. "La fonction tribunitienne et la députation créditiste à l'Assemblée Nationale du Québec: 1970-3." ["The Tribunicial Function and the Créditiste Group in the Quebec National Assembly, 1970-1973."] Canadian Journal of Political Science 8:1 (1975): 3-21. Analysis of behavior and attitudes in the Quebec National Assembly of the Créditiste group since it first appeared in 1970-1973.

1652. Hargrove, E.C. "Nationality, Values, and Change. Young Elites in French Canada." Comparative Politics 2:3 (1970): 473-499.

1653. Heintzmann, Ralph. "The Political Culture of Quebec, 1840-1960." Canadian Journal of Political Science 16:1 (1983): 3-60.

1654. Irvine, William P. "Recruitment to Nationalism: New Politics or Normal Politics?" Canadian Journal of Political Science 5:4 (1972):P 503-520. A formal modelling attempt to decide whether nationalism in Quebec is a "new" or a "normal" phenomenon.

1655. Isajiw, Wsevolod "Towards a Theory of Ideological Movements: Nationalism and Community Change in Quebec and Flanders." Canadian Review of Studies in Nationalism 12:1 (1985): 141-159. Compares "radical" nationalism of Quebec and Flanders with "liberal" nationalism which has developed elsewhere.

1656. Knopff, Rainer. "Quebec's `Holy War' as `Regime' Politics: Reflections on the Guibord Case." Canadian Journal of Political Science 12:2 (1979): 315-332. The Guibord case was an 1890 suit dealing with the church-state conflict and the right of the city to influence the decision of who is buried in church graveyards.

French Canada and Quebec   157

1657. Kornberg, Allan, and Archer, Keith. "Note on Quebec Attitudes Toward Constitutional Options." Law and Contemporary Problems 45:4 (1982): 71-86.

1658. Kwavnick, David. "Quebec and the Two Nations Theory: A Reexamination." Queen's Quarterly 81:3 (1974): 357-376.

1659. Lachance, Gabrielle. "La coopération au développement: Le point de vue des organisations non gouvernementales québécoises." ["Development Cooperation: The Point of View of Quebec Non-Governmental Organizations."] Canadian Journal of Development Studies 7:1 (1986): 117-129.

1660. Laczko, Leslie. "English Canadians and Québécois Nationalism: An Empirical Analysis." Canadian Review of Sociology and Anthropology 15:2 (1978): 206-217. Analysis of Anglophones in terms of social class and nationalism in Quebec.

1661. Lamonde, Pierre, and Julien, Pierre André. "Economie et nouveau nationalisme: de la nostalgie agriculturiste au souverainisme." ["Economy and New Nationalism: From Agricultural Nostalgia to Sovereignty."] Canadian Review of Studies in Nationalism 5:2 (1978): 208-236.

1662. Landry, Réjean. "L'Hydro-électricité du Québec: Produire pour consommer ou produire pour exporter?" ["Quebec's Hydro-Electricity: Production for Consumption or for Exportation."] Études internationales 15:1 (1984): 95-120. Study examines the use options dealing with Hydro-Quebec's surplus power.

1663. LaPonce, Jean A. "Assessing the Neighbour Effect on the Vote of Francophone Minorities in Canada." Political Geography Quarterly 6:1 (1987): 77-87. Studies how "fragments" of ethnic minorities vote, using data from 1945-1982.

1664. LaPonce, Jean A. "The French Language in Canada: Tensions Between Geography and Politics." Political Geography Quarterly 3:2 (1984): 91-104. The policies of the Canadia government to prevent the "coincidence" of linguistic and provincial boundaries works against the needs of minority languages to control specific territories for their own survival.

1665. LaPonce, Jean A. "Protecting the French Language in Canada: From Neurophysiology to Geography to Politics: The Regional Imperative." Journal of Commonwealth and Comparative Politics 23:2 (1985): 157-170. The geographic concentration of minority languages, needed for their survival, has neurophysiological underpinnings. Examines federal language policies, especially since the constitutional reform of 1982, in light of these factors.

1666. LaTouche, Daniel. "Anti-séparatisme et messianisme au Québec depuis 1960." ["Anti-separatism and Messianism in Quebec Since 1960."] Canadian Journal of Political Science 3:4 (1970): 559-578. Intellectual history of the anti-separatist movement in Quebec.

1667. LaTouche, Daniel. "Les effets pervers de l'entre-dépendence: Le Canada et son problème québécois." ["Negative Effects of Interdependence: Canada and the Quebec Problem."] Canadian Journal of Political and Social Theory 7:3 (1983): 68-81. Relations between Quebec and Canada after the 1980 rejection of the "Sovereignty-Association" referendum.

1668. LaTouche, Daniel. "Jeunesse et nationalisme au Québec: Une idéologie peut-ell mourir?" ["Youth and Nationalism in Quebec: Can an Ideology Die?"] Revue Français de Science Politique 35:2 (1985): 236-261.

1669. LaTouche, Daniel. "The Organizational Culture of Government: Myths, Symbols, and Rituals in a Quebecois Setting." International Social Science Journal 35:2 (1983): 257-278. Study of political offices in Quebec from an organization theory perspective.

1670. LaTouche, Daniel. "La vrai nature de...la révolution tranquille." Canadian Journal of Political Science 7:3 (1974): 525-535. Empirical analysis of some of the effects of the "Quiet Revolution" in Quebec.

1671. Latouche, D. "Quebec and the North American Subsystem: One Possible Scenario." International Organization 28:4 (1974): 931-960.

1672. Lecomte, Patrick. "A New Term of Office for the Parti Québécois: The Test of Power." Pouvoirs 21 (1982): 159-168.

1673. Legaré, Anne. "Social Classes and the Parti Québécois Government in Québec." Canadian Review of Sociology and Anthropology 15:2 (1978): 218-226.

1674. Lemieux, Vincent. "Le conflit dans les organisations biculturelles." ["Conflict in Bicultural Organizations."] Recherches sociographiques 14:1 (1973): 41-57.

1675. Lemieux, Vincent. "Québec contre Ottawa: axiomes et jeux de la communication." ["Québec versus Ottawa: Axioms and Communications Games."] Études internationales 9:2 (1978): 323-336. In the game theory of politics, "primary concern is focused on tactical possibilities rather than on the usefulness of outcomes." This study seeks to explain Quebec-Ottawa communications in game theory terms.

1676. Lemieux, Vincent. "Quel Etat du Québec?" ["What State of Quebec?"] Études internationales 8:2 (1977): 254-265. Discusses economic and social aspects of a future Quebec, and how it would be perceived by the Quebec public.

1677. Lemieux, Vincent. "The Quiet Revolution: From Patronage to Adjustment." Recherches sociographiques 23:3 (1982): 335-346.

1678. Lemieux, Vincent, and Duchesneau, Paule. "Public Interest Laws Adopted in Quebec from 1945 to 1980." Recherches sociographiques 22:3 (1981): 379-390.

1679. Lemieux, Vincent, and LeDoux, Genevieve. "Le Controle de L'Information Gouvernementale: Le Cas Du Quebec." ["The Control Of Governmental Information: The Case Of Quebec.] Canadian Public Administration 26:3 (1983): 402-419. Study of how the government of Quebec has acted to regulate information to reflect its actions in a more positive way.

1680. Lemieux, Vincent, and Turgeon, Jean. "La décentralisation: une analyze structurale." ["Decentralization: A Structural Analysis."] Canadian Journal of Political Science 13:4 (1980): 691-710.

1681. Lévesque, René. "For an Independent Québec." Foreign Affairs 54:4 (1976): 734-744.

1682. Levine, Marc V. "Institutional Design and the Separatist Impulse: Quebec and the Antebellum American South." Annals of the American Academy of Political and Social Science 433 (1977): 60-72.

1683. Loh, Wallace D. "Nationalist Attitudes in Quebec and Belgium." Journal of Conflict Resolution 19:2 (1975): 217-249. Discussion of results of survey research using scales of political and cultural nationalism and measuring effects of ethnicity and social class.

1684. Luetkens, W.L. "Nationalism in Quebec." Europäische Rundschau 5:3 (1977): 141-148.

1685. McKinsey, Lauren S. "Dimensions of National Political Integration and Disintegration: The Case of Quebec Separatism, 1960-1975." Comparative Political Studies 9:3 (1976): 335-360..

1686. McRoberts, Kenneth. "Internal Colonialism: The Case of Quebec." Ethnic and Racial Studies 2:3 (1979): 293-318.

1687. McRoberts, Kenneth. "Quebec and the Canadian Political Crisis." Annals of the American Academy of Political and Social Science 433 (1977): 19-31.

1688. McRoberts, Kenneth. "The Sources of Neo-nationalism in Quebec." Ethnic and Racial Studies 7:1 (1984): 55-85.

1689. McWhinney, Edward. "Constitutional Solutions for the Racial-Linguistic Crisis in French-Canada." Jahrbuch des öffentlichen Rechts der Gegenwart 23 (1974): 489-504.

1690. McWhinney, Edward. "French-Canadian Nationalism and Separatism and Contemporary Canadian Federalism." Jahrbuch des Öffentlichen Rechts der Gegenwart 21 (1972): 571-590.

1691. McWhinney, Edward. "The `Language' Problem in Quebec." American Journal of Comparative Law 29:3 (1981): 413-427.

1692. No entry

1693. McWhinney, Edward. "Self-Determination for Québec and the French Language Question." Jahrbuch des öffentlichen Rechts der Gegenwart 26 (1977): 513-538.

1694. McWhinney, Edward. "The `Quiet Revolution' in French Canada and Its Constitutional Implications for Canadian Federalism." Jahrbuch des öffenlichen Rechts der Gegenwart 19 (1970): 331-353.

1695. Mallen, Pierre-Louis. "Québec: l'année de la décision." ["Quebec: The Year of the Decision."] Defense nationale (1979): 69-82.

1696. Mascotto, Jacques, and Soucy, Pierre Yves. "The Quebec Workers' Movement and the Constitutional Crisis of the Canadian State: A Survey of Some Practical and Theoretical Issues." Journal of Area Studies 5 (1982): 30-33.

1697. Massicotte, Louis. "Provincial By-Elections in Quebec Since 1867. A Good Thermomenter, a Bad Barometer?" Recherches sociographiques 22:1 (1981): 105-124.

1698. Monière, Denis. "The Parti Québécois and Social Change in Quebec." Australian and New Zealand Journal of Sociology 14:3 (1978): 340-346.

1699. Moreux, Colette. "Spécificité culturelle du leadership en milieu rural canadien-français." ["Cultural Specificity of Leadership in French-Canadian Areas."] Sociologie et Sociétés 3:2 (1971): 229-258.

1700. Moreux, Colette. "Religious Ideologies and Power: the Example of Quebec Catholicism." Cahiers internationaux de Sociologie 64 (1978): 35-62.

1701. Murray, Vera. "The Parti québécois: Tensions Within the Independentist Coalition." Politique aujourd'hui 1978 (7-8): 55-67.

1702. Myhul, Ivan M. "Quebec Language Legislation." Res Publica 23:4 (1981): 497-508. Development of a French language bureau in Quebec, and the incremental expansion of language legislation in Quebec.

1703. Neatby, H. Blair. "Mackenzie King and French Canada." Journal of Canadian Studies 11:1 (1976): 3-13.

1704. Olzak, Susan. "Ethnic Mobilization in Quebec." Ethnic and Racial Studies 5 (1982): 253-275. Linguistic boundaries and federal-state activities must be taken into account when analyzing ethnic political movements.

1705. Ornstein, Michael D., and Stevenson, H. Michael. "Elite and Public Opinion Before the Quebec Referendum: A Commentary on the State in Canada." Canadian Journal of Political Science 14:4 (1981): 745-774. Study of opinions to be found among various Canadian "elite" in relation to sovereignty-association referendum before the public vote.

1706. Painchaud, Paul. "Territorialization and Internationalism: The Case of Quebec." Publius 7:4 (1977): 161-175. Historical discussion of nationalism in Quebec and possible Quebec-Canadian economic and diplomatic relations if nationalist trends in Quebec were to continue.

1707. Paquot, Annette. "Le Peuple Problematique du Canada. Les Definitions de Canada et Quebec dans le Discours Journalistique Quebecois Post-Referendaire." ["The Problematic People Of Canada. The Definitions Of Canada And Quebec in the Quebecois Newspapers' Discourse After the Referendum."] Mots 7 (1983): 7-29. Study of definitions of the words "Canada" and "Quebec" and the words used to define them.

1708. Pelletier, Réjean. "Nationalisme et étatisme au Québec dans les anées 60: Une hypothese de travail pour l'analyse des programmes des partis politiques." ["Nationalism and Statism in Quebec in the 1960'sf: A Working Hypothesis for an Analysis of Political Party Platforms."] Canadian Review of Studies in Nationalism 7:2 (1980): 329-350.

1709. Penner, Norman. "Quebec Explodes a Bombshell: René Levesque and the Challenge of Separatism." Round Table 266 (1977): 153-160. Analysis of 1976, vote in Quebec compared to the 1970 and 1973 votes. Provides a brief background, and discussion of "reforms" after the "Quiet Revolution", as well as a discussion of other reasons for the PQ victory.

1710. Philip, Christian. "La situation politique et constitutionnelle au Québec après les élections du 29 octobre 1973." ["The Political and Constitutional Situation in Quebec After the Elections of October 29, 1973."] Revue du Droit Publque et de la Science Politique 90:2 (1974): 465-499.

1711. Philip, Christian. "Quebec: The Time for Choice." Revue du Droit public et de la Science politique 94:5 (1978): 1351-1371.

1712. Pinard, Maurice. "Working Class Politics: An Interpretation of the Quebec Case." Canadian Review of Sociology and Anthropology 7:2 (1970): 87-109. The Union Nationale's success cannot be explained in the normal context of working class politics.

1713. Pinard, Maurice, and Hamilton, Richard. "The Class Bases of the Quebec Independence Movement: Conjectures and Evidence." Ethnic and Racial Studies 7:1 (1984): 19-54.

1714. Pious, Richard. "Canada and the Crisis of Quebec." Journal of International Affairs 27:1 (1973): 53-65. Discusses the "crisis of Quebec," including the constitutional understandings of Quebec, the rise of Quebec nationalism, and relations between the federal government and Quebec since that time.

1715. Plasse, Micheline. "Les chefs de cabinets ministériels au Québec: la transition du gouvernement libéral au gouvernement péquiste (1976-1977)." ["The Ministerial `chefs de cabinet' in Quebec: The Transition from the Liberal to the PQ Government (1976-1977)."] Canadian Journal of Political Science 14:2 (1981): 309-335. Role of personal aides of ministers ("chefs de cabinet") in Quebec and their influence upon existing tension between ministers and higher civil servants.

1716. Rawkins, Phillip. "The Role of the State in the Transformation of the Nationalist Movements of the 1960s: Comparing Wales and Quebec." Ethnic and Racial Studies 7:1 (1984): 86-105.

1717. Raynauld, André. "La propriété et la performance des entreprises établies au Québec." ["Property and the Performance of Established Enterprises in Quebec."] Études Internationales 2:1 (1971): 81-109.

1718. Reid, Malcolm. "Canadian Socialists, Politics in Quebec." Dissent 24:4 (1977): 351-354.

1719. Reny, Paul, and Rouleau, Jean-Paul. "Charismatics and Socio-Politics in the Quebec Catholic Church." Social Compass 25:1 (1978): 125-143. Discussion of the movement of Catholicism and its effect on Quebec politics.

1720. Rogel, Jean-Pierre. "La presse québécoise et l'information sur la politique internationale." ["The Quebec Press and Information on International Politics."] Études Internationales 5:4 (1974): 693-710. Study of whether the "Quiet Revolution" resulted in greater Quebec awareness of international politics and a better informed Quebec public. Found that Quebeckers were slightly better informed than before the Quiet Revolution, but Quebec newspapers accord issues related to international affairs little importance.

1721. Roy, Jean-Louis. "The French Fact in North America: Quebec-United States Relations." International Journal 31:3 (1976): 470-487.

1722. Roy, Jean-Louis. "Le nationalisme Québécois." ["Quebec Nationalism."] Canadian Review of Studies in Nationalism 5:2 (1978): 161-162.

1723. Sabourin, Louis. "La recherche d'un statut endogène québécois: trois stades de connaissance mutuelle." ["Research of an Endogenous Quebec Statute: Three Stages of Mutual Knowledge."] Études internationales 8:2 (1977): 231-239. Discusses the Quiet Revolution and the growth of Quebec attitudes supporting the French language and independence for Quebec.

1724. Saint-Germain, Maurice. "Dépendance économique et freins au développement: Le cas du Québec." ["Economic Dependence and Brakes on Development: The Case of Quebec."] Recherche sociale 49 (1974): 93-98.

1725. Shaffir, William. "Hassidic Jews and Quebec Politics." Jewish Journal of Sociology 25:2 (1983): 105-118. Studies reactions of two large Hassidic communities in Montreal to issues in Quebec politics, primarily Bill 101, the Charter of the French Language.

1726. Sigler, John. "Stabilité, changement social et séparatisme dans les sociétés développées: le cas québécois." ["Stability, Social Change, and Separatism in Developed Societies: The Case of Quebec."] Études internationales 8:2 (1977): 282-291. Studies how these three factors interact in contemporary Quebec politics.

1727. Simard, Jean-Jacques. "Fragments of a Tired Discourse on Quebecois Identities." Recherches sociographiques 21:1-2 (1980): 163-179.

1728. Simeon, R. "Quebec 1970: The Dilemma of Power." Queen's Quarterly 79:1 (1972): 100-107.

1729. Stein, Michael B. "Le Bill 22 et la population non-francophone au Québec: les attitudes du groupe minoritaire face à la legislation de la langue." ["Bill 22 and the Non-Francophone Population of Quebec: The Attitudes of a Minority Group Facing Language Legislation."] Canadian Review of Studies in Nationalism 5:2 (1978): 163-188.

1730. Stein, Michael B. "Le rôle des Québécois non francophones dans le débat actuel entre le Québec et le Canada." ["The Role of non-Francophone Quebeckers in the Debate Between Quebec and Canada."] Études internationales 8:2 (1977): 292-306. Describes self-perceptions of the more than one million non-French speaking citizens of Quebec, and the role that they can play in the linguistic battles there.

1731. Stone, Alec. "The New Québec Challenge to North American Diplomacy." SAIS Review 3:2 (1983): 119-132.

1732. Tancelin, Maurice. "La justice contractuelle: expérience et perspectives au Quebec." ["Contractual Justice: Experiences and Perspectives in Quebec."] Revue internationale de Droit comparé 30:4 (1978): 1009-1028.

1733. Thibaut, F., and Amboise, Jean-Claude. "L'étrange paradoxe d'une liberté devenue obligatoire: la loi 101 sur l'usage exclusif du français dans l'État du Québec." ["The Strage Paradox of a Now Compulsory Right: Law 101 on the Exclusive Use of French in the Province of Quebec."] Revue du Droit public et de la Science politique (1987): 149-172.

1734. Thibeault, A., and Wynant, L. "Investor Reaction to the Political Environment in Quebec." Canadian Public Policy 5:2 (Spring, 1979): 236-247.

1735. Thomson, Dale C. "Quebec and the Bicultural Dimension." Proceedings of the Academy of Political Science 32:2 (1976): 27-39.

1736. Tiryakian, Edward A. "Quebec, Wales, and Scotland: Three Nations in Search of a State." International Journal of Comparative Sociology 21:1-2 (1980): 1-13. Description of nationalist movements in these settings.

1737. Treddenick, J.M. "Quebec and Canada: Some Economic Aspects of Independence." Journal of Canadian Studies 8:4 (1973): 16-31.

1738. Vaillancourt, F. "La Charte de la Langue Français du Québec." ["The Charter of the French Language of Quebec."] Canadian Public Policy 4:3 (Summer, 1978): 284-308.

1739. Vaillancourt, F. "La situation démographique et socio-économique des francophones du Québec: une revue." ["The Demographic and Socio-Economic Situation of Francophones of Quebec: A Review."] Canadian Public Policy 5:4 (Autumn, 1979): 542-558.

1740. Verney, Douglas V. "Canada and Quebec: A New Regime?" India International Centre Quarterly 7:1 (1980): 3-14.

1741. Zorgbibe, C. "Québec: scénarios pour l'independance." ["Quebec: Scenarios For Independence."] Défense Nationale (1975): 67-77. Examines several possibilities for an independent Quebec, with a focus upon Quebec diplomacy with Canada, the United States, the Commonwealth, and the Francophonie.

7
Public Opinion and Citizen Participation

Books

1742. Armstrong, P., and Armstrong, H. The Double Ghetto: Women and Their Work in Canada. Toronto: McClelland and Stewart, 1978.

1743. Bashevkin, Sylvia B. Toeing the Lines: Women and Party Politics in English Canada. Toronto: University of Toronto Press, 1985. History and increasing role of women in English-Canadian political parties and political behavior.

1744. Bélanger, André. A Framework for Political Sociology. Toronto: University of Toronto Press, 1985. The role of social classes in political interactions, including interest groups, patterns of communication, and governance.

1745. Black, Derek. Winners and Losers: The Book of Canadian Political Lists. Toronto: Methuen, 1984.

1746. Brody, Janine. Women and Politics in Canada. McGraw-Hill Ryerson, 1985.

1747. Buchbinder, H., Hunnius, G., and Stevens, E. Citizen Participation: A Research Framework and Annotated Bibliography. Ministry of State, Urban Affairs Canada, 1974.

1748. Cairns, Alan, and Williams, Cynthia. The Politics of Gender, Ethnicity, and Language in Canada. Toronto: University of Toronto Press, 1986.

1749. Campbell, Colin. Canadian Political Facts, 1945-1976. Toronto: Methuen, 1977. Compendium of facts and figures related to Canadian political institutions and political practices.

1750. Canadian Advisory Council on the Status of Women. 10 Years Later: An Assessment of the Federal Government's Implementation of the Recommendations Made by the Royal Commission on the Status of Women. Ottawa: The Council, 1979.

1751. Carter, A. Direct Action and Liberal Democracy. Don Mills, Ont.: Musson, 1973.

1752. Chapin, Henry, and Deneau, Denis. Citizen Involvement in Public Policy-Making: Access and the Policy-Making Process. Ottawa: Canadian Council on Social Development, 1978.

1753. Cochrane, Jean. Women in Canadian Life: Politics. Don Mills, Ontario: Fitzhenry and Whiteside, 1977.

1754. Cochrane, Jean. Women in Canadian Politics. Toronto: Fitzhenry & Whiteside, 1977.

1755. Cocking, Clive. Following the Leaders: A Media Watcher's Diary of Campaign '79. Toronto: Doubleday Canada, 1980. Analysis of the political actors and events which proved to be significant in the 1979 federal election.

1756. Cohen, Yolande, ed. Femmes et Politique. [Women and Politics] Montreal: Le Jour, 1981. Discussion of feminism and its impact upon contemporary politics.

1757. Dion, L. Société et politique: la vie des groups. Dynamique de la société libérale. [Society and Politics: The Life of Groups. Dynamics of a Liberal Society] Québec: Les Presses de l'Université Laval, 1972.

1758. Draper, J.A., ed. Citizen Participation in Canada. Toronto: New Press, 1971.

1759. Environment Conservation Authority (Alberta). Involvement and Environment: Proceedings of the Canadian Conference on Public Participation, Banff, Alberta, October 4th-7th, 1977. Edmonton: Environment Council of Alberta, 1978-1979.

1760. Gibbons, Kenneth M., and Rowat, Donald C., eds. Political Corruption in Canada: Cases, Causes, and Cures. Toronto: McClelland and Stewart in association with the Institute of Canadian Studies, Carleton University, 1976. Case studies, analysis of causes and effects of political corruption, and suggestions for preventative actions that could affect political corruption.

1761. Hunnius, G. Participatory Democracy for Canada. Montreal: Black Rose, 1971.

1762. Jabbra, Joseph G., and Landes, Ronald G. The Political Orientations of Canadian Adolescents: Political Socialization and Political Culture in Nova Scotia. Halifax, N.S.: Saint Mary's University, 1976.

1763. Johnston, Richard. Public Opinion and Public Policy in Canada: Questions of Confidence. Toronto: University of Toronto Press, 1986.

1764. Keating, D. The Power to Make It Happen. Toronto: Green Tree, 1977.

1765. Kome, Penney. Women of Influence: Canadian Women and Politics. Toronto: Doubleday, Canada, 1985. Study of the growth of the women's rights movement in Canada since suffrage, and the issues which have been important in the increasingly visible role of women in politics in Canada.

1766. No entry

1767. Kornberg, Allan, and Clarke, Harold, eds. Political Support in Canada: The Crisis Years. Durham, N.C.: Duke University Press, 1983. Essays discussing the nature of political support, agents creating political support, government policies affecting support, and other issues generating "crises" of political support.

1768. Kornberg, Allan, Mishler, William, and Clarke, Harold. Representative Democracy in the Canadian Provinces. Scarborough, Ont.: Prentice Hall Canada, Inc., 1982. Study of political participation and political culture in Canada, including discussion of the roles of political parties, interest groups, formal governmental structures, and public policy in representative democracy.

1769. Kornberg, Allan, Smith, Joel, and Clarke, Harold. Citizen Politicians -- Canada : Party Officials in a Democratic Society. Durham, N.C.: Carolina Academic Press, 1979. Study of political socialization, social background, and political activities of a range of "citizen politicians" in Canada, and how they became active in politics.

1770. Levitt, Morris. Dissertations in Political Science on Women. Monticello, Ill.: Vance Bibliographies, 1982.

1771. Lovenduski, Joni, and Hills, Jill, eds. The Politics of the Second Electorate: Women and Public Participation. London: Routledge and Kegal Paul, 1981. A collection of essays on the role of women in politics in thirteen different countries. One chapter is on women in Canadian politics.

1772. Lyon, Noel. *Aboriginal Self-Government: Rights of Citizenship and Access to Governmental Services.* Kingston, Ont.: Institute of Intergovernmental Relations, 1984.

1773. McClain, Paula Denice. *Alienation and Resistance: The Political Behavior of Afro-Canadians.* Palo Alto, Calif.: R&E Research Associates, 1979.

1774. MacKinnon, F. *Postures and Politics: Some Observations on Participatory Democracy.* Toronto: University of Toronto Press, 1973.

1775. Massey, J.H., and Godfrey, C. *People and Places.* Toronto: Copp Clark, 1972.

1776. Matheson, G., ed. *Women in the Canadian Mosaic.* Toronto: Peter Martin, 1976

1777. Miles, Angela R., and Finn, Geraldine, eds. *Feminism in Canada: From Pressure to Politics.* Montreal, Black Rose Books, 1982.

1778. Mishler, William T. E. *Political Participation in Canada: Prospects for Democratic Citizenship.* Toronto: Macmillan of Canada, 1979. Study of various components of political participation in Canada, including political psychology, sociological variables, and the consequences of political participation.

1779. Pammett, Jon H., and Whittington, Michael S., eds. *Foundations of Political Culture: Political Socialization in Canada.* Toronto: Macmillan of Canada, 1976.

1780. Pateman, C. *Participation and Democratic Theory.* Toronto: Macmillan of Canada, 1970.

1781. Pelletier, R. *Les militants du R.I.N.* [*The Militants of the R.I.N.*] Ottawa: Éditions de l'Université d'Ottawa, 1974.

1782. Presthus, Robert. *Elite Accommodation in Canadian Politics.* Toronto: Macmillan of Canada, 1973.

1783. Presthus, Robert. *Elites in the Policy Process.* Toronto: Macmillan of Canada, 1974.

1784. Pross, A. Paul, ed. *Pressure Group Behaviour in Canadian Politics.* Scarborough, Ont.: McGraw-Hill Ryerson, 1975. Articles dealing with pressure groups as instruments of political communication and their role in the policy-making of the federal government, in foreign policy, and in the bureaucracy.

1785. Roald, J.B., et al. *Political Life in Canada.* Prentice-Hall, 1983.

1786. Royal Commission on the Status of Women in Canada. *What's Been Done? Assessment of the Federal Government's Implementation of the Recommendations of the Royal Commission on the Status of Women: A Report.* Ottawa: Advisory Council on the Status of Women, 1974.

1787. Shackleton, D. *Powertown: Democracy Discarded.* Toronto: McClelland and Stewart, 1977.

1788. Siegel, Arthur. *Politics and the Media in Canada.* Toronto: McGraw-Hill Ryerson, 1983.

1789. Somerville, David. *Trudeau Revealed by His Actions and Words.* Richmond Hill, Ont.: BMG Pub., 1978. Critical analysis of Trudeau's first ten years in power.

1790. Stephenson, M., ed. *Women in Canada.* Toronto: New Press, 1973.

1791. Stewart, Walter. *Trudeau in Power.* New York: Outerbridge and Dienstfrey, 1971. Critical history of Trudeau's first several years in office.

1792. Stinson, Arthur, ed. *Canadians Participate.* Ottawa: Centre for Social Welfare Studies, Carleton University, 1979.

1793. Swanick, M. Lynne Struthers. *Women in Canadian Politics and Government: A Bibliography.* Monticello, Ill.: Council of Planning Librarians, 1974.

1794. Tardif, G. *Police et politique au Québec.* [*Police and Politics in Quebec*] Montréal: Les éditions de l'aurore, 1974.

1795. Taylor, Charles. *The Pattern of Politics.* Toronto: McClelland and Stewart, 1970.

1796. Thompson, F., and Stanbury, W.T. *The Political Economy of Interest Groups in the Legislative Process in Canada.* Toronto: Butterworths, 1979.

1797. Thorburn, Hugh. *Interest Groups in the Canadian Federal System.* Toronto: University of Toronto Press, 1985. Examination of how federalism affects interest groups, and how interest groups affect federalism.

1798. Tremblay, R. *L'économie québécoise: histoire, développement, politiques.* [*The Quebec Economy: History, Development, Politics*] Montréal: Les Presses de l'Université de Québec, 1976.

1799. Verwey, Norma Ellen. <u>Radio Call-Ins and Covert Politics: A Verbal Unit and Role Analysis Approach</u>. Brookfield, Vt., U.S.A.: Gower, 1987.

1799a. Wilson, W.A. <u>The Trudeau Question, Election 1972</u>. Don Mills, Ont.: Paperjacks, 1972.

1800. Zureik, Elia, and Pike, Robert, eds. <u>Socialization and Values in Canadian Society</u>. 2 vols. Toronto: McClelland and Stewart, 1975. Study of the agents, actors, periods, and relationships in the process of political socialization.

Articles

1801. Alexander, A. "Local Politics and Decision-Making: A Hypothesis-Generating Case Study." <u>British Journal of Political Science</u> 5:1 (1975): 112-123. Discusses hypotheses which will lead to the construction of a general theory of non-partisan civic government in Canada.

1802. Alexander, Malcolm. "Business Elites, National Development, and Problems of Comparative and World-System Approaches: A Comment on Teichman's Study of Argentina and Canada." <u>Canadian Journal of Political Science</u> 15:3 (1982): 589-604.

1803. Anderson, John C. "A Comparative Analysis of Local Union Democracy." <u>Industrial Relations</u> 17:3 (1978): 278-295. Study of individual characteristics and social variables on the democratic processes of local unions.

1804. Archibald, Clinton, and Paltiel, K.Z. "On the Passage from Intermediary Bodies to Pressure Groups: the Transformation of an Idea Illustrated by the Desjardins Cooperative Movement." <u>Recherches sociographiques</u> 18:1 (1977): 59-91.

1805. Armstrong, J. "Canadians in Crisis: The Nature and Source of Support for Leadership in a National Emergency." <u>Canadian Review of Sociology and Anthropology</u> 9:4 (1972): 299-324. Content analysis of letters to the editor of several newspapers related to the October, 1970 period of crisis in Quebec and the response of the federal government with the War Measures Act.

1806. Atkinson, Michael, Coleman, William, and Lewis, Thomas. "Regime Support in Canada: A Comment." <u>British Journal of Political Science</u> 10:3 (1980): 402-410. Criticism of article by Kornberg et al. dealing with regime support, saying that Kornberg article did not validly operationalize the concept of regime support.

1807. Atkinson, Michael, and Mancuso, Maureen. "Do We Need a Code of Conduct for Politicians? The Search for an Elite Political Culture of Corruption in Canada." Canadian Journal of Political Science 18:3 (1985): 459-480.

1808. Babin, Ronald. "Antinuclear Movement in Canada." Sociologie et Sociétés 13:1 (1981): 131-145.

1809. Bashevkin, Sylvia B. "Social Change and Political Partisanship: The Development of Women's Attitudes in Quebec, 1965-1979." Comparative Political Studies 16:2 (1983): 147-172.

1810. Bauer, Julien. "L'attitude des syndicats." ["The Attitude of Unions."] Études internationales 8:2 (1977): 307-319. Describes the views of several Quebec unions to the November 1976 election of the Parti Quebec to power.

1811. Bernier, Léon. "The Political Attitudes of Youths and Their Parents: A Longitudinal Study." Recherches sociographiques 19:1 (1978): 103-134.

1812. Bird, Florence. "Experience with Women's Rights." International Perspectives (January/February, 1978): 20-25.

1813. Bird, Florence. "The Great Decade for Canadian Women." Current History 72:426 (1977): 170-172.

1814. Black, Edwin. "Turning Canadian Politics Inside Out." Political Quarterly 51:2 (1980): 141-153.

1815. Black, Edwin. "Opposition Research: Some Theories and Practice." Canadian Public Administration 15:1 (Spring, 1972): 24-41.

1816. Black, Jerome H., and McGlen, Nancy. "Male-Female Political Involvement Differentials in Canada, 1965-1974." Canadian Journal of Political Science 12:3 (1979): 471-497. Changing role of women in Canadian politics in the decade; involvement of women at the "elite" level has changed.

1817. Blais, André, and Crête, Jean. "The Press and Local Politics in Two Cities of Quebec." Politique 2 (1982): 41-67.

1818. Bouchard, Pierrette. "Féminisme et marxisme: Un dilemme pour la Ligue communiste canadienne." ["Feminism and Marxism: A Dilemma for the Canadian Communist League."] Canadian Journal of Political Science 20:1 (1987): 57-78.

1819. Brooks, Joel E. "Democratic Frustration in the Anglo-American Polities: A Quantification of Inconsistency Between Mass Public Opinion and Public Policy." Western Political Quarterly 38:2 (1985): 250-261. Studies the relationship between mass public opinion and public policy in Canada, Great Britain, and the United States.

1820. Bryden, Kenneth. "Public Input into Policy-Making and Administration: The Present Situation and Some Requirements for the Future." Canadian Public Administration 25:1 (1982): 81-107.

1821. Burke, Mike, et al. "Federal and Provincial Political Participation in Canada: Some Methodological and Substantive Considerations." Canadian Review of Sociology and Anthropology 15:1 (1978): 61-75. Development and analysis of scales of political participation rates shows that there is strong correlation between federal and provincial participation rates at the individual level.

1822. Burt, Sandra. "Different Democracies? A Preliminary Examination of the Political Worlds of Canadian Men and Women." Women and Politics 6:4 (1986): 57-79.

1823. Caron, André, Mayrand, Chantal, and Payne, David. "L'Imagerie politique à la télévision: Les derniers jours de la campagne référendaire." ["Political Imagery on Television: The Final Days of the Referendum Campaign."] Canadian Journal of Political Science 16:3 (1983): 473-488.

1824. Clark, John. "Canadian Labour Congress as an International Actor." International Perspectives (September-October, 1980): 9-12. The role of the CLC in achieving an understanding of social and political developments outside of Canada.

1825. Clarke, Harold, et al. "Ontario Student Party Activists: A Note on Differential Participation in a Voluntary Organization." Canadian Review of Sociology and Anthropology. 12:2 (1975): 213-220. Studies rates and types of participation within university clubs in several Ontario universities.

1826. Clarke, Harold, and Kornberg, Allan. "Moving Up the Political Escalator: Women Party Officials in the United States and Canada." Journal of Politics 41:2 (1979): 442-477.

1827. Clarke, Harold, Price, Richard, Stewart, Marianne, and Krause, Robert. "Motivational Patterns and Differential Participation in a Canadian Party: The Ontario Liberals." American Journal of Political Science 22:1 (1978): 130-151. Variables which affect party activity in Ontario Liberal party.

1828. Clift, Dominique. "L'État et les groupes d'intérêts: Perspectives d'avenir." ["The State and Interest Groups: Perspectives of the Future."] Canadian Public Administration 25:2 (1982): 265-277.

1829. Coleman, William D "Analysing the Associative Action of Business: Policy Advocacy and Policy Participation." Canadian Public Administration 28:3 (1985): 413-433. Defines the two types of roles that business associations might play in lobbying or pressure-group activities.

1830. Coleman, William D. "The Capitalist Class and the State: Changing the Roles of Business Interest Associations." Studies in Political Economy 20 (1986): 135-159.

1831. Coleman, William, and Jacek, Henry. "The Roles and Activities of Business Interest Associations in Canada." Canadian Journal of Political Science 16:2 (1983): 257-280.

1832. Conley, Marshall, and Smith, Patrick. "Political Recruitment and Party Activists: British and Canadian Comparisons." International Political Science Review 4:1 (1983): 48-56. Data from both Canada and England are analyzed to indicate distinctive styles of behavior, outlook, and motivation in two different political settings.

1833. Dalpé, Robert. "Les politiques canadiennes de l'industrie aérospatiale." ["Canadian Politics of the Aerospace Industry."] Politique 8 (1985): 103-129.

1834. Dawson, Helen Jones. "Canadian and Australian Farm Interest Groups." Politics 17:2 (1982): 10-22.

1835. Dion, Léon. "Anti-Politics and Marginals." Government and Opposition 9:1 (1974): 28-41.

1836. Dion, Léon, and de Sève, Micheline. "Quebec: Interest Groups and the Search for an Alternative Political System." Annals of the American Academy of Political and Social Science 413 (1974): 124-144.

1837. Donneur, André. "La presse du Québec et les pays étrangers." ["The Press in Quebec and Foreign Countries."] Études internationales 2:3 (1971): 410-423.

1838. Dunn, M.J., et al. "A Test of the Unidimensionality of Various Political Scales Through Factor Analysis: A Research Note." Canadian Journal of Political Science 6:4 (1973): 664-669.

1839. Eckhart, W. "Attitudes of Canadian Peace Groups." *Journal of Conflict Resolution* 16:3 (1972): 341-352. Reports the results of a survey of personality traits of members of five "peace groups" in Canada, and compares these attitudes with those of members of control groups.

1840. Fox, John, and Ornstein, Michael. "The Canadian State and Corporate Elites in the Post-War Period." *Canadian Review of Sociology and Anthropology* 23:4 (1986): 481-506. Study examines links between the boards of the largest Canadian corporations and public offices in Canadian politics.

1841. Frank, J.A., and Kelly, Michael. "A Middle-Level Model of Collective Protest in Canada." *International Journal of Comparative Sociology* 21:1 (1980): 118-150.

1842. Frank, J.A., and Kelly, Michael . "Etude préliminaire sur la violence collective en Ontario et au Québec, 1963-1973." ["Preliminary Study of Collective Violence in Ontario and Quebec, 1963-1973."] *Canadian Journal of Political Science* 10:1 (1977): 145-157. Analysis of collective violence in Ontario and Quebec between 1963 and 1973.

1843. Frank, J.A., and Kelly, Michael. "'Street Politics' in Canada: An Examination of Mediating Factors." *American Journal of Political Science* 23:3 (1979): 593-614. Analysis of factors affecting collective violence in Ontario and Quebec, 1963-1975.

1844. Fulton, M Jane, and Stanbury, W. T. "Comparative Lobbying Strategies in Influencing Health Care Policy." *Canadian Public Administration* 28:2 (1985): 269-300. Argues that lobbying behavior of groups is affected by whether they are "output-oriented" or "process-oriented."

1845. Gay, Daniel. "French Language Papers in Quebec and Latin America: An Inventory of Editorials and Para-Editorials." *Études internationales* 7:3 (1976): 359-392.

1846. Gilsdorf, Robert. "Cognitive and Motivational Sources of Voter Susceptibility to Influence." *Canadian Journal of Political Science* 6:4 (1973): 624-638. Study of electoral and other forms of participation in Edmonton, Alberta, and the susceptibility of voters to information and the media.

1847. Grabb, Edward G. "Class, Conformity, and Political Powerlessness." *Canadian Review of Sociology and Anthropology* 18:3 (1981): 362-369. Link between occupation as cause of class differences and literature demonstrating negative relationship between social class and subjective political powerlessness.

1848. Grabb, Edward G. "Relative Centrality and Political Isolation: Canadian Dimensions." *Canadian Review of Sociology and Anthropology* 16:3 (1979): 343-365. An analysis of Canadian feelings of isolation from political institutions and the relationship to region of residence, language affiliation, and socioeconomic status.

1849. Grayson, L.M., and Grayson, J. Paul. "Interest Aggregation and Canadian Politics: The Case of the Central Bank." *Canadian Public Administration* 16:4 (1973): 557-571.

1850. Grayson, Paul. "Plant Closures and Political Despair." *Canadian Review of Sociology and Anthropology* 23:3 (1986): 331-349. Studies the effect that plant closures has had upon the political attitudes of the unemployed.

1851. Hartnagel, Timothy, Creechan, James, and Silverman, Robert. "Public Opinion and the Legalization of Abortion." *Canadian Review of Sociology and Anthropology* 22:3 (1985): 411-430. Study of variations in public opinion in Edmonton, Alberta, related to the issue of legalized abortion.

1852. Hodgetts, J.E. "Government Responsiveness to the Public Interest: Has Progress Been Made?" *Canadian Public Administration* 24:2 (1981): 216-231.

1853. Hudon, Raymond. "La poursuite des fins organisationnelles par une groupe de pression: la CSN et les unités nationales de negociation dans l'affaire Lapalme." ["The Pursuit of Organizational Ends by a Pressure Group: The CSN and the National Unions of Negotiation in the LaPalme Affair."] *Canadian Journal of Political Science* 7:2 (1974): 328-334.

1854. Hudon, Raymond. "Pour une analyse politique du patronage." ["Towards a Political Analysis of Patronage."] *Canadian Journal of Political Science* 7:3 (1974): 484-501. Traces practice of party patronage in Quebec between 1944 and 1972, defines meaning of concept of "patronage," and examines differences in behavior between the Liberal Party and the Union Nationale in respect to party patronage.

1855. Jabbra, Joseph, and Ronald G. Landes. "Political Orientations Among Adolescents in Nova Scotia: An Exploratory Analysis of a Regional Political Culture in Canada." *Indian Journal of Political Science* 37:4 (1976): 75-96. Analysis of concepts of political community, political awareness, political trust, political efficacy, and political involvement in Nova Scotia.

1856. Jacek, Henry. "Pluralist and Corporatist Intermediation, Activities of Business Interest Associations, and Corporate Profits: Some Evidence from Canada." Comparative Politics 18:4 (1986): 419-438.

1857. Johnston, William, and Ornstein, Michael. "Class, Work, and Politics." Canadian Review of Sociology and Anthropology 19:2 (1982): 196-214.

1858. Kornberg, Allan, Clarke, Harold, and LeDuc, Lawrence. "Some Correlates of Regime Support in Canada." British Journal of Political Science 8:2 (1978): 199-216. Study of the distribution of public support for the political regime in Canada.

1859. Kornberg, Allan, Smith, Joel, and Clarke, Harold. "Attributes of Ascribed Influence in Local Party Organization in Canada and the United States." Canadian Journal of Political Science 5:2 (1972): 206-233. The distribution, characteristics, and location of influence in local party organizations in Vancouver, Winnipeg, Seattle, and Minneapolis.

1860. Kornberg, Allan, and Smith, Joel. "Self-Concepts of American and Canadian Party Officials." Polity 3:1 (1970): 70-99.

1861. Kornberg, A., et al. "Participation in Local Party Organizations in the United States and Canada." American Journal of Political Science 17:1 (1973): 23-47. Analysis of different types and degrees of participation in various party organizations in two American and two Canadian cities.

1862. Kornberg, A., et al. "Political Elite and Mass Perceptions of Party Locations in Issue Space: Some Tests of Two Positions." British Journal of Political Science 5:2 (1975): 161-185. Although parties are capable of being ordered on left-right scales in Canada, there is not a single scale which will accomodate all of the major issues.

1863. Kwavnick, David. "Pressure Group Demands and the Struggle for Organizational Status: the Case of Organized Labour in Canada." Canadian Journal of Political Science 3:1 (1970): 56-72. Demands upon government by interest group leaders for organizational recognition may overshadow the demands they make in pursuit of the group's interests.

1864. Kwavnick, David. "Pressure-Group Demands and Organizational Objectives: The CNTU, the LaPalme Affair, and National Bargaining Units." Canadian Journal of Political science 6:4 (1973): 582-601. The process by which pressure groups bring "their" issues to the attention of decision makers; suggests that in one particular case the CNTU sacrificed the interests of its members for the ambitions of its leaders.

1865. Lamont, Michèle. "Political Relations Within the Quebec Women's Movement." Politique 5 (1984): 75-107.

1866. Landes, Ronald G. "Political Socialization Among Youth: A Comparative Study of English-Canadian and American School Children." International Journal of Comparative Sociology 18:1-2 (1977): 63-80. Summary of the major findings of the first comparative study of political socialization in Canada and the U.S.

1867. Landes, Ronald G. "Pre-Adult Orientations to Multiple Systems of Government: A Comparative Study of English-Canadian and American Schoolchildren in Two Cities." Publius 7:1 (1977): 27-39. A comparison of Canadian and American children's understandings of and attachment to their respective federal political systems.

1868. Landes, Ronald, and Jabbra, Joseph. "The Impact of Socio-Political Cleavages on Support for Democratic Orientations Among Canadian Adolescents in Nova Scotia." Indian Political Science Review 15:2 (1981): 158-174. Study of survey research variables affecting fundamental democratic attitudes in Nova Scotia. Stresses value of civic culture.

1869. Landes, Ronald, and Jabbra, Joseph. "Partisan Identity Among Canadian Youth: A Case Study of Nova Scotian Adolescents." Journal of Commonwealth and Comparative Politics 17:1 (1979): 60-76. Discussion of poliical socialization process in Nova Scotia, and its effect upon the development of party preferences.

1870. Lawson, Edwin D. "Canadian and American Perception of World Powers." Peace Research Reviews 6:2 (1974): 25-38. Empirical study of American and Canadian college students rating world powers and reference concepts using an Osgood Semantic Differential measure. Discussion of differences found in patterns of responses.

1871. Leduc, Lawrence, Jr. "Measuring the Sense of Political Efficacy in Canada: Problems of Measurement Equivalence." Comparative Political Studies 8:3 (1975): 490-515.

1872. Lee, J.S., and Kornberg, A. "A Computer Simulation Model of Multiparty Recruitment." Simulation and Games 4:1 (1973): 37-58.

1873. Lemieux, Vincent. "Le patronage politique dans l'ile d'Orléans." ["Political Patronage on the Island of Orleans."] Homme 10:2 (1970): 22-44. Offers a definition of patronage and studies the various power relationships which may exist and their influence on the political system.

1874. Leonard, Jean-François, and Hamel, Pierre. "Les groupes populaires dans la dynamique socio-politique québécois." ["Popular Groups in Quebec's Socio-Political Dynamic."] Politique aujourd'hui 1978 (7-8): 155-164.

1875. Long, J. Anthony, and Slemko, Brian. "The Recruitment of Local Decision-Makers in Five Canadian Cities: Some Preliminary Findings." Canadian Journal of Political Science 7:3 (1974): 550-559. Processes involved in the recruitment of candidates for local office in five Canadian cities (all in Alberta).

1876. Lovink, J.A.A. "Is Canadian Politics Too Competitive?" Canadian Journal of Political Science 6:3 (1973): 341-379. Development of a theory based upon mathematical analysis of electoral competition in Canada.

1877. McBride, Stephen. "Public Policy as a Determinant of Interest Group Behaviour: The Canadian Labour Congress' Corporatist Initiative, 1976-1978." Canadian Journal of Political Science 16:3 (1983): 501-518.

1878. McDonald, Virginia. "Participation in the Canadian Context." Queen's Quarterly 84:3 (1977): 457-475. Study of Canadian political culture, social culture, and the political system reveals that political participation is not prevalent in the Canadian setting.

1879. MacInnis, G. "Women and Politics" Parliamentarian 53:1 (1972): 8-12.

1880. Maghami, Farhat Ghaem. "Political Knowledge Among Youth: Some Notes on Public Opinion Formation." Canadian Journal of Political Science 7:2 (1974): 334-340. Examines the impact of religion, socioeconomic characteristics, education, and the like on degree of political knowledge among Canadian university students.

1881. Mahler, Gregory. "Political Socialization and Political Interest in Israeli and Canadian Legislators: A Comparative Examination." Political Science Review 19:3 (1980): 361-383. The effects of environmental and political variables upon the socialization process are evaluated and discussed.

1882. Mahler, Gregory. "Political Consciousness and Political Events: A Study of Israeli and Canadian Members of Parliament." Political Science 31:2 (1979): 89-107. The importance of the political environment upon the development of a political consciousness of individuals.

1883. Martin, Robert. "The Law Union of Ontario." Law and Policy 7:1 (1985): 51-60. History of Ontario's Law Union, a group of lawyers which seeks to "engage in organized progressive political and legal work." Decribes structure of organization and its political views.

1884. Martinez, Michael. "Intergenerational Transfer of Canadian Partisanships." Canadian Journal of Political Science 17:1 (1984): 133-144. Data from 1974 Canadian national election show the relationships between voter partisanships and parental partisanships.

1885. Mishler, W., et al. "Patterns of Political Socialization. Simulating the Development of Party Identification in Two Political Elites." Comparative Political Studies 6:4 (1974): 399-430.

1886. Monroe, Kristen, and Erickson, Lynda. "The Economy and Political Support: The Canadian Case." Journal of Politics 48:3 (1986): 616-647.

1887. Munton, Donald J. "Public Opinion and the Media in Canada from Cold War to Detente to New Cold War." International Journal 39:1 (1983-1984): 171-213.

1888. Ornstein, Michael. "The Political Ideology of the `Inner Group' of Canadian Capital." Journal of Political and Military Sociology 13:2 (1985): 219-238. Using data from a 1981 survey of chief executives of the largest Canadian corporations and governmental officials, discovers differences between executives and state officials and discusses the implications of these findings.

1889. Ornstein, Michael. "The Political Ideology of the Canadian Capitalist Class." Canadian Review of Sociology and Anthropology 23:2 (1986): 182-209. Presents results of 1977 national survey of corporation executives, federal and provincial politicians and civil servants, and union leaders.

1890. Ornstein, Michael, Stevenson, H., and Williams, A. Paul M. "Public Opinion and the Canadian Political Crisis." Canadian Review of Sociology and Anthropology 15:2 (1978): 158-205. Political ideology is important in the understanding of the current political crisis in Canada.

1891. Page, Don. "Participation d'un groupe de pression canadien à la conférence mondiale de l'alimentation, 1974." ["Participation of a Canadian Pressure Group in the World Food Conference, 1974."] Études internationales 15:2 (1984): 329-349. Description of how a Canadian pressure group exerted a great deal of influence at the World Conference on Food in 1974.

1892. Paltiel, Khayyam Z. "The Changing Environment and Role of Special Interest Groups." Canadian Public Administration 25:2 (Summer, 1982): 198-210.

1893. Paltiel, Khayyam Z. "The Changing Environment and Role of Special Interest Groups." Canadian Public Administration 24:4 (1981): 612-632.

1894. Pammett, Jon H. "The Development of Political Orientations in Canadian School Children." Canadian Journal of Political Science 4:1 (1971): 132-140. Measured development of political knowledge and political attitudes of children in Ontario schools.

1895. Pratt, Geraldine. "Class, Home, and Politics." Canadian Review of Sociology and Anthropology 24:1 (1987): 39-57. Explores the influence of housing stability on political ideals of Canadians.

1896. "Pressure Groups in Canada." Parliamentarian 51:1 (1970): 11-20.

1897. Presthus, Robert. "Interest Groups and the Canadian Parliament: Activities, Interaction, Legitimacy, and Influence." Canadian Journal of Political Science 4:4 (1971): 444-460.

1898. Presthus, Robert. "Interest Group Lobbying: Canada and the United States." Annals of the American Academy of Political and Social Science 413 (1974): 44-57.

1899. Pross, A. Paul. "Canadian Pressure Groups in the 1970's: Their Role and Their Relations With the Public Service." Canadian Public Administration 18:1 (1975): 121-135.

1900. Reilly, Wayne G. "Political Attitudes Among Law Students in Quebec." Canadian Journal of Political Science 4:1 (1971): 122-131. Exploration of political attitudes of French- and English-speaking law students to study the level of support for the Canadian political system of the two groups.

1901. Reilly, W.O. "Incipient Elites in Quebec. A Panel Analysis of Political Attitudes." International Journal of Group Tensions 5:1-2 (1975): 67-94.

1902. Renaud, F. "Les motivations dans une organisation partisane de circonscription." ["Motivations in a Partisan Constituency Organization."] Recherches sociographiques 14:1 (1973): 59-79.

1903. Richert, Jean Pierre. "Political Socialization in Quebec: Young People's Attitudes Toward Government." Canadian Journal of Political Science 6:2 (1973): 303-313. English- and French-Canadian children differ in their perception of government.

1904. Roback, Leo, and Tremblay, Louise-Marie. "Le nationalisme au sein des syndicats Québécois." ["Nationalism in the Heart of Quebec Unions."] Canadian Review Of Studies in Nationalism 5:2 (1978): 237-257.

1905. Saumier, André. "Business Lobbying." Canadian Public Administration 26:1 (1983): 73-79.

1906. Skogstad, Grace. "Agrarian Protest in Alberta." Canadian Review of Sociology and Anthropology 17:1 (1980): 55-73. Study of the links between the protests of individual farmers and economic discontent, populist beliefs, and political alienation.

1907. Smith, Joel, and Kornberg, Allan. "Self-Concepts of American and Canadian Party Officials: Their Development and Consequences." Social Forces 49:2 (1970): 210-225.

1908. Smith, Joel, and Zipp, John F. "The Party Official Next Door: Some Consequences of Friendship for Political Involvement." Journal of Politics 45:4 (1983): 958-978. Impact of a personal relationship with a party official on the political involvement of a group of Canadians in Winnipeg and Vancouver who reside near the officials and are like them with respect to sex, age, and occupational status.

1909. Soderlund, Walter C., et al. "Output and Feedback: Canadian Newspapers and Political Integration." Journalism Quarterly 57:2 (1980): 316-321. Analysis of press treatment of political integration issues in the differing regions o Canada.

1910. Sproule-Jones, M., and Hart, K.D. "A Public-Choice Model of Political Participation." Canadian Journal of Political Science 6:2 (1973): 175-194.

1911. Thorburn, Hugh. "Canadian Pluralist Democracy in Crisis." Canadian Journal of Political Science 11:4 (1978): 723-738. Analysis of application of the term "pluralism" to contemporary democratic political behavior in Canada.

1912. Truman, Tom. "A Scale for Measuring a Tory Streak in Canada and the United States." Canadian Journal of Political Science 10:3 (1977): 597-614. Describes the making and testing of an attitude scale which can be used to measure toryism/conservatism in both English Canada and the United States.

1913. Uhlaner, Carole Jean. "The Consistency of Individual Political Participation Across Government Levels in Canada." American Journal of Political Science 26:2 (1982): 298-311. Canadians who participate at one level of government will participate in the same way at other levels of government.

1914. Van Loon, Richard. "Political Participation in Canada: The 1965 Election." *Canadian Journal of Political Science* 3:3 (1970): 376-399. Study of socio-economic factors which have the greatest influence on voting behavior in Canada.

1915. Wallace, Donald C., and Fletcher, Frederick J. *Canadian Politics Through Press Reports*. Oxford University Press, 1984.

1916. Weimann, Gabriel, and Winn, Conrad. "The Misperception of Public Opinion: The Canadian Nazi Trials and Their Implications." *PS* 19:3 (1986): 641-645.

1917. Welch, Susan. "Dimensions of Political Participation in a Canadian Sample." *Canadian Journal of Political Science* 8:4 (1975): 553-559. Study of sample of Toronto families focusing upon different degrees and qualities of political activity.

1918. Winn, Conrad. "Affirmative Action for Women: More than a Case of Simple Justice." *Canadian Public Administration* 28:1 (Spring, 1985): 24-46.

1919. Young, Walter D. "The Voices of Democracy: Politics and Communication in Canada." *Canadian Journal of Political Science* 14:4 (1981): 683-700. The importance of communications for Canadian politics; the nature and style of political communications in Canada have had important effects upon both federal and provincial politics.

1920. Zaborszky, D. "Feminist Politics: The Feminist Party of Canada." *Women's Studies International Forum* 10:6 (1987): 613-621.

8
Political Parties, Ideology, and Elections

Books

1921. Abella, I.M. Nationalism, Communism, and Canadian Labour: The CIO, the Communist Party, and the Canadian Congress of Labour, 1935-1956. Toronto: University of Toronto Press, 1973.

1922. Alexander, Robert J., ed. Political Parties of the Americas: Canada, Latin America, and the West Indies. Greenwood Press, 1982.

1923. Anwar, Muhammad. Ethnic Minorities and the 1983 General Election: A Research Report. London: Commission for Racial Equality, 1984.

1924. Aucoin, Peter, ed. Party Government and Regional Representation in Canada. Toronto: University of Toronto Press, 1985. Essays covering party government and national integration, the role of national party caucuses, and regionalism and party and national government.

1925. Avakumovic, Ivan. The Communist Party in Canada: A History. Toronto: McClelland and Stewart, 1975. Political history of the Canadian communist party.

1926. Avakumovic, Ivan. Socialism in Canada: A Study of the CCF-NDP in Federal and Provincial Politics. Toronto: McClelland and Stewart, 1978. A political history of the Cooperative Commonwealth Federation which became the New Democratic Party, and its development as a force in Canadian socialism.

1927. Barr, J.J. The Dynasty: The Rise and Fall of Social Credit in Alberta. Toronto: McClelland and Stewart, 1974.

1928. Bashevkin, Sylvia. _Toeing the Lines: Women and Party Politics in English Canada_. Toronto: University of Toronto Press, 1985. Study of the experiences of women in English Canadian political parties.

1929. Baum, G. _Catholics and Canadian Socialism: Political Thought in the Thirties and Forties_. Toronto: Lorimer, 1980.

1930. Beder, E. A. _The Missing Political Party_. Toronto: Wilton Agencies, 1972.

1931. Bercuson, David Jay, Granatstein, J. L, and Young, W. R. _Sacred Trust? Brian Mulroney and the Conservative Party in Power_. Toronto: Doubleday Canada 1986.

1932. Berkowitz, Stephen. _Models and Myths in Canadian Society_. Toronto: Butterworths, 1981.

1933. Boyer, J. Patrick. _Money and Message: The Law Governing Election Financing, Advertising, Broadcasting, and Campaigning in Canada_. Toronto: Butterworths, 1983.

1934. Boyer, J. Patrick. _Political Rights: The Legal Framework of Elections in Canada_. Toronto: Butterworth's, 1981. A highly detailed and legalistic study of all aspects of Canadian elections, including (but not limited to) election statutes, common law, constitutional legal issues, and the rights of citizens to vote, to free speech, to run for office, and to form parties.

1935. Broadbent, John Edward. _The Liberal Rip-off: Trudeauism vs. the Politics of Equality_. Toronto: New Press, 1970.

1936. Brodie, M. Janine. _Women and Politics in Canada_. Toronto: McGraw-Hill Ryerson, 1985.

1937. Brodie, M. Janine, and Jenson, Jane. _Crisis, Challenge, and Change: Party and Class in Canada_. Toronto: Methuen, 1980. A political history of the development of the various provincial and federal party systems in Canada. Among many other factors, this study pays particular attention to the effects of social class on the party system.

1938. Brooks, Stephen, ed. _Political Thought in Canada: Contemporary Perspectives_. Toronto, Ontario: Irwin Publications, 1984. Collection of original essays describing a number of different perspectives of contemporary political thought in Canada, including such questions as religion and politics, democratic values, French Canada, and historical evidence and contemporary insights.

Political Parties, Ideology, and Elections   187

1939. Brown, P., Chodos, R., and Murphy, R. Winners,
       Losers: The 1976 Tory Leadership Convention.
       Toronto: Lorimer, 1976.

1940. Buck, T. Lenin and Canada. Toronto: Progress
       Books, 1970.

1941. Camp, Dalton. Points of Departure. Ottawa: Deneau
       and Greenberg, 1979. Discussion of the Canadian
       Parliament and the parliamentary election and
       campaign of 1979 in Canada.

1942. Caplan, G.L. The Dilemma of Canadian Socialism:
       The CCF in Ontario. Toronto: McClelland and
       Stewart, 1973.

1943. Christian, William, and Campbell, Colin. Political
       Parties and Ideologies in Canada: Liberals, Conser-
       vatives, Socialists, Nationalists. Toronto: McGraw-
       Hill Ryerson, 1974. Investigation of ideology
       appearing in Canadian political party platforms, and
       the degree to which there is a substantial
       "Canadian" component to this ideology.

1944. Clarke, Harold, et al. Absent Mandate: The
       Politics of Discontent in Canada. Toronto: Gage,
       1984. Data-based study of Canadian electoral behav-
       ior primarily in the 1974, 1979, and 1980 election
       years, with specific discussion of the party system,
       federalism, economic issues, leadership, and
       partisanship.

1945. Clarke, Harold D., et al. Political Choice in
       Canada. Toronto: McGraw-Hill Ryerson, 1979. Data-
       based study of political participation, political
       choice, and voting behavior in recent Canadian fed-
       eral elections.

1946. Clarke, H.D., and Price, R.G. Recruitment and
       Leadership Selection in Canada. Toronto: Holt,
       Rinehart and Winston, 1973.

1947. Courtney, John C. The Selection of National Party
       Leaders in Canada. Toronto: Macmillan of Canada,
       1973. Historical and comparative study of party
       leader selection, with special attention paid to the
       national leadership conventions and the politics of
       the selection process.

1948. Cross, M.S. The Decline and Fall of a Good Idea:
       CCF-NDP Manifestoes, 1932 to 1969. Toronto: New
       Hogtown Press, 1974.

1949. Cunningham, F. Understanding Marxism: A Canadian
       Introduction. Toronto: Progress Books, 1978.

188   Contemporary Canadian Politics

1950. Drouilly, Pierre. Le Paradoxe Canadien: Le Québec et les élections fédérales. [The Canadian Paradox: Quebec and Federal Elections] Montréal: Parti Pris, 1978. Discussion of Quebec voting patterns in the federal elections of 1972 through 1979.

1951. Electoral Boundaries Commission for British Columbia. Report of the Electoral Boundaries Commission for the Province of British Columbia, 1976. Ottawa: Information Canada, 1976.

1952. Engelmann, Frederick C., and Schwartz, Mildred A. Canadian Political Parties: Origin, Character, Impact. Scarborough, Ont.: Prentice-Hall of Canada, 1975. Discussion of the history of Canadian parties, their role in a democratic state, their relation to the Government, interaction with elites, the mass media, and interest groups, their internal organization and platforms, and how they behave in elections.

1953. Finlay, J.L. Social Credit: The English Origins. Montreal: McGill-Queen's University Press, 1972.

1954. Fotheringham, Allan. Malice in Blunderland: or, How the Grits Stole Christmas. McClelland and Stewart, 1983.

1955. Frizzell, Alan, and Westell, Anthony. The Canadian General Election of 1984: The Parties, Politicians, Polls, and Press. Don Mills, Ontario: Oxford University Press, 1985. Using national polls and other data, authors evaluate the Conservative victory in this election as well as shifts in patterns of voting behavior.

1956. Gargrave, A., and Hull, R.M. How to Win an Election: The Complete Practical Guide to Organizing and Winning Any Election Campaign. Toronto: Macmillan, 1979.

1957. Glassford, Larry A., Clark, Robert J., and Chud, Larry. Challenge of Democracy: Ideals and Realities in Canada. Nelson and Sons, 1984.

1958. Heggie, Grace F. Canadian Political Parties, 1867-1968: A Historical Bibliography. Toronto: Macmillan of Canada, 1977.

1959. Hiemstra, John L. Trudeau's Political Philosophy: Its Implications for Liberty and Progress. Institute for Christian Studies, 1983.

1960. Horn, M. The League for Social Reconstruction: Intellectual Origins of the Democratic Left in Canada, 1930-1942. Toronto: University of Toronto Press, 1980.

1961. Irvine, William P. Does Canada Need a New Electoral System? Kingston, Ont.: Institute of Intergovernmental Relations, Queen's University, 1979. Analysis of some of the political and policy-related consequences of Canada's current electoral system, and discussion of proposed reforms in the electoral system and what their effect would be.

1962. Kavic, L.J. The 1200 Days, A Shattered Dream: Dave Barrett and the NDP in B.C., 1972-1975. Coquitlam, B.C.: Kaen Publishers, 1979.

1963. Kelly, Fraser, ed. The Canadian Voter's Guide: Election '79. Toronto: McClelland and Stewart, 1979. Examination of issues, actors, and events in the 1979 federal election campaign.

1964. Kornberg, Allan, Smith, Joel, and Clarke, Harold D. Semi-Careers in Political Work: The Dilemma of Party Organizations. Beverly Hills, Calif.: Sage Publications, 1970. Develops a typology of careers for party organization office-holders in four cities, two in Canada and two in the United States. Investigates social and political backgrounds of party leaders.

1965. LaPierre, L., et al. Essays on the Left. Toronto: McClelland and Stewart, 1971.

1966. Laxer, James, and Laxer, Robert. The Liberal Idea of Canada: Pierre Trudeau and the Question of Canada's Survival. Toronto: J. Lorimer, 1977. Describes policies of the Trudeau government in political, economic, and ideological areas.

1967. Lemieux, V., Gilbert, M., and Blais, A. Une élection réalignment: l'élection générale du 29 avril 1970 du Québec. [A Realigning Election: The Quebec General Election of April 29, 1970] Montréal: Éditions du Jour, 1970.

1968. Lyons, William E. One Man, One Vote. Toronto: McGraw-Hill Co. of Canada, 1970. Analysis of the 1964 redistribution of seats in the House of Commons, the effects of which were first felt in the 1968 federal election.

1969. McCall-Newman, Christina. Grits: An Intimate Portrait of the Liberal Party. Toronto: Macmillan of Canada, 1982. Historical study of the federal Liberal Party from 1957 through 1979.

1970. MacDonald, J., and MacDonald, J., eds. The Canadian Voter's Guidebook. Don Mills, Ont.: Fitzhenry and Whiteside, 1972.

1971. McDonald, Lynn. The Party that Changed Canada: The New Democratic Party, Then and Now. Toronto: Macmillan of Canada, 1987.

1972. Marchak, M. Patricia. Ideological Perspectives on Canada. Toronto: McGraw-Hill Ryerson, 1981. Discussion of major currents in contemporary Canadian ideology, including individualism and equality, free enterprise, and social class.

1973. Martin, Patrick, Gregg, Allan, and Perlin, George. Contenders: The Tory Quest for Power. Scarborough, Ont.: Prentice-Hall Canada, 1983.

1974. Masson, J.K., and Anderson, J.D., eds. Emerging Party Politics in Urban Canada. Toronto: McClelland and Stewart, 1972.

1975. Meisel, John. Working Papers on Canadian Politics. Montreal: McGill-Queen's University Press, 1975. Collection of four essays. The first three are based upon national survey data, and deal with party support in the 1968 election, party image, and political values. The fourth paper deals with national unity.

1976. Morton, Desmond. NDP: Social Democracy in Canada. 2nd Ed. Toronto: Hakkert, 1977. Political history of the New Democratic Party, examination of its foundations, and analysis of its political successes and failures.

1977. Morton, Desmond. The New Democrats, 1961-1986: The Politics of Change. Toronto: Copp Clark Pitman, 1986.

1978. Nurgitz, Nathan, and Segal, Hugh. No Small Measure. Ottawa: Deneau, 1983. Study of the process of constitutional reform in Canada and the role played by the Official Opposition at the time, the Progressive Conservative party.

1979. Osborne, Stephen, and Osborne, Tom. Social Credit for Beginners: An Armchair Guide. Vancouver: Pulp Press Book Publishers, 1986.

1980. O'Toole, R. The Precipitous Path: Studies in Political Sects. Toronto: Peter Martin Associates, 1976.

1981. Paltiel, K.Z. Political Party Financing in Canada. Toronto: McGraw-Hill Ryerson, 1970.

1982. Parti Liberal (Quebec). Choose Quebec and Canada: A Working Document for the Members of the Quebec Liberal Party. Montréal: Quebec Liberal Party, 1979.

1983. Pelletier, Réjean, ed. _Partis politiques au Québec._ [_Political Parties in Quebec_] Montréal: Hurtubise, 1976. Description of general ideologies of parties in Quebec, with individual studies of different Quebec political parties.

1984. Penner, N. _The Canadian Left: A Critical Analysis._ Toronto: Prentice-Hall of Canada, 1977.

1985. Penniman, Howard Rae, ed. _Canada at the Polls: The General Election of 1974._ Washington: American Enterprise Institute for Public Policy Research, 1975. Essays dealing with the 1974 party system, public opinion, campaign finance, the media, and individual essays on each of the four major parties in the campaign.

1986. Penniman, Howard Rae, ed. _Canada at the Polls, 1979 and 1980: A Study of The General Elections._ Washington: American Enterprise Institute for Public Policy Research, 1981. Collection of essays dealing with these two elections, focusing on external events, candidate selection, financing, and the campaigns.

1987. Penniman, Howard, ed. _Canada at the Polls, 1984: A Study of the Federal General Elections._ Durham, NC: Duke University Press, 1988.

1988. Perlin, George. _The Tory Syndrome: Leadership Politics in the Progressive Conservative Party._ Montreal: McGill-Queen's University Press, 1980. Political history of the federal Progressive-Conservative party, from the Diefenbaker era through the 1976 leadership convention.

1989. Persky, S. _Son of Socred: Has Bill Bennett's Government Gotten B.C. "Moving Again"?_ Vancouver: New Star, 1979.

1990. Pinard, Maurice. _The Rise of a Third Party: A Study in Crisis Politics._ Englewood Cliffs, N.J.: Prentice Hall, 1971. Socio-political explanation of the remarkable increase in political support of the right-wing Social Credit Party in the 1962 federal election.

1991. Pocklington, T.C., ed. _Liberal Democracy in Canada and the United States: An Introduction to Politics and Government._ Toronto: Holt, Rinehart, and Winston, 1984.

1992. Qualter, Terence. _The Election Process in Canada._ Toronto: McGraw Hill of Canada, 1970. Concise study of the electoral process, focusing on the voters, candidates, and mechanics of the voting process itself.

1993. Roberts, John. _Agenda for Canada: Towards a New Liberalism_. Toronto: Lester and Orpen Dennys, 1985.

1994. Roussopoulos, D., ed. _The New Left in Canada_. Montreal: Our Generation Press, 1970.

1995. Saywell, John. _The Rise of the Parti Québécois, 1967-1976_. Toronto: University of Toronto Press, 1977. Political history of the evolution of the P.Q. from the Lévesque-Liberal separation in 1967 through the November, 1976 election in which the PQ captured control of the Quebec government.

1996. Simpson, Jeffrey. _Discipline of Power: The Conservative Interlude and the Liberal Restoration_. Toronto: Personal Library, 1980. Analysis of the brief period of Conservative rule, 1979- 1980.

1997. Smillie, Benjamin G., ed. _Political Theology in the Canadian Context_. Waterloo, Ontario: Wilfrid Laurier University Press, 1982.

1998. Smith, David E. _Prairie Liberalism: The Liberal Party in Saskatchewan, 1905-71_. Toronto: University of Toronto Press, 1975. Political history of the Liberal Party in Saskatchewan during this period of time, explaining its increasing and decreasing support.

1999. Smith, D.E. _Feminism and Marxism: A Place to Begin, A Way to Go_. Vancouver: New Star, 1977.

2000. Smith, David. _The Regional Decline of a National Party: Liberals on the Prairies_. Toronto: University of Toronto Press, 1981.

2001. Soderlund, Walter C., et al. _Media and Elections in Canada_. Toronto: Holt, Rinehart and Winston, 1984.

2002. Stanfield, Robert L. _National Political Parties and Regional Diversity_. Kingston, Ont.: Institute of Intergovernmental Relations, 1985.

2003. Stein, M. _The Dynamics of Right-Wing Protest: Social Credit in Quebec_. Toronto: University of Toronto Press, 1973.

2004. Stewart, Walter. _Divide and Con: Canadian Politics at Work_. Toronto: New Press, 1973. Study of the 1972 federal election, with much personal interpretation of issues and events in the campaign.

2005. Swanick, Eric L. _Public Funding of Political Parties in Canada, An Introductory Bibliography_. Monticello, Ill.: Vance Bibliographies, 1979.

2006. Taylor, Charles. _Radical Tories: The Conservative Tradition in Canada_. Toronto: Anansi, 1982.

2007. Thorburn, Hugh, ed. _Party Politics in Canada_. 5th ed. Scarborough, Ont.: Prentice Hall, 1985. Essays on the party systems of each of the provinces.

2008. Wagner, Jonathan F. _Brothers Beyond the Sea: National Socialism in Canada_. Wilfrid Laurier University Press, 1981.

2009. Wearing, Joseph. _The L-Shaped Party: The Liberal Party of Canada, 1958-1980_. Toronto: McGraw-Hill Ryerson, 1981.

2010. Whitaker, R. _The Government Party: Organizing and Financing the Liberal Party of Canada, 1930-1958_. Toronto: University of Toronto Press, 1977.

2011. Wilson, Barry. _Politics of Defeat: The Decline of the Liberal Party in Saskatchewan_. Saskatoon, Sask.: Western Producer Prairie Books, 1980. Political history of the Saskatchewan Liberal party from the 1950's through the end of the 1970's.

2012. Winn, Conrad, and McMenemy, John, eds. _Political Parties in Canada_. Toronto: McGraw-Hill Ryerson, 1976. Origins of parties, social cleavages represented by parties, the electoral process, party personnel, and the party policy-making process.

2013. Woods, H.D. _Labour Policy in Canada_. Toronto: Macmillan of Canada, 1973.

2014. Woodward, C.A. _A History of New Brunswick Provincial Election Campaigns and Platforms, 1866-1974_. Toronto: Micromedia, 1976.

2015. Young, Walter D. _Democracy and Discontent: Progressivism, Socialism and Social Credit in the Canadian West_. Toronto: McGraw-Hill Ryerson, 1978. Political history of the development of protest movements and political parties in the Canadian west.

Articles

2016. Adelman, H. "The Canadian New Left as an American Daimonion." _Social Theory and Practice_ 1:3 (1971): 73-85.

2017. Albert, Alain. "Conditions économiques et élections: le cas de l'élection provinciale de 1976 au Québec." ["Economic Conditions and Elections: The 1976 Provincial Election in Quebec."] _Canadian Journal of Political Science_ 13:2 (1980): 325-346.

2018. Albert, Alain. "La participation politique: les contributions monétaires aux partis politiques québécois." ["Political Participation: Monetary Contributions to Quebec Political Parties."] Canadian Journal of Political Science 14:2 (1981): 397-410. Reasons for public participation in the financing of political parties.

2019. Angell, Harold. "Duverger, Epstein, and the Problem of the Mass Party: The Case of the Parti Québécois." Canadian Journal of Political Science 20:2 (1987): 363-378.

2020. Archer, Keith. "The Failure of the New Democratic Party: Unions, Unionists, and Politics in Canada." Canadian Journal of Political Science 18:2 (1985): 353-366.

2021. Aube, N., Hudon, R., and Lemieux, V. "L'étude du patronage des partis provinciaux du Québec, de 1944 à 1970." ["The Study of Patronage of Provincial Parties of Quebec, from 1944 to 1970."] Recherches sociographiques 13:1 (1972): 125-138.

2022. Aucoin, Peter. "The 1970 Nova Scotia Provincial Election: Some Observations on Recent Party Performance and Electoral Support." Journal of Canadian Studies 7:3 (1972): 27-37.

2023. Baer, Doug, Grabb, Edward, and Johnston, William. "Class, Crisis, and Political Ideology in Canada: Recent Trends." Canadian Review of Sociology and Anthropology 24:1 (1987): 1-22.

2024. Barrett, Stanley R. "Fascism in Canada." Contemporary Crises: Crime, Law, and Social Policy 8:4 (1984): 345-378.

2025. Beck, Nathaniel, and Pierce, John. "Political Involvement and Party Allegiances in Canada and the United States." International Journal of Comparative Sociology 18:1-2 (1977): 23-43. Comparison between the Canadian and American electorates in terms of their political involvement and partisan allegiances.

2026. Black, E. "Political Realignment in Canada." Monthly Review 39:6 (1987): 33-39.

2027. Black, Jerome H. "The Multicandidate Calculus of Voting: Application to Canadian Federal Elections." American Journal of Political Science 22:3 (1978): 609-638. Tests probability components in the multicandidate calculus of voting examining 1968 and 1972 Canadian federal elections.

2028. Blais, André, Cantin, H., and Crète, J. "Les élections comme phénomène de décision collective: Les élections fédérales de 1957 à 1965 au Québec." ["Elections as the Product of Collective Decision: Federal Elections from 1957 to 1965 in Quebec."] Canadian Journal of Political Science 3:4 (1970): 522-539. How ridings in Quebec collectively make a choice among a number of different electoral possibilities.

2029. Blais, André, Crète, Jean, and Lachapelle, Guy. "L'élection québécoise de 1985: Un bilan des sondages." ["The Quebec Election of 1985: A Summary of Polls."] Canadian Journal of Political Science 19:2 (1986): 325-336.

2030. Blais, André, Desrosiers, Rachel, and Renaud, François. "L'effet en amont de la carte électorale: le cas de la Région de Québec à l'élection fédérale de 1968." ["The Effect of Redistributing Municipalities: The Case of Quebec in the Federal Election of 1968."] Canadian Journal of Political Science 7:4 (1974): 648-671. The effect on voting results of shifting municipalities from one constituency to another, and inter-party differences in results.

2031. Blake, Donald E. "The Consistency of Inconsistency: Party Identification in Federal and Provincial Politics." Canadian Journal of Political Science 15:4 (1982): 691-710.

2032. Blake, Donald E. "Constituency Contexts and Canadian Elections: An Exploratory Study." Canadian Journal of Political Science 11:2 (1978): 279-305. Examines differences in 264 ridings which make up a single "federal election" result; shows that ridings are not always similar in either their demographics or in the issues of major concern to their publics.

2033. Blake, Donald E. "`The Land is Strong(?)': An Interpretation of the 1972 Canadian Election." The Australian Journal of Politics and History 19:1 (1973): 48-62. Analysis of 1972 federal election discussing major issues and provincial voting patterns.

2034. Blake, Donald E. "The Measurement of Regionalism in Canadian Voting Patterns." Canadian Journal of Political Science 5:1 (1972): 55-81. Uses multiple regression analysis to test the impact of regionalism on Canadian voting behavior to develop models of support for the Liberal and Progressive Conservative parties in English Canada for several federrall elections since 1908.

2035. Blake, Donald E. "1896 and All That: Critical Elections in Canada." Canadian Journal of Political Science 12:2 (1979): 259-280. Focus on electoral changes over time. Argues that the theme of electoral change is important in itself in the study of Canadian politics.

2036. Bourque, Gilles. "The Parti Québécois in Class Relations." Politique aujourd'hui 1978 (7-8): 83-91.

2037. Casstevens, Thomas W., and Morris, William D. "The Cube Law and the Decomposed System." Canadian Journal of Political Science 5:4 (1972): 521-532. Mathematical analysis of the effect of the structure of the Canadian electoral system on Canadian political parties.

2038. "Caucus Reform in the Canadian Conservative Party." Parliamentarian 65:1 (1984): 39-42.

2039. Chandler, William M. "Canadian Socialism and Policy Impact: Contagion from the Left?" Canadian Journal of Political Science 10:4 (1977): 755-780. Extent to which Canadian provincial parties have all moved to the left in order to maintain their positions of power and influence.

2040. Churchill, G. "Recollections and Comments on Election Strategy." Queen's Quarterly 77:4 (1970): 499-511.

2041. Clarke, Harold. "The Parti Québécois and Sources of Partisan Realignment in Contemporary Quebec." Journal of Politics 45:1 (1983): 64-85.

2042. Clarke, Harold, Hildebrandt, Kai, LeDuc, Lawrence, and Pammett, Jon. "Issue Volatility and Partisan Linkages in Canada, Great Britain, The United States, and West Germany." European Journal of Political Research 13:3 (1985): 237-264. The role of issues in elections is studied, focusing upon issue-change and issue-stability over time.

2043. Clarke, Harold, and Stewart, Marianne. "Partisan Inconsistency and Partisan Change in Federal States: The Case of Canada." American Journal of Political Science 31:2 (1987): 383-407.

2044. Clarke, Harold, and Stewart, Marianne. "Short Term Forces and Partisan Change in Canada: 1974-1980." Electoral Studies 4:1 (1985): 15-35. Studies partisan change in Canada between 1974 and 1980, and seeks to understand why partisan loyalties are less stable than previously believed.

2045. Clarke, Harold, and Zuk, Gary. "The Politics of Party Popularity: Canada, 1974-1979." Comparative Politics 19:3 (1987): 299-315.

2046. Clarke, Harold, et al. "Voting Behaviour and the Outcome of the 1979 Federal Election: The Impact of Leaders and Issues." Canadian Journal of Political Science 15:3 (1982): 517-552.

2047. Cloutier, Edouard. "Les conceptions américaine, canadienne-anglaise, et canadienne-française de l'idée d'égalité." ["American, English-Canadian, and French-Canadian Conceptions Of The Idea of Equality."] Canadian Journal of Political Science 9:4 (1976): 581-604. There are different conceptions of the idea of equality among these three groups, but the nature and significance of the difference depends upon one's interpretation of the data.

2048. Conway, J.F. "Populism in the United States, Russia, and Canada: Explaining the Roots of Canada's Third Parties." Canadian Journal of Political Science 11:1 (1978): 99-124. Argues that the study of populism is necessary for a thorough understanding of Canadian third parties.

2049. Conway, M. M., and Feigert, F.B. "Incentives and Task Performance Among Party Precinct Workers." Western Political Quarterly 27:4 (1974): 693-709.

2050. Copes, Parzival. "The Fishermen's Vote in Newfoundland." Canadian Journal of Political Science 3:4 (1970): 579-604. How the Newfoundland fishermen's vote -- the dominant voting block at the time -- was harnessed by electoral leaders.

2051. Courtney, John C. "Reflections on Reforming the Canadian Electoral System." Canadian Public Administration 23:3 (1980): 427-457.

2052. Courtney, John C. "Recognition of Canadian Political Parties in Parliament and in Law." Canadian Journal of Political Science 11:1 (1978): 33-60. Tests the common assumption that political parties don't "official" exist in law and shows that, in fact, there are many legal and parliamentary practices which are "officially" based on political party organizations.

2053. Crête, Jean. "Analyse stratégique du choix d'un candidat dans une circonscription urbaine." ["Strategic Analysis of Candidate Choice in an Urban Constituency."] Canadian Journal of Political Science 6:2 (1973): 254-270. Game-theoretical approach to the question of how candidates for office are chosen.

2054. Croisat, Maurice. "Centralisation et décentralisation au sein des partis politiques canadiens." ["Centralization and Decentralization within the Canadian Political Parties."] Revue français de science politique 20:3 (1970): 483-502. Adopts and "institutional" approach to show the effects of both federalism and a parliamentary-style government on Canadian political parties. These political structures lead to a dual party system.

2055. Croisat, Maurice. "Le Parti québécois: la fin d'une époque." ["The Parti Quebecois: The End of an Era."] Revue juridique et politique: Indépendance et Coopération 40:1-2 (1986): 99-112. Study of the PQ from its birth in 1967 through its negotiating with the Government of Canada over the Canada Bill in 1985.

2056. Croisat, Maurice. "Le système des partis québécois à la lumière des dernières élections legislatives." ["The System of Quebec Parties in the Light of the Last Legislative Elections."] Revue juridique et politque 28:3 (1974): 423-440.

2057. Cunningham, Robert. "The Impact of the Local Candidate in Canadian Federal Elections." Canadian Journal of Political Science 4:2 (1971): 287-290.

2058. Curtis, James E., and Lambert, Ronald. "Voting, Election Interest, and Age: National Findings for English and French Canadians." Canadian Journal of Political Science 9:2 (1976): 293-307. Relationship of age, voting, and election interest, controlling for subcultures of samples and membership in political organizations.

2059. Daly, J.W. "Toward a Philosophic Basis for Canadian Conservatism." Journal of Canadian Studies 5:4 (1970): 50-57.

2060. Dobell, W.M. "A Limited Corrective to Plurality Voting." Canadian Public Policy 7:1 (Winter, 1981): 75-81.

2061. Dobell, W.M. "Updating Duverger's Law." Canadian Journal of Political Science 19:3 (1986): 585-596. The uniqueness of Canada and India as federal parliamentary nations using plurality electoral systems lies in the dominance of a single national party.

2062. Dofny, Jacques. "Towards a Quebec Socialist Movement." Politique aujourd'hui 1978 (7-8): 179-190.

2063. Elkins, David J. "Party Identification: A Conceptual Analysis." Canadian Journal of Political Science 11:2 (1978): 419-436. Usefulness of term "party identification" in Canada as compared with its usefulness in the United States.

2064. Elkins, David J. "The Perceived Structure of the Canadian Party Systems." Canadian Journal of Political Science 7:3 (1974): 502-524. Analysis of the degree to which the "classical" left-right continuum accurately describes Canadian political parties.

2065. Elkins, David J., and Blake, Donald . "Voting Research in Canada: Problems and Prospects." Canadian Journal of Political Science 8:2 (1975): 313-325. Bibliographic review article describing the state of the literature in the study of Canadian voting behavior.

2066. Falcone, David. "Minority Government in Canada." Round Table 255 (1974): 259-276. Why Canada has had as many minority governments as it has for several decades. Includes discussion of characteristics of minority governments in Canada and how they affect the parliamentary process.

2067. Fitzmaurice, John. "The Quebec General Election of December, 1985." Electoral Studies 5:1 (1986): 186-189.

2068. Fletcher, F. J. "Mass Media and Parliamentary Elections in Canada." Legislative Studies Quarterly 12:3 (1987): 341-372.

2069. Forbes, H. D. "Hartz-Horowitz at Twenty: Nationalism, Toryism, and Socialism in Canada and the United States." Canadian Journal of Political Science 20:2 (1987): 287-315.

2070. Forcese, Dennis, and De Vries, John. "Occupation and Electoral Success in Canada: the 1974 Federal Election." Canadian Review of Socioloy and Anthropology 14:3 (1977): 331-340. An examination of occupational data for all candidates for Parliament in 1974. Data showed that the candidates contained a higher proportion of high-status people than the population as a whole.

2071. Frohlich, Norman, and Boschmann, Irvin. "Partisan Preference and Income Redistribution: Cross-National and Cross-Sexual Results." Canadian Journal of Political Science 19:1 (1986): 53-69. Study of Canadian and American college students and the relationship between attitudes toward income redistribution and partisan preferences.

2072. Gagnon, Gabriel. "Populism and Progress: Social Credit in Quebec." Recherches sociographiques 17:1 (1976): 23-34.

2073. "The General Election." Parliamentarian 61:2 (1980): 96-98.

2074. "General Elections in Canada." *Journal of Constitutional and Parliamentary Studies* 4:4 (1970): 659-665. Review of rules, regulations, and procedures of Canadian federal elections.

2075. Gerber, Linda. "The Federal Election of 1968: Social Class Composition and Party Support in the Electoral Districts of Ontario." *Canadian Review of Sociology and Anthropology* 23:1 (1986): 118-135.

2076. Gibbins, Roger, and Nevitte, Neil. "Canadian Political Ideology: A Comparative Analyis." *Canadian Journal of Political Science* 18:3 (1985): 577-598.

2077. Gibbins, Roger, Knopff, Rainer, and Morton, F.L "Canadian Federalism, the Charter of Rights, and the 1984 Election." *Publius* 15:2 (1985): 155-168. The 1984 election created a climate that allowed for the change of the Canadian political agenda away from "territorial politics" to national, nonterritorial issues for the first time in decades.

2078. Grayson, J.P. "Social Position and Interest Recognition: The Voter in Broadview, or, Are Voters Fools?" *Canadian Journal of Political Science* 6:1 (1973): 131-139. The extent to which voters perceive the link between their interests and the party which supports their interests.

2079. Hagy, James W. "Le Parti québécois in the 1970 election." *Queen's Quarterly* 77:2 (1970): 266-273.

2080. Hamel, J.M. "Registering Voters in Canada: A Responsibility of the State." *National Civic Review* 61:7 (1972): 336-340.

2081. Hamel, J.M. "An Election Expenses Act for Canada." *National Civic Review* 63:11 (1974): 565-568.

2082. Hamel, J.M. "Native Participation in Free Elections: The Case of the Northwest Territories." *Electoral Studies* 2:2 (1983): 149-154. The means by which elections to the Council of the Northwest Territories are carried out.

2083. Hamilton, Richard E., and Pinard, Maurice. "The Bases of Parti Québécois Support in Recent Quebec Elections." *Canadian Journal of Political Science* 9:1 (1976): 3-26. Explanation of the drastic decline in electoral support for the Union National and correspondingly great increase in electoral support for the Parti Québécois and the Liberals in Quebec in 1973.

2084. Happy, J.R. "Voter Sensitivity to Economic Conditions: A Canadian-American Comparison." *Comparative Politics* 19:1 (1986): 45-56.

2085. Harris, Richard. "The Canadian New Left in Urban Politics." Queen's Quarterly 92:3 (1985): 572-589.

2086. Horowitz, Gad. "Notes on `Conservatism, Liberalism, and Socialism in Canada'." Canadian Journal of Political Science 11:2 (1978): 383-400. Defends his 1966 essay "Conservatism, Liberalism, and Socialism in Canada," against subsequent critics. The article first appeared in the Canadian Jouranal of Economics and Political Science 32 (1966): 143-171.

2087. Howell, Susan. "Candidates and Attitudes: Revisiting the Question of Causality." Journal of Politics 48:2 (1986): 450-461.

2088. Hudon, Raymond. "Electoral Studies in Quebec: Major Directions and Debates." Recherches sociographiques 17:3 (1976): 283-322.

2089. Hudon, Raymond. "The 1976 Quebec Election." Queen's Quarterly 84:1 (1977): 18-30. An examination of the aftereffects of the 1976 election was well as discussion of the election itself.

2090. Hunter, Alfred A., and Denton, Margaret A. "Do Female Candidates `Lose Votes?' The Experience of Female Candidates in the 1979 and 1980 Canadian General Elections." Canadian Review of Sociology and Anthropology 21:4 (1984): 395-406.

2091. Irvine, William P. "Does the Candidate Make a Difference? The Macro-Politics and Micro-Politics of Getting Elected." Canadian Journal of Political Science 15:4 (1982): 755-782.

2092. Irvine, William P. "Explaining the Religious Basis of the Canadian Partisan Identity: Success on the Third Try." Canadian Journal of Political Science 7:3 (1974): 560-563. The "traditional" association between religion and party identification in Canada is a spurious one. Analysis here shows why.

2093. Irvine, William P. "The Puzzle of Liberal Party Success." Queen's Quarterly 89:2 (1982): 340-346. An exploration of the Liberal Party's success in the face of its organizational weakness.

2094. Irvine, William P., and Gold, H. "Do Frozen Cleavages Ever Go Stale? The Bases of the Canadian and Australian Party Systems." British Journal of Political Science 10:2 (1980): 187-218. Examines the relationships between social cleavages and party choice over time in these two nations.

2095. Isajiw, Wsevolod. "Towards a Theory of Ideological Movements: Nationalism and Community Change in Quebec and Flanders." Canadian Review of Studies in Nationalism 12:1 (1985): 141-160.

2096. Isenberg, Seymour. "Can You Spend Your Way into the House of Commons?" Optimum 11:1 (1980): 28-39. Study of electoral expenses.

2097. Jacek, Henry. "Party Loyalty and Electoral Volatility: A Comment on the Study of the Canadian Party System." Canadian Journal of Political Science 8:1 (1975): 144-145. Calls into question the "brokerage" interpretation of Canada's two major parties.

2098. Jacek, Henry, et al. "The Congruence of Federal-Provincial Campaign Activity in Party Organizations: The Influence of Recruitment Patterns in Three Hamilton Ridings." Canadian Journal of Political Science 5:2 (1972): 190-205. Campaign activities of provincial party organizations are affected by federalism, and there are differences between the political party organizations in the nature of these effects.

2099. Jacek, Henry, et al. "Social Articulation and Aggregation in Political Party Organizations in a Large Canadian City." Canadian Journal of Political Science 8:2 (1975): 274-298. Studies social bases of party organization of three political parties in Hamilton, Ontario.

2100. Jackman, Robert W. "Political Parties, Voting, and National Integration: The Canadian Case." Comparative Politics 4:4 (1972): 511-536.

2101. Jenson, Jane. "Comment: The Filling of Wine Bottles is Not Easy." Canadian Journal of Political Science 11:2 (1978): 437-446. Role of theory in developing causal models related to party identification and voting behavior in Canada.

2102. Jenson, Jane. "Party Loyalty in Canada: The Question of Party Identification." Canadian Journal of Political Science 8:4 (1975): 543-552. Party identification and voting behavior in Canada are not the same thing.

2103. Jenson, Jane. "Party Strategy and Party Identification: Some Patterns of Partisan Allegiance." Canadian Journal of Political Science 9:1 (1976): 27-48. Tests predictions of Canadian electoral behavior derived from various models of voting choice.

2104. Jenson, Jane, and Regenstreif, Peter. "Some Dimensions of Partisan Choice in Quebec, 1969." Canadian Journal of Political Science 3:2 (1970): 308-317. Results of 1969 telephone survey in Quebec analysing socio-economic correlates of party support at the time.

2105. Johnston, R.J. "Campaign Spending and Votes: A Reconsideration." *Public Choice* 33:3 (1978): 83-92.

2106. Johnston, Richard. "The Reproduction of the Religious Cleavage in Canadian Elections." *Canadian Journal of Political Science* 18:1 (1985): 99-118.

2107. Johnston, Richard, and Percy, Michael. "Reciprocity, Imperial Sentiment, and Party Politics in the 1911 Election." *Canadian Journal of Political Science* 13:4 (1980): 711-730.

2108. Johnston, William, and Ornstein, Michael. "Social Class and Political Ideology in Canada." *Canadian Review of Sociology and Anthropology* 22:3 (1985): 369-393. Studies class differences, measured along Marxist lines, in political ideology in Canada.

2109. Kavanagh, Dennis. "Do Opinion Polls Influence Elections?" *Parliamentarian* 62:3 (1981): 199-203.

2110. Kay, Barry J. "By-Elections as Indicators of Canadian Voting." *Canadian Journal of Political Science* 14:1 (1981): 37-52. Study of 147 by-election contests between 1940 and 1980, seeking to understand how accurately these by-elections reflected the national mood at the time.

2111. Kay, Barry. "An Examination of Class and Left-Right Party Images in Canadian Voting." *Canadian Journal of Political Science* 10:1 (1977): 127-143. Relationship of class and perceived images of political parties, and voting behavior in the 1965 and 1968 federal elections.

2112. Keddie, Vincent. "Class Identification and Party Preference Among Manual Workers : The Influence of Community, Union Membership, and Kinship." *Canadian Review of Sociology and Anthropology* 17:1 (1980): 24-36. Analysis of class identification and party preference using community differences, union membership, and kinship as explanatory variables.

2113. Kopinak, Kathryn. "Gender Differences in Political Ideology in Canada." *Canadian Review of Sociology and Anthropology* 24:1 (1987): 23-38.

2114. Krashinsky, Michael, and Milne, William. "Additional Evidence on the Effect of Incumbency in Canadian Elections." *Canadian Journal of Political Science* 18:1 (1985): 155-165.

2115. Krashinsky, Michael, and Milne, William. "The Effect of Incumbency in the 1984 Federal and 1985 Ontario Elections." *Canadian Journal of Political Science* 19:2 (1986): 337-344. Examines riding by riding the results of the 1984 federal election and the 1985 Ontario provincial election.

2116. Krashinsky, Michael, and Milne, William. "Some Evidence on the Effect of Incumbency in Ontario Provincial Elections." Canadian Journal of Political Science 16:3 (1983): 489-500.

2117. Krause, Robert, and LeDuc, Lawrence. "Voting Behavior and Electoral Strategies in the Progressive Conservative Leadership Convention of 1976." Canadian Journal of Political Science 12:1 (1979): 97-136. Survey data from interviews with delegates to the Progressive Conservative leadership convention is analyzed.

2118. LaChapelle, Guy. "Les répondants-discrets et l'élection québécoise de 1985." ["Discreet Respondents and the Quebec Election of 1985."] Politique 10 (1986): 31-54.

2119. Laflamme, Simon. "Des motifs des électeurs au scrutin fédéral de 1984: Le cas de Sudbury." ["Motives of Voters in the Federal Election of 1984: The Case of Sudbury."] Canadian Journal of Political Science 19:3 (1986): 565-572.

2120. Laflamme, Simon. "La politique fédérale canadienne au singulier et au pluriel." ["Canadian Federal Politics in the Singular and in the Plural."] Canadian Journal of Political Science 18:4 (1985): 697-714. Studies the similarities and differences between the different political parties in Canada.

2121. Lambert, Ronald, Curtis, James, Brown, Steven, and Kay, Barry. "In Search of Left/Right Beliefs in the Canadian Electorate." Canadian Journal of Political Science 19:3 (1986): 541-564.

2122. Lambert, Ronald D., and Hunter, Alfred A. "Social Stratification, Voting Behavior, and the Images of Canadian Federal Political Parties." Canadian Review of Sociology and Anthropology 16:3 (1979): 287-304. Analysis of Canadian electoral behavior and a comparison with previous studies.

2123. Lambert, Ronald, et al. "Effects of Identification with Governing Parties on Feelings of Political Efficacy and Trust." Canadian Journal of Political Science 19:4 (1986): 705-728. Using data from the 1984 National Election Study, the authors test the effects of party identification on feelings towards the government in power.

2124. Landes, Ronald G. "The Canadian General Election of 1980." Parliamentary Affairs 34:1 (1981): 95-109. Study of the Clark Administration and the factors leading to its demise in 1980.

2125. Landes, Ronald. "The Canadian General Election of 1984." Parliamentary Affairs 38:1 (1985): 86-96.

2126. Laponce, J.A. "Dieu- à droite ou à gauche?" ["God - Right or Left?"] Canadian Journal of Political Science 3:2 (1970): 257-274. Analysis of the value of the "traditional left-right" scale for understanding religious and profane concepts.

2127. Laponce, J.A. "Measuring Party Preference: The Problem of Ambivalence." Canadian Journal of Political Science 11:1 (1978): 139-152. Suggests that when there is reason to expect ambivalence in the study of party preference one should measure separately both the positive and negative attitudes related to party preference and voting behavior.

2128. Laponce, J.A. "Post-Dicting Electoral Cleavages in Canadian Federal Elections, 1949-1968: Material for a Footnote." Canadian Journal of Political Science 5:2 (1972): 270-286. Overall view of the association between socio-demographic factors and party preference in Canadian elections.

2129. Laponce, J.A., and Uhler, R.S. "Measuring Electoral Cleavages in a Multiparty System: The Canadian Case." Comparative Political Studies 7:1 (1974): 3-25.

2130. Laskin, Richard, and Baird, Richard . "Factors in Voter Turnout and Party Preference in a Saskatchewan Town." Canadian Journal of Political Science 3:3 (1970): 450-462. Analysis of 1960-1962 data on voluntary organizations and social participation in Biggar, Saskatchewan, forcusing upon the importance of social class, and ethnic and religious politics.

2131. LeDuc, Lawrence. "The Dynamic Properties of Party Identification: A Four-Nation Comparison." European Journal of Political Research 9:3 (1981): 257-268. A comparison of Great Britain, Canada, the Netherlands, and America, and the measurement and nature of individual partisanship

2132. LeDuc, Lawrence. "Partisan Change and Dealignment in Canada, Great Britain, and the United States." Comparative Politics 17:4 (1985): 379-398. Differences among political parties in the three countries are more impressive than the similar patterns of movement among them.

2133. LeDuc, Lawrence. "Party Decision-Making: Some Empirical Observations on the Leadership Selection Process." Canadian Journal of Political Science 4:1 (1971): 97-118. The 1968 Liberal Leadership convention is studied to describe the internatal party politics of a national convention.

2134. LeDuc, Lawrence, "Political Behavior and the Issue of Majority Government in Two Federal Elections." Canadian Journal of Political Science 10:2 (1977): 311-339. The degree to which fear of or support for the issue of a minority government influenced voting behavior in the 1965 and 1974 federal elections.

2135. LeDuc, Lawrence, et al. "A National Sample Design." Canadian Journal of Political Science 7:4 (1974): 701-708. How to establish a reliable and valid national sampling design.

2136. LeDuc, Lawrence, et al. "Partisan Instability in Canada: Evidence from a New Panel Study." American Political Science Review 78:2 (1984): 470-484. Studies properties of party identification in Canada and compares levels of partisan stability in Canada with those in Britain and the United States.

2137. LeDuc, Lawrence, et al. "Partisanship, Voting Behavior, and Election Outcomes in Canada." Comparative Politics 12:4 (1980): 401-417. Study of patterns of voting behavior of Canadians in recent federal elections.

2138. LeDuc, Lawrence, and White, Walter L. "The Role of Opposition in a One-Party Dominant System: The Case of Ontario." Canadian Journal of Political Science 7:1 (1974): 86-100. The pattern of one-party dominance in Ontario affects the nature of legislative opposition there, in terms of backgrounds, attitudes, and behavior of Ontario legislators.

2139. Lemieux, Vincent. "Les élections fédérales de 1957 à 1965 au Québec: Une réinterprétation." ["Federal Elections From 1957 to 1965 in Quebec: A Reinterpretation."] Canadian Journal of Political Science 4:3 (1971): 395-397.

2140. Lemieux, Vincent, and Lavoie, Marie. "La réforme du système électoral." ["The Reform of the Electoral System."] Politique 6 (1984): 33-50. Discusses electoral systems and the way that a proportional representation ballot and a single transferable vote ballot would affect the electoral system.

2141. Levesque, Terrence. "On the Outcome of the 1983 Conservative Leadership Convention: How They Shot Themselves in the Other Foot." Canadian Journal Of Political Science 16:4 (1983): 779-784. Study of the 1983 Conservative Leadership Convention, concluding that it produced a "nonoptimal" outcome.

2142. Levesque, Terrence, and Norrie, Kenneth. "Overwhelming Majorities in the Legislature of Alberta." Canadian Journal of Political Science 12:3 (1979): 451-470. Effect of large electoral majorities on the party system of Alberta.

2143. Lightbody, James. "Electoral Reform in Local Government: the Case of Winnipeg." *Canadian Journal of Political Science* 11:2 (1978): 307-332. Develops theme that reform in local electoral systems has had a great effect on local government in Canada.

2144. Lightbody, James. "The Rise of Party Politics in Canadian Local Elections." *Journal of Canadian Studies* 6:1 (1971): 39-44.

2145. Lightbody, James. "Swords and Ploughshares: The Election Prerogative in Canada." *Canadian Journal of Political Science* 5:2 (1972): 287-290. Environmental limitations on the prime minister's prerogative power to dissolve the legislative assembly and call for a general election.

2146. Lijphart, Arend. "Language, Religion, Class, and Party Choice: A Four-Country Comparison." *Rivista italiana di Scienza politica* 8:1 (1978): 77-111. Comparative analysis of Belgium, Canada, South Africa, and Switzerland, with the use of three variables: importance of social class and religion, disagreement on which is more important, and neglect of a potentially powerrful determinant, language.

2147. Loree, D.J., and Pullman, D.R. "Socio-Political Facets of a Plural Province -- Reasons for the Failure of `Third Parties' in New Brunswick, Canada." *Plural Societies* 10:3-4 (1979): 85-102. Study of why it is difficult for a third party to build organized support in New Brunswick.

2148. Loveday, P., and Jaensch, D. "Indigenes and Electoral Administration: Australia and Canada." *Electoral Studies* 6:1 (1987): 31-40. Study of the Aboriginal voters and how they differ fom the "traditional" voters in these countries. This article complements the paper by J.-M. Hamel, "Native Participation in Free Elections: The Case of the Northwest Territories (Canada)," *Electoral Studies* 2:2 (1983): 149-154.

2149. Lovink, J.A.A. "On Analyzing the Impact of the Electoral System on the Party System in Canada." *Canadian Journal of Political Science* 3:4 (1970): 497-516. Further study of Alan Cairns' 1968 study of "The Electoral System and the Party System in Canada," supporting Cairns' views and taking his theories of the impact of the electoral system upon political parties even further than Cairns had done.

2150. McDonald, L. "Attitude Organization and Voting Behavior in Canada." *Canadian Review of Sociology and Anthropology* 8:3 (1971): 164-184. Whether Ontario voters organize their attitudes into identifiable sets, and how those attitudes affect voting.

2151. McDonald, L. "Social Class and Voting: A Study of the 1968 Canadian Federal Election in Ontario." British Journal of Sociology 22:4 (1971): 410-422. Studies degree to which voting behavior is influenced by social class, living and working conditions, personality characteristics and attitudes, and status in general.

2152. McRae, K.D. "Le Concept de la societé fragmentaire de Louis Hartz et son application a l'exemple canadien." ["The Concept of the Fragmentary Society of Louis Hartz and Its Application to the Canadian Example."] Canadian Journal of Political and Social Theory 3:3 (1979): 69-82.

2153. Massicotte, Louis. "L'incidence Partisane des Inégalités de la Carte Electorale Quebecois Depuis 1900." ["Party Incidence of Inequalities of the Quebec Electoral Map Since 1900."] Recherches sociographiques 24:2 (1983): 155-170. The overrepresentation of rural areas in Quebec between 1900 and 1972.

2154. Matthews, Robin. "Susanna Moodie, Pink Toryism, and Nineteenth Century Ideas of Canadian Identity." Journal of Canadian Studies 10:3 (1975): 3-14.

2155. Mayer, Lawrence. "Federalism and Party Behavior in Australia and Canada." The Western Political Quarterly 23:4 (1970): 795-807.

2156. Mellos, Koula. "Quantitative Comparison of Party Ideology." Canadian Journal of Political Science 3:4 (1970): 540-558. Formal modelling analysis of political party ideologies analysing content of political action programs of parties.

2157. Miles, Simon. "Parties Introduced in Metro Toronto." National Civic Review 59:4 (1970): 212-215.

2158. Morris, Eleanor B. "Maoist `Contraditions' in Canada." Journal of Social and Political Studies 3:2 (1978): 155-172. Examination of some of the similarities between Maoist theory in China and some of the politics and attitudes manifested by the Trudeau government.

2159. Morrison, K.L. "The Businessman Voter in Thunder Bay: The Catalyst to the Federal-Provincial Voting Split?" Canadian Journal of Political Science 6:2 (1973): 219-229. Why Canadian voters so often vote for one party on the federal level and a different party on the provincial level. Study of Ontario voters.

2160. Morton, Desmond. "Canada's Democratic Left Inches Ahead." Dissent 34:1 (1987): 27-33.

2161. Murray, Donald. "The Ralliement des Creditistes in Parliament, 1970-1971." Journal of Canadian Studies 8:2 (1973): 13-30.

2162. Myles, John F. "Differences in the Canadian and American Class Vote: Fact or Pseudofact." American Journal of Sociology 84:5 (1979): 1232-1242. Suggests that traditional assumption that Canada has less class voting than the U.S. is incorrect; class voting in two nations is virtually identical.

2163. Nassmacher, Karl-Heinz. "Party Finance in Canada: A Model for Germany?" Seitschrift für Parlamentstragen 13:3 (1982): 338-359.

2164. Nevitte, N., and Gibbins, R. "Neoconservatism: Canadian Variations on an Ideological Theme?" Canadian Public Policy 10:4 (December, 1984): 384-394.

2165. Ogmundson, Richard. "Liberal Ideology and the Study of Voting Behavior." Canadian Review of Sociology and Anthropology 17:1 (1980): 45-54. Article which replies to criticisms of Ogmundson's position and an attempt to arrange a confrontation between the two perspectives.

2166. Ogmundson, Richard. "A Note on the Ambiguous Meanings of Survey Research Measures Which Use the Words `Left' and `Right'." Canadian Journal of Political Science 12:4 (1979): 799-805. The assumption that the average Canadian understands the terms "left" and "right" is mistaken.

2167. Ogmundson, Richard. "Party Class Images and the Class vote in Canada." American Sociological Review 40:4 (1975): 506-512. Re-examines the importance of the class vote in Canada using a new approach which considers voter perceptions of the political parties' class orientations.

2168. "Ontario: Blind Can Now Vote in Private." Parliamentarian 60:1 (1979): 35.

2169. Ornstein, M.D., and Stevenson, H.M. "Ideology and Public Policy in Canada." British Journal of Political Science 14:3 (1984): 313-344. Indicates that there is considerable ideological heterogeneity rather than homogeneity among Canadian political elites.

2170. Palda, K. Filip, and Palda, Kristian. "Ceilings on Campaign Spending: Hypothesis and Partial Test with Canadian Data." Public Choice 45:3 (1985): 313-331. Tests proposition that ceilings on campaign spending do in fact limit outlays, and thus lessen the anxiety of incumbents.

2171. Palda, Kristian. "Does Advertising Influence Votes? An Analysis of the 1966 and 1970 Quebec Elections." Canadian Journal of Political Science 6:4 (1973): 638-655. Study of whether advertising expenditures had a measurable and significant impact upon the outcomes of these two elections.

2172. Palda, Kristian. "Does Canada's Election Act Impede Voters' Access to Information." Canadian Public Policy 11:3 (1985): 533-542. Do the provisions of the 1977 Elections Act concerning campaign expenditure limits and advertising limit information for voters?

2173. Palda, Kristian. "The Effect of Expenditure on Political Success." Journal of Law and Economics 18:3 (1975): 745-771. Mathematical models were constructed to try to measure the impact of campaign expenditures on voting behavior.

2174. Paltiel, Khayyam Z. "The Impact of Election Expenses Legislation in Canada, Western Europe, and Israel." Sage Electoral Studies Yearbook 5 (1979): 15-39. Analysis of legislative attempts to limit party funding for campaigns and campaign financing in general.

2175. Paltiel, Khayyam Z. "Party and Candidate Expenditures in the Canadian General Election of 1972." Canadian Journal of Political Science 7:2 (1974): 341-351. Distribution of party spending in the 1972 election.

2176. Paltiel, Khayyam Z., and Kzosa, L.G. "The Structure and Dimensions of Election Broadcasting in Canada." Jahrbuch des öffenlichen Rechts der Gegenwart 19 (1970): 355-382.

2177. Pammett, John. "Class Voting and Class Consciousness in Canada." Canadian Review of Sociology and Anthropology 24:2 (1987): 269-290.

2178. Pammett, Jon H., LeDuc, Lawrence, Jenson, Jane, and Clarke, Harold. "The Perception and Impact of Issues in the 1974 Federal Election." Canadian Journal of Political Science 10:1 (1977): 93-126. Studies the pattern of voting and vote-switching in the 1974 federal election and the effect of some of the major issues in the campaign on individual voting behavior.

2179. Pasis, Harvey. "Achieving Population Equality Among thg Constituencies of the Canadian House, 1903-1976." Legislative Studies Quarterly 8:1 (1983): 111-116.

2180. Perlin, George, and Peppin, Patti . "Variations in Party Support in Federal and Provincial Elections: Some Hypotheses." Canadian Journal of Political Science 4:2 (1971): 280-286.

2181. Pinard, Maurice. "Third Parties in Canada Revisited: A Rejoinder and Elaboration of the Theory of One-Party Dominance." Canadian Journal of Political Science 6:3 (1973): 439-460. Review of his earlier research on the causes for the development of third parties in Canada.

2182. Pinard, Maurice, and Hamilton, Richard . "The Independence Issue and the Polarization of the Electorate: The 1973 Quebec Election." Canadian Journal of Political Science 10:2 (1977): 215-259. Uses survey data to examine 1970-1973 forces leading to a polarization between the Liberals and the Parti Québécois in Quebec voting behavior.

2183. Pinard, Maurice, and Hamilton, Richard . "The Parti Québécois Comes to Power: An Analysis of the 1976 Quebec Election." Canadian Journal of Political Science 11:4 (1978): 739-776. Study of 1976 Quebec election results with focus on Parti Québécois attitudes and behavior as well as public attitudes.

2184. Preece, Rod. "The Myth of the Red Tory." Canadian Journal of Political and Social Theory 1:2 (1977): 3-28. The concept of the "Red Tory," often used to explain elements of conservatism, is explained and denied. A different understanding of conservatism is offered.

2185. Punnett, R.M. "Leadership Selection in Opposition: The Progressive-Conservative Party of Canada." The Australian Journal of Politics and History 17:2 (1971): 188-201. Discusses Conservative Party leaders, 1867-1967, their candidacies, party choice mechanisms, and the party conventions which chose them.

2186. Punnett, R.M. "Selection of Party Leaders: A Canadian Example." Journal of Commonwealth Political Studies 8:1 (1970): 54-69. Analysis of 1968 Liberal leadership convention which chose Pierre Trudeau to succeed Lester Pearson and lead the Liberal party.

2187. Rayside, David M. "Federalism and the Party System: Provincial and Federal Liberals in the Province of Quebec." Canadian Journal of Political Science 11:3 (1978): 499-528. How federal-provincial tensions are reflected in differences between federal and provincial Liberals in Quebec.

2188. Regenstreif, Peter. "Canadian Parties and Politics." Current History 66:392 (1974): 173-176.

2189. Regenstreif, Peter. "An Electoral Turnaround in Canada." Current History 79:460 (1980): 113-116.

2190. Rempel, Henry David. "The Practice and Theory of the Fragile State: Trudeau's Conception of Authority." Journal of Canadian Studies 10:4 (1975): 24-38.

2191. Resnick, Philip. "La gauche et la question nationale." ["The Left and the National Question."] Canadian Journal of Political Science 13:2 (1980): 377-388.

2192. Rich, Harvey. "One-Party Dominance in Alberta, Canada." Political Science 31:2 (1979): 117-124. Case study of plebiscitorian-style democracy where elitist rule is tempered by frequent popular consultations.

2193. Ricketts, Edmond F., and Waltzer, Herbert. "Electoral Arrangements and Party System: The Case of Canada." Western Political Quarterly 23:4 (1970): 695-714.

2194. Sankoff, David, and Mellos, Koula. "La régionalisation électorale et l'amplification des proportions." ["Electoral Regionalization and the Swing Ratio."] Canadian Journal of Political Science 6:3 (1973): 380-398. Mathematical analysis of the effect of Canada's electoral system upon party legislative seat distribution in Canada.

2195. Santos, C.R. "Some Collective Characteristics of the Delegates to the 1968 Liberal Party Leadership Convention." Canadian Journal of Political Science 3:2 (1970): 299-308. Description using interview data on demographic and socio-economic characteristics of delegates to the 1968 Liberal Party leadership convention.

2196. Scammon, Richard. "Election of the Canadian House of Commons, May 29, 1979." World Affairs 142:2 (1979): 135-137. Presents the results of the May 22, 1979 by-elections.

2197. Scammon, Richard. "International Election Notes: By-Election to the Canadian House of Commons, October 16, 1978." World Affairs 141:3 (1979): 277-278. Presents the results of the October, 1978 by-elections.

2198. Schneck, Rodney, Russell, Douglas, and Scott, Ken. "The Effects of Ruralism, Bureaucratic Structure, and Economic Role on Right-wing Extremism." Canadian Journal of Political Science 7:1 (1974): 155-165. Study of Edmonton, Alberta, 1969-1970, to see the way right wing extremism varied as a result of several different independent variables.

2199. Schreiber, E.M. "Class Awareness and Class Voting in Canada: A Reconsideration of the Ogmundson Thesis." Canadian Review of Sociology and Anthropology 17:1 (1980): 37-44. Critique of the thesis that class voting would be higher in Canada if one party offered a "for the working class" choice to the electorate.

2200. Segal, David R. "Status Inconsistency and Party Choice in Canada: An Attempt to Replicate." Canadian Journal of Political Science 3:3 (1970): 471-474. The effect of status variables is statistically inconsistent as predictors of political party choice.

2201. Smith, David E. "The Canadian General Election of 1979." Parliamentary Affairs 33:1 (1980): 92-106.

2202. Sniderman, Paul, Forbes, H.D., and Melzer, Ian. "Party Loyalty and Electoral Volatility: A Study of the Canadian Party System." Canadian Journal of Political Science 7:2 (1974): 268-288. Voting in Canada is not especially volatile; party identification is a long-term commitment. Party identification is a useful concept of analysis of the vote in Canada.

2203. Soderlund, Walter C., and Wagenberg, Ronald H. "A Content Analysis of Editorial Coverage of the 1972 Election Campaigns in Canada and the United States." Western Political Quarterly 28:1 (1975): 85-107.

2204. Soderlund, Walter C., and Wagenberg, Ronald H. "The Editor and External Affairs: The 1972 and 1974 Election Campaigns." International Journal 31:2 (1976): 244-253.

2205. Soderlund, Walter C., et al. "Regional and Linguistic Agenda-Setting in Canada: A Study of Newspaper Coverage of Issues Affecting Political Integration in 1976." Canadian Journal of Political Science 13:2 (1980): 347-356.

2206. Spafford, Duff. "The Electoral System of Canada." The American Political Science Review 64:1 (1970): 168-176. Identifies factors which influence the share of seats in House of Commons elections. Uses mathematical models to analyze elections between 1921 and 1965.

2207. Spafford, Duff. "Highway Employment and Provincial Elections." Canadian Journal of Political Science 14:1 (1981): 135-142. Examination of historical record of highway employment and its relation to the cycle of provincial elections in seven provinces.

2208. Stanbury, W.T. "The Mother's Milk of Politics: Political Contributions to Federal Parties in Canada, 1974-1984." Canadian Journal of Political Science 19:4 (1986): 795-821. Studies the three major national parties at the federal level during this period of time focusing upon both regulated and unregulated financing activities.

2209. Stein, Michael B. "Le Crédit social dans la province du Québec: Sommaire et développements." ["Social Credit in the Province of Quebec: Summary and Developments."] Canadian Journal of Political Science 6:4 (1973): 563-581. Historical analysis of the Social Credit movement in Quebec, with suggestions about the relationship between Social Credit and the later Parti Québécois movement.

2210. Stevenson, Paul. "Class and Left-Wing Radicalism." Canadian Review of Sociology and Anthropology 14:3 (1977): 269-284. An examination of the relationship between various background factors and left-wing radicalism in Winnipeg.

2211. Stewart, Ian. "Of Customs and Coalitions: The Formation of Canadian Federal Parliamentary Alliances," Canadian Journal of Political Science 13 (1980): 451-481.

2212. Stewart, Ian. "Friends at Court: Federalism and Provincial Elections on Prince Edward Island." Canadian Journal of Political Science 19:1 (1986): 127-150. Studies why only Prince Edward Island has found voters tending to regularly elect provincial governments from the same party as federal governments.

2213. Taylor, K.W., and Wiseman, Nelson. "Class and Ethnic Voting in Winnipeg: The Case of 1941." Canadian Review of Sociology and Anthropology 14:2 (1977): 174-187. An examination of class versus ethnic determinants of voting behavior in Winnipeg.

2214. Wagenberg, Ronald, and Soderlund, Walter C. "The Effects of Chain Ownership on Editorial Coverage: The Case of the 1974 Canadian Federal Election." Canadian Journal of Political Science 9:4 (1976): 682-689. Content analysis of effects of chain ownership on newspaper editorials relative to editorials in the 1974 federal election.

2215. Ward, Norman. "Money and Politics: The Costs of Democracy in Canada." Canadian Journal of Political Science 5:3 (1972): 335-347. Reviews developments in Canadian electoral system and tries to measure the direct monetary costs of the Canadian parliamentary and electoral system.

Political Parties, Ideology, and Elections   215

2216. Ward, Norman. "The Representative System and the Calling of Elections." Canadian Journal of Political Science 6:4 (1973): 655-660. Study of the 1972-1973 minority government of Pierre Trudeau and its decision to call for an election in 1973.

2217. Wattenberg, Martin P. "Party Identification and Party Images: A Comparison of Britain, Canada, Australia, and the United States." Comparative Politics 15:1 (1982): 23-40.

2218. White, Graham. "One-Party Dominance and Third Parties: The Pinard Theory Reconsidered." Canadian Journal of Political Science 6:3 (1973): 399-421. Tests theory that third parties arise duiring times of strain and only in systems which have had one-party dominance.

2219. Wilson, John, and Hoffman, David. "The Liberal Party in Contemporary Ontario Politics." Canadian Journal of Political Science 3:2 (1970): 177-204. Explanation of the success of federal Liberals but weakness of provincial Liberals.

2220. Wilson, R. Jeremy. "Geography, Politics, and Culture: Electoral Insularity in British Columbia." Canadian Journal of Political Science 13:4 (1980): 751-774.

2221. Wilson, R. Jeremy. "The Impact of Communications Developments on British Columbia Electoral Patterns, 1903-1975." Canadian Journal of Political Science 13:3 (1980): 509-536.

2222. Winer, Stanley. "Money and Politics in a Small Open Economy." Public Choice 51:2 (1986): 221-239. Shows a relationship between monetary growth and the standing in the Gallop Poll of political parties and candidates.

2223. Winham, Gilbert R., and Robert B. Cunningham. "Party Leader Images in the 1968 Federal Election." Canadian Journal of Political Science 3:1 (1970): 37-55. Importance of voters' perceptions of party leaders as compared to other factors which influence electoral behavior.

2224. Winkler, John D., Judd, Charles M., and Kelman, Herbert C. "Determinants of Political Participation in a Canadian and a United States City." Political Psychology 3:3-4 (1981-1982): 140-161.

2225. Wiseman, Nelson, and aylor, K. Wayne. "Class and Ethnic Voting in Winnipeg During the Cold War." Canadian Review of Sociology and Anthropology 16:1 (1979): 60-76. Examination of the strength of ethnic and class determinants of the voting patterns in the Winnipeg provincial elections of 1949 and 1953.

2226. Wiseman, Nelson, and Taylor, K. Wayne. "Ethnic vs. Class Voting: The Case of Winnipeg, 1945." Canadian Journal of Political Science 7:2 (1974): 314-327. Class status is an important determinant of voting behavior in Winnipeg.

2227. Wiseman, Nelson, and Taylor, K. Wayne. "Voting in Winnipeg During the Depression." Canadian Review of Sociology and Anthropology 19:2 (1982): 215-236.

2228. Zipp, John F. "Left-Right Dimensions of Canadian Federal Party Identification: A Discriminant Analysis." Canadian Journal of Political Science 11:2 (1978): 251-278. Asks whether a standard "left-right" continuum really fit the four national Canadian political parties, and whether parties are better represented by the standard "left-right" scale, or by a "major party - minor party" differentiation.

2229. Zipp, John F., and Smith, Joel. "A Structural Analysis of Class Voting." Social Forces 60:3 (1982): 738-759. Analysis of class voting that claims non-voting in constituencies without an NDP candidate is the same as class voting.

2230. Zipp, John F., and Smith, Joel. "The Structure of Electoral Political Participation." American Journal of Sociology 85:1 (1979): 167-177. Results of this new method of examination show that recruitment to participate increases the likelihood of campaign activity.

9
The Executive

Books

2231. Berkeley, H. The Power of the Prime Minister. Toronto: Methuen, 1971.

2232. Bom, Philip C. Trudeau's Canada: Truth and Consequences. St. Catharine's, Ont.: Guardian Publishing Co., 1977. Analysis of Trudeau's first decade as prime minister, with considerable references to Trudeau's speeches and writings.

2233. Butler, Rick, and Carrier, Jean-Guy, eds. The Trudeau Decade. Toronto: Doubleday Canada, 1979. News articles, editorials, and cartoons covering 1968 - 1978.

2234. Campbell, Colin. Governments Under Stress: Political Executives and Key Bureaucrats in Washington, London, and Ottawa. Toronto: University of Toronto Press, 1983. Relationships between executives and bureaucrats in three governments.

2235. Canada. Library of Parliament. Information and Reference Branch. Governors General of Canada, 1867-1975: Select Bibliography. Ottawa: Queen's Printer, 1975.

2236. D'Aquino, T.P. Organization of Ministerial Offices -- An Organizational Study of Ministerial Offices in Aid of Ministers and Staff. Ottawa: Prime Minister's Office, 1970.

2237. Donaldson, Gordon. Sixteen Men: The Prime Ministers of Canada. Toronto: Doubleday of Canada, 1980.

2238. Gibson, Frederick W., ed. Cabinet Formation and Bicultural Relations: Seven Case Studies. Ottawa: Information Canada, 1970.

2239. Gossage, Patrick. *Close to the Charisma: My Years Between the Press and Pierre Elliott Trudeau*. Toronto: McClelland and Stewart, 1986.

2240. Hockin, Thomas A., ed. *Apex of Power: The Prime Minister and Political Leadership in Canada*. Scarborough, Ont.: Prentice-Hall of Canada, 1977. Collection of articles dealing with the Prime Minister and Cabinet, including discussion of party politics, other governmental sources of influence, and case studies in decision-making.

2241. Maillet, Lise. *Provincial Royal Commissions and Commissions of Inquiry, 1867-1982: A Selective Bibliography*. Ottawa: National Library of Canada, 1986.

2242. Martin, Lawrence. *The Presidents and the Prime Ministers: Washington and Ottawa Face to Face: The Myth of Bilateral Bliss, 1867-1982*. Toronto: Doubleday Canada, 1982.

2243. Matheson, William A. *The Prime Minister and the Cabinet*. Toronto: Methuen, 1976. Study of the growth of cabinet government in Canada, what the cabinet does and how it is organized, and case studies of the role of the Cabinet under prime ministers through Pierre Trudeau.

2244. Miller, John, and Hurst, Donald. *Exercising Power: Government in Canada*. Don Mills, Ont.: Longman, Canada, 1977.

2245. Monet, Jacques. *The Canadian Crown*. Toronto: Clarke, Irwin, 1979. Constitutional history of the Head of State in Canada and the development of the office of the Governor General. Elementary level book with many pictures.

2246. Punnett, Robert M. *The Prime Minister in Canadian Government and Politics*. Toronto: Macmillan of Canada, 1977. Analysis of the evolution of the office of prime minister, the men who have held the position, and the powers exercised by incumbents of the office today.

2247. Robertson, Gordon. *The Changing Role of the Privy Council Office*. Ottawa, Information Canada, 1971.

2248. Rock, Paul Elliott. *A View from the Shadows: The Ministry of the Solicitor General of Canada and the Making of the Justice for Victims of Crime Initiative*. New York: Oxford University Press, 1986.

2249. Schultz, R., et al. *The Cabinet as a Regulatory Body: The Case of the Foreign Investment Review Act*. Ottawa: Economic Council of Canada, 1980.

2250. Troyer, Warner. 200 Days: Joe Clark in Power: The Anatomy of the Rise and Fall of the 21st Government. Toronto: Personal Library Publisher, 1980. Study of the Clark government interregnum, 1979-1980.

2251. Wilson, Barbara M., Gillis, Peter, and Wright, Glenn T, eds. Records of the Privy Council Office. Ottawa: Public Records Division, Public Archives Canada, 1977.

Articles

2252. Benoît, Paul. "Remembering the Monarch." Canadian Journal of Political Science 15:3 (1982): 575-588.

2253. Chenier, John A. "Ministers of State to Assist: Weighing the Costs and Benefits." Canadian Public Administration 28:3 (1985): 397-412. Examines some of the problems associated with the use of ministers of state to assist in the Canadian federal government.

2254. Clark, Ian D. "Recent Changes in the Cabinet Decision-Making System in Ottawa." Canadian Public Administration 28:2 (1985): 185-201. Describes changes instituted by Prime Ministers Turner and Mulroney in the context of other changes in the Prime Minister's Office since the Second World War.

2255. Clark, Joseph. "The Canadian Prime Ministership." Presidential Studies Quarterly 11:1 (1981): 32-43.

2256. Cooper, Albert. "The Canadian Auditor-General and Access to Cabinet Documents." Parliamentarian 68:1 (1987): 10-15.

2257. Courtney, John C. "`An Alternative View' of Mackenzie King: A Rejoinder." Canadian Journal of Political Science 9:2 (1976): 308-309. Defends the use of political psychology to analyze prime ministerial behavior.

2258. Courtney, John C. "Has the Canadian Prime Minister Become `Presidentialized'?" Presidential Studies Quarterly 14:2 (1984): 238-241.

2259. Courtney, John C. "Leadership Conventions in Canada: A Comment." Presidential Studies Quarterly 11:1 (1981): 44-47.

2260. Courtney, John C. "Prime Ministerial Character: An Examination of Mackenzie King's Political Leadership." Canadian Journal of Political Science 9:1 (1976): 77-100. Self image, world view, and style of MacKenzie King as Prime Minister.

2261. Crowley, Ronald W. "A New Power Focus in Ottawa: The Ministry of State for Economic and Regional Development." Optimum 13:2 (1982): 5-12.

2262. D'Aquino, Thomas. "The Prime Minister's Office: Catalyst or Cabal? Aspects of the Development of the Office in Canada and Some Thoughts About Its Future." Canadian Public Administration 17:1 (1974): 55-79.

2263. Deutsch, John. "Governments and Their Advisors," Canadian Public Administration 16:1 (1973): 25-34.

2264. Donneur, André. "Politique et technique: le rôle du groupe d'analyse politique du ministère canadien des affaires extérieures." ["Politics and Techniques: the Role of the Political Analysis Group of the Canadian Minister of External Affairs."] Res Publica 16:2 (1974): 209-220. Description of the function of the political analysis group, with an example of its work in Canadian politics regarding the United States.

2265. Esberey, J.E. "Personality and Politics: A New Look at the King-Byng Dispute." Canadian Journal of Political Science 6:1 (1973): 37-55. Study of the 1926 dispute between the Governor General and the prime minister over the nature of prime ministerial "advice".

2266. Esberey, J.E. "Prime Ministerial Character: An Alternative View." Canadian Journal of Political Science 9:1 (1976): 101-106. Criticism of previous attempts to use political psychology to analyze prime ministerial behavior.

2267. Faulkner, J. Hugh. "Pressuring the Executive." Canadian Public Administration 25:2 (1982): 240-253.

2268. Fay, James S. "Restraints on Executive Emergency Power in the United States and Canada." Hastings International and Comparative Law Review 3:1 (1979): 127-150. Examines constitutional and statutory dimensions of emergency powers for executives in both nations, and discusses potential legislative and judicial checks on such powers.

2269. Forsey, Eugene. "The Role of the Crown in Canada Since Confederation." Parliamentarian 60:1 (1979): 14-20.

2270. Forsey, Eugene. "The Role and Position of the Monarch in Canada." Parliamentarian 64:1 (1983): 6-11.

2271. Gagnon, Yvan. "Should Canada Copy the American System of Checks and Balances," Presidential Studies Quarterly 11 (1981): 335-341.

2272. Godbout, Alain. "Une note d'accompagnement au ministre." ["A Note of Accompanyment for a Minister."] Canadian Public Administration 27:3 (1984): 437-441.

2273. Irvine, William P., and R. E. Simeon. "The Prime Minister's Mailbag." Canadian Public Administration 19:2 (1976): 279-294.

2274. Johnson, A.W. "Management Theory and Cabinet Government." Canadian Public Administration 14:1 (Spring, 1971): 73-81.

2275. Kirkwood, David. "Accountability and the [Canadian] Deputy Minister." Optimum 13:2 (1982): 17-26.

2276. Lalonde, M. "The Changing Role of the Prime Minister's Office." Canadian Public Administration 14:4 (1971): 509-537.

2277. Lammers, William, and Nyomarkay, Joseph. "The Canadian Cabinet in Comparative Perspective." Canadian Journal of Political Science 15:1 (1982): 29-46.

2278. Leger, Paul. "The Cabinet Committee System of Policy-making and Resource Allocation in the Government of New Brunswick." Canadian Public Administration 26:1 (1983): 16-35.

2279. Lower, Arthur. "The Prime Minister and the Premiers." Queen's Quarterly 87:4 (1980): 560-565. Analysis of the positions of the Prime Minister and the Premiers in the Constitutional conflict.

2280. Mallory, J.R. "Mackenzie King and the Origins of the Cabinet Secretariat." Canadian Public Administration 19:2 (1976): 254-266.

2281. Mallory, J.R. "Parliament, the Cabinet, and the Bureaucracy in Canada." Politics 15:2 (1980): 249-263. Asks whether the cabinet can regain control over the bureaucracy. Suggests that this may still be possible, but there are risks associated with necessary action.

2282. Mallory, J.R. "The Two Clerks: Parliamentary Discussion of the Role of the Privy Council Office." Canadian Journal of Political Science 10:1 (1977): 3-19. Discussion of the privy council office casts some light on the inner workings of the parliament.

2283. Monet, Jacques. "La Coronne du Canada." ["The Crown of Canada."] Journal of Canadian Studies 11:4 (1976): 27-32.

2284. Normand, Robert. "Les rélations entre les haut fonctionnaires et le ministre." ["The Relations Between High Civil Servants and the Minister."] Canadian Public Administration 27:4 (1984): 522-541.

2285. O'Neil, Daniel J. "The French Canadian Prime Ministers: Their Route to Power." Political Science 30:1 (1978): 1-14. Biographical analysis of Lilfrid Laurier, Louis St. Laurent, and Pierre Trudeau as prime ministers, and description of the pattern in the accession of the three French-Canadian prime ministers.

2286. Rabinovitch, Arthur. "The Political Dimension: (What Information Should Officials Provide to Assist Ministerial Policy Making?)" Optimum 11:3 (1980): 59-70. Study of the information currently given to the Minister and what else he may need.

2287. Robertson, G. "The Changing Role of the Privy Council Office." Canadian Public Administration 4:4 (1971): 487-508.

2288. Savoie, Donald. "The Minister's Staff: The Need for Reform." Canadian Public Administration 26:4 (1983): 509-524. Studies the staffs of ministers and investigates how the staffs affect the capacities of ministers to provide policy directions to their departments and to assess policy advice coming from permanent public servants.

2289. Sharp, Mitchell. "Decision-Making in the Federal Cabinet." Canadian Public Administration 19:1 (1976): 1-7.

2290. Smith, Denis. "Comments on `The Prime Minister's Office: Catalyst or Cabal?'" Canadian Public Administration 17:1 (Spring, 1974): 80-84.

2291. Soldatos, P. "La problématique de l'incompatibilité des fonctions ministérielles et du mandat de député en système politique étatique de type parlementaire. ["The Problem of the Incompatibility of Ministerial Functions with the Deputy's Mandate in Political Systems of the Parliamentary Type."] Canadian Journal of Political Science 5:2 (1972): 252-269. Sociological factors shape the decision-making capacities of the system's authorities.

2292. Spencer, Samia. "The Female Cabinet Members of France and Quebec: Token Women?" Contemporary French Civiliation 9:2 (1985): 166-191. Based upon biographies by former cabinet members, discusses role of women in government in two polities.

2293. Stark, Frank. "The Prime Minister as Symbol: Unifier or Optimizer?" Canadian Journal of Political Science 6:3 (1973): 514-515. Discussion of Hockin's book Apex of Power.

2294. Sutherland, Sharon. "The Politics of Audit: The Federal Office of the Auditor General in Comparative Perspective." Canadian Public Administration 29:1 (1986): 118-148. Traces the development of the Office from its creation in 1977 to its state in 1985.

2295. Tellier, Paul M. "L'évolution du rôle du Bureau du Conseil privé et du Bureau du Premier Ministre: commentaire." ["The Evolution of the Role of the Privy Council Office and Prime Minister's Office: Commentary." Canadian Public Administration 15:2 (Summer, 1972): 378-382.

2296. Ward, Norman. "The Changing Role of the Privy Council Office and Prime Minister's Office: A Commentary." Canadian Public Administration 15:2 (Summer, 1972): 375-377.

2297. Weller, Patrick. "Do Prime Ministers' Departments Really Create Problems?" Public Administration 61:1 (1983): 59-78.

2298. Weller, Patrick. "The Vulnerability of Prime Ministers: A Comparative Perspective." Parliamentary Affairs 36:1 (1983): 96-117.

10
The Legislature

Books

2299. Aiken, B. The Backbencher -- Trials and Tribulations of a Member of Parliament. Toronto: McClelland and Stewart, 1974.

2300. Aster, Howard. House on the Hill. Toronto: McClelland and Stewart, 1972. Study of the House of Commons, its institutions and procedures.

2301. Aucoin, Peter. Institutional Reforms for Representative Government. Toronto: University of Toronto Press, 1985. Four essays on the size of the House of Commons, parliamentary reform, reform of the electoral system, and the role of future referenda in the Canadian democratic system.

2302. Bain, George. Canada's Parliament. Ottawa: Information Canada, 1972.

2303. Bejermi, John. Canadian Parliamentary Handbook. Ottawa: Borealis Press, 1982.

2304. Bejermi, John. How Parliament Works. Ottawa: Borealis Press, 1979.

2305. Campbell, Colin. The Canadian Senate: A Lobby from Within. Toronto: Macmillan of Canada, 1978. Classic study of the Canadian Senate and the interaction between Senators and Canadian corporate interests. Discusses the role and function of the Senate, and the entrenchment of business interests there. Includes comparisons of Senators and Members of Parliament, and discussion of proposals to abolish the Senate.

2306. Canada's 28th Parliament: A Guide to the Members, Their Constituencies, and Their Government. Toronto: Methuen, 1971.

2307. Canadian Study of Parliament Group. Seminar on Accountability to Parliament. Ottawa: Queen's Printer for Canada, 1978.

2308. Clarke, Harold, et al. Parliament, Policy, and Representation. Toronto: Methuen, 1980. Articles covering linkages with the public and representation, policy involvement and accountability, staff and legislative structures, and a comparative perspective of the Canadian parliament.

2309. Commonwealth Parliamentary Association. Canadian Branch. Fourth Canadian Regional Parliamentary Seminar: Ottawa, Ontario, October 31-November 3, 1977. Ottawa: Commonwealth Parliamentary Association, Canadian Branch, 1977.

2310. Commonwealth Parliamentary Association.; Canadian Branch. Third Canadian Regional Seminar on Parliamentary Practice and Procedure, Ottawa, October 31-November 5, 1976. Ottawa: Commonwealth Parliamentary Association, Canadian Region, 1976.

2311. Commonwealth Parliamentary Association, Canadian Region. Second Canadian Regional Seminar on Parliament at Work: Parliament Buildings, Ottawa, Canada, November 18-22, 1974. Ottawa: The Association, Canadian Region, 1975.

2312. Commonwealth Parliamentary Association. Canadian Branch. First Canadian Regional Seminar on Parliamentary Practice and Procedure. Ottawa: Commonwealth Parliamentary Association, Canadian Region, 1974.

2313. Courtney, John C., ed. The Canadian House of Commons: Essays in Honour of Norman Ward. Calgary: University of Calgary Press, 1985. Essays covering question period, parliamentary procedure, parliamentary reform, cabinet government, the role of the courts, elections expenses, and the media and campaigns.

2314. Cramer, Jack. Parliamentary Experience and Legislative Behavior. Toronto: Macmillan of Canada, 1976.

2315. D'Aquino, Thomas, et al. Parliamentary Democracy in Canada: Issues for Reform. Toronto: Methuen, 1983.

2316. Fleming, Robert J. A Comparative Study of the Administrative Structures of Canadian Legislatures. Toronto: Office of the Assembly, 1980.

2317. Fleming, Robert J., and Mitchinson, J. Thomas, eds. Canadian Legislatures: the 1981 Comparative Study. Toronto: Office of the Assembly, 1981.

The Legislature   227

2318. Franks, C.E.S. Parliament and Security Matters: A Study. Ottawa: Commission of Inquiry, 1980. The Report of the Commission of Inquiry Concerning Certain Activities of the Royal Canadian Mounted Police. Covers the role of Parliament as a watchdog, case studies of questionable police behavior, and a section dealing with recommendations for change.

2319. Gaboury, Jean Pierre, and Hurley, James Ross, eds. The Canadian House of Commons Observed: Parliamentary Internship Papers. Ottawa: University of Ottawa Press, 1979. Papers written by Parliamentary Interns on parliamentary procedure, legislative history, committees, parliamentary services, information and the press, parties, and parliamentary actors.

2320. Gander, Barry. Legislative Handbook: A Citizen's Guide to the Canadian Parliamentary System. Ottawa: Canadian Construction Association, 1978.

2321. Hoffman, David, and Ward, Norman. Bilingualism and Biculturalism in the Canadian House of Commons. Ottawa: Queen's Printer, 1970. Document prepared for the Royal Commission on Bilingualism and Biculturalism. Discusses the history of the House, how it operates, how Members perceive their roles, and how bilingualism and biculturalism affect it.

2322. Hurley, James R., ed. The Canadian House of Commons Observed: Parliamentary Internship Papers. Ottawa: University of Ottawa Press, 1979.

2323. Jackson, Robert J. The Canadian Legislative System: Politicians and Policy-Making. Toronto: MacMillan of Canada, 1980. Study of individual legislative behavior in the Canadian legislature, with an emphasis upon how the legislature as a body is able to respond to policy-making demands in its environment.

2324. Jerome, James. Mr. Speaker. Toronto: McClelland and Stewart, 1985. Description of role and duties of the Speaker of the House of Commons written by a former Speaker.

2325. Johnston, Donald J. Up the Hill. Montreal: Optimum, 1986.

2326. Kelly, John, and Hanson, Hugh. Improving Accountability: Canadian Public Accounts Committees and Legislative Auditors. Ottawa: Canadian Comprehensive Auditing Foundation, 1981.

2327. Kornberg, Allan, and Mishler, William T. E. Influence in Parliament, Canada. Durham, N.C.: Duke University Press, 1976. Survey-based analysis of Canadian Members of Parliament, their behavior, and description of those factors which affect participation and influence in the House of Commons.

2328. Lalonde, Marc. *Constitutional Reform: House of the Federation*. Ottawa: Govt. of Canada Unity Information Office, 1978. Description of proposed new upper house of the Canadian Parliament, and how its functions and structures would differ from those of the current Senate.

2329. Levy, Gary. *Speakers of the House of Commons*. Ottawa: Library of Parliament, 1984. History of the development of the office of Speaker and the incumbents of that office over its existence.

2330. MacDonald, Brian, ed. *Parliament and Defence Policy: Preparedness or Procrastination?* Toronto: Canadian Institute of Strategic Studies, 1982. Essays covering a variety of defense-related questions, with a special focus on the role of parliament in the preparation of defense policy independent of government policy in that area.

2331. MacEachen, Allan J. *Members of Parliament and Conflict of Interest*. Ottawa: Information Canada, 1973.

2332. McGrath, James. *Report of the Special Committee on Reform of the House of Commons*. Ottawa: Queen's Printer for Canada, 1985. Special parliamentary committee recommending wide reforms in procedure, committee behavior, and more opportunities for backbenchers to have an important role in the legislative process.

2333. MacGuigan, Mark. *Reform of the Senate: A Discussion Paper*. Ottawa: Government of Canada, 1983.

2334. March, Roman R. *The Myth of Parliament*. Scarborough, Ontario: Prentice-Hall of Canada, 1974.

2335. Neilson, William A. W., and MacPherson, James C., eds. *The Legislative Process in Canada: The Need for Reform*. Montreal: Institute for Research on Public Policy, 1978.

2336. *Parliament and Foreign Affairs: A Seminar Sponsored Jointly with the Canadian Institute of International Affairs, Ottawa*. Ottawa, Ontario: Canadian Institute of International Affairs, 1984.

2337. Resnick, Philip. *Parliament vs. People: An Essay on Democracy and Canadian Political Culture*. New Star Books, 1984.

2338. Robinson, A. *Parliament and Public Spending*. Toronto: Book Society of Canada, 1978.

2339. Slatter, Frans F. _Parliament and Administrative Agencies: A Study Paper_. Ottawa: Law Reform Commission of Canada, 1982. Role of administrative agencies in the parliamentary system, role of parliament in the administrative system, and points of contact between parliament and administrative agencies.

2340. Stewart, John B. _The Canadian House of Commons: Procedure and Reform_. Montreal: McGill-Queen's University Press, 1977. Comprehensive study of the House, its functions, procedures, the legislative process, committees, and taxation questions.

2341. Taras, David, ed. _Parliament and Canadian Foreign Policy_. Toronto: Canadian Institute of International Affairs, 1985. Examines Parliament's foreign policy committees, the Standing Committee on External Affairs, Parliament's role in Canada-China relations, and the Senate's role in defense policy.

2342. Walkland, S.Z., ed. _The House of Commons in the Twentieth Century_. Oxford: Oxford University Press, 1979.

Articles

2343. Atkinson, Michael, and Kim R. Nossal. "Executive Power and Committee Autonomy in the Canadian House of Commons: Leadership Selection, 1968-1979." _Canadian Journal of Political Science_ 13:2 (1980): 287-308.

2344. Balls, Herbert R. "The Watchdog of Parliament: The Centenary of the Legislative Audit." _Canadian Public Administration_ 21:4 (1978): 584-617.

2345. Bayefsky, Anne F. "Parliamentary Sovereignty and Human Rights in Canada: The Promise of the Canadian Charter of Rights and Freedoms." _Political Studies_ 31:2 (1983): 239-263.

2346. Bishop, P.V. "Restoring Parliament to Power." _Queen's Quarterly_ 77:2 (1970): 149-156.

2347. Briggs, E.D. "Federalism and Reform of the Senate: A Commentary on Recent Governmental Proposals." _Queen's Quarterly_ 77:1 (1970): 56-71.

2348. Burns, R. M. "Second Chambers: German Experience and Canadian Needs." _Canadian Public Administration_ 18:4 (Winter, 1975): 541-568.

2349. Byers, R.B. "Perceptions of Parliamentary Surveillance of the Executive: The Case of Canadian Defense Policy." Canadian Journal of Political Science 5:2 (1972): 234-250. Views of parliamentarians about the adequacy of parliamentary surveillance over defense policy, and analysis of inter-party variations in these views.

2350. Byrne, D. "Some Attendance Patterns Exhibited by Members of Parliament During the 28th Parliament." Canadian Journal of Political Science 5:1 (1972): 135-141. Descriptive essay which shows that some members of Parliament are taking a more active part than others in the legislative process, studying recorded divisions and records of committee attendance.

2351. Caley, Rodney. "Canada: Parliamentary Reporting." Parliamentarian 60:4 (1979): 219-222.

2352. Campbell, Colin. "The Interplay of Institutionalization and Assignment of Tasks in Parliamentary and Congressional Systems: The House of Commons and the House of Representatives." International Journal of Comparative Sociology 18:1-2 (1977): 127-153.

2353. Campbell, Colin. "'The Protestant Ethic,' 'Rationality,' and Canada's Political Elite: Ethnic and Religious Influences on Senators." Social Science Journal 12:3 (1975): 159-173. Ethnic and religious backgrounds influence the behavior and perspective of Canadian Senators.

2354. Campbell, Colin, and Clarke, Harold. "Editors' Introduction: The Contemporary Canadian Legislative System." Legislative Studies Quarterly 3:4 (1978): 529-536.

2355. Campbell, Colin, and Kornberg, Allan. "Parliament in Canada: A Decade of Published Research." Legislative Studies Quarterly 3 (1978): 555-581. Comprehensive review of the literature dealing with the Canadian Parliament.

2356. "Canada: The Parliamentary and Scientific Committee." Parliamentarian 58:3 (1977): 187-188.

2357. "Canada: Unparliamentary Language." Parliamentarian 55:2 (1974): 134.

2358. "Canadian Senate - Abolition or Reform," Parliamentarian 54 (1973): 162-164.

2359. Carman, Robert D. "Accountability of Senior Public Servants to Parliament and Its Committees." Canadian Public Administration 27:4 (1984): 542-555.

2360. Cassidy, Michael. "Crown Corporations and the Canadian Legislatures -- a Vain Search for Accountability." Parliamentarian 63:3 (1982): 129-138.

2361. Casstevens, Thomas, and Denham, William III. "Turnover and Tenure in the Canadian House of Commons, 1867-1968." Canadian Journal of Political Science 3:4 (1970): 655-661. Analysis of what theory predicted and what happened in turnover in House of Commons elections during this period.

2362. Champagne, Maurice. "Written Questions in the Parliamentary Process." Politique 2 (1982) 143-152.

2363. Clark, Joseph. "The Standing of Parliament in Canada." Parliamentarian 57:4 (1976): 227-234.

2364. Clarke, Harold. "Determinants of Provincial Constituency Service Behaviour: A Multivariate Analysis." Legislative Studies Quarterly 3:4 (1978): 601-628.

2365. Clarke, Harold. "The Ideological Self-Perceptions of Provincial Legislators." Canadian Journal of Political Science 11:3 (1978) 617-634. Opinions of provincial legislators are examined related to ideology and party position in all ten provinces.

2366. Clarke, Harold, et al. "Constituency Service Among Canadian Provincial Legislators: Basic Findings and a Test of Three Hypotheses." Canadian Journal of Political Science 8:4 (1975): 520-542. The extent of constituency service work among provincial legislators in all ten provinces.

2367. Clarke, Harold, Kornberg, Allan, and Stewart, Marianne. "Parliament and Political Support in Canada." American Political Science Review 78:2 (1984): 452-469. How support for legislatures and legislators influences support for the regime.

2368. Clarke, Harold, and Price, Richard. "Parliamentary Experience and Representational Role Orientations in Canada." Legislative Studies Quarterly 6:3 (1981): 373-390. A study of the effect of legislative experience on role orientations in Canadian MPs.

2369. Clarke, Harold, and Price, Richard. "Freshman MPs' Job Images: The Effects of Incumbency, Ambition, and Position." Canadian Journal of Political Science 13:3 (1980): 583-606.

2370. Clarke, Harold, and Price, Richard. "A Note on the Pre-Nomination Role Socialization of Freshmen Members of Parliament." Canadian Journal of Political Science 10:2 (1977): 391-406. How holders of legislative positions develop their values, attitudes, and "cognitive maps" prior to their nominations.

232   Contemporary Canadian Politics

2371. Clayton, Alan. "The Information Revolution Comes to Parliament." Optimum 10:3 (1979): 5-15. A major reform in the Canadian Parliament is access to increased government information and increased services to maintain and analyze information.

2372. Comeau, C.A. "Quebec: The Sword and the Mace." Parliamentarian 60:1 (1979): 36.

2373. Connolly, John. "The Senate of Canada," Parliamentarian 53:2 (1972): 96-103.

2374. Dawson, W.F. "Resignation and Removal of Canadian Senators." Parliamentarian 56:1 (1975): 12-20.

2375. Dobell, W.M. "Foreign Policy in Parliament." International Perspectives (January-February, 1985): 9-11. Discusses the traditional role of Parliament in this area and new changes in procedure and behavior that may increase the power of Parliament.

2376. Dowding, Gordon H. "The Selection of Mr. Speaker: A Canadian Comment." Parliamentarian 59:3 (1978): 200-201..

2377. Eglington, G.G. "Scrutiny of Delegated Legislation in the Parliament of Canada." Parliamentarian 59:4 (1978): 271-274.

2378. Ellis, J.R. "Information Technology and the Canadian House of Commons." Parliamentarian 67:3 (1986): 93-96.

2379. "Experiment on Improving Parliamentary Efficiency in Canada." Parliamentarian 64:2 (1983): 113-115.

2380. Falcone, David. "Legislative Change and Policy Change: A Deviant Case analysis of the Canadian House of Commons." Journal of Politics 41:2 (1979): 611-633.

2381. Falcone, David, and Mishler, William . "Legislative Determinants of Provincial Health Policy in Canada: A Diachronic Analysis." Journal of Politics 39:2 (1977): 345-367.

2382. Finsten, Hugh. "New Conflict of Interest Rules for Canadian Parliamentarians." Parliamentarian 60:1 (1979): 29-33.

2383. Fleming, R.J., and Hulmes, F.G. "Canadian Legislatures: The 1986 Comparative Study." Canadian Journal of Political Science 20:3 (1987): 649-650. A Book Review of the new study put out by the Ontario Legislative Research Service.

2384. Fletcher, Fredrick J., and Goddard, Arthur M. "Government and Opposition: Structural Influences on Provincial Legislators." Legislative Studies Quarterly 3:4 (1978): 647-670.

2385. Forsey, Eugene. "Dissolution of Parliament in Canada." Parliamentarian 58:1 (1977): 5-11.

2386. Forsey, Eugene. "Dissolution of Parliament in Canada." Parliamentarian 55:4 (1974): 229-233.

2387. Fortier, Robert. "A New Initiative in Canadian Senate Procedure." Journal of Parliamentary Information 21:3 (1975): 607-611. Basic discussion of recent changes in Senate procedure to give the Senate a more meaningful role in the Canadian legislative system.

2388. Franks, C.E.S. "The Dilemma of the Standing Committees of the Canadian House of Commons," Canadian Journal of Political Science 4 (1971): 461-477.

2389. Gaboury, Jean-Pierre. "Pour un Parlement fédéral plus démocratique." ["For a More Democratic Federal Parliament."] Politique 6 (1984): 127-144. How changes in parliament could enable it to better perform its function.

2390. Gillies, James, and Pigott, Jean. "Participation in the Legislative Process." Canadian Public Administration 25:2 (1982): 254-264.

2391. Guppy, N., Freeman, S., and Buchan, S. "Representing Canadians: Changes in the Economic Backgrounds of Federal Politicians, 1965-1984." Canadian Review of Sociology and Anthropology 24:3 (1987): 417-430.

2392. Hales, Alfred D. "What's an MP Worth? The Review of the Salaries and Allowances of Canadian Senators and MPs." Parliamentarian 61:4 (1980): 243-245.

2393. Happy, J. R., and Kyba, J. P. "The `Myth' of Business Over-Representation in the Canadian House of Commons." Journal of Commonwealth and Comparative Politics 24:3 (19986): 278-283.

2394. Hockin, Thomas A. "The Advance of Standing Committees in Canada's House of Commons: 1965 to 1970." Canadian Public Administration 13:2 (1970): 185-202.

2395. Huntington, Ron. "Effective Parliamentary Influence and Better Government." Parliamentarian 65:2 (1984): 99-103.

2396. Hyson, R.V. Stewart. "The Role of the Backbencher -- an Analysis of Private Members' Bills in the Canadian House of Commons." Parliamentary Affairs 27:3 (1974): 262-272.

2397. Ivany, Ranall. "The Ombudsman and the Elected Member." Parliamentarian 64:4 (1983): 197-203. Results of new policy in Alberta which established the office of Ombudsman in 1967.

2398. Jerome, James A. "The Office of Speaker in the Canadian House of Commons." Journal of Parliamentary Information 21:3 (1975): 590-595. Very basic overview of the development of the Office of Speaker and his role in the contemporary House of Commons.

2399. Jerome, James A. "The Speakership in Canada." Parliamentarian 59:2 (1978): 77-84.

2400. Johansen, Peter W. "Televising Parliament: What the Commons Report Left Out." Journal of Canadian Studies 8:4 (1973): 39-51.

2401. Kay, Barry J. "Voting Patterns in a Non-Partisan Legislature: A Study of Toronto City Council." Canadian Journal of Political Science 4:2 (1971): 224-242.

2402. Kornberg, Allan, and Campbell, Colin. "Parliament in Canada: A Decade of Published Research." Legislative Studies Quarterly 3:4 (1978): 555-580.

2403. Lapointe, Renaude. "The Role of the Canadian Senate." Journal of Parliamentary Information 21:3 (1975): 596-606. Very basic review of the organization and functions of the Canadian Senate in contemporary Canadian politics.

2404. Laundy, Philip. "Comment on Professor C.E.S. Frank' `The Dilemma of the Standing Committees of the Canadian House of Commons.'" Canadian Journal of Political Science 5:3 (1972): 437-438. Discusses role of Library of Parliament and its Research Branch in assisting Members of Parliament.

2405. Laundy, Philip. "The Future of the Canadian Speakership," Parliamentarian 53 (1972): 113-118.

2406. Laundy, Philip. "A New Direction for Canada." Parliamentarian 59:4 (1978): 211-215.

2407. Lemco, Jonathan. "Senate Reform: A Fruitless Endeavour." Journal of Commonwealth and Comparative Politics 24:3 (1986): 269-277. Brian Mulroney supported Senate reform when he was elected to office. This hasn't happened. This article explains why, although it suggests that calls for reform of the Senate will reemerge in the future.

2408. Levy, Gary. "Delegated Legislation and the Standing Joint Committee on Regulations and Other Statutory Instruments," Canadian Public Administration 22:3 (1979): 349-366.

2409. Lovink, J.A.A. "Parliamentary Reform and Governmental Effectiveness in Canada." Canadian Public Administration 16:1 (1973): 35-54.

2410. Lovink, J.A.A. "Who Wants Parliamentary Reform?" Queen's Quarterly 79:4 (1972): 505-513.

2411. MacDonald, Donald S. "Change in the House of Commons -- New Rules." Canadian Public Administration 13:1 (1970): 30-39.

2412. McGovern, Josephine. "The Library: Parliament of Victoria," Parliamentarian 53 (1972): 17-21.

2413. MacGuigan, Mark. "Parliamentary Reform: Impediments to an Enlarged Role for the Backbencher." Legislative Studies Quarterly 3:4 (1978): 671-682.

2414. McInnes, Simon. "Improving Legislative Surveillance of Provincial Public Expenditures: The Performance of the Public Accounts Committees and Auditors General." Canadian Public Administration 20:1 (Spring, 1977): 36-86.

2415. Macleod, Alex. "The Reform of the Standing Committees of the Quebec National Assembly: A Preliminary Assessment." Canadian Journal of Political Science 8:1 (1975): 22-39. Studies the 29th legislature in Quebec and changes in behavior of the Standing Committees there.

2416. MacMinn, George. "Police Powers and Confidentiality Between Constituent and His Member of Parliament," Parliamentarian 63 (1982): 92-96.

2417. McWhinney, Edward. "Parliamentary Privilege and the Media, Parliamentarian 56 (1975): 96-105.

2418. Mallory, J.R. "Parliamentary Scrutiny of Delegated Legislation in Canada: A Large Step Forward and a Small Step Back." Public Law (London) (1972): 30-42.

2419. Mallory, J. R., and Smith, B.A. "The Legislative Role of Parliamentary Committees in Canada: The Case of the Joint Committee on the Public Service Bills." Canadian Public Administration 15:1 (Spring, 1972): 1-23.

2420. Massicotte, Louis. "Le Parlement du Quebec en transition." ["The Quebec Parliament in Transition."] Canadian Public Administration 28:4 (1985): 550-574. Examines first the period from 1867 to 1960, and then evolution from the early 1960s through 1980.

2421. "Members' Salaries and Allowances Raised in Canada."
Parliamentarian 62:4 (1981): 278.

2422. Mishler, William. "Nominating Attractive Candidates for Parliament: Recruitment to the Canadian House of Commons." Legislative Studies Quarterly 3:4 (1978): 581-600.

2423. Nolan, Cathal. "The Influence of Parliament on Human Rights in Canadian Foreign Policy." Human Rights Quarterly 7:3 (1985): 373-390.

2424. Nossal, Kim, and Atkinson, Michael. "Executive Power and Committee Autonomy in Canadian House of Commons," Canadian Journal of Political Science 13 (1980): 287-309.

2425. "Ontario: Nomination of Officers of Parliament," Parliamentarian 61 (1980): 164-167.

2426. "Parliamentary Task Forces in the Canadian House of Commons: A New Approach to Committee Activity." Parliamentarian 66:1 (1985): 28-31.

2427. Pasis, Harvey. "The Inequal Distribution in the Canadian Provincial Assemblies." Canadian Journal of Political Science 5:3 (1972): 433-436. Study of the degree of deviation from the principle of an equal number of voters for all constituencies to be found in provincial assemblies in Canada.

2428. Pelletier, Marcel R. "Privilege in the Canadian Parliament." Parliamentarian 54:3 (1973): 143-152.

2429. Pelletier, Réjean. "Les fonctions du député: bilan des réformes parlementaires à Québec." ["The Deputies' Functions: An Assessment of Parliamentary Reforms in Quebec."] Politique 6 (1984): 145-164. Discusses three major roles of the Deputy, and the contributions to politics that contemporary representatives can make.

2430. Penikett, Tony. "A `Meeting Man': A Member in Canada's North." Parliamentarian 65:3 (1984): 195-198.

2431. Penikett, Tony, and Michael, Patrick. "Yukon Legislative Assembly: Report of Special Committee on Privileges on Wiretapping of a Member's Telephone." Parliamentarian 63:1 (1982): 51-55.

2432. Pigott, Jean, and Gillies, James. "Participation in the Legislative Process," Canadian Public Administration 25 (1982): 254-265.

2433. Pitfield, P.M. "The Office of the Auditor General as a Way to Parliamentary Reform." Optimum 15:1 (1984): 22-38.

2434. Presthus, Robert. "Aspects of Political Structure and Legislative Behavior: U.S. and Canada," International Journal of Comparative Sociology 18 (1977): 7-23.

2435. Price, Richard, and Clarke, Harold. "Freshman MPs' Job Images: The Effects of Incumbency, Ambition, and Position," Canadian Journal of Political Science 13 (1980): 583-.

2436. Price, Richard, and Clarke, Harold. "Parliamentary Experience and Representational Role Orientations in Canada," Legislative Studies Quarterly 6 (1981): 373-391.

2437. Pross, A. Paul. "Parliamentary Influence and the Diffusion of Power." Canadian Journal of Political Science 18:2 (1985): 235-266.

2438. "Question Period Weapon in Canada," Parliamentarian 63 (1982): 344-348.

2439. "Question Time in the Legislative Assembly, Victoria," Parliamentarian 55 (1974): 59-60.

2440. "Reform of the Canadian Senate." Parliamentarian 65:1 (1984): 47-51.

2441. Reid, Patrick. "Public Accountants Committee: Ontario Legislature." Parliamentarian 61:4 (1980): 247-252.

2442. "Report of the Joint Committee on the Reform of the Canadian Senate." Parliamentarian 65:3 (1984): 204-207.

2443. Rose, Joseph. "Legislative Support for Multi-Employer Bargaining: The Canadian Experience." Industrial and Labor Relations Review 40:1 (1986): 3-18.

2444. Rush, Michael. "The Development of the Committee System in the Canadian House of Commons -- Diagnosis and Revitalization." Parliamentarian 55:2 (1974): 86-94.

2445. Rush, Michael. "The Development of the Committee System in the Canadian House of Commons -- Reassessment and Reform." Parliamentarian 55:3 (1974): 149-158.

2446. Rush, Michael. "Parliamentary Committees and Parliamentary Government: The British and Canadian Experience." Journal of Commonwealth and Comparative Politics 20:2 (1982): 138-154. Discusses legislative reform in the two parliaments, and the value of increasing the role of committees as a means of giving the parliament more power.

2447. Sancton, Andrew. "The Application of the `Senatorial Floor' Rules to the Latest Redistribution of the House of Commons: The Peculiar Case of Nova Scotia." Canadian Journal of Political Science 6:1 (1973): 56-64. Study of the British North America rules determining how to compute the distribution of seats in the House of Commons.

2448. Sancton, Andrew. "The Representation Act, 1974," Canadian Journal of Political Science 8:3 (1975): 467-469. Analysis of the 1974 formula for distribution of seats in the House of Commons among Canadian provinces.

2449. Sigelman, Lee, and Vanderbok, William. "Legislators, Bureaucrats, and Canadian Democracy: The Long and the Short of It." Canadian Journal of Political Science 10:3 (1977): 615-623. Comparison of political attitudes of Canadian bureaucrats and legislators.

2450. Skogstad, Grace. "Interest Groups, Representation, and Conflict Management in the Standing Committees of the House of Commons." Canadian Journal of Political Science 18:4 (1985): 739-772. Argues that representation of regional interests is not necessarily compatible with acoommodation of conflicts between competing interests.

2451. Smiley, Donald. "The McRiver Report: Parliamentary Majoritarian Democracy and Human Rights," Journal of Canadian Studies 5 (1970): 3-10.

2452. "Speaker and the Clerk: Practice and Procedure," Parliamentarian 52 (1976): 287-293.

2453. Spicer, Erik J. "Research Service to Party Caucuses in the Canadian Federal Parliament." Politics 9:2 (1974): 209-212. Historical discussion of the expansion of scope of mandate of parliamentary research service to assist party caucuses in Canada as well as MPs.

2454. Sproule-Jones, Mark. "The Enduring Colony? Political Institutions and Political Science in Canada." Publius 14:1 (1984): 93-108. Suggests that the notion of "parliamentary supremacy", although existing in theory in Canada, has never really been seriously practiced. Canada has a "colonial political system;" the foreign colonial masters have left, but parliament has -- through its own actions -- yielded much of its sovereignty to the executive and the bureaucracy.

2455. Thomas, Paul. "The Influence of Standing Committees of Parliament on Government Legislation," Legislative Studies Quarterly 3 (1978): 683-704.

2456. Thomas, Paul. "The Role of House Leaders in the Canadian House of Commons." Canadian Journal of Political Science 15:1 (1982): 125-144.

2457. Vaugeois, Denis. "The Parliament of Quebec and Delegated Legislation." Parliamentarian 66:1 (1985): 14-19.

2458. Verney, Douglas. "The Reconciliation of Parliamentary Supremacy and Federalism in Canada," Journal of Commonwealth and Comparative Politics 21 (1983): 22-45.

2459. "Victoria: Register of Members' Interests," Parliamentarian 60 (1979): 154-156.

2460. Walker, John. "Foreign Policy Formulation -- a Parliamentary Breakthrough." International Perspectives (May-June, 1982): 10-13. The House of Commons is beginning to take a new role in Canadian foreign policy.

2461. White, Graham. "Committees in the Ontario Legislature." Parliamentarian 61:1 (1980): 9-23. Study of the Ontario legislature's institutions with respect to British, American, and domestic influences.

2462. Wilson, R. Jeremy. "Continuity Despite Change: Reform of the British Columbia Legislature." Parliamentarian 62:1 (1981): 27-38. Analysis of the failure of the Social Credit regime in British Columbia to implement reforms adopted elsewhere.

2463. Winn, Conrad, and Twiss, James. "The Spatial Analysis of Political Cleavages and the Case of the Ontario Legislature." Canadian Journal of Political Science 10:2 (1977): 287-310. Uses spatial analysis to identify similarities and differences between and among parties in the Ontario legislature based upon survey data of political attitudes of Ontario provincial legislators.

2464. Wright, Anthony. "Pages in the Canadian Parliament and Legislatures," Parliamentarian 53 (1972): 13-15.

2465. Young, H.P., and Balinski, M.L. "Parliamentary Representation and the Amalgam Method," Canadian Journal of Political Science 14 (1981): 797-813.

11
The Administrative Process

Books

2466. Adie, Robert F., and Thomas, Paul G. Canadian Public Administration: Problematical Perspectives. Scarborough, Ont.: Prentice-Hall of Canada, 1982. Discussion of organization theory, how public policy is made, the process of budgeting, and federalism and administration.

2467. Archibald, K. Sex and the Public Service. Ottawa: Queen's Printer, 1970.

2468. Atkinson, Michael, and Chandler, Marsha, eds. The Politics of Canadian Public Policy. Toronto: University of Toronto Press, 1983. Essays on resource policy, language policy, legal aid, industrial policy, fisheries policy, taxation policy, health policy, and northern development.

2469. Aucoin, P., ed. The Politics and Management of Restraint in Government. Montreal: Institute for Research on Public Policy, 1981.

2470. Baccigalupo, A. Les grands rouages de la machine administrative québécoise. [The Big Wheels of the Quebec Administrative Machine] Montréal: Éditions Agence d'Arc, 1978.

2471. Baker, W. Organization Under Stress: The Reorganization of Canada's Department of Public Works, 1970-1973. Ottawa: Centre for Policy and Management Studies, 1980.

2472. Beattie, C. Minority Men in a Majority Setting: Middle-Level Francophones in the Canadian Public Service. Toronto: McClelland and Stewart, 1975.

242 Contemporary Canadian Politics

2473. Bernier, Ivan, and Lajoie, Andree, eds. Regulations, Crown Corporations, and Administrative Tribunals. Toronto: University of Toronto Press, 1985. Essays on legal aspects of crown corporations, understanding regulations, and the evolution of administrative tribunals in Canada.

2474. Bird, Richard Miller. The Growth of Public Employment in Canada. Toronto: Butterworths, 1979.

2475. Bird, Richard Miller. Financing Canadian Government: A Quantitative Overview. Toronto: Canadian Tax Foundation, 1979. Analysis of government spending, financing government activities, deficits and the public debt, fiscal decentralization, with some international perspectives and discussion of why the government has grown as large as it has.

2476. Brown-John, C. Lloyd. Canadian Regulatory Agencies. Toronto: Butterworths, 1981. Includes discussion of the context within which regulation takes place, the creation and operation of regulatory agencies, the actors being regulated, the politics of "the public interest," and the question of deregulation.

2477. Campbell, Colin, and Szablowski, George J. The Superbureaucrats: Structure and Behaviour in Central Agencies. Toronto: Macmillan of Canada, 1979. Study of five central agencies of Canadian federal government: the Prime Minister's Office, the Privy Council Office, the Federal-Provincial Relations Office, the Finance Department, the Treasury Board.

2478. Channing, J.G. The Effects of Transition to Confederation on Public Administration in Newfoundland. Toronto, Ontario: Institute of Public Administration of Canada, 1982.

2479. Christensen, S. Unions and the Public Interest: Collective Bargaining in the Government Sector. Vancouver: Fraser Institute, 1980.

2480. Doerr, Audrey. The Machinery of Government in Canada. Toronto: Methuen, 1981. Analysis of the practice of public administration, with discussion of machinery of government and how public policy is made.

2481. Foot, D.K., ed. Public Employment and Compensation in Canada: Myths and Realities. Toronto: Butterworths, 1978.

2482. Fox, D. Public Participation in the Administrative Process. Ottawa: Law Reform Commission, 1980.

2483. Friedmann, K.A. Complaining: Comparative Aspects of Complaint Behavior and Attitudes Toward Complaining in Canada and Britain. Beverly Hills: Sage, 1974.

2484. Garant, P. La Fonction publique canadienne et québécoise. [Canadian and Quebec Public Administration] Québec: Les Presses de l'Université Laval, 1973.

2485. Gélinas, A., ed. L'enterprise publique et l'intérêt public. [The Public Enterprise and the Public Interest] Toronto: Institute of Public Administration of Canada, 1977. Published in English in 1978 by the Institute of Public Administration of Canada.

2486. Glenday, D.E., et al. Modernization and the Canadian State. Toronto: Macmillan of Canada, 1978.

2487. Granatstein, J.L. The Ottawa Men: The Civil Service Mandarins, 1935-1957. Toronto: Oxford University Press, 1982. Political analysis of the growth of the federal civil service during this 20-year period, and the changing role of the "Mandarins."

2488. Grasham, W. E., and Julien, Germain. Canadian Public Administration: Bibliography. Toronto: Institute of Public Administration of Canada, 1972.

2489. Hodgetts, J.E. The Canadian Public Service: A Physiology of Government, 1867-1970. Toronto: University of Toronto Press, 1973. A Historical-Analytic survey of the organizational structure and management practices of Canadian government.

2490. Hodgetts, J.E., and Dwivedi, O.P. Provincial Governments as Employers. Montreal: McGill-Queen's University Press, 1974.

2491. Jain, H.C., and Kanungo, R.N. Behavioural Issues in Management: The Canadian Context. Toronto: McGraw-Hill Ryerson, 1977.

2492. Janisch, H.N., et al. The Regulatory Process of the Canadian Transport Commission. Ottawa: Law Reform Commission, 1978.

2493. Johnston, Richard. Bureaucrats and Elections. Toronto: University of Toronto, Institute for Policy Analysis, 1977.

2494. Kernaghan, W.D.K., ed. Bureaucracy in Canadian Government. Toronto: Methuen, 2nd ed., 1973.

2495. Kernaghan, W.D.K., ed. Canadian Cases in Public Administration. Toronto: Methuen, 1977.

2496. Kernaghan, Kenneth, ed. Canadian Public Administration: Discipline and Profession. Toronto: Butterworths, 1983. Articles covering a variety of subjects related to public administration, including organization theory, provincial application, municipal application, and the question of regulation.

2497. Kernaghan, K., ed. Executive Manpower in the Public Service: Make or Buy. Toronto: Institute of Public Administration of Canada, 1977.

2498. Kernaghan, W. D. K., ed. Public Administration in Canada: Selected Readings. 4th Ed. Toronto: Methuen, 1982. Readings on public administration, grouped into units dealing with organization theory, formal governmental structures, problems of management, financial administration, personnel, bureaucracy, and administrative responsibility.

2499. Lavoie, J. Le protecteur du citoyen du québec. [The Protector of the Citizen in Quebec] Paris: Presses Universitaires, 1977.

2500. Lemieux, V. Les cheminements de l'influence: systémes, strategies et structures du politique. [The Approaches to Influence: Systems, Strategies, and Structures of Politics] Québec: Les Presses de l'Université Laval, 1979.

2501. Marchand, Edward. Working for Canadians: A Study of Local, Provincial, and Federal Government. Scarborough, Ont.: Prentice-Hall of Canada, 1979.

2502. Niemann, Lindsay. Wage Discrimination and Women Workers: The Move Towards Equal Pay for Work of Equal Value in Canada. Ottawa, Ontario: Labour Canada, 1984.

2503. Olsen, Dennis. The State Elite. Toronto: McClelland and Stewart, 1980. Study of the various elite in contemporary Canadian politics: political elite, judicial elite, and bureaucratic elite.

2504. Poncelet, M. Le management public. [Public Management] Montréal: Les Presses de l'Université du Québec, 1979.

2505. Rowat, D.C., ed. Global Comparisons in Public Administration. Ottawa: Carleton University, 1981.

2505a. Rowat, D.C., ed. Administrative Secrecy in Developed Countries. New York: Columbia University Press, 1979.

2506. Self, P. Administrative Theories and Politics. Toronto: University of Toronto Press, 1973.

2507. Sinclair, S. Cordial But Not Cosy: A History of the Office of Auditor General. Toronto: McClelland and Stewart, 1979.

2508. Smart, C.F., and Stanbury, W.T., eds. Studies on Crisis Management. Toronto: Butterworths, 1978.

2509. Stevens, Thomas J. *The Business of Government: An Introduction to Canadian Public Administration*. Toronto: McGraw-Hill Ryerson, 1978.

2510. Sutherland, Sharon, and Doern, G. Bruce. *Bureaucracy in Canada: Control and Reform*. Toronto: University of Toronto Press, 1985. Discussion of the nature of bureaucracy, how the bureaucracy is organized, the growth and scope of bureaucracy, and how political parties affect bureaucracies.

2511. Swanick, Eric L. *Canadian Provincial Regulatory Agencies: An Introductory Bibliography*. Monticello, Ill.: Vance Bibliographies, 1979.

2512. Swanick, Eric L. *Decentralization of Government Services in Canada*. Monticello, Ill.: Vance Bibliographies, 1979.

2513. Swanick, M. Lynne Struthers. *Municipal Administration in Canada: An Introductory Checklist of Secondary Sources*. Monticello, Ill.: Vance Bibliographies, 1978.

2514. Trebilcock, M.J. *The Choice of Governing Instruments*. Ottawa: Economic Council of Canada, 1982.

2515. Vandervort, Lucinda. *Political Control of Independent Administrative Agencies: A Study Paper*. Ottawa: Law Reform Commission of Canada, 1979. Analysis of development of independent regulatory bodies in Canada and the structures which exist to oversee and control their actions.

Articles

2516. Allen, John R., and Yurchuk, Nestor. "Managing by Results in the Province of Ontario." *Governmental Finance* 13:3 (1984): 17-20. Ontario's "output-oriented" management style of "management by results."

2517. Anderson, John C. "Determinants of Bargaining Outcomes in the Federal Government of Canada." *Industrial and Labor Relations Review* 32:2 (1979): 224-241.

2518. Anderson, John C., and Kochan, Thomas A. "Impasse Procedures in the Canadian Federal Service: Effects on the Bargaining Process." *Industrial and Labor Relations Review* 30:3 (1977): 283-301.

2519. Antoft, Kell. "In-Service Education for Municipal Administrators in Nova Scotia." *Governmental Finance* 2:2 (1973): 18-22. Efforts made in Nova Scotia and other Atlantic provinces to deal with "upgrading" the quality of municipal administrators.

2520. Archibald, K.A. "Men, Women, and Persons." Canadian Public Administration 16:1 (1973): 14-24.

2521. Arpin, Roland. "La Gestion Des Ressources Humaines au Sein de l'Administration Publique: Un Art Bien Complexe!" ["The Management of Human Resources in the Quebec Civil Service: A Very Complex Art!"] Canadian Public Administration 26(3): 1983: 344-359.

2522. Arsenault, Frederic J., and Malone, Kevin. "L'innovation dans le secteur public." ["Innovation in the Public Sector."] Canadian Public Administration 28:1 (1985): 143-149.

2523. Atkinson, Michael, and Coleman, William. "Bureaucrats and Politicians in Canada: An Examination of the Political Administration Model." Comparative Political Studies 18:1 (1985): 58-80.

2524. Atkinson, Michael, and Nossal, Kim R. "Bureaucratic Politics and the New Fighter Aircraft Decisions." Canadian Public Administration 24:4 (Winter, 1981): 531-562.

2525. Aucoin, Peter. "Organizational Change in the Machinery of Canadian Government: From Rational Management to Brokerage Politics." Canadian Journal of Political Science 19:1 (1986): 3-28.

2526. Baar, Carl. "Patterns and Strategies of Court Administration in Canada and the United States." Canadian Public Administration 20:2 (1977): 242-274

2527. Baccigalupo, Alain. "La consultation dans l'administration de la planification au Québec." ["Consultation in Quebec Planning Administration."] International Review of Administrative Sciences 42:4 (1976): 382-397. The opportunities for public participation in the planning process in Quebec.

2528. Baccigalupo, Alain. "L'informatique dans les administrations publiques et para-publiques québécoises." ["Information in Quebec Public and Para-Public Administrations."] Canadian Public Administration 17:4 (1974): 542-552.

2529. Baccigalupo, Alain. "Police Administration in Quebec." Revue Administrative 174 (1976): 648-659.

2530. Baccigalupo, Alain. "Problèmes actuels de l'enseignement et de la recherche sur les administrations publiques dans les universités québécoises." ["Problems of Teaching and Research of Public Administration in Quebec Universities."] International Review of Administrative Science 40:4 (1974): 322-328. This article examines the way public administration is taught in Quebec and the kind of research that is done in this field.

2531. Baccigalupo, Alain. "Le protecteur du citoyen." ["The Protector of the Citizen."] Recherches Sociographiques 16:3 (1975): 353-373.

2532. Baccigalupo, Alain. "The Quebec Citizen's Protector." International Review of Administrative Sciences 41:2 (1975): 128-134. Attitudes held by parliamentarians, bureaucrats, and the public related to the Citizen's Protector (ombudsman) in Quebec.

2533. Baccigalupo, Alain. "Vie administrative à l'étranger: Administrations publiques territoriales et planification régionale dans la province du Québec." ["Administrative Life Abroad: Territorial Public Administration and Regional Planning in the Province of Quebec."] La Revue Administrative 25:145 (1972): 61-66.

2534. Baccigalupo, Alain. "Vie administrative à l'étranger: Les cabinets ministériels dans l'administration publique québécois." ["Administrative Life Abroad: Ministerial Cabinets in Quebec Public Administration."] La Revue Administrative 26:153 (1973): 317-328.

2535. Baccigalupo, Alain. "Vie administrative à l'étranger: Les grands technocrates québécois." ["Administrative Life Abroad: Major Quebec Technocrats."] La Revue Administrative 29:169 (1976): 76-86.

2536. Baccigalupo, Alain, and Groulx, Elise. "Vie administrative à l'étranger: Le protecteur du citoyen dans la province de Québec." ["Administrative Life Abroad: The Protector of the Citizen in the Province of Quebec."] La Revue Administrative 25:150 (1972): 640-646.

2537. Bairstow, Frances. "Final Position Arbitration." Canadian Public Administration 18:1 (Spring, 1975): 55-64.

2538. Baker, Walter. "Accountability, Responsiveness, and Public Sector Productivity." Canadian Public Administration 23:4 (1980): 542-557.

2539. Baker, Walter. "Administrative Reform in the Federal Public Service: The First Faltering Steps." Canadian Public Administration 16:3 (1973): 381-398.

2540. Baker, Walter. "Power and the Public Service." Canadian Public Administration 30:1 (1987): 14-33.

2541. Baker, Walter. "The `Triple E' Movement and Productivity in Canada's Federal Public Service." Optimum 11:3 (1980): 5-20. A study of the movement in the Canadian public service towards directing managerial attention to effectiveness, efficiency, and economy.

2542. Bakvis, Herman. "French Canada and the `Bureaucratic Phenomenon'." Canadian Public Administration 21:1 (1978): 103-124.

2543. Balls, Herbert. "Common Services in Government." Canadian Public Administration 17:2 (1974): 226-241.

2544. Balls, Herbert. "Decision-Making: The Role of the Deputy Minister." Canadian Public Administration 19:3 (1976): 417-431.

2545. Balls, Herbert. "Improving Performance of Public Enterprises through Financial Management and Control." Canadian Public Administration 13:1 (Spring, 1970): 100-123.

2546. Bartha, Peter F. "Organizational Competence in Business-Government Relations: A Managerial Perspective." Canadian Public Administration 28:2 (1985): 202-220. Article examines impediments to business-government cooperation and effective decision-making.

2547. Bauer, Julien. "La représentativité dans l'administration consultative." ["Representation in Consultative Administration."] Canadian Public Administration 24:3 (1981): 452-468.

2548. Bergeron, Gérard. "Walking the Labor-Relations Tightrope." Public Management 52:10 (1970): 6-7. Municipal labor relations in Ontario.

2549. Blais, André, and Dion, Stéphane. "Les employés du secteur public: sont-ils différents?" ["Are {Quebec} Public Sector Employees Different?"] Revue français de Science politique 37:1 (1987): 76-97.

2550. Blakeney, Allan. "Goal-Setting Politicians' Expectations of Public Administrators." Canadian Public Administration 24:1 (1981): 1-7.

2551. Bolduc, Roch. "Les questions d'éthique dans les anées 1980." ["Questions of Ethics in the 1980's"] Canadian Public Administration 24:2 (1981): 200-215.

2552. Bordeleau, Yvan. "Le style de gestion du personnel chez les administrateurs publics et privés: une question d'efficacité?" ["The Style of Personnel Administration of Public and Private Administrators: A Question of Effectiveness?"] Canadian Public Administration 26:4 (Winter, 1983): 577-590.

2553. Borins, Sanford. "Language Use in the Federal Public Service: Some Recent Survey Results." Canadian Public Administration 27:2 (1984): 262-268.

2554. Bortha, Peter. "Organizational Competence in Business-Government Relations: A Managerial Perspective." Canadian Public Adminisration 28:2 (1985): 202-220.

2555. Bostock, William. "The Commissioner of Official Languages: A Canadian Response to a Situation of Ethno-Linguistic Cleavage." Ethnic and Racial Studies 3:4 (1980): 415-426.

2556. Bourgault, Jacques. "Les hauts fonctionnaires québécois: Paramètres synergiques de puissance et de servitude." ["Quebec High Functionaries: Indicators of Power and Servitude."] Canadian Journal of Political Science 16:2 (1983): 227-256.

2557. Breton, Albert, and Wintrobe, Ronald. "Bureaucracy and State Intervention: Parkinson's Law." Canadian Public Administration 22:2 (Summer, 1979): 208-226.

2558. Brophy, J., and McGimpsey, L.M. "Internal Audit and Program Evaluation in the Government of Canada." Optimum 11:2 (1980): 16-25. An attempt to clarify the roles, responsibilities, and relationships of internal auditing and program evaluation.

2559. Brown, M. Paul. "A Lesson in Bureaucratic Persistence: The Provision of Rehabilitation and Resource Management Services in the Maritimes, 1943-1981." Canadian Public Administration 25:1 (1982): 130-146.

2560. Brown-John, C. Lloyd. "Advisory Agencies in Canada: An Introduction." Canadian Public Administration 22:1 (1979): 72-91.

2561. Brown-John, C. Lloyd. "On Parlons Français Ici: The Challenge of Administration in Two Languages, a Canadian Experience." Indian Journal of Public Administration 23:2 (1977): 298-318. The issues, costs, and problems that have developed in the effort to implement the policy of bilingualism.

2562. Brown-John, C. Lloyd. "Party Politics and the Canadian Federal Public Service." Public Administration (Great Britain) 52 (1974): 79-93.

2563. Brunet, Jacques. "La croissance de la machine gouvernementale fédérale et le développement de la région de la capitale." ["The Growth of the Federal Government Machine and the Development of the Capital Region."] Canadian Public Policy 1:2 (Spring, 1975): 148-157.

2564. Brunet, Jacques, Houde, Jean-Guy, and Savard, Gabriel. "La gestion ministérielle et les organismes centraux." ["Ministerial Administration and Central Organizations."] Canadian Public Administration 17:2 (1974): 321-327.

2565. Bryce, R.B. "Reflections on the Lambert Report." Canadian Public Administration 22:4 (Winter, 1979): 572-580.

2566. Cabatoff, Kenneth. "Personnel Management Reorganization in the Government of Québec, 1965-1975." International Review of Administrative Sciences 44:3 (1978): 283-end.

2567. Cabatoff, Kenneth. "Radio Québec: A Case Study of Institution-Building." Canadian Journal of Political Science 11:1 (1978): 125-138. Changes in Radio Québec's behavior and goals can be explained by its perceived need to obtain political and financial support.

2568. Cabatoff, Kenneth, and Iezoni, Massimo. "La professionnalisation de la fonction du personnel comme instrument de réforme de la fonction publique québécoise." ["The Professionalization of Personnel Management as a Means for Reform of the Quebec Civil Service."] Politiques et Management public 3:2 (1985): 33-42.

2569. Cameron, David. "The Discipline and the Profession of Public Administration: An Academic's Perspective." Canadian Public Administration 25:4 (1982): 496-506.

2570. Cameron, David. "Power and Responsibility in the Public Service: Summary of Discussions." Canadian Public Administration 21:3 (Fall, 1978): 358-372.

2571. Campbell, Colin. "The Never-Ending Task of Administrative Reform in the United Kingdom: Some Very Canadian Reflections." Canadian Public Administration 24:3 (1981): 486-494.

2572. Carrothers, Alfred. "Collective Bargaining as Public Policy: Let us Not Pre-empt Disaster." Canadian Public Administration 18:4 (Winter, 1975): 527-540.

2573. Carrothers, Alfred. "The Cuckoo's Egg in the Mare's Nest -- Arbitration of Interests Disputes in Public Service Collective Bargaining: Problems of Principle, Policy, and Process." Canadian Public Administration 20:3 (Fall, 1977): 499-512.

2574. Carson, John J. "Bilingualism in the Public Service." Canadian Public Administration 15:2 (Summer, 1972): 190-193.

2575. Carson, John J. "Bilingualism Revisited: Or the Confessions of a Middle-Aged and Belated Francophile." Canadian Public Administration 21:4 (1978): 539-547.

2576. Carson, John J., and McCloskey, William. "Manpower and Educational Planning in the Canadian Federal Public Service." Administration 22:3 (1974): 271-277. Describes the growth and identification of manpower needs and the training and development of executives in the federal public service.

2577. Carter, Richard. "Les entreprises publiques: pourquoi et pour qui?" ["Public Enterprises: Why, and For Whom?"] Canadian Public Administration 26:2 (Summer, 1983): 239-254.

2578. Carvey, Davis. "Gifts and Bribes: The Purchasing Agent." Canadian Public Administration 29:4 (1986): 598-600.

2579. Cassidy, Frank. "Closed or Open Government: The Public Servant and the Public." Canadian Public Administration 29:4 (1986): 583-584.

2580. Cassidy, Michael. "Political Rights for Public Servants: A Federal Perspective (I)." Canadian Public Administration 29:4 (1986): 653-664.

2581. Cassidy, R. Gorden, and Neave, Edwin H. "Accountability and Control in the Federal Government." Queen's Quarterly 87:1 (1980): 53-62. Analysis of the success of government control mechanisms in Canada.

2582. Chackerian, R. "Community Influence and Bureaucratic Structure." Canadian Public Administration 16:4 (1973): 652-661.

2583. Chandler, Marsha, and Chandler, William. "Public Administration in Canada's Provinces." Canadian Public Administration 25:4 (1982): 580-602.

2584. Chant, J.F., and Acheson, K. "The Choice of Monetary Instruments and the Theory of Bureaucracy." Public Choice 12 (1972): 13-33.

2585. Chantal, R. "Quelques réflexions sur le style administratif: le français dans l'administration fédérale canadienne." ["Reflections on Administrative Style: French in Federal Canadian Administration"] La Revue administrative 23:137 (1970): 536-542.

2586. Chapman, Richard. "The Development of the Academic Study of Public Administration in the United Kingdom, the United States, Canada, and Ireland." International Review of Administrative Sciences 44:1-2 (1978): 40-49. Background of academic study of public administration in these countries; suggests strengths and weaknesses of these studies.

2587. Clift, D. "Le fonctionnaire et le droit du public à l'information." ["The Civil Servant and the Right of the Public to Information."] Canadian Public Administration 14:1 (1971): 53-57.

2588. Conti, Raymond. "La planification des effectifs dans la fonction publique québécois." ["Planning of Figures in Quebec Public Administration."] Canadian Public Administration 15:4 (1972): 631-640.

2589. Corbett, Christopher. "Expert Systems: The Pros and Cons." Canadian Public Administration 29:4 (1986): 568-570.

2590. Corbett, D.C. "The Politics of Bureaucracy in Canada." Public Administration (Sydney) 32:1 (1973): 42-55. The importance of the Treasury Board and the Privy Council Office in Canadian politics.

2591. Coulombe, Pierre E. "Evolution de la gestion des ressources humaines dans la fonction publique québécoise." ["The Evolution of Administration of Human Resources in the Quebec Public Administration."] Canadian Public Administration 27:3 (1984): 418-428.

2592. Courville, Léon. "L'Etat et ses problèmes d'organisation: la taille ou la ceinture?" ["The State and Its Organizational Problems: The Figure or the Belt?"] Canadian Public Administration 21:4 (Winter, 1978): 548-557.

2593. Crerar, Alistair, and Kelly, Michael. "Managing for Failure and Alternatives for Managing for Success." Canadian Public Administration 29:1 (1986): 149-154.

2594. Crispo, John. "Collective Bargaining in the Public Service." Canadian Public Administration 16:1 (Spring, 1973): 1-13.

2595. Cutt, James. "The Program Budgeting Approach to Public Expenditure: A Conceptual Review." Canadian Public Administration 13:4 (1970): 396-425.

2596. Dahamni, Ahmed. "Quelques aspects du management du Ministère des Affaires extérieures du Canada." ["Some Aspects of Management of the Ministry of Foreign Affairs of Canada."] Canadian Public Administration 18:2 (1975): 171-188.

2597. Daquin, Michel. "La rationalisation des politiques publiques: un état de la question." ["The Rationalization of Public Politics: A State of the Question."] Canadian Public Administration 20:2 (1977): 305-316.

2598. D'Aquino, Thomas. "The Public Service of Canada: The Case for Political Neutrality." Canadian Public Administration 27:1 (1984): 14-23.

2599. Davidson, Jill. "Tech Change: Boon or Bane for Professionals, Supervisors, and Middle Managers." Canadian Public Administration 29:4 (1986): 562-566.

2600. Debanneé, J. G. "Management Education for Tomorrow's Society." Canadian Public Administration 14:3 (Fall, 1971): 354-372.

2601. Denham, Ross. "The Canadian Auditors General -- What Is Their Role?" Canadian Public Administration 17:2 (1974): 259-273.

2602. Denham, Ross. "New Public-Sector Audit Legislation in Canada." Canadian Public Policy 4:4 (Autumn, 1978): 474-488.

2603. Dingle, J.F. "Management Information Systems, Economic Theory, and Public Policy." Canadian Public Policy 1:4 (Autumn, 1975): 536-545.

2604. Dion, Stéphane. "Les partis de gouvernement et les administrations publiques: un champ d'interactions mal connu." ["The Parties of Government and Public Administrations: An Unknown Field of Interaction."] Canadian Public Administration 23:3 (Fall, 1980): 400-426.

2605. Dion, Stéphane. "La politisation des administrations publiques: Eléments d'analyse strategique." ["The Politicization of Public Administrations: Elements of Strategic Analysis."] Canadian Public Administration 29:1 (1986): 95-117.

2606. Dobell, A.R. "The Public Servant as God: Taking Risks with the Public." Canadian Public Administration 29:4 (1986): 601-616.

2607. Dobell, Rodney. "The Senior Public Service and Responsibility: Some Reflections in Summary." Canadian Public Administration 27:4 (1984): 617-639.

2608. Dobell, Rodney, and Zussman, David. "An Evaluation System for Government: If Politics is Theatre, then Evaluation is (Mostly) Art." Canadian Public Administration 24:3 (1981): 404-427.

2609. Doern, G. Bruce. "The Political Administration of Government Reorganization: The Merger of DREE and ITC." Canadian Public Administration 30:1 (1987): 34-56.

2610. Dorscht, Alex, et al. "Canada's Foreign Energy Policy." International Perspectives 1986 (May-June): 3-6.

2611. Dussault, René. "L'équilibre entre les pouvoirs judiciare, législatif, et exécutif: rupture ou évolution?" ["The Equilibrium Between Judicial, Legislative, and Executive Powers: Separation or Evolution?"] Canadian Public Administration 22:2 (1979): 196-207.

2612. Dussault, René. "L'evolution du professionalisme au Québec." ["The Evolution of Professionalism in Quebec."] Canadian Public Administration 20:2 (1977): 275-290.

2613. Dussault, René. "L'officier de justice au carrefour des valeurs administratives et judiciares." ["The Judicial Official at the Intersection of Administrative and Judicial Values."] Canadian Public Administration 25:3 (1982): 354-365.

2614. Dussault, René. "The Public Servant and the Citizen." Canadian Public Administration 13:4 (Winter, 1970): 313-315.

2615. Dussault, René. "Le rôle du juriste fonctionnaire dans l'aménagement des ralations entre l'administration et les citoyens." ["The role of the Judicial Administrator in the Resolution of Relations Between the Administration and the Citizens."] Canadian Public Administration 24:1 (1981): 8-17.

2616. Dussault, René, and Bernatchez, R. "La fonction publique canadienne et québécoise." ["Canadian and Quebec Public Administration."] Canadian Public Administration 15:1 (1972): 74-159.

2617. Dussault, René, and Bernatchez, R. "La fonction publique canadienne et québécoise: suite." ["Canadian and Quebec Public Administration: Continued."] Canadian Public Administration 15:2 (1972): 251-374.

2618. Dussault, René, and Borgeat, Louis. "Le droit administratif: Une réalité omniprésente pour l'administrateur publique." ["Administrative Law: An Omnipresent Reality for the Public Administrator."] Canadian Public Administration 25:4 (1982): 653-673.

2619. Dussault, René, and Borgeat, Louis. "La réforme des professions au Québec." ["The Reform of Professions in Quebec."] Canadian Public Administration 17:3 (Fall, 1974): 407-442.

2620. Dwivedi, O.P. "Accountability of Public Servants: Recent Developments in Canada." Journal of Public Administration 26:3 (1980): 757-778.

2621. Dwivedi, O.P. "Administrative Reforms in Canada: Reflections." Indian Journal of Public Administration 31:3 (1985): 1041-1058.

The Administrative Process   255

2622. Feldman, Lionel, and McInnis, Peter. "Continuing Education and Training Programs for Municipal Administrators: A Case Study in Selected Provinces." Canadian Public Administration 16:4 (Winter, 1973): 613-626.

2623. Fera, Norman. "Review of Administrative Decisions Under the Federal Court Act (1970)." Canadian Public Administration 14:4 (1971): 580-594.

2624. Forget, Claude E. "L'administration publique: sujet ou objet du pouvoir politique?" ["Public Administration: Subject or Object of Political Power?"] Canadian Public Administration 21:2 (Summer, 1978): 234-242.

2625. Fournier, André. "Gestion de l'information dans la fonction publique: Diffusion et partage de l'information." ["Administration of Information in the Public Service: Distribution and Division of Information."] Canadian Public Administration 29:1 (1986): 45-60.

2626. Fowke, Donald V. "Toward a General Theory of Public Administration for Canada." Canadian Public Administration 19:1 (1976): 34-40.

2627. Franks, C.E.S. "Administrative Accountability in Canada." Indian Journal of Public Administration 29:3 (1983): 690-701. Discusses the concept and philosophy of accountability, problems in the present system, and possible changes designed to improve the system.

2628. Franks, C.E.S. "The Public Service in the North." Canadian Public Administration 27:2 (1984): 210-241.

2629. Friedmann, Karl A. "Controlling Bureaucracy: Attitudes in the Alberta Public Service Towards the Ombudsman." Canadian Public Administration 19:1 (1976): 51-87. The ombudsman is a recent example of a political institution crossing institutional boundaries.

2630. Friedmann, Karl A. "The Public and the Ombudsman: Perceptions and Attitudes in Britain and in Alberta." Canadian Journal of Political Science 10:3 (1977): 497-525. Types and content of information about the ombudsman and attitudes toward the ombudsman held by the public.

2631. Friedrich, Carl. "Bureaucracy Faces Anarchy," Canadian Public Administration 13 (1970): 219-232.

2632. Gagnon, Jacques. "Les communications administratives." ["Administrative Communications."] Canadian Public Administration 17:3 (1974): 495-504.

2633. Gagnon, Jacques. "Humour et administration." ["Humor and Administration."] Canadian Public Administration 28:3 (Fall, 1985): 434-439.

2634. Gagnon, Yvan. "Le fonctionnaire et l'information." ["The Administrator and Information."] Canadian Public Administration 14:1 (1971): 51-52.

2635. Gallant, Edgar. "Political Rights for Public Servants: A Federal Perspective II." Canadian Public Administration 29:4 (1986): 665-668.

2636. Garant, Patrice. "The Control of Public Administration in Quebec." International Review of Administrative Sciences 39:3 (1973): 225-235. Growth of Quebec's public service and the changes in laws designed to improve both its structures and its operation.

2637. Garant, Patrice. "L'Ethique dans la fonction publique: un essai de théorie générale." ["Ethics in Public Work: An Essay of General Theory."] Canadian Public Administration 18:1 (Spring, 1975): 65-90.

2638. Gardner, C. James. "Organization and Methods Development in the Government of Canada." Public Administration (Great Britain) 54 (1976): 283-318.

2639. Garneau, Raymond. "Quelques jalons dans l'analyse de la relation fonctionnaire-citoyen." ["Some Landmarks in the Analysis of Citizen-Administrator Relations."] Canadian Public Administration 13:4 (1970): 331-336.

2640. Gélinas, André. "Le cadre général des institutions administratives et la déconcentration territoriale." ["The General Body of Administrative Institutions and Territorial Deconcentration."] Canadian Public Administration 18:2 (1975): 253-268.

2641. Gélinas, André. "La commission parlementaire: méchanisme d'imputabilité à l'égard des sous-ministres et des dirigeants d'organismes." ["The Parliamentary Commission: A Mechanism of Overseeing Sub-Ministers and Directors of Agencies."] Canadian Public Administration 27:3 (1984): 372-398.

2642. Gélinas, André. "Le rapport Lambert: les organismes de la couronne." ["The Lambert Report: Organizations and the Crown."] Canadian Public Administration 22:4 (1979): 541-556.

2643. Goodings, Stewart. "Making Public Comment: When is it Acceptable?" Canadian Public Administration 29:4 (1986): 670-673.

2644. Gopalakrishnan, K.C. "Financial and Personnel Administration in Canada." Indian Journal of Public Administration 20:2 (1974): 383-407. Describes the financial agencies in Canada and appraises their effectiveness, the administration of personnel, and the way governmental machinery affects bureaucracy.

2645. Gow, Donald. "The Setting of Canadian Public Administration." Public Administration Review 33:1 (1973): 5-13. Describes features of the Canadian federal system, executive dominance, the federal cabinet, civil servants and ministers, and the relative position of civil servants.

2646. Gow, James I. "L'administration québécoise de 1867 à 1900: un Etat en formation." ["The Quebec Administration from 1867 to 1900: A State in the Making."] Canadian Journal of Political Science 12:3 (1979): 555-620. Growth and development of the Quebec government during this historical period.

2647. Gow, James I. "Histoire administrative du Québec et théorie administrative." ["Administrative History of Quebec and Administrative Theory."] Canadian Journal of Political Science 4:1 (1971): 141-145. Attempt to develop a paradigm of public administration in the Quebec provincial government.

2748. Gow, James I. "L'histoire de l'administration publique québécoise." ["The History of Quebec Public Administration."] Recherches sociographiques 16:3 (1975): 385-411.

2649. Gow, James I. "The Modernization of the Quebec Civil Service." Administration 19:1 (1971): 79-81. An explanation of the Civil Service Reform of 1965 and its implications.

2650. Gow, James I. "La modernisation de la fonction publique du Québec." ["The Modernization of Public Administration in Quebec."] International Review of Administrative Sciences 36:3 (1970): 234-242. Changes in structure and organization of Quebec public service.

2651. Gow, James I. "One Hundred Years of Quebec Administrative History, 1867-1970." Canadian Public Administration 28:2 (1985): 244-268. Examines role of the Catholic church, the development of bureaucracy, and the role of civil servants in Quebec.

2652. Gow, James I. "La réforme institutionnelle de la fonction publique de 1983: contexte, contenu et enjeux." ["The 1983 Institutional Reform of the Civil Service: Context, Content, and Stake."] Politique 6 (1983): 1-101. Study of 1983 reform of the Civil Service in Quebec, and the crisis from 1981-1983 which led to the reform.

2653. Gray, William. "Formalized Mentoring." Canadian Public Administration 29:4 (1986): 636-638.

2654. Grusec, Ted. "Office Automation Trials in the Federal Government: Lessons for Managers." Canadian Public Administration 29:4 (1986): 556-562.

2655. Gunton, T.I. "The Role of the Professional Planner." Canadian Public Administration 27:3 (Fall, 1984): 399-417.

2656. Haché, Jean-Guy. "The Management of Canada Government Projects." Optimum 12:3 (1981): 16-31.

2657. Hardy, Cynthia. "Fighting Cutbacks: Some Issues for Public Sector Administrators." Canadian Public Administration 28:4 (Winter, 1985): 531-549.

2658. Hartle, D. G. "The Public Servant as Advisor: The Choice of Policy Evaluation Criteria." Canadian Public Policy 2:3 (Summer, 1976): 424-438.

2659. Hartle, D. G. "Techniques and Processes of Administration." Canadian Public Administration 19:1 (Spring, 1976): 21-33.

2660. Heeney, A.D.P. "Independence and Partnership: The Search for Principles." International Journal 27:2 (1972): 159-171.

2661. Hehner, Eric. "The Public Servant and the Legalistic Mentality." Canadian Public Administration 13:4 (1970): 324-330.

2662. Henderson, Cyril McC. "Case Study / Halifax: The Role of the Professional Adminstrator in Canada." Public Management 52:10 (1970): 13-15. Brief history of the search of Halifax, N.S., for a city manager.

2663. Hicks, Michael. "Cutback Management in Canada." Australian Journal of Public Administration 42:2 (1983): 193-206. Ontario's experience in cutting back its budget, with an emphasis upon administrative techniques.

2664. Hicks, Michael. "The Treasury Board of Canada and Its Clients: Five Years of Change and Administrative Reform, 1966-71." Canadian Public Administration 16:2 (1973): 182-205.

2665. Hodge, Gerald. "The Roots of Canadian Planning." Journal of the American Planning Association 51:1 (1985): 8-22. Historical, social, and cultural examination of Canadian planning policy, describing goals and tools used in the planning process.

2666. Hodgetts, J.E. "Implicit Values in the Administration of Public Affairs." Canadian Public Administration 25:4 (1982): 471-483.

2667. Hodgetts, J.E. "Managing Money and People in the Public and Private Sectors: Are There More Similarities Than Differences?" Canadian Public Administration 26:1 (1983): 80-83.

2668. Hodgetts, J.E. "The Public Service: Its Past and the Challenge to Its Future." Canadian Public Administration 17:1 (1974): 17-25.

2669. Hodgson, J.S. "The Impact of Minority Government on the Senior Civil Servant." Canadian Public Administration 19:2 (1976): 227-237.

2670. Hodgson, J.S. "Management by Objectives -- The Experience of a Federal Government Department." Canadian Public Administration 16:3 (1973): 422-431.

2671. Holloway, Donald G. "Indicative Planning: Failure or Success?" Canadian Public Administration 14:2 (Summer, 1971): 204-216.

2672. Hull, W.H.N. "Captive or Victim: The Board of Broadcast Governors and Bernstein's Law, 1958-1968." Canadian Public Administration 26:4 (1983): 544-562. Ten year study of the relationship between the Board of Broadcast Governors and the industry it is supposed to regulate.

2673. Hurtubise, Rolland A. "La conception d'un mini-système intégré d'information pour la gestion." ["The Idea of an Integrated Information Mini-System for Administration."] Canadian Public Administration 16:2 (Summer, 1973): 267-283.

2674. Irvine, A.G. "The Delegation of Authority to Crown Corporations." Canadian Public Administration 14:4 (Winter, 1971): 556-579.

2675. Islam, N., and Paquet, M. "Les étudiants et la fonction publique: une étude des perceptions, des valeurs professionnelles et de l'attrait comparatif." ["Students and Public Administration: A Study of Perceptions, Professional Values, and Comparative Attraction."] Canadian Public Administration 18:1 (1975): 38-54.

2676. Jacques, Jocelyn, and Ryan, Edward J. "Does Management by Objectives Stifle Organizational Innovation in the Public Sector?" Canadian Public Administration 21:1 (Spring, 1978): 16-25.

2677. Jaffary, Karl D. "The Role of the State in a Technological Society." Canadian Public Administration 15:3 (Fall, 1972): 428-441.

2678. Johnson, A.W. "Education and the Development of Senior Executives." Canadian Public Administration 15:4 (Winter, 1972): 539-557.

2679. Johnston, John. "Public Servants and Private Contractors: Managing the Mixed Service Delivery System." Canadian Public Administration 29:4 (1986): 549-553.

2680. Jones, J.C.H. "The Bureaucracy and Public Policy: Canadian Merger Policy and the Combines Branch, 1960-71." Canadian Public Administration 18:2 (1975): 269-296.

2681. Julien, J., and Trudel, D. "Bilan de la recherche sur l'administration publique québécoise." ["Statement of Research on Quebec Public Administration."] Recherches Sociographiques 16:3 (1975): 413-438.

2682. Kee, Herbert W. "Incentives and Rewards in the Public Sector." Canadian Public Administration 29:4 (1986): 545-548.

2683. Kernaghan, Kenneth. "Canadian Public Administration: Progress and Prospects." Canadian Public Administration 25:4 (1982): 444-470.

2684. Kernaghan, Kenneth. "Changing Concepts of Power and Responsibility in the Canadian Public Service." Canadian Public Administration 21:3 (1978): 389-406.

2685. Kernaghan, Kenneth. "Codes of Ethics and Administrative Responsibility." Canadian Public Administration 17:4 (1974): 527-541.

2686. Kernaghan, Kenneth. "The Conscience of the Bureaucrat: Accomplice or Constraint?" Canadian Public Administration 27:4 (1984): 576-591.

2687. Kernaghan, Kenneth. "The Ethical Conduct of Canadian Public Servants." Optimum 4:3 (1973): 5-18. Primary emphasis on the federal level of government.

2688. Kernaghan, Kenneth. "Political Rights and Political Neutrality: Finding the Balance Point." Canadian Public Administration 29:4 (1986): 639-652.

2689. No entry

2690. Kernaghan, Kenneth. "Representative Bureaucracy: The Canadian Perspective." Canadian Public Administration 21:4 (1978): 489-512.

2691. Kernaghan, Kenneth. "Responsible Public Bureaucracy: A Rationale and a Framework for Analysis." Canadian Public Administration 16:4 (Winter, 1973): 572-603.

2692. Kernaghan, Kenneth. "The Statement of Principles of the Institute of Public Administration of Canada: The Rationale for Its Development and Content." Canadian Public Administration 30:3 (1987): 331-351.

2693. Kernaghan, Kenneth, and Kuruvilla, P.K. "Merit and Motivation: Public Personnel Management in Canada." Canadian Public Administration 25:4 (1982): 696-713.

2694. King, Alexander. "Change and Uncertainty: The Challenge to the Administration." Canadian Public Administration 21:4 (1978): 2-22.

2695. Kingsley, Jean-Pierre. "Conflict of Interest: A Modern Antidote." Canadian Public Administration 29:4 (1986): 585-592.

2696. Kuruvilla, P.K. "Administrative Culture in Canada: Some Perspectives." Canadian Public Administration 16:2 (1973): 284-297.

2697. Kuruvilla, P.K. "The Career Concept in the Canadian Public Service." International Review of Administrative Sciences 39:1 (1973): 49-55. Examines the extent to which the career concept has been present at the higher levels of the Canadian public service.

2698. Kuruvilla, P.K. "Collective Bargaining in the Canadian Public Service." Philippine Journal of Public Administration 18:4 (1974): 279-296. Development of the right of Canadian public servants to collective bargaining, with suggestions for future changes.

2699. Kuruvilla, P.K. "Language Training in the Canadian Public Service: Some Perspectives and Problems." Indian Journal of Public Administration 23:2 (1977): 283-297. Costs and effectiveness of programs to promote bilingualism in the federal civil service.

2700. Kuruvilla, P.K. "The Problem of Bilingualism in the Canadian Public Service." Res Publica 14:4 (1972): 785-802. Difficulties involved when an administrative apparatus must adapt itself to operating in two languages. Includes data on degree of bilingualism in various areas of the civil service.

2701. Kuruvilla, P.K. "The Problem of Secrecy in Canadian Public Administration: Some Perspectives." Indian Journal of Public Administration 25:4 (1979): 1036-1054. Analysis of Governmental abuse of the concept of secrecy and the pattern and value of classification of documents, with discussion of steps toward greater freedom of information.

2702. Kuruvilla, P.K. "Public Service Recruitment in Canada: Some Perspectives and Problems." Harvard Law Review 26:1 (1980): 62-90.

2703. Kuruvilla, P.K. "Representation of Women in the Public Service: The Canadian Experience." <u>Indian Journal of Public Administration</u> 29:1 (1983): 97-113. Discusses the historical background of the problem, difficulties in reaising representation of women, attitudinal difficulties, and impediments due to the merit system.

2704. Kuruvilla, P.K. "Training and Development in Public Service: The Canadian Experience." <u>Indian Journal of Public Administration</u> 26:3 (1980): 814-826. Describes the structures involved in the training and development of the Canadian public service.

2705. Laberge, Edouard P. "Collective Bargaining in the Public Service of Canada." <u>International Review of Administrative Sciences</u> 36:3 (1970): 227-233. Discussion of the "Public Service Staff Relations Act, 1967," and its potential impact upon collective bargaining in the public service.

2706. Lacampagne, Suzanne. "The Public Sector Right to Strike in Canada and the United States: A Comparative Analysis." <u>Boston College International and Comparative Law Review</u> 6:2 (1983): 509-532. Examines the right to strike in Canada, especially at the federal level, and contrasts the American policy of not permitting federal, and some state, employees the right to strike. Focuses upon the Canadian Public Service Staff Relations Act, as well as Canadian Government's actions during the postal workers' strike of 1968, and compares the latter to the 1980 strike by the Professional Air Traffic Controllers Organization in the United States.

2707. LaFramboise, H.L. "Administrative Reform in the Federal Public Service: Signs of a Saturation Psychosis." <u>Canadian Public Administration</u> 14:3 (1971): 303-325.

2708. LaFramboise, H.L. "Conscience and Conformity: The Uncomfortable Bedfellows of Accountability." <u>Canadian Public Administration</u> 26:3 (1983): 325-343. Study of Canadian federal bureaucracy and how the emphasis on conformity damaged the role of discretion in the value system of the federal civil service.

2709. LaFramboise, H.L. "The Future of Public Administration in Canada." <u>Canadian Public Administration</u> 25:4 (1982): 507-519.

2710. LaFramboise, H.L. "The Responsibilities of a Senior Public Servant: Organization, Profession and Career." <u>Canadian Public Administration</u> 27:4 (1984): 592-600.

2711. Lahey, Jim, and Gratias, Alan. "Accountability Through Evaluation: A Case Study." Optimum 9:4 (1978): 55-63. Case study of the Indian Arts and Crafts program and how an evaluation helped strengthen the Department of Indian Affairs.

2712. Langford, John W. "The Identification and Classification of Federal Public Corporations: A Preface to Regime Building." Canadian Public Administration 23:1 (1980): 76-104.

2713. Langford, John W. "Public Corporations in the 1980s: Moving From Rhetoric to Analysis." Canadian Public Administration 25:4 (1982): 619-637.

2714. Langford, John W. "The Question of Quangos: Quasi-Public Service Agencies in British Columbia." Canadian Public Administration 26:4 (1983): 563-576. Examines the use of private organizations as vehicles for delivering social policy to the public.

2715. Langford, John W. "Responsibility in the Senior Public Service: Marching to Several Drummers." Canadian Public Administration 27:4 (1984): 513-521.

2716. Langford, John W., and Huffman, Kenneth. "Fear and Ferment: Public Sector Management Today: Introduction." Canadian Public Administration 29:4 (1986): 511-527.

2717. Leclair, François. "D'un pouvoir responsable pour l'administrateur public." ["On Responsible Power for the Public Administrator."] Canadian Public Administration 21:3 (Fall, 1978): 418-440.

2718. Leger, Jacques. "Le Controleur Ministeriel." ["The Ministerial Controller."] Optimum 14:1 (1983): 43-51. Describes the ideas behind the creation of the Office of the Ministerial Comptroller.

2719. Leger, Paul. "A New Approach to Management Philosophy: Implications for Canadian Public Administration." Canadian Public Administration 26:3 (1983): 462-488.

2720. Leger, Paul. "A Note on Responsibility and the Senior Public Service." Canadian Public Administration 27:4 (1984): 640-641.

2721. Lemelin, Claude. "Les contrôles doivent procéder de la finalité du secteur public." ["Controls Should Precede Finality in the Public Sector."] Canadian Public Administration 19:1 (Spring, 1976): 41-50.

2722. Lemieux, Vincent. "L'information administrative au Québec: faits et interprétations." ["Administrative Information in Quebec: Facts and Interpretations."] Canadian Public Administration 18:3 (1975): 409-427.

2723. Lemire, Jean-Marc, and Rehill, Dave. "Model of a Social Research Function for Social Programming Organizations." Canadian Public Administration 17:1 (Spring, 1974): 142-152.

2724. Levin, Benjamin. "Squaring a Circle: Strategic Planning in Government." Canadian Public Administration 28:4 (Winter, 1985): 600-605.

2725. Love, J.D. "Personnel Reorganization in the Canadian Public Service: Some Observations on the Past." Canadian Public Administration 22:3 (1979): 402-414.

2726. McCallum, Sandra K. "Personal Liability of Public Servants: An Anachronism." Canadian Public Administration 27:4 (1984): 611-616.

2727. MacDonald, Bruce. "Information Management in the Public Service: Summary of Discussions." Canadian Public Administration 29:1 (1986): 1-34.

2728. MacDonald, Bruce, and Guruprasad, G. "Organizational Change for Better Information Management." Canadian Public Administration 29:1 (1986): 78-94.

2729. MacDonald, H.I. "Evolving Patterns of Government Organization." Queen's Quarterly 83:3 (1976): 454-463. A discussion of problems that face Ontario public administrators.

2730. McKie, Craig. "American Managers in Canada: A Comparative Profile." International Journal of Comparative Sociology 18:1-2 (1977): 44-62.

2731. McLeod, T.H. "The Special National Seminar on Financial Management and Accountability: An Appraisal." Canadian Public Administration 23:1 (Spring, 1980): 105-134.

2732. McQueen, Jennifer. "Integrating Human Resource Planning with Strategic Planning." Canadian Public Administration 27:1 (1984): 1-13.

2733. Mallory, J.R. "The Lambert Report: Central Roles and Responsibilities." Canadian Public Administration 22:4 (1979): 517-529.

2734. Mann, Bruce. "The Federal Information Coordinator as Meat in the Sandwich." Canadian Public Administration 29:4 (1986): 579-582.

2735. Mansbridge, Stanley H. "The Lambert Report: Recommendations to Departments." Canadian Public Administration 22:4 (1979): 530-540.

2736. Martin, Louis. "Contrôle de la qualité dans l'information pour la prise de décision." ["Quality Control of Information for Decision-Making."] Canadian Public Administration 29:1 (1986): 35-44.

2737. Meisel, John. "Citizen Demands and Government Response." Canadian Public Policy 2:4 (Autumn, 1976): 564-571.

2738. Mercier, Jean. "`Le phénomène bureaucratique' et le Canada français: Quelques données empiriques et leur interprétation." ["`The Bureaucratic Phenomenon' and French Canada: Some Empirical Themes and Their Interpretation."] Canadian Journal of Political Science 18:1 (1985): 31-56.

2739. Mercier, Jean. "`Le phénomène bureaucratique' et le Canada français: une réponse au professeur Bakvais." ["`The Bureaucratic Phenomenon' and French Canada: A Response to Professor Bakvais."] Canadian Public Administration 22:3 (1979): 453-467.

2740. Meredith, Harry, and Martin, Joe. "Management Consultants in the Public Sector." Canadian Public Administration 13:4 (1970): 383-395.

2741. Milligan, Frank. "The Canada Council as a Public Body." Canadian Public Administration 22:2 (1979): 269-289.

2742. Morley, D. "The Career Assignment Program." Canadian Public Administration 14:1 (Spring, 1971): 100-111.

2743. Morley, J. Terrence. "The Justice Development Commission: Overcoming Bureaucratic Resistance to Innovative Policy-Making." Canadian Public Administration 19:1 (Spring, 1976): 121-139.

2744. Morton, F.L, and Pal, Leslie A "The Impact of the Charter of Rights on Public Administration." Canadian Public Administration 28:2 (1985): 221-243. The principal change in the practice of Canadian public administration of the new Charter of Rights will be that jdges will have the final say on many issues formerly controlled by other administrators.

2745. Neilson, William A.W. "Service at the Pleasure of the Crown: The Law of Dismissal of Senior Public Servants." Canadian Public Administration 27:4 (1984): 556-575.

2746. Nicholson, Oliver. "Case Study/Quebec: The C-M Plan and How It Grew." Public Management 52:10 (1970): 10-12. Discussion of how the council-manager form of government works in Quebec municipalities.

2747. Nottage, Raymond. "Canadian and British Public Administration: Thoughts on a Brief Visit too Ottawa and Toronto." Canadian Public Administration 15:1 (Spring, 1972): 163-166.

2748. Ola, R.O.F. "Two Commonwealth Watchdogs: A Comparative Study of the Evolution and Position of the Auditors-General of Nigeria and Canada." International Review of Administrative Sciences 45:1 (1979): 35-40. Examines the evolution of the office of Auditor-General in two stages of development, Nigeria and Canada, "the former still struggling to accommodate an administrative culture" and the latter having accepted it.

2749. Ostry, Bernard. "Making Deals: The Public Official as Politician." Canadian Public Administration 29:4 (1986): 674-681.

2750. O'Sullivan, James, and Galimberti, Joseph. "The Institute of Public Administration of Canada." Canadian Public Administration 17:1 (Spring, 1974): 1-16.

2751. Ouellette, Y. "La responsabilité civile personnelle du fonctionnaire." ["The Civil Personnel Responsibility of the Civil Servant."] Canadian Public Administration 18:1 (1975): 1-16.

2752. Paquet, Gilles. "An Agenda for Change in the Federal Public Service." Canadian Public Administration 28:2 (1985): 455-462.

2753. Paquin, Michel. "La rationalisation des politiques publiques: un état de la question." ["The Rationalization of Public Politics: A Statement of the Question."] Canadian Public Administration 20:2 (Summer, 1977): 305-316.

2754. Paquin, Michel, and Hurtubise, Rolland. "L'utilisation de la méthode des cas et des jeux de simulation dans l'enseignement de l'administration publique." ["The Use of the Case Method and of Simulation Games in the Instruction of Public Administration."] Canadian Public Administration 17:2 (Summer, 1974): 242-258.

2755. Parenteau, Roland. "Une nouvelle approche dans la formation des administrateurs publics: l'École nationale d'administration publique." ["A New Approach in the Formation of Public Administrators: The National School of Public Administration."] Canadian Public Administration 15:3 (Fall, 1972): 465-480.

2756. Picard, Laurent. "Canada: Strategy in a Modern Society," La Revue Administrative 24 (1971): 210-215.

2757. Picard, Laurent. "La Vie Administrative Canadienne: L'Administration publique au Canada." ["Canadian Administrative Life: Public Administration in Canada."] La Revue Administrative 24:139 (1971): 77-79.

2758. Pickersgill, J.W. "Bureaucrats and Politicians." Canadian Public Administration 15:3 (1972): 418-427.

2759. Pickersgill, J.W. "Responsible Government in a Federal State," Canadian Public Administration 15:4 (1972): 520-528.

2760. Pitfield, Michael. "The Discipline and the Profession of Public Administration: A Practitioner's Perspective." Canadian Public Administration 25:4 (1982): 484-495.

2761. Plouffe, Jean-Pierre. "International Arrangements Entered into by Canadian Departments and Agencies." Canadian Yearbook of International Law 21 (1983): 176-216.

2762. Presthus, Robert, and Monopoli, William . "Bureaucracy in the United States and Canada: Social, Attitudinal, and Behavioral Variables." International Journal of Comparative Sociology 18:1-2 (1977): 176-204.

2763. Prost, R. "Knowledge and Action: Or the Two Contrary Aspects of Governmental Reform." Canadian Journal of Political Science 10:1 (1977): 43-63.

2764. Rawson, Bruce. "The Responsibilities of the Public Servant to the Public: Accessibility, Fairness, and Efficiency." Canadian Public Administration 27:4 (1984): 601-610.

2765. Reddy, V. Madan Mohan. "Role of Higher Civil Servants in Canada and Pakistan: A Comparative Study of Two Commonwealth Countries." Indian Journal of Public Administration 22:2 (1976): 155-173. Shows how bureaucracies based on the same British model vary widely in their roles in their respective governments.

2766. Relyea, Harold. "The Provisions of Government Information: The Federal Freedom of Information Act Experience." Canadian Public Administration 20:2 (Summer, 1977): 317-341.

2767. Rich, Harvey. "The Canadian Case for a Representative Bureaucracy." Political Science 27:1-2 (1975): 97-110. Describes the concept of "representativeness" as it might be applied to a bureaucracy and how that is both relevant and important in the Canadian case.

2768. Rich, Harvey. "Career Patterns and Role Conceptions of Higher Civil Servants in Ontario, Canada." Indian Journal of Public Administration 21:4 (1975): 711-726. Relationship between role conceptions of senior civil servants in Ontario and their career patterns, focusing upon career profiles, interagency mobility, and role conceptions of actors involved.

2769. Rich, Harvey. "From a Study of Higher Civil Servants in Ontario." Canadian Public Administration 17:2 (1974): 328-334.

2770. Rich, Harvey. "Higher Civil Servants and the Political Process: Ontario, Canada." Administration 23:2 (1975): 143-149. Staffing the senior public service and the degree of politics involved in the bureaucracy.

2771. Rich, Harvey. "Higher Civil Servants in Ontario, Canada: An Administrative elite in Comparative Perspective." International Review of Administrative Sciences 41:1 (1975): 67-74. Compares socio-economi background and recruitment data of Ontario civil servants with American, French, British, and German data.

2772. Rivet, J. "Administration publique et communication civique: le cas du Canada." ["Public Administration and Civic Communication: The Canadian Case."] International Review of Administrative Sciences 50:1 (1984): 10-16. The creation of office of Ombudsman in 1968 made clear that new steps in civic communication were needed.

2773. Robinson, Ivan "Managing Retrenchment in a Public Service Organization." Canadian Public Administration 28:4 (1985): 513-530.

2774. Rogers, Harry. "Management Control in the Public Service." Optimum 9:3 (1978): 14-28. The need to increase the speed of change in financial management and control isn't easy, because of difficulties in establishing control techniques and measurement of results.

2775. Rogers, H.G. "Comptrollership in Departments and Agencies of the Federal Government." Optimum 14:3 (1983): 5-19. The Controller General of Canada discusses the evolution of the concept of the comptroller.

2776. Rogers, H.G., Ulrick, M.A., and Traversy, K.L. "Evaluation in Practice: The State of the Art in Canadian Governments." Canadian Public Administration 24:3 (1981): 371-386.

2777. No entry

2778. Rudnick, Johan. "ATI [Access to Information Act] -- Access and the Bureaucratic Milieu." Optimum 13:2 (1982): 49-56.

2779. Russell, Terry. "Challenges and Promises of Technological Innovations: An Executive View." Canadian Public Administration 29:1 (1986): 61-77.

2780. Ryan, Claude. "[Can Governments Govern?] Un cas pertinent: le Quebec." ["A Pertinent Case: Quebec."] Canadian Public Policy 2:4 (Autumn, 1976): 587-594.

2781. Santos, Conrado. "A Theory of Bureaucratic Authority." Canadian Public Administration 21:2 (Summer, 1978): 243-267.

2782. Savoie, Donald. "The General Development Agreement Approach and the Bureaucratization of Provincial Governments in the Atlantic Provinces." Canadian Public Administration 24:1 (1981): 116-132.

2783. Savoie, Donald. "Government Decentralization: A Review of Some Management Considerations." Canadian Public Administration 28:3 (Fall, 1985): 440-446.

2784. Schultz, Richard. "Regulation and Public Administration." Canadian Public Administration 25:4 (1982): 638-652.

2785. Segsworth, R.V. "P.P.B.S. and Policy Analysis: The Canadian Experience," International Review of Administrative Sciences 38:4 (1972): 419-425. Evaluation of the "Planning-Programming-Budgeting System" as an effective bureaucratic tool in Canada.

2786. Sharma, G.B. "The Federal Privacy Commissioner of Canada: Defender of the Peoples' Privacy." Indian Journal of Public Administration 25:4 (1979): 1055-1081. Discusses privacy legislation in Canada in general, and the Canadian Human Rights Act in particular, with relation to the right to privacy.

2787. Sharma, G.B. "The Office of the Ombudsman in Nova Scotia Province: A Conceptual Empirical Analysis." Indian Journal of Public Administration 24:4 (1978): 1100-1129. Review of the development of the office of ombudsman, and its popularity, followed by a discussion of the office of ombudsman in Nova Scotia.

2788. Simard, Jean-Jacques. "The Long March of the Technocrats." Recherches sociographiques 18:1 (1977): 93-132.

2789. Snell, James G. "The Deputy Head in the Canadian Bureaucracy: A Case Study of the Registrar of the Supreme Court of Canada." Canadian Public Administration 24:2 (1981): 301-334.

2790. Strick, J.C. "Recent Developments in Canadian Financial Administration." Public Administration 48 (1970): 69-85.

2791. Sutherland, Sharon. "On the Audit Trail of the Auditor General: Parliament's Servant, 1973-1980." Canadian Public Administration 23:4 (1980): 616-644.

2792. Sutherland, Sharon. "Public Employment in Canada." Canadian Public Administration 30:1 (1987): 110-117.

2793. Swan, H. F. "Personnel Induced Frustration: An Instrument for the Selection of Senior Executives." Canadian Public Administration 14:4 (Winter, 1971): 621-636.

2794. Szabo, D. "Loi et ordre: Perspectives théorique et quelques implications pratiques." ["Law and Order: Theoretical Perspectives and Some Practical Implications."] Canadian Public Administration 13:4 (1970): 360-369.

2795. Tardi, Gregory. "The Appointment of Federal Regulatory Commissioners: A Case Study of the CRTC." Canadian Public Administration 24:4 (1981): 587-595.

2796. Taylor, Maureen, and Filmer, Alan. "Moonlighting: The Practical Problems." Canadian Public Administration 29:4 (1986): 593-597.

2797. Tennyson, Brian D. "Mackenzie King and Patronage in the Public Service: An Historical Footnote." Journal of Canadian Studies 6:1 (1971): 56-60.

2798. Théberge, Ghislain. "Relations, politico administratives en période de décroissance." ["Politico-Administrative Relations in a Period of Cutbacks."] Canadian Public Administration 28:3 (1985): 447-454.

2799. Thomas, Paul. "The Lambert Report: Parliament and Accountability." Canadian Public Administration 22:4 (1979): 557-571.

2800. Thomas, Paul. "Public Administration and Expenditure Management." Canadian Public Administration 25:4 (1982): 674-695.

2801. Thomas, Paul. "Secrecy and Publicity in Canadian Government." Canadian Public Administration 19:1 (1976): 158-182.

2802. Tremblay, Arthur. "Le fonctionnaire à l'avant-garde ou à la remorque de l'évolution sociale?" ["The Administrator: At the Front or the Rear of Social Evolution?"] Canadian Public Administration 13:4 (1970): 316-323.

2803. Vaillancourt-Martin, Nicole. "La Loi 51 ou la difficulté de décentraliser l'administration publique." ["Law 51 or the Difficulty in Decentralizing Public Administration."] Canadian Public Administration 29:2 (1986): 304-311.

2804. Wallersteiner, Ulrika. "System Ergonomics: Enhancing the People-Technology Relationships in Offices." Canadian Public Administration 29:4 (1986): 566-567.

2805. Watson, Ian C. "Identifying and Reducing Manpower Imbalances in the Public Service of Canada." Public Personnel Management 3:4 (1974): 258-264.

2806. Whittington, M.S. "Territorial Bureaucracy: Trends in Public Administration in the Northwest Territories." Canadian Public Administration 27:2 (1984): 242-252.

2807. Williams, Colin H. "Official-Language Districts: `A Gesture of Faith in the Future of Canada'." Ethnic and Racial Studies 4:3 (1981): 334-347.

2808. Williams, Roger, and Bates, David. "Technical Decisions and Public Accountability." Canadian Public Administration 19:4 (Winter, 1976): 603-632.

2809. Wilson, Douglas. "Disability and Employment: A Guide for Managers in the Public Sector." Canadian Public Administration 29:4 (1986): 634-636.

2810. Wilson, H.T. "The Dismal Science of Organization Reconsidered." Canadian Public Administration 14:1 (Spring, 1971): 82-99.

2811. Wilson, V. Seymour. "The Influence of Organizational Theory in Canadian Public Administration." Canadian Public Administration 25:4 (1982): 545-563.

2812. Wilson, V. Seymour. "Mandarins and Kibitzers: Men in and Around the Trenches of Political Power in Ottawa." Canadian Public Administration 26:3 (1983): 446-461.

2813. Wilson, V. Seymour, and Mullins, Willard A. "Representative Bureaucracy: Linguistic/Ethnic Aspects in Canadian Public Policy." Canadian Public Administration 21:4 (1978): 513-538.

2814. Woodward, C.H.L. "Regionalization and the Classification of Government Responsibilities." Governmental Finance 4:2 (1975): 11-15. Description of a British Columbia program to deal with the problem of ever-increasing municipal bureaucracy.

2815. Wronski, W. "The Public Servant and Protest Groups." Canadian Public Administration 14:1 (Spring, 1971): 65-72.

2816. Yeomans, D.R. "Decentralization of Authority," *Canadian Public Administration* 12 (1969): 9-26.

2817. Young, Robert. "Reining in James: The Limits of the Task Force," *Canadian Public Administration* 24 (1981): 596-612.

2818. Zussman, David. "The Image of the Public Service in Canada." *Canadian Public Administration* 25:1 (1982): 63-80.

12
General Works on Foreign Policy

Books

2819. Barrett, Jane R., and Beaumont, Jane. _A Bibliography of Works on Canadian Foreign Relations, 1976-1980_. Toronto: Canadian Institute of International Affairs, 1982.

2820. Barrett, Jane R., Beaumont, Jane, and Broadhead, Lee-Anne. _A Bibliography of Works on Canadian Foreign Relations, 1981-1985_. Toronto: Canadian Institute of International Affairs, 1987.

2821. Blanchette, Arthur E., ed. _Canadian Foreign Policy, 1955-65: Selected Speeches and Documents_. Toronto: McClelland and Stewart, 1977. Items dealing with the United Nations, NATO, North American defense, Canadian-American relations, Commonwealth relations, the Far East, international economic policy, and the Canadian provinces and foreign policy.

2822. Blanchette, Arthur, ed. _Canadian Foreign Policy, 1966-1976: Selected Speeches and Documents_. Agincourt, Ontario: Gage Publishing, 1980. Items dealing with the United Nations, NATO, Canadian-American relations, the Far East, the Commonwealth, international economic policy, international development, the environment, the provinces and foreign policy, and the 1968-1970 review of Canadian foreign policy.

2823. Brewin, Andrew. _Foreign Policy for Canadians: Comments on the White Paper_. Toronto: Canadian Institute of International Affairs, 1970.

2824. Campbell, Allan, and Fretts, Gerald. _Canada in the World: Choosing a Role_. Regina, Saskatchewan: Weigl Educational Publishers, 1985. Examination of Canadian policies with other powers in terms of general foreign policy.

2825.   Canada; Department of External Affairs. Perspectives on World Affairs and Foreign Policy Issues: A Research Report for External Affairs Canada. Ottawa: External Affairs Canada, 1979.

2826.   Canada. Parliament. Special Joint Committee on Canada's International Relations. Independence and Internationalism: Report of the Special Joint Committee of the Senate and of the House of Commons on Canada's International Relations. Ottawa: Canadian Publishing Centre, Supply and Services Canada, 1986.

2827.   Chaney, Michael P., ed. Sources for the Study of Canadian-American Relations: Manuscripts at the University of Vermont Library. Burlington, VT: University of Vermont, Bailey/Howe Library, 1986.

2828.   Dewitt, David, and Kirton, John. Canada as a Principal Power: A Study in Foreign Policy and International Relations. Toronto: John Wiley, 1983. General discussion of Canadian foreign policy, theory, major doctrines and decisions, and activities, with several detailed case studies covering immigration policy, energy policy, space policy, and Canada's policy toward the Middle East.

2829.   Dobell, Peter C. Canada's Search for New Roles: Foreign Policy in the Trudeau Era. London: Oxford University Press, 1972. Discussion of Canada's role in the world, its perceptions of external threats, and its relations with Europe.

2830.   Donneur, Andre. Politique Étrangere du Canada: Bibliographie 1976-1977. [Foreign Policy of Canada: Bibliography 1976-1977] Montréal: Université du Québec à Montréal, 1978.

2831.   Eayrs, James. In Defense of Canada: Volume IV; Growing up Allied. Toronto: University of Toronto Press, 1980. Series studies Canadian Defense and Foreign Policies since 1918; this volume focuses upon Canada's role in the creation of the North Atlantic Treaty Organization.

2832.   Evans, Allan Stewart, and Martinello, I. L. Canada's Century. Toronto: McGraw-Hill Ryerson, 1978.

2833.   Friedenberg, E.Z. Deference to Authority: The Case of Canada. White Plains, N.Y.: M.E. Sharpe, 1980.

2834.   Goldfarb Consultants. Perspectives on World Affairs and Foreign Policy Issues: A Research Report for External Affairs Canada. Ottawa: External Affairs Canada, 1979.

General Works on Foreign Policy   275

2835.   Gosselin, Guy, and Hervouet, Gerard. Les Politique
        étrangeres régionales du Canada: elements et
        materiaux. [Regional Foreign Relations of Canada:
        Elements and Materials.] Montréal, Québec: Les
        Presses de l'Université de Laval, 1983.

2836.   Gosselin, Guy. La politique étrangère du Canada:
        approches bilaterale et régionale. [The Foreign
        Policy of Canada: Bilateral and Regional
        Approaches] Laval: Centre québécois de rélations
        internationales, 1984.

2837.   Granatstein, J. L. Canada, 1957-1967: The Years
        of Uncertainty and Innovation. Toronto: McClelland
        and Stewart, 1986.

2838.   Granatstein, J.L., ed. Canadian Foreign Policy:
        Historical Readings. Toronto: Copp Clark Pitman,
        1986. Collection of articles dealing with govern-
        ment policy, and with academic interpretations of
        policy from the 1930's into the 1980's.

2839.   Halstead, John, and Jarvis, Michael. Canada's
        International Relations: The Report of a Working
        Group of the National Capital Branch. Toronto:
        Canadian Institute of International Affairs, 1986.

2840.   Hockin, Thomas A., et al. The Canadian Condominium:
        Domestic Issues and External Policy. Toronto:
        McClelland and Stewart, 1972. Essays discussing
        Canadian external relations and domestic develop-
        ments for the 1970's, including provincial power,
        Quebec's special demands, economic patterns, and
        Canadian-American trade and economic relations.

2841.   Keating, Tom, and Munton, Don, eds. The Provinces
        and Canadian Foreign Policy. Toronto: Canadian
        Institute of International Affairs, 1985. Essays on
        foreign policy activities of the provinces, includ-
        ing trade policy, energy policy, federalism and for-
        eign policy, environmental relations, fisheries and
        boundaries, and comparative perspectives on feder-
        alism and foreign policy.

2842.   Lyon, Peyton V., and Tomlin, Brian W. Canada as an
        International Actor. Toronto: Macmillan of Canada,
        1979. Contemporary review of Canada's role in the
        international community, its foreign policy objec-
        tives, and its relations with the United States, the
        third world, and international organizations.

2843.   Matthews, Geoffrey J., and Morrow, Robert Jr.
        Canada and the World: An Atlas Resource. Scar-
        borough, Ontario: Prentice-Hall of Canada, 1985.
        Wide range of maps and diagrams.

2844.   Maxwell, Judith, ed. A Time For Realism. Montreal:
        C. D. Howe Research Institute, 1978.

2845. Munton, Don, ed. Groups and Governments in Canadian Foreign Policy. Toronto: Canadian Institute of International Affairs, 1985.

2846. Nossal, Kim Richard, ed. An Acceptance of Paradox. Toronto: Canadian Institute of International Affairs, 1982. Essays focusing upon the maturation and practice of Canadian diplomacy.

2847. Ollivant, Simon. Canada: How Powerful an Ally? London: Institute for the Study of Conflict, 1984.

2848. Page, Donald M. A Bibliography of Works on Canadian Foreign Relations, 1971-1975. Toronto: Canadian Institute of International Affairs, 1977.

2849. Painchaud, Paul. Le Canada et le Québec sur la scène internationale. [Canada and Quebec on the International Scene] Québec: Centre québécois de rélations internationales, Faculté des sciences sociales, Université Laval: diffusé par les Presses de l'Université du Québec, 1977. Discussion of all aspects of the Canadian-Quebec relationship in international relations, including examination of federalism, general Canadian foreign policy, the role of provinces, monetary policy, cultural and scientific relations. A second section focuses on international relations including Canadian-American, Canadian-European, Canadian-Pacific, and Canadian-Middle East relations. A final section focuses on Quebec's relations with France, the United States, and other international actors.

2850. Riddell-Dixon, Elizabeth. The Domestic Mosaic: Domestic Groups and Canadian Foreign Policy. Toronto: Canadian Institute of International Affairs, 1985.

2851. Rotstein, A., and Lax, G., eds. Getting It Back: A Program for Canadian Independence. Toronto: Clarke, Irwin, 1974.

2852. Rugman, A.M. Multinationalism in Canada: Theory, Performance, and Economic Impact. Boston: Martinus Nijhoff, 1980.

2853. Stacey, C. P. Canada and the Age of Conflict: A History of Canadian External Policies. Toronto: Macmillan of Canada, 1977. Extremely comprehensive history of Canadian external relations.

2854. Stairs, Denis, and Winham, Gilbert, eds. Selected Problems in Formulating Foreign Economic Policy. Toronto: University of Toronto Press, 1985. Discussion of bureaucratic politics, the nature of the foreign service, and the defense and procurement practice in Canada and how they affect Canadian foreign economic policy.

General Works on Foreign Policy   277

2855. Thomson, Dale, and Swanson, Roger. <u>Canadian Foreign Policy: Options and Perspectives</u>. Toronto: McGraw-Hill Ryerson, 1971. Discusses sources of Canadian foreign policy, and Canadian relations with Europe, the Third World, the Pacific, and the United States.

2856. Thordarson, Bruce. <u>Trudeau and Foreign Policy</u>. Toronto: Oxford University Press, 1972. Study of several of Trudeau's major foreign policy decisions and how they were reached.

2857. Tomlin, Brian, ed. <u>Canada's Foreign Policy: Analysis and Trends</u>. Toronto: Methuen, 1978. Essays covering reasons for Canadian foreign policy, the "Third Option," and future policy alternatives.

2858. Tomlin, Brian, and Molot, Maureen, eds. <u>Canada Among Nations: 1984, A Time of Transition</u>. Toronto: Lorimer, 1985.

2859. Tucker, Michael. <u>Canadian Foreign Policy: Contemporary Issues and Themes</u>. Toronto: McGraw-Hill Ryerson, 1980.

2860. Turner, Carol. <u>Directory of Foreign Document Collections</u>. New York: American Library Association, 1985.

2861. Wyse, Peter. <u>Canadian Foreign Aid in the 1970's: An Organizational Audit</u>. Montreal: Centre for Developing-Area Studies, McGill University, 1983. After examining the degree to which foreign aid is in the Canadian interest, the book studies the domestic politics of foreign aid.

<u>Articles</u>

2862. Balthazar, Louis. "Approaches to Foreign Policy." <u>International Perspectives</u> (Special Issue, 1976): 18-22.

2863. Balthazar, Louis. "Le style canadien et la politique étrangère." ["Canadian Style and Foreign Policy."] <u>Politique étrangère</u> 38:2 (1973): 131-148. The experiences of English Canadians, American influence, and internationalism, have all combined to give Canada new perspectives on foreign policy.

2864. Bergeron, Gérard. "Dissenting on Canadian Foreign Policy." <u>International Perspectives</u> (November/December, 1975): 57-62.

2865. Black, J.B., and Blanchette, A.E. "Media Influence in the Conduct of Foreign Policy." <u>International Perspectives</u> (July/-August, 1974): 42-46.

2866. Bonenfant, Jean-Charles. "Les relations extérieures du Québec." ["Foreign Relations of Quebec"] Études internationales 2:1 (1971): 137-146. ; 2:2 (1971): 317-346.

2867. Bromke, Adam, and Nossal, Kim. "Canada: Foreign Policy Outlook after the Conservative Victory." World Today 40:11 (1984): 462-470.

2868. Carver, Humphrey. "A New Presence for External Affairs." International Perspectives (November-December, 1972): 48-50.

2869. Chapdelaine, Jean. "Esquisse d'une politique extérieure d'un Québec souverain - Genèse et prospective." ["Discourse on a Foreign Policy of a Sovereign Quebec: Basis and Prospective."] Études internationales 8:2 (1977): 342-355. What a sovereign Quebec's foreign policy might be, and its effect on Canadian-American relations.

2870. Chapin, P.H. "The Canadian Public and Foreign Policy." International Perspectives 1986 (January-February): 14-17.

2871. Cox, David. "Leadership Change and Innovation in Canadian Foreign Policy: The 1979 Progressive Conservative Government." International Journal 37:4 (1982): 555-583.

2872. Dobell, Peter C. "The Management of a Foreign Policy for Canadians." International Journal 26:1 (1971): 202-220.

2873. Dobell, Peter C. "La Politique extérieure canadienne." ["Canadian Foreign Policy."] Rivista di Studi politici internazionali 38:4 (1971): 585-600.

2874. Dobell, W. M. "Is External Affairs a Central Agency? A Question of Leadership Controls." International Perspectives (May-June-July-August, 1979): 8-12. Analysis of organization and role of External Affairs in the governmental hierarchy.

2875. Dobell, W. M. "Interdepartmental Management in External Affairs." Canadian Public Administration 21:1 (1978): 83-102.

2876. Dobell, W.M. "The Ministry of External Affairs: A Central Agency?" International Perspectives (May-August, 1979): 22-26.

2877. Donneur, André. "Étude bibliographique: La politique étrangère canadienne: De l'internationalisme au réalisme." ["Bibliographic Essay: Canadian Foreign Policy: From Internationalism to Realism."] Études internationales 15:1 (1984): 213-221. Book review essay on Canadian foreign policy.

2878. Donneur, André, et al. "L'évaluation des politiques en rélations internationales: Le cas de la coopération franco-québecoise en éducation." ["The evaluation of Policies in International Relations: The Case of Cooperation Between France and Quebec in the Field of Education."] Études internationales 14:2 (1983): 237-254.

2879. Dorscht, Axel, Keating, Tom, Legare, Gregg, and Rious, Jean-François. "Canada's International Role and `Realism'." International Perspectives 1986 (September-October): 6-10.

2880. Doxey, Margaret. "Canada's International Connections: The Canadian Foreign Policy Review in Review." Year Book of World Affairs 32 (1978): 43-63. Criticisms of Canadian foreign policy.

2881. Fleurot, J. "Ambitions et limits de la politique extérieure du Canada." ["Ambitions and Limits of Foreign Politics of Canada."] Défense Nationale (July, 1974): 85-93. Discusses major historical themes of Canadian relations with the United States and Canada's plans to increase ties with the European Economic Community.

2882. Fox, Annette Baker, and Fox, William T. "Domestic Capabilities and Canadian Foreign Policy." International Journal 39:1 (1983-1984): 23-46.

2883. Gilpin, R. "Will Canada Last?" Foreign Policy 10 (1973): 117-131.

2884. Gow, James I. "Les Québécois, la guerre, et la paix, 1945-1960." ["Quebec and External Affairs, 1945-1960."] Canadian Journal of Political Science 3:1 (1970): 88-122. Description and analysis of opinions of French-speaking residents of Quebec on questions related to war and peace during the 1945-1960 period.

2885. Graham, John W. "Canadian Studies Abroad." International Perspectives (September-October, 1976): 38-42.

2886. Head, Ivan L. "The Foreign Policy of the New Canada." Foreign Affairs 50:2 (1972): 237-252.

2887. Held, Robert. "Canadian Foreign Policy - An Outsider's View." International Journal 33:2 (1978): 448-456.

2888. Holmes, J.W. "Les institutions internationals et la politique extérieure." ["International Institutions and Foreign Politics."] Études Internationales 2 (1970): 20-40.

2889. Jacomy-Millette, Annemarie. "The Federal State in Contemporary International Relations: The Case of Canada." _Canadian Yearbook of International Law_ 14 (1976): 3-56.

2890. Jewett, Pauline. "Toward an Independent Foreign Policy." _International Perspectives_ (November-December, 1985): 9-10. The New Democratic Party foreign policy would move Canada further away from United States control to greater independence.

2891. Johannson, P.R. "Provincial International Activities." _International Journal_ 33:2 (1978): 357-378.

2892. Keenleyside, T.A. "The Generalist Versus the Specialist: The Department of External Affairs." _Canadian Public Administration_ 22:1 (1979): 51-71.

2893. Kirton, John. "Canadian Foreign Policy in the 1980s." _Current History_ 83:493 (1984): 193-196.

2894. Kirton, John. "Foreign Policy Decision-making in the Trudeau Government: Promise and Performance." _International Journal_ 33:2 (1978): 287-311.

2895. Kirton, John. "Realism and Reality in Canadian Foreign Policy." _International Perspectives_ 1987 (January-February): 3-9.

2896. Kirton, John, and Dimock, Blair. "Domestic Access to Government in the Canadian Foreign Policy Process, 1968-1982." _International Journal_ 39:1 (1983-1984): 68-98.

2897. Lande, Ellen Beth. "Quebec's International Personality." _Fletcher Forum_ 3:2 (1979): 22-45. Examines recent conduct of Quebec external affairs, and focuses on the question of how effective Quebec is in developing an international personality and furthering nationalist goals both at home and overseas.

2898. LeDuc, Lawrence, and Murray, J.A. "Attitudes Towards Foreign Policy." _International Perspectives_ (May-June, 1976): 38-41.

2899. Lyon, Peyton V. "The Canadian Perspective." _Proceedings of the Academy of Political Science_ 32:2 (1976): 14-26.

2900. Lyon, Peyton V. "New Directions in Canada's Foreign Policy." _Round Table_ 277 (1980): 28-32. Pessimistic assessment of the future of Canadian foreign policy under Flora MacDonald, given her inclination to virtually dismiss the "contractual link" as government foreign policy, and her downgrading of the Third Option, and her subsequent stressing of the need to intensify relations with the United States.

General Works on Foreign Policy   281

2901. MacEachen, Allan J. "Directions for Canadian Foreign Policy." International Perspectives (November/December, 1975): 62-66.

2902. MacGuigan, Mark. "Federalism and Canada's International Relations." Politique internationale 12 (1981): 189-200.

2903. MacLaren, Alasdair. "Reconciling Foreign and Defence Policies." International Perspectives (March/April, 1977): 22-26.

2904. McLaren, Robert. "Provincial Priorities and Foreign Affairs." International Perspectives (September/October, 1978): 28-30.

2905. Madar, Daniel. "Foreign Policy Objectives, Country Studies, and Planning Theory." Canadian Public Administration 23:3 (Fall, 1980): 380-399.

2906. Manor, F.S. "Canada's Crisis: The Causes." Foreign Policy 29 (1977-78): 43-55.

2907. Marchand, de Montigny. "Foreign Policy and Public Interest." International Perspectives (July-August, 1984): 6-9. Although foreign policy should generally reflect public opinion, Canadian public opinion is often not in agreement, and the government cannot permit this to lead to a state of inaction.

2908. Maybee, Jack. "Foreign Service Consolidation." International Perspectives (July-August, 1980): 17-20. The reorganization of the Canadian foreign service.

2909. Miller, A.J. "The Functional Principle in Canada's External Relations." International Journal 35:2 (1980): 309-328.

2910. Morin, Claude. "La politique extérieure du Québec." ["Foreign Policy of Quebec."] Études internationales 9:2 (1978): 281-289. Quebec's Minister of Intergovernmental Affairs explains the specific objectives of Quebec foreign policy, as well as its broad orientations.

2911. Munton, Donald J. "Les pussances secondaires et l'influence des attributs relationnels: le cas du Canada et de sa politique extérieure." ["Lesser Powers and the Influence of Relational Attributes: The Case of Canadian Foreign Policy Behavior."] Études internationales 10:3 (1979): 471-502. Examines foreign policy behavior of Canada as a lesser power, explaining Canadian foreign policy as a function of a number of attributes.

2912. Murray, J. Alex, and LeDuc, Lawrence. "Public Opinion and Foreign Policy Options in Canada." Public Opinion Quarterly 40:4 (1976-1977): 488-496.

2913. Newman, Peter. "The Thawing of Canada." The Atlantic Community Quarterly 9:2 (1971): 219-228. Canadian nationalism and anti-Americanism.

2914. Nossal, Kim. "Allison through the (Ottawa) Looking Glass: Bureaucratic Politics and Foreign Policy in a Parliamentary System." Canadian Public Administration 22:4 (1979): 610-626.

2915. Nossal, Kim. "Analyzing the Domestic Sources Of Canadian Foreign Policy." International Journal 39:1 (1983-1984): 1-22.

2916. O'Neil, Pierre. "Les relations extérieures du Canada." ["Foreign Relations of Canada."] Études internationales 2:1 (1971): 131-136.

2917. Osbaldesten, Gordon. "Reorganizing Canada's Department of External Affairs." International Journal 37:3 (1982): 453-466.

2918. Page, Donald. "Public Influence on Foreign Policy." International Perspectives (May/June, 1978): 21-25.

2919. Painchaud, Paul. "Le rôle international du Québec: possibilités et contraintes." ["The International Role of Quebec: Possibilities and Constraints."] Études internationales 8:2 (1977): 374-392. Speculates about Quebec foreign policy, given a range of premises about Quebec's role in a future Canadian federation.

2920. Pearson, G.A.H. "Order Out of Chaos? Some Reflections on Foreign Policy Planning in Canada." International Journal 32:4 (1977): 756-768.

2921. Pratt, Cranford. "Dominant Class Theory and Canadian Foreign Policy: The Case of the Counter-Consensus." International Journal 39:1 (1983-1984): 99-135.

2922. "Québec's Foreign Policy: An Interview with Claude Morin, Minister of Intergovernmental Affairs, Province of Québec." Fletcher Forum 4:1 (1980): 127-134. Morin attempt to define the future course of Quebec's foreign policy. This was written prior to the Sovereignty-Association referendum.

2923. Ranger, Robin. "Canadian Foreign Policy in an Era of Super-Power Détente." The World Today 28:12 (1972): 546-554.

2924. Regenstreif, Peter. "Canada's Foreign Policy." Current History 72:426 (1977): 150-153.

2925. Reuber, Grant L. "Canadian Independence in an Asymmetrical World Community: A National Riddle." International Journal 29:4 (1974): 535-556.

2926. Reuber, Grant L. "The Trade-Offs Among the Objectives of Canadian Foreign Aid." International Journal 25:1 (1969-1970): 129-141.

2927. Roche, Douglas. "Reflections on Canada's Foreign Policy During the 1980's." International Perspectives (May-August, 1979): 3-8.

2928. Roche, Douglas. "Towards a Foreign Policy for Canada in the 1980s." International Perspectives (May-June-July-August, 1979): 3-7.

2929. Rutan, Gérard F. "Provincial Participation in Canadian Foreign Relations." Journal of Interamerican Studies and World Affairs 13:2 (1971): 230-245. Role of provinces in international agreements.

2930. Sabourin, Louis. "L'influence des facteurs internes sur la politique étrangère canadienne." ["The Influence of Domestic Factors on Canadian Foreign Policy."] Études internationales 2 (1970): 41-63.

2931. Sabourin, Louis. "Quebec's International Competence." International Perspectives (March/April, 1977): 3-8.

2932. Smith, Arnold. "The New Department of External Affairs." International Perspectives (May-June, 1982): 13-14.

2933. No entry

2934. Soldatos, Panayotis. "Les données fondamentales du devenir de la politique étrangère canadienne: Essai de synthèse." ["The Basic Orientations of a Canadian Foreign Policy in the Making: An Essay of Synthesis."] Études internationales 14 (1983): 5-22.

2935. Soward, F.H. "The Descent From the Lonely Heights." International Journal 26:1 (1971): 194-201.

2936. Soward, F.H. "Inside a Canadian Triangle: The University, the CIIA, and the Department of External Affairs -- A Personal Record." International Journal 33:1 (1977-1978): 66-87.

2937. Stairs, Denis. "Responsible Government and Foreign Policy." International Perspectives (May/June, 1978): 26-29.

2938. Stairs, Denis. "Pierre Trudeau and the Politics of the Canadian Foreign Policy Review," Australian Outlook 26:3 (1972): 274-290. External changes and internal pressures on Canadian foreign policy.

2939. Stairs, Denis. "The Press and Foreign Policy in Canada." *International Journal* 31:2 (1976): 223-243.

2940. Stairs, Denis. "Public Opinion and External Affairs: Reflections on the Domestication of Canadian Foreign Policy." *International Journal* 33:1 (1977-1978): 128-149.

2941. Stairs, Denis. "Publics and Policy-Makers: The Domestic Environment of the Foreign Policy Community." *International Journal* 26:1 (1971): 221-248.

2942. Starnes, John. "Foreign Policy in the 'New' Quebec." *International Perspectives* (March-April, 1980): 3-6. Analysis of the foreign policy implications of the Quebec Government's White Paper "Quebec-Canada: A New Deal."

2943. Stethem, Nicholas. "Canada's Crisis: The Dangers." *Foreign Policy* 29 (1977-1978): 56-64.

2944. Strempel, Ulrich. "Canada's New External Relations Under Mulroney." *Aussenpolitik* 37:3 (1986): 239-252.

2945. Thakur, Ramesh. "Change and Continuity in Canadian Foreign Policy." *India Quarterly* 33:4 (1977): 401-418. Determinants of Canadian foreign policy, the Trudeau Doctrine, and relations with India.

2946. Thomson, Dale C. "Foreign Policy and Domestic Politics of Canada at the Present Time." *Revista de Politica internacional* 152 (1977): 119-126.

2947. Thordarson, Bruce. "Posture and Policy: Leadership in Canada's External Affairs." *International Journal* 31:4 (1976): 666-691.

2948. Tomlin, Brian W., et al. "Foreign Policies of Subordinate States in Asymmetrical Dyads." *Jerusalem Journal of International Relations* 5:4 (1981): 14-40. Analysis of the foreign policies that weak states use in dealing with powerful states.

2949. Torelli, M. "Les relations extérieures du Québec." ["Foreign Relations of Quebec."] *Annuaire français de Droit international* 16 (1970): 275-303.

2950. Vaugeois, Denis. "La coopération du Québec avec l'extérieur." ["Quebec's Cooperation With Foreign Powers."] *Études internationales* 5:2 (1974): 376-387.

2951. Von Riekhoff, Harold. "The Impact of Prime Minister Trudeau on Foreign Policy." *International Journal* 33:2 (1978): 267-286.

2952. Warden, William T. "The Foreign Policy of Canada." Pakistan Horizon 36:1 (1983): 13-27.

2953. Wilson, W.A. "Canadians View Foreign Affairs." International Perspectives (May/June, 1980): 11-14.

13
"High" Foreign Policy Issues: Traditional Diplomacy and National Security

Books

2954. American Bar Association. <u>Settlement of International Disputes Between Canada and the USA: Resolutions Adopted by the American Bar Association on 15 August 1979 and by the Canadian Bar Association on 30 August 1979, with Accompanying Reports and Recommendations</u>. Chicago: Section of International Law of the American Bar Association, 1979.

2955. Armstrong, Willis C., et al. <u>Canada and the United States</u>. Cambridge, Ma.: Ballinger, 1982. Discussion of several aspects of Canadian-American relations, including comparing federal structures, and examination of energy relations, investment relations, trade relations, environmental issue relations, defense relations, and the issue of Quebec.

2956. Aronsen, Lawrence, and Kitchen, Martin. <u>The Origins of the Cold War in Comparative Perspective: American, British, and Canadian Relations with the Soviet Union, 1941-48</u>. New York: St.Martin's, 1988.

2957. Azmi, M. Raziullah. <u>Pakistan-Canada Relations, 1947-1982: A Brief Survey</u>. Islamabad: Quiad-i-Azam University, 1982.

2958. Balawyder, Aloysius. <u>Canadian-Soviet Relations Between the World Wars</u>. Toronto: University of Toronto Press, 1972.

2959. Balawyder, Aloysius, ed. <u>Canadian-Soviet Relations, 1939 - 1980</u>. Oakville, Ont.: Mosaic Press, 1981. Articles highlighting the political history of the development and continuity of relations between Canada and the Soviet Union.

288   Contemporary Canadian Politics

2960. Bercuson, David J. _Canada and the Birth of Israel: A Study in Canadian Foreign Policy_. Toronto: University of Toronto Press, 1985. Argues that Canada was unenthusiastic in response to the Zionist efforts to involve Canada in the Palestine Question.

2961. Boardman, Robert, and Keeley, James, eds. _Nuclear Exports and World Politics: Policy and Regime_. New York: St. Martin's Press, 1983. Essays on nuclear policy. One chapter deals with Canada and international nuclear security.

2962. Boyd, Gavin, ed. _Region Building in the Pacific_. New York: Pergammon Press, 1982. One essay in this reader deals with Canadian and American perspectives on the subject.

2963. Bridle, Paul. _Canada and the International Commissions in Indochina, 1954-1972_. Toront: Canadian Institute of International Affairs, 1973.

2964. Bromke, Adam. _Canada's Response to the Polish Crisis_. Toronto: Canadian Institute of International Affairs, 1982.

2965. Burns, Eedson Louis Millard. _Defence in the Nuclear Age: An Introduction for Canadians_. Toronto: Clarke, Irwin, 1976. Discussion of national security from several different perspectives. Gives historical foundation, and then discusses Canadian membership in multi-national organizations such as NATO, peacekeeping, and arms control, among other topics.

2966. Byers, R.B., ed. _Canada and Western Security: The Search for New Options_. Toronto: Atlantic Council of Canada, 1982. Focuses upon the North Atlantic Alliance, and examines the degree to which Alliance responses are in Canada's best interests.

2967. Canada. Parliament. House of Commons. Standing Committee on External Affairs and National Defence. _Tenth Report of the Standing Committee on External Affairs and National Defence Respecting Maritime Forces_. Ottawa: Queen's Printer for Canada, 1970.

2968. Canada. Parliament. House of Commons. Standing Committee on External Affairs and National Defence. _Eleventh Report of the Standing Committee on External Affairs and National Defence Respecting Canada-U.S. Relations_. Ottawa: Queen's Printer for Canada, 1970.

2969. Collins, Ralph. _Jerusalem: The Canadian Experience_. Washington, D.C.: Middle East Institute, 1980. Analysis of Canadian foreign relations with Israel and Canada's position on the question of jurisdiction over Jerusalem.

2970. Egyed, Peter. _National Approaches to the Development of Economic Relations with the U.S.S.R. and China: Comparison of Recent Canadian and French Experience_. Ottawa: Institute of Soviet and East European Studies, Carleton University, 1981.

2971. Eustace, Marilyn D. _Canada's Participation in Political NATO_. Kingston, Ont.: Centre for International Relations, Queen's University, 1976.

2972. Griffiths, Franklyn. _A Northern Foreign Policy_. Toronto: Canadian Institute of International Affairs, 1979. Discussion of what Canada's foreign policy should be with regard to the Arctic Circle.

2973. Harbron, John D. _Canada Recognizes China: The Trudeau Round 1968-1973_. Toronto: Canadian Institute of International Affairs, 1974.

2974. Hillmer, Norman, and Stevenson, Garth, eds. _A Foremost Nation: Canadian Foreign Policy and a Changing World_. Toronto: McClelland and Stewart, 1977. Essays discussing Canada's relations with Europe, the United States, multinational corporations, the United Nations, Africa, Latin America, China, and Japan.

2975. Holmes, John Wendell. _The Better Part of Valour: Essays on Canadian Diplomacy_. Toronto: McClelland and Stewart, 1970. Essays on Canadian foreign policy in general, on international organizations, the Commonwealth, the Atlantic community, Canada and the United States, the Pacific arena, and the Western Hemisphere.

2976. Holmes, John Wendell. _Canada and the United States: Political and Security Issues_. Toronto: Canadian Institute of International Affairs, 1970.

2977. Holmes, John W. _Life With Uncle: The Canadian-American Relationship_. Toronto: University of Toronto Press, 1981. Discussion of the role of the United States in the world, and the implications that role has for Canada.

2978. Holmes, John Wendell. _The Shaping of Peace: Canada and the Search for World Order, 1943-1957_. Toronto: University of Toronto Press, 1979. Comprehensive political history of Canadian foreign relations in the post-World War Two era.

2979. Ichikawa, Akira, Ph.D. _The "Helpful Fixer": Canada's Persistent International Image_. Toronto: Canadian Institute of International Affairs, 1979.

2980. Innis, Hugh R., ed. _International Involvement_. Toronto: McGraw-Hill Ryerson, 1972.

2981. Ismael, Tareq, ed. Canadian-Arab Relations: Policy and Perspectives. Ottawa: Jerusalem International Publishing House, 1984.

2982. Jacomy-Millette, Anne-Marie. L'introduction et l'application des traités internationaux au Canada. [The Introduction and Application of International Treaties to Canada] Paris, Librairie générale de droit et de jurisprudence, 1971. Study of the treaty-making power in Canada, and how it has affected international, provincial, and municipal law in Canada as well as Canadian foreign relations.

2983. Kavic, Lorne J. Canada and the Pacific: Prospects and Challenges. Toronto: Canadian Institute of International Affairs, 1970.

2984. Kay, Zachariah. Canada and Palestine: The Politics of Noncommitment. Jerusalem: Israel Universities Press, 1978.

2985. Kohler, Gernot, Hakim, Antjie, and Bisci, Rosina. Arms Control and Disarmament: A Bibliography of Canadian Research, 1965-1980. Ottawa: Department of National Defense, 1981.

2986. Levant, Victor. Quiet Complicity: Canadian Involvement in the Vietnam War. Toronto: Between the Lines, 1986.

2987. Ludz, Peter. Dilemmas of the Atlantic Alliance: Two Germanys, Scandinavia, Canada, NATO and the EEC. New York: Praeger, 1975.

2988. Lyon, Peter, ed. Britain and Canada: Survey of a Changing Relationship. London: Cass, 1976. Essays of a political-historical nature of British-Canadian relations, from the time of World War I into the 1970's.

2989. Lyon, Peyton V., and Ismael, Tareq Y., eds. Canada and the Third World. Toronto: Macmillan of Canada, 1976.

2990. Massey, H.J. The Canadian Military. Toronto: Copp Clark, 1972.

2991. Massey, H.J. People or Planes. Toronto: Copp Clarke, 1972.

2992. Matthews, Robert O., and Pratt, Cranford, eds. Church and State: The Christian Churches and Canadian Foreign Policy. Toronto: Canadian Institute of International Affairs, 1982.

2993. Morton, Desmond. *Canada and War: A Military and Political History*. Toronto: Butterworths, 1981. Analysis of the relationship of Canada to war, attitudes of Canadians and Canadian government, and Canada's role in the contemporary Cold War era.

2994. Morton, Desmond. *A Peculiar Kind of Politics: Canada's Overseas Ministry in the First World War*. Toronto: University of Toronto Press, 1982.

2995. Oervik, Nils. *Our Neighbours to the East*. Kingston, Ont.: Centre for International Relations, Queen's University, 1979.

2996. Porter, Gerald. *In Retreat: The Canadian Forces in the Trudeau Years*. Ottawa: Deneau & Greenberg, 1978.

2997. Reford, Robert William, ed. *Lester Pearson's Diplomacy*. Toronto: Canadian Institute of International Affairs, 1974.

2998. Rosenblum, Simon. *Misguided Missiles: Canada, the Cruise, and "Star Wars"*. Toronto: Lorimer, 1985. Development of the Cruise missile and Canada's involvement both in the Cruise missile project.

2999. Shragge, Eric, Babin, Ronald, and Vaillancourt, Jean-Guy, eds. *Roots of Peace: The Movement Against Militarism in Canada*. Toronto: Between The Lines, 1986.

3000. Smith, Arnold. *Stitches in Time: The Commonwealth in World Politics*. General, 1981.

3001. Stein, Janice, and Dewitt, David, eds. *The Middle East at the Crossroads: Regional Forces and External Powers*. Oakville, Ont.: Mosaic Press, 1983.

3002. Stiles, John A. *Developing Canada's Relations Abroad*. Sackville, N.B.: Mt. Allison University, 1980. Study of Canadian relations with the United States, Europe, Pacific nations, Korea, Latin America, the Commonwealth Caribbean, and developing nations.

3003. Swanson, Roger F., ed. *Canadian-American Summit Diplomacy, 1923-1973: Selected Speeches and Documents*. Toronto: McClelland and Stewart, 1975. Organized by prime minister, with units on W.B. Bennett, Mackenzie King, Louis St. Laurent, John Diefenbaker, Lester Pearson, and Pierre Trudeau.

3004. Taylor, Charles. *Snow Job: Canada, the United States, and Vietnam: 1954 to 1973*. Toronto: Anansi, 1978. Discusses Canada's role in the Vietnam conflict and its relations with the United States during that period.

3005. Tennyson, Brian. <u>Canadian Relations with South Africa: A Diplomatic History</u>. Washington, D.C.: University Press of America, 1982.

3006. Warnock, J.W. <u>Partner to Behemoth</u>. Toronto: New Press, 1970. Study of Canadian military policy.

3007. Wiktor, Christian. <u>Canadian Treaty Calendar, 1928-1978</u>. London: Oceana Publications, 1983.

3008. Willoughby, William R. <u>The Joint Organizations of Canada and the United States</u>. Toronto: University of Toronto Press, 1979. Provides detailed descriptions of the major joint institutions in Canadian-American relations, including the International Joint Commission, the International Fisheries Commission, the International Boundary Commission, the Permanent Joint Board on Defense, and others.

3009. Zubrzycki, Jack. <u>Canadian Public Opinion and Government Policy Toward the Middle East</u>. Kingston, Ont.: Near East Cultural and Educational Foundation of Canada, 1986.

<u>Articles</u>

3010. Ali, Mehrunnisa. "Pakistan-Canada Relations." <u>Pakistan Horizon</u> 27:1 (1974): 77-82.

3011. Andrew, Arthur. "Canada and Asia: Evolving Awareness and Deepening Links." <u>Pacific Affairs</u> 45:3 (1972): 403-408.

3012. Andrew, A. J. "The Diplomat and the Manager." <u>International Journal</u> 30:1 (1974-1975): 45-56.

3013. Andrew, A. J. "Role of a Canadian Diplomat Abroad." <u>International Perspectives</u> (March/April, 1974): 54-58.

3014. April, Serge. "Examining the Right of Asylum." <u>International Perspectives</u> (May/June, 1974): 39-44.

3015. Arkin, William. "Canada -- Too Close for Comfort." <u>Bulletin of the Atomic Scientists</u> 42:3 (1986): 4-6.

3016. Atkey, Ronald. "The Role of the Provinces in International Affairs." <u>International Journal</u> 26:1 (1971): 249-273.

3017. Barrett, John, and Ross, Douglas. "The Air-Launched Cruise Missile and Canadian Arms Control Policy." <u>Canadian Public Policy</u> 11:4 (December, 1985): 711-730.

3018. Barton, W.H. "Canada on the Security Council." *International Perspectives* (May-August, 1979): 12-16.

3019. Beaton, L. "The Strategic and Political Issues Facing America, Britain, and Canada." *Atlantic Community Quarterly* 9:4 (1971): 476-492. Discussion of possible future challenges facing the three nations, and what they will have to do to maintain their traditional associations.

3020. Berry, G.R. "The West Indies in Canadian External Relations: Present Trends and Future Prospects." *Canadian Public Policy* 3:1 (Winter, 1977): 50-62.

3021. Bishop, Neil. "What Does the Future Hold for Canada-France Relations?" *International Perspectives* (January-February, 1979): 16-19 Review of relations between the two countries and speculation about future relationship.

3022. Bishop, Neil B. "Future of Canada-France Relations." *International Perspectives* (January/February, 1979): 16-18.

3023. Bothwell, Robert, and English, John. "The View from Inside Out: Canadian Diplomats and Their Public." *International Journal* 39:1 (1983-1984): 47-67.

3024. Bouvier, François. "Changing World Power Relationships: A Consensus Was too Easy." *International Perspectives* (July/August, 1973): 14-16.

3025. Bromke, Adam, and Nossal, Kim Richard. "Tensions in Canada's Foreign Policy." *Foreign Affairs* 62:2 (1983-1984): 335-353. Tensions in Canada's foreign policy with respect to the two superpowers.

3026. Bromke, Adam, and Nossal, Kim Richard. "Trudeau Rides the 'Third Rail'." *International Perspectives* (March-April, 1984): 3-6. Discussion of Trudeau's 1983 speech announcing his peace initiative to speed an agreement between East and West.

3027. Browne, Evan. "Canada and the Seas: Sovereignty in the Arctic." *International Perspectives* (July-August, 1980): 7-12.

3028. Browne, Evan. "Sovereignty Questions Remain After Century in the Arctic." *International Perspectives* (July-August, 1980): 7-11. Discusses Canadian sovereignty over Arctic lands.

3029. Byers, R.B. "Canadian Defence: The ASW Dilemma." *Survival* 18:4 (1976): 154-161. Discusses Canadian priorities in defense in light of the status quo of the early 1960's, priorities, and Canada's anti-submarine role in maritime defense.

3030. Byers, R.B. "Canadian Defense: The Genesis of a Debate." Current History 83:493 (1984): 197-201.

3031. Byers, R.B. "The Canadian Military." Current History 72:426 (1977): 173-183.

3032. Byers, R.B. "The Canadian Military and the Use of Force: End of an Era?" International Journal 30:2 (1975): 284-298.

3033. Byers, R.B. "Defence and Foreign Policy in the 1970's: The Demise of the Trudeau Doctrine." International Journal 33:2 (1978): 312-338.

3034. Byers, R.B. "Structural Change and the Policy Process in the Department of National Defence: Military Perceptions." Canadian Public Administration 16:2 (1973): 220-242.

3035. Byers, R.B., and Leyton-Brown, D. "The Strategic and Economic Implications for the United States of a Sovereign Quebec." Canadian Public Policy 6:2 (Spring, 1980): 325-341.

3036. Cadieux, Marcel. "Canada and Europe: The Key to Closer Relations." International Perspectives (November/December, 1976): 3-8.

3037. Calkin, G.A. "Development of Canada-Mexico Relations." International Perspectives (May/June, 1973): 55-58.

3038. "Canadian Policy Towards Southern Africa: Brief From the Task Force on the Churches and Corporate Responsibility." Canadian Review of African Studies 16:1 (1982): 113-126. Review by Task Force on past Canadian Governmental actions toward South Africa, and recommendations for future action.

3039. Canby, Steven, and Smith, Jean Edward. "Canada's Role in NATO: The Laggard Who Can Rescue the Alliance." Strategic Review 13:3 (1985): 47-59. At the present Canada does only slightly more than Luxembourg for NATO, but if Canada would begin to play its proper role it could give NATO a genuine deterrent force.

3040. Chohan, Muhammad Anwar. "The Evolution of Canadian Foreign Policy towad the Middle East (1945-1967)." Pakistan Horizon 38:3 (1985): 12-32.

3041. Clark, Joe. "Canada and NATO in the 1990s." NATO Review 34:3 (1986): 1-6.

3042. Clark, Joe. "Canada and the Commonwealth." Round Table 296 (1985): 306-310.

3043. Copithorne, M.D. "The Settlement of International Claims Between Canada and China: A Status Report." Pacific Affairs 48:2 (1975): 230-end.

3044. Cox, David. "The Aftermath of the Korean Airline Incident: Gathering Intelligence about Intelligence Gathering." Queen's Quarterly 92:1 (1985): 36-50. Canada may face the choice between ignorance of intelligence operations or the "dependence that arises from alliance," and should be concerned about the implications of the KAL affair.

3045. Cox, David. "Canadian-American Military Relations: Some Present Trends and Future Possibilities." International Journal 36:1 (1980-1981): 91-116.

3046. Cox, David. "The Cruise Testing Agreement." International Perspectives (July-August, 1984): 3-5. Explains the decision by the Canadian government to permit Cruise missile testing in Canada.

3047. Cox, David. "Renewal of NORAD." International Perspectives (July/August, 1975): 13-18.

3048. Cox, David. "Trudeau's Foreign Policy Speeches." International Perspectives (November-December, 1982): 7-9. Trudeau's positions on North-South relations, arms control, and the Caribbean.

3049. Curtis, John. "Bilateralism in a Multilateral World." International Perspectives (March-April, 1985): 23-26. Whether Canada and the United States should negotiate new trade arrangements.

3050. Dai, Poeliu. "The United Nations Interim Force in Lebanon and Canadian Participation." Canadian Yearbook of International Law 17 (1979): 304-313. Study of Canadian participation in UNIFIL in 1978.

3051. David, Charles-Philippe. "Canada and the Superpowers." International Perspectives (November-December, 1985): 10-12. Reviews Canada's security problems and offers suggestions for improving communication between Washington and Moscow.

3052. Delvoie, L.A. "Canada's International Security Policy." International Perspectives (July-August, 1985): 25-27. Traces the four complementary and reinforcing elements of Canada's security policy over the last forty years.

3053. Dewitt, David, and Kirton, John. "Canada and Mideast Realities." International Perspectives (January-February, 1984): 19-23. During the Trudeau years Canadian policy shifted toward greater sympathy with the Palestinians.

3054. Dickey, John Sloan. "Canada Independent." Foreign Affairs 50:4 (1972): 684-697.

3055. Dobell, Peter C. "A Matter of Balance." International Journal 28:2 (1973): 315-324.

3056. Dobell, Peter C. "Europe: Canada's Last Chance?" International Journal 27:1 (1972): 113-133.

3057. Dobell, Peter C. "Une première étape: les liens avec l'Europe: une réévaluation." ["A First Stage: Ties with Europe: A Reevaluation."] Études Internationales 2 (1970): 64-75.

3058. Dobell, W.M. "Canada's Record at UNCTAD," International Perspectives (1972): 21-29.

3059. Dobell, W.M. "Defence Procurement Contracts and Industrial Offset Packages." International Perspectives (January-February, 1981): 14-18. Subcontracting to Canadian companies has become a major component of Canadian policy in buying defence supplies outside of Canada.

3060. Dobell, W.M. "Parliament's Role in Choosing the New Fighter Aircraft." International Perspectives (September-October, 1981): 10-13. Examines the role of Parliament in the selection of the F-18A fighter for Canada.

3061. Donneur, André. "Changing World Power Relationships: The Emerging International Order." International Perspectives (July/August, 1973): 3-8.

3062. Donneur, André. "European Image of Canada." International Perspectives (March/April, 1977): 16-20.

3063. Donneur, André. "Les relations franco-canadiennes: bilan et perspectives." ["Franco-Canadian Relations: Balance and Perspectives."] Politique étrangère 38:2 (1973): 179-199. An explanation of past relations between the two countries, and a description of perspectives of future relations.

3064. Douglas, W.A.B. "Why Does Canada Have Armed Forces?" International Journal 30:2 (1975): 259-283.

3065. Dupras, Maurice. "Canada and the OAS." International Perspectives (January-February, 1984): 15-17. Canadian interests in the Caribbean area are more diverse and more intense than in any other part of the Third World.

3066. Eayrs, James. "Canada's Emergence as a Foremost Power." International Perspectives (May/June, 1975): 15-22.

3067. Eayrs, James. "Canada's Emergence as a Foremost Power." International Perspectives (November/December, 1981): 3-9.

3068. Eayrs, James. "Defining a New Place for Canada in the Hierarchy of World Power." International Perspectives (1981): 3-9.

3069. Edwards, L.J. "Canada and the New Pacific." International Perspectives (September-October, 1983): 15-17. The Pacific region has an enormous development potential for Canada, and Canada should pay more attention to this area.

3070. Epstein, William. "Canada's Disarmament Initiatives Mark Return to Active Role." International Perspectives (March-April, 1979): 3-8 Review of recent Trudeau activities both in United Nations and outside of that context.

3071. Epstein, William. "Canada's Interest in Disarmament." International Perspectives (March/April, 1980): 13-18.

3072. Farrell, R. Barry. "Canada and the United States." Atlantic Community Quarterly 14:1 (1976): 69-75. Discussion of the "deteriorating" relationship between Canada and the United States, the issues of contention, and what can be done to repair bilateral relations.

3073. Fisher, Douglas. "The Canadian-Soviet Hockey Series." International Perspectives (November-December, 1972): 13-20.

3074. Fohlen, Claude. "Has France a Canadian Policy?" Politique internationale 12 (1981): 239-251.

3075. Ford, Robert A.D. "The Canadian Perception of East-West Relations." Politique internationale 12 (1981): 217-224.

3076. Fox, Annette Baker. "The Range of Choice for Middle Powers: Australia and Canada Compared." Australian Journal of Politics and History 26:2 (1980): 193-203. Examines Canada's and Australia's behavior in multinational organizations (e.g. NATO) and in areas of trade, foreign investment, natural resources, and arms control.

3077. Freeman, Linda. "Canada and Africa in the 1970's." International Journal 35:4 (1980): 794-820. A study of Canadian foreign policy toward Africa, and how this policy might be forced to change due to international pressure.

3078. Freeman, Linda. "L'ouverture sur le marché africain: Le Canada et l'Afrique dans les années 80." ["The Opening to the African Market: Canada and Africa in the 1980's."] Études internationales 14:1 (1983): 103-130.

3079. Garigue, Philippe. "La politique de défense du Canada et ses priorités stratégiques." ["Canadian Defense Politics and Her Strategic Priorities."] Canadian Journal of Political Science 13:3 (1980): 537-564.

3080. Garner, Lord. "Canadian Diplomacy: The Memoirs of Two Public Servants." Round Table 253 (1974): 85-94. Book review of memoirs of Lester Pearson and Arnold Heeney.

3081. Gay, Daniel. "La présence du Québec en Amérique latine." ["Quebec's Latin American Presence."] Politique 7 (1985): 33-52.

3082. Gellner, John. "Defending the Continent." International Perspectives (Special Issue, 1976): 27-30.

3083. Gellner, John. "Future of International Peacekeeping." International Perspectives (September/October 1973): 23-26.

3084. Gellner, John. "Strategic Analysis in Canada." International Journal 33:3 (1978): 493-505.

3085. Gervais, Myriam. "La politique "africaine" du Québec, de 1960 à 1984." Politique 7 (1985): 53-66.

3086. Godfrey, Steve. "Canadian Sanctions and Southern Africa." International Perspectives (November-December, 1985): 13-19. Traces Canadian government record in the area of sanctions and advocates greater measures.

3087. Goldblatt, Murray. "Canada and Europe: Canada and European Security." International Perspectives (January/February, 1973): 35-38.

3088. Goldblatt, Murray. "Canadian-Soviet Relations." International Perspectives (January/February, 1972): 19-24.

3089. Gordon, J. King. "Canada at the U.N.: Return to a Global Perspective." International Perspectives (September-October, 1976): 3-7.

3090. Gotlieb, Allan E., and Legault, Léonard H. "Law and Diplomacy: New Borders of Canada." Politique internationale 12 (1981): 263-285.

3091. Goumois, Michel de. "Le Canada et la Francophonie." ["Canada and the Francophonie."] Études internationales 5:2 (1974): 355-366. Discusses bilateral ties with France, Belgium, and French Africa, and the major international francophonic institutions which exist and the programs they support.

3092. Graham, Gerald. "An Arctic Foreign Policy for Canada." International Perspectives 1987 (March-April): 11-14.

3093. Green, Leslie C. "Le rôle du Canada dans le développement du droit en matière de conflit armé." ["The Canadian Contribution to the Law of Armed Conflict."] Études internationales 11:3 (1980): 489-503. The general assumption that Canadian courts always followed the edicts of courts in the UK is not entirely correct. Describes the evolution of Canadian attitudes in this area, and Canada's role in the development of the law of armed conflict through contemporary times.

3094. Green, L.C. "The Case for Diplomatic Immunity." International Perspectives (March/April, 1980): 19-23.

3095. Green, Lorne. "Arms, Arms Control, and Security." International Perspectives 1987 (January-February): 15-17.

3096. Grenon, Jean-Yves. "The Framework Agreement Between Canada and the European Communities: A Legal Breakthrough." Canadian Yearbook of International Law 16 (1978): 304-314.

3097. Grossman, L.I. "United Nations: Canadian Voting on Mideast Questions." International Perspectives (May/June, 1978): 9-13.

3098. Guy, James. "Canada and Latin America." World Today 32:10 (1976): 376-386.

3099. Guy, James. "Canada and the Americas." International Perspectives (July/August, 1977): 3-6.

3100. Guy, James. "Canadian-Brazilian Relations." International Perspectives (May/June, 1978): 18-20.

3101. Halstead, John. "A Canadian View of NATO." Atlantic Community Quarterly 22:1 (1984): 52-58. Discussion of Canada's perception of problems in NATO alliance, and suggestion of how Canada's NATO policy should be shaped.

3102. Halstead, John. "Changing World Power Relationships: Implications for Canada." International Perspectives (July/August, 1973): 9-11.

3103. Halstead, John G. H. "Trudeau Abroad: Restoring Franco-Canadian Relations." International Perspectives (January/February, 1975): 3-6.

3104. Harbron, John D. "Canada and Brazil: Comparing Two Hemispheric Giants." International Perspectives (1982): 20-22.

3105. Harbron, John D. "Canada in Caribbean America: Technique for Involvement." Journal of Inter-American Studies and World Affairs 12:4 (1970): 475-484. Traces pattern of Canadian political and economic relationships with countries in the Caribbean.

3106. Harbron, John D. "The New Links With Latin America." International Perspectives (May-June, 1972): 25-29.

3107. Harker, John. "Canada at the U.N.: Labour and the New Economic Order." International Perspectives (September-October, 1976): 11-15.

3108. Harnetty, P. "Canada's Asian Policy: The Case of Pakistan." South Asian Review 3:2 (1970): 117-129. Since 1947 the relationship between the two countries has developed rapidly. Discussion and analysis of various Canadian aid programs and their significance is offered.

3109. Hawkins, Gordon. "Changing World Power Relationships: Encounter with the Diplomats." International Perspectives (July/August, 1973): 12-14.

3110. Head, I.L. "Canada's Pacific Perspective." Pacific Community 6:1 (1974): 6-21.

3111. Hero, Alfred, Jr. "Quelques réactions américaines au régime du parti québecois depuis le 15 novembre 1976." ["Some American Reations to the Parti Québécois Regime Since November 15, 1976."] Études internationales 8:2 (1977): 356-373. Discusses American reactions to Quebec in the areas of defense and security policy, and what implications these reactions will have on Canadian-American relations.

3112. Hervouet, Gérard. "L'Asie orientale: Une option régionale pour le Canada?" ["East Asia: A Regional Option for Canada?"] Études internationales 14:1 (1983): 59-82.

3113. Hilborn, Kenneth. "Canada and South Africa." International Perspectives (July-August, 1975): 50-55.

3114. Hillmer, Norman. "Defence and Ideology: The Anglo-Canadian Military `Alliance' in the 1930's." International Journal 33:3 (1978): 588-612.

3115. Hnatyshyn, Ray. "Canada: Its Recommitment to NATO." Atlantic Community Quarterly 22:3 (1984): 200-203. Reasertion of Canada's commitment to NATO.

3116. Hockin, Thomas. "Atlantic Alliance: NATO's Structural Problems Remain." International Perspectives (September/October, 1974): 36-40.

3117. Holmes, J.W. "After 25 Years." International Journal 26:1 (1970-1971): 1-4.

3118. Holmes, John W. "Canada and the Pacific." Pacific Affairs 44:1 (1971): 5-17.

3119. Holmes, John W. "Canada and the United States: Political and Security Issues." The Atlantic Community Quarterly 8:3 (1970): 398-416. Discussion of Canada's relationship with the U.S., the implications of the NATO/NORAD alliances, and alternative policies which might be considered.

3120. Holmes, John W. "Canada: The Reluctant Power." Orbis 15:1 (1971): 292-304.

3121. Holmes, John W. "Most Safely in the Middle." International Journal 39:2 (1984): 366-388.

3122. Houndjahove, Michel. "Characteristics of Canadian Bilateral Assistance to Francophone Africa, 1968-1980." Revue juridique et politique: Indépendance et Coopération 38 (1984): 821-832.

3123. Houndjahoudé, Michel. "La coopération bilatérale entre le Canada et les pays francophones de l'Afrique de l'Ouest: une évaluation de l'offre entre 1961 et 1975." ["Bilateral Cooperation Between Canada and Francophone West Africa: An Analysis of their State Between 1961 and 1975."] Canadian Journal of African Studies 15:1 (1981): 77-91. Analyzes the bases of Canadian aid to Francophone West Africa between 1961 and 1975, with an evaluation of these programs.

3124. Humphreys, David. "Linking Canada to Europe." International Perspectives (March/April, 1976): 32-37.

3125. Ignatieff, Goerge. "Canada at the U.N.: Security Council Hot Seat." International Perspectives (September-October, 1976): 7-11.

3126. Ignatieff, George. "NATO, Nuclears and Canada's Interests." International Perspectives (November/December, 1978): 3-9.

3127. Ignatieff, George. "NATO, Nuclear Weapons, and Canada's Interests." International Perspectives (1981): 14-18.

3128. Ing, Stanley. "Greenland Home Rule and Canada." International Perspectives (January-February, 1984): 24-26. Although Canada and Greenland share a common heritage, they have not been especially close in the past.

3129. Inglis, Alex I. "Review of Canadian Peacekeeping Commitment." International Perspectives (January/February, 1975): 31-35.

3130. Jackson, Geoffrey, et al. "Canada's Royal Commission on Conditions of Foreign Service." International Journal 37:3 (1982): 378-412.

3131. Jacomy-Millette, A.-M. "Canada at the U.N.: Canada's Voting Pattern." International Perspectives (September-October, 1976): 21-26.

3132. Jewett, Pauline. "Toward an Independent Foreign Policy." International Perspectives 1985 (November-December): 9-10.

3133. Jockel, Joseph T. "Canada and Defence of Norway." International Perspectives (January/February, 1980): 21-24.

3134. Jockel, Joseph. "Canada's Other Commitment: the Defense of Norway." International Perspectives (January-February, 1980): 21-24, The Norwegian-Canadian defence relationship has become closer over the last several years.

3135. Jockel, Joseph T. "Un Québec souverain et la défense de l'Amérique du Nord contre une attaque nucléaire (Note de recherche)." ["A Sovereign Quebec and the Defense of North America Against a Nuclear Attack."] Études internationales 11:2 (1980): 303-316. Importance of Quebec's geographic location in nuclear strategy of NORAD.

3136. Johannson, P.R. "British Columbia's Relations with the United States." Canadian Public Administration 21:2 (1978): 212-233.

3137. Johnson, Leonard. "Military Cooperation with the U.S. and Canadian Independence." International Perspectives 1986 (July-August) 3-6.

3138. Joxe, Alain. "Sécurité de l'Europe occidentale et du Canada dans le système atlantique: rétrospectives et perspectives." ["Security of West Europe and Canada in the Atlantic System: Retrospectives and Perspectives."] Politique étrangère 38:2 (1973): 201-212. Discussion of economic relationships, political ties, the importance of the Atlantic Alliance, and military understandings.

3139. Kapur, Ashok. "The Canada-India Nuclear Negotiations: Some Hypotheses and Lessons." World Today 34:8 (1978): 311-320.

3140. Kasurak, Peter C. "Civilianization and the Military Ethos: Civil-Military Relations in Canada." Canadian Public Administration 25:1 (1982): 108-129.

3141. Kavic, Lorne J. "Canada and Asia: Evolving Awareness and Deepening Links." Pacific Affairs 45:4 (1972): 521-534. Review of attitudes toward the Commonwealth, and the institutional links between Canada and the Commonwealth nations, especially in terms of trade, support, and cultural relations.

3142. Kavic, Lorne J. "Canada and the Commonwealth." Round Table 257 (1975): 37-50.

3143. Kavic, Lorne J. "Canada-Japan Relations." International Journal 26:3 (1971): 567-580.

3144. Keenleyside, T.A. "Canada and the Pacific: Perils of a Policy Paper." Journal of Canadian Studies 8:2 (1973): 31-49.

3145. Keenleyside, T.A. "Career Attitudes of Canadian Foreign Service Officers." Canadian Public Administration 19:2 (1976): 208-226.

3146. Kilgour, David. "Canada and Latin America." International Perspectives 1986 (January-February): 19-21.

3147. King, Henry T, Jr. "Joint Bar Association Proposal for Canadian-U.S. Dispute Settlement." American Journal of International Law 74:2 (1980): 454-456. Proposal put forth by the Canadian and American Bar Associations for the establishment of a mechanism for resolving policy disputes.

3148. Kinsman, Jeremy. "Canada and Europe: Canada-EEC Relations." International Perspectives (January-February, 1973): 22-27.

3149. Kirton, John. "Trudeau and the Diplomacy of Peace." International Perspectives (July-August, 1984): 3-5.

3150. Kirton, John. "Les contraintes du milieu et la gestion de la politique étrangère canadienne de 1976 à 1978." ["External Constraints and Foreign Policy Coordination: The Case of Canada's U.S. Affairs: 1976-1978."] Études internationales 10:2 (1979): 321-349. The effects of environmental change on governmental policy between 1976 an 1978. The approach of a federal election, the PQ victory in Quebec, economic pressures, and a decline in relations with the United States all led to a reorganization of the Department of External Affairs.

3151. Lalande, Gilles. "Les relations avec les pays du Pacifique: constantes et perspectives." ["Relations with the Countries of the Pacific: Constants and Perspectives."] International Journal 26:1 (1971): 151-177.

3152. Langley, James. "Canada and the European Community: Problems in Canada's Dialogue with the EEC." International Perspectives (January-February, 1974): 28-31.

3153. LaTouche, Daniel. "Une prospective des relations France-Québec." ["An Examination of France-Quebec Relations."] Politique 7 (1985): 67-86.

3154. Law, Carl Edgar. "Freedom of Innocent Passage versus Territorial Expansion." International Perspectives (1980): 13-16.

3155. Leach, Richard. "Canada and the Commonwealth." International Perspectives (May/June, 1973): 24-29.

3156. Legault, Albert. "L'organisation de la défense au Canada." ["The Organization of Defense in Canada."] Études internationales 3:2 (1972): 198-220. Discussion of the 1971 Government White Paper titled "Defense in the 1970's" which was distributed by the government. The essay describes the principles expounded in the White Paper, the organization of the Defense hierarchy, and the Defense budget, including analysis of the growth of the defense budget over time.

3157. Legault, Albert. "La position stratégique du Canada et la décennie 1970." ["The Strategic Position of Canada in the 1970 Decade."] International Journal 26:1 (1971): 82-108.

3158. Léger, Jean-Marc. "The Emergence of La Francophonie." International Perspectives (November/December, 1975): 50-57.

3159. Lemco, Jonathan. "Canadian Foreign Policy Interests in Central America: Some Current Issues." Journal of Interamerican Studies and World Affairs 28:2 (1986): 119-146.

3160. Lemelin, Claude. "Canada and the European Community: Ottawa's Objectives Viewed as too Vague." International Perspectives (January-February, 1974): 32-36.

3161. Lentner, Howard H. "Foreign Policy Decision-Making: The Case of Canada and Nuclear Weapons." World Politics 29:1 (1976): 29-66.

3162. Levy, Gary. "Le Canada, le Québec, et l'Association internationale des parlementaires de langue français." ["Canada, Quebec, and the International Association of Parliamentarians of the French Language."] Études internationales 7:3 (1976): 447-456. Describes the formation of the AIPLF and the role of Quebec in its founding, as well as the general use of these parliamentary associations.

3163. Levy, Gary. "Canadian Participation in Parliamentary Associations." Canadian Journal of Political Science 7:2 (1974): 352-357. Study of six informal international organizations to which Canadian parliamentarians belong.

3164. Licari, Wilfrid-Guy. "L'élaboration et la pratique de la politique canadienne en Afrique." ["The Elaboration and Practice of Canadian Politics in Africa."] Canadian Journal of African Studies 18:2 (1984): 417-422. Analysis of Canadian foreign policy in Africa.

3165. Lloyd, Trevor. "Some International Aspects of Arctic Canada." International Journal 25:4 (1970): 717-725.

3166. Longmuir, D. Gordon. "Canada and Japan." International Perspectives (May/June, 1972): 30-32.

3167. Loomis, D.G. "Canada at the U.N.: Sovereignty and Peacemaking." International Perspectives (September-October, 1976): 15-21.

3168. Lucy, R.V. "Jerusalem: The Holy City. Canadian Position." International Perspectives (March/April, 1978): 24-27.

3169. Lyon, Peyton. "Canada at the United Nations." International Perspectives (September-October, 1985): 15-19. How other United Nations member countries see Canada's positions at the U.N.

3170. Lyon, Peyton. "Canada, Britain, and the EEC." International Perspectives (March/April, 1972): 26-30.

3171. Lyon, Peyton. "Canada's Middle East Tilt." International Perspectives (September-October, 1982): 3-5. Although Canada has traditionally been one of Israel's strongest supporters, new directions of policy are leading toward a greater balance.

3172. Lyon, Peyton V. "Second Thought on the Second Option." International Journal 30:2 (1975): 646-670.

3173. Lyon, Peyton V. "The Trudeau Doctrine." International Journal 26:1 (1971): 19-43.

3174. Macdonald, Hugh. "Canada, NATO, and the Neutron Bomb." International Perspectives (March-April, 1979): 9-11 Canada's position on the existence, deployment, and use of the neutron bomb.

3175. Mahant, E.E. "Canada and the European Community: The First Twenty years." Revue d'Intégration européenne 4:3 (1981): 263-279. Summarization of the developments leading to the signing of the Canada-European Community Framework Agreement.

3176. Mahant, E.E. "Canada and the European Community: The New Policy." International Affairs (Great Britain) 52:4 (1976): 551-564. Discussion of the "Framework Agreement for Commercial and Economic Cooperation" signed by Canada and the European Economic Community in 1976.

3177. Mahant, Edelgard. "Institutional Aspects of Canada-European Community Relations." Canadian Yearbook of International Law 23 (1985): 285-296.

3178. Marshall, C.J. "Atlantic Alliance: The Consensus of the Ottawa Declaration." International Perspectives (September/October, 1974): 32-36.

3179. Matejko, Alexander. "Canada and Poland: Two Countries, Two `Big Brothers'." Jerusalem Journal of International Relations 4:4 (1980): 31-55. Comparison of the Soviet style socialist system of Poland and the Canadian market economy and what they mean for the standard of living.

3180. Matthews, Robert. "Africa in Canadian Affairs." International Journal 26:1 (1970-1971): 122-150.

3181. Matthews, Robert. "L'Afrique noire dans la politique étrangère du Canada." ["Black Africa in Canadian Foreign Policy."] Études internationales 1:4 (1970): 59-72.

3182. Matthews, Robert O. "Canada's Relations With Africa." International Journal 30:3 (1975): 536-568.

3183. Matthews, Roy A. "National Interests and the International System." International Perspectives (September-December, 1979): 12-14.

3184. Maybee, J.R. "Protection of Canadians in Foreign Countries." International Perspectives (May/June, 1974): 39-44.

3185. Mégélas, Roger. "The New Canada-Cuba Dialogue." International Perspectives (July/August, 1976): 19-22.

3186. Meret, Livia. "Canada and Namibia." Canadian Yearbook of International Law 17 (1979): 314-323. Discussion of Canada's position on UN Security Council decisions concerning Namibia.

3187. Merle, Marcel. "Saying Farewell to Arms." International Perspectives (November/December, 1978): 10-13.

3188. Molot, Maureen Appel. "Canada-U.S. Relations: The Politics of Attraction and Distance." Jerusalem Journal of International Relations 6:2 (1982): 88-107.

3189. Morales, Cecilio. "A Canadian Role in Central America." International Perspectives (January-February, 1985): 12-15. Past Canadian policy in this area and possible directions of future activity.

3190. Morin, Jacques-Yvan. "Le développement Africain - L'engagement du Québec." ["African Development - The Entry of Quebec."] Canadian Journal of African Studies 18:2 (1984): 423-428. Discussion of Quebec's growing relations with Africa.

3191. Mount, Graeme S., and Mahant, Edelgard E. "Review of Recent Literature on Canadian-Latin American Relations." Journal of Inter-American Studies and World Affairs 27:2 (1985): 127-151. Reviews literature published on Canada's relations with Latin America between 1976 and 1983. Includes much thematic discussion, and many references.

3192. Moxon-Browne, Edward P. "Canadian Crisis Diplomacy." Orbis 14:4 (1971): 1044-1048.

3193. Mueller, David. "Inescapable SDI." International Perspectives 1986 (September-October): 14-16.

3194. Munton, Donald. "The Canadian Winter of Nuclear Discontent." Current History 83:493 (1984): 202-205.

3195. Munton, Don, and Slack, Michael. "Canadian Attitudes on Disarmament." International Perspectives (July-August, 1982): 9-12. The threat of nuclear war is the dominant international concern of Canadians.

3196. Murray, D.R. "The Bilateral Road: Canada and Latin America in the 1980s." International Journal 37:1 (1981-1982): 108-131.

3197. Murray, D.R. "Canada's First Diplomatic Missions in Latin America." Journal of Interamerican Studies and World Affairs 16:2 (1974): 153-172. History of Canadian diplomacy in Latin America.

3198. Nailor, Peter. "Canada's External Relations in the 1980's." The Round Table 298 (1986): 123-128.

3199. Nevitte, Neil, and Gibbins, Roger. "Foreign Policy Debates and Sleeping Dogs: All Quiet on the Public Front." Canadian Public Policy 12:3 (1986): 401-412. Uses data from students at nine Canadian universities to study why there has been so little public discussion of foreign policy issues in Canada.

3200. Noble, Paul. "Canada and the Palestinian Question." International Perspectives (September-October, 1984): 3-7. Review of Canadian policy in this area and suggestion that Canada needs to be more active.

3201. Noble, John J. "Canada's Search for Nuclear Safeguards." International Perspectives (July-August, 1978): 42-47.

3202. Ogelsby, J.C.M. "A Trudeau Decade: Canadian-Latin American Relations 1968-1978." Journal of Inter-American Studies and World Affairs 21:2 (1979): 187-208. Trudeau's interest in Latin America, and how policy changed during his tenure of office.

3203. Ogelsby, J.C.M. "Relaciones Canadiense-Latinoamericanas, pasadas, presentes, y futuras." ["Canadian-Latin American Relations: Past, President, and Future."] Estudios internacionales 5:18 (1972): 68-87.

3204. Ogelsby, Jack. "Canada-Cuba Relations." International Perspectives (September, 1975): 34-38.

3205. Okuma, Tadayuki. "Passive Japan -- Active Canada." International Journal 33:2 (1978):443-447.

3206. Ollivant, Simon. "Canada: How Powerful an Ally?" Conflict Studies 159 (1984): 3-20. Do specific political factions in Quebec (such as the separatist movement) concern Canada's allies in NORAD and NATO, because an independent Quebec could compromise these associations.

3207. O'Neill, R. Constraint With Honor." International Journal 29:3 (1974): 350-355.

3208. Orvik, Nils. "Canadian Security and 'Defense Against Help'." International Perspectives (May-June, 1984): 3-7. Canada should initiate more cooperative agreements on its own rather than waiting for American undertakings.

3209. Orvik, Nils. "A Defense Doctrine for Canada." Orbis 27:1 (1983): 185-206. Five major criteria reflect the major elements in the Canadian defence posture, some of which are symbolic rather than functional.

3210. Orvik, Nils. "Semi-Neutrality and Canada's Security." *International Journal* 29:2 (1974): 186-215.

3211. Painchaud, Paul. "Canadian-Danish Relations." *International Perspectives* (May/June, 1978): 39-43.

3212. Painchaud, Paul. "Trudeau Abroad: Franco-Canadian Rapprochement." *International Perspectives* (January/February, 1975): 6-8.

3213. Pearson, Geoffrey. "Trudeau Peace Initiative Reflections." *International Perspectives* (March-April, 1985): 3-6. Discussion of Trudeau's attitudes and behavior by a participant in some of his meetings.

3214. Pearson, Michael, Mackinnon, Gregor, and Sapardanis, Christopher. "`The World is Entitled to Ask Questions': The Trudeau Peace Initiative Reconsidered." *International Journal* 41:1 (1985-1986): 129-158.

3215. Pelletier, Jean-Guy. "Les relations entre le Québec et l'Afrique, 1880-1905." ["The Relations Between Quebec and Africa, 1880-1905."] *Canadian Journal of African Studies* 15:1 (1981): 117-120. Historical review of the relations between Quebec and Africa during this period of time.

3216. Pentland, Charles. "Linkage Politics: Canada's Contract and the Development of the European Community's External Relations." *International Journal* 32:2 (1977): 207-231.

3217. Pentland, Charles. "L'option européenne du Canada dans les années 80." ["Canada's European Option in the 1980's."] *Études internationales* 14:1 (1983): 39-58.

3218. Perron, Bruno. "Les contraintes dans les relatons entre le Québec et les États Unis." ["Constraints in the Relations Between Quebec and the United States."] *Politique* 7 (1985): 9-31.

3219. Pilisi, Paul. "Canada and Europe: Both Can Benefit from the Link." *International Perspectives* (November/December, 1976): 8-12.

3220. Pillay, P.D. "Minus the Spectacular, Commonwealth Proves a Plus." *International Perspectives* (November-December, 1973): 3-8.

3221. Pleuger, G. "The Relations Between the European Community and Canada. A `Special Relationship'." *Europa-Archiv* 30:8 (1975): 269-276.

3222. Pratt, Cranford. "Canadian Policies Towards South Africa: An Exchange Between the Secretary of State for External Affairs and the Task Force of the Churches and Corporate Responsibility." Canadian Journal of African Studies 17:3 (1983): 497-525. Recommendations by the Task Force of the Churches and Corporate Responsibility for Canadian policy to South Africa, and responses by the Department of External Affairs.

3223. Pratt, Cranford. "South Africa Liberation Movements: Assessment of Canadian Policy." International Perspectives (November-December, 1974): 38-43.

3224. Preston, A. "The Profession of Arms in Postwar Canada, 1945-1970. Political Authority as a Military Problem." World Politics 23:2 (1971): 189-214.

3225. Quo, F.Q., and Ichikawa, Akira. "Sino-Canadian Relations: A New Chapter." Asian Survey 12:5 (1972): 386-398. Discussion of change in Canadian-Chinese relations, including historical analysis and discussion of implications of new China policy for Canadian foreign relations.

3226. Radwanski, George. "Trudeau in Latin America." International Perspectives (May-June, 1976): 6-11.

3227. Redekop, John H. "A Reinterpretation of Canadian-American Relations." Canadian Journal of Political Science 9:2 (1976): 227-243. Argues that "conventional approaches" to the study of Canadian-American relations are inadequate; suggests an alternative approach.

3228. Reford, Robert. "Canada and Europe: Dealing with a Divided Continent." International Perspectives (January/February, 1973): 28-34.

3229. Reford, Robert. "Lester Pearson's Diplomacy." International Journal 29:1 (1973-1974): 1-153.

3230. Reford, Robert. "Our Seat at the Table: A Canadian Menu for Arms Control." International Journal 36:3 (1981): 657-679.

3231. Reford, Robert. "The UN Disarmament Conference and Canada." International Perspectives (July-August, 1982): 6-8. Opportunities are open to Canada to encourage disarmament talks.

3232. Reford, Robert. "UNSSOD II and Canada." International Perspectives (July/August, 1982): 6-9.

3233. Reid, Escott. "Negotiating the Atlantic Pact." International Perspectives (September/October, 1981): 16-19.

3234. Reid, Escott. "Strengthening the North Atlantic Alliance." International Perspectives (November-December, 1985): 3-6. A NATO "summit" is needed to clarify treaty obligattions and goals.

3235. Rohrlich, Paul. "Canada and Star Wars." International Perspectives (May-June, 1985): 17-20. Whether Canadian participation in U.S. space research is a meaningful option, and how participation might affect Canada's ability to influence U.S. policy.

3236. Ross, David J. "Official Canadian Attitudes Towards the Commonwealth." Australian Journal of Politics and History 26:2 (1980): 183-192. Discusses the wide range of Canadian attitudes from Mackenzie King's strong opposition to a centralized Commonwealth to Trudeau's vision of the Commonwealth in a favorable light.

3237. Ross, Douglas A. "Middlepowers as Extra-Regional Balancer Powers: Canada, India, and Indo-china, 1954-1962." Pacific Affairs 55:2 (1982): 185-209.

3238. Rossetto, Luigi. "A Final Look at the 1971 White Paper on Defence." Queen's Quarterly 84:1 (1977): 61-74. An examination of the poor state of Canada's defence and what might be done to improve the situation.

3239. Sabourin, Louis. "Le Canada et le tiers monde: origines et originalite d'une politique." ["Canada and the Third World: Origins and Originality of Politics."] Studia Diplomatica 31:5 (1978): 527-544.

3240. Sabourin, Louis. "Quebec and Africa: Language and Politics." Africa Report 15:4 (1970): 16-17.

3241. Sabourin, Louis. "Quebec Courts Francophone Africa." Africa Report 15:4 (1970): 16-17. Focus primarily upon Ottawa's reactions to Quebec's actions in Francophone Africa.

3242. Sabourin, Louis. "Les programmes canadiens de coopération avec les Etats de l'Afrique (particulièrement avec l'Afrique francophone)." ["Canadian Programs of Cooperation with the States of Africa (Particularly With Francophone Africa)."] Études internationales 1:4 (1970): 73-87.

3243. Sanger, Clyde. "Canada and Africa: Aid and Politics." Africa Report 15:4 (1970): 12-15.

3244. Sanger, Clyde. "What Does Canada Care About Africa?" Africa Report 15:4 (1970): 12-15. The Trudeau Government's concern about Africa is based upon domestic political pressures.

3245. Saywell, William. "Pierre and the Pacific: A Post-Mortem." International Journal 33:2 (1978): 408-414.

3246. Schlegal, John P. "A Successful Alternative? Canada and the European Community." Round Table 269 (1978): 55-64. Evaluation of new trend of Canadian interest in the European Community and the "contractual link" policy first articulated in the early 1970's.

3247. Schlegal, John P. "Ottawa's Achilles Heel: Formulating Policies in Southern Africa." Round Table 274 (1979): 142-153. Discussion of Canada's relations with Tanzania, Rhodesia, and South Africa.

3248. Schlegal, John P. "Patterns of Diplomacy: Canada and Australia in the Third World." Australian Journal of Politics and History 30:1 (1984): 7-18. The issues of independence and trade and resources, their perceptions as "middle powers", and then discusses some specific policies of the two countries.

3249. Schneider, Fred D. "Exploring the Third Option: Canadian Foreign Policy and Defense." Current History 79:460 (1980): 121-124.

3250. Schreiner, John. "Jamieson in Southeast Asia." International Perspectives (May/June, 1976): 11-15.

3251. Schwartz, Alan, and Jockel, Joseph. "Increasing Power of IJC." International Perspectives (November-December, 1983): 3-7. The International Joint Commission's power needs to be increased.

3252. Scott, Stephen. "MacEachen in Middle East." International Perspectives (May/June, 1976): 3-6.

3253. Shadwick, Martin. "Canadian Defence Policy." International Perspectives (September/October, 1983): 7-11.

3254. Shadwick, Martin. "Canadian Defense Policy." International Perspectives (September-October, 1984): 7-10. Canada must move away from the status quo in defence policy and modernize its defense resources significantly.

3255. Shadwick, Martin. "Star Wars and Canadian Air Defense." International Perspectives (March-April, 1985):11-16. Canada's role in North American air defense from the 1950's to the present time.

3256. Sharp, Mitchell. "Canada in the World Community." The Atlantic Community Quarterly 10:1 (1972): 66-70. Canada's contributions to the easing of East-West tensions through discussions with the U.S.S.R. and China.

3257. Sharp, Mitchell. "Reflections on Foreign Policy During the Trudeau Years." International Perspectives 1986 (November-December): 3-7.

3258. Shaw, Timothy. "Nigerian Coups and Foreign Policy." International Perspectives 1985 (November-December): 17-19.

3259. Shea, Michael. "Canada and East Germany." International Perspectives 1986 (July-August): 9-11.

3260. Skinner, G.R. "Canada's Approach to Disarmament Session." International Perspectives (May/June, 1978): 30-34.

3261. Small, A. Douglas. "Dialogue Between Canada and ASEAN." International Perspectives (March/April, 1978): 28-31.

3262. Smith, Arnold. "Evolution of the Commonwealth." International Perspectives (November/December, 1975): 43-50.

3263. Smith, Malcolm. "A Pacific Community: Prospects for Canadian Participation." Pacific Affairs 55:4 (1983): 660-670.

3264. Smith, Stuart. "The Pacific Challenge." International Perspectives (September/October, 1984): 11-13.

3265. Smythe, Elizabeth. "International Relations Theory and the Study of Canadian-American Relations." Canadian Journal of Political Science 13:1 (1980): 121-148.

3266. Sokolsky, Joel J. "Canada in NATO; The Perceptions of a Middle Power in Alliance." Fletcher Forum 4:2 (1980): 203-226. Canada's position in NATO has been an ambiguous one; this article examines the strengths and weaknesses of Canada's NATO participation over the years.

3267. Sokolsky, Joel. "Changing Strategies, Technologies and Organization: The Continuing Debate on NORAD and the Strategic Defense Initiative." Canadian Journal of Political Science 19:4 (1986): 751-774. Studies the renewal of the Canada-U.S. North American Aerospace Defence (NORAD) agreement in March of 1986, and discusses potential sources of tension that will not go away in this relationship.

3268. Sokolsky, Joel, and Jockel, Joseph. "Canada: The Not So Faithful Ally." The Washington Quarterly 7:4 (1984): 159-169. Canada has not only neglected the interests of its allies in NATO and the United States specifically over the last decade, but as well Canada has neglected its own interests.

3269. Spicer, Keith. "Clubmanship Upstaged: Canada's Twenty Years in the Colombo Plan." International Journal 25:1 (1969-1970): 23-33.

3270. Stairs, Denis. "Canada and the Korean War." International Perspectives (November, 1972): 25-32.

3271. Stanford, Joseph. "Canadian Policy Options in East-West Relations." International Perspectives 1986 (July-August), 6-9.

3272. Stevens, Geoffrey. "Mr. Trudeau Woos Europe: Canada's Attempts to Lessen Dependence on the United States." Round Table 260 (1975): 401-409. Analysis of the policy of the "contractual link," Trudeau's goal in negotiating closer ties for Canada with the European Economic Community to lessen Canada's economic dependence upon the United States.

3273. Stigger, P. "A Study in Confusion: Canadian Diplomatic Staffing Practices in Africa and the Middle East." Canadian Journal of African Studies 5:3 (1971): 241-262. Decries lack of consideration given to a foreign policy for Africa.

3274. Swanson, Roger F. "An Analytical Assessment of the United States-Canadian Defense Issue Area." International Organization 28:4 (1974): 781-802.

3275. Swanson, Roger F. "Canadian Consular Representation in the United States." Canadian Public Administration 20:2 (1977): 342-369.

3276. Swanson, Roger F. "Canadian Diplomatic Representation in the United States." Canadian Public Administration 18:3 (1975): 366-398.

3277. Swanson, Roger F. "Deterrence, Détente, and Canada?" Proceedings of the Academy of Political Science 32:2 (1976): 100-112.

3278. Swanson, Roger K. "NORAD: Choices for Canada." International Perspectives (November/December, 1972): 8-12.

3279. Swanson, Roger K. "NORAD: Origins and Operations." International Perspectives (November/December, 1972): 3-7.

3280. Swanson, Roger F. "The United States Canadiana Constellation, I: Washington D.C." International Journal 27:2 (1972): 185-218.

3281. Taras, David. "Brian Mulroney's Foreign Policy: Something for Everyone." The Round Table 293 (1985): 35-46. Analysis of whether Prime Minister Mulroney will be able to please all of his different constituencies in the field of foreign policy.

3282. Tennyson, Brian D. "Canadian Policy Towards South Africa." Africa Today 29:1 (1982): 3-20. Describes beginning of policies toward South Africa, and examines future trade and investment policies.

3283. Tenzer, Nicolas, and Rouah, Eric. "Entre le Canada et la France, de nouveax liens privilégiés." ["Between Canada and France: New Privileged Links."] Défense nationale (1987): 69-82.

3284. Thakur, Ramesh. "Peacekeeping and Foreign Policy: Canada, India, and the International Commission in Vietnam, 1954-1965." British Journal of International Studies 6:2 (1980): 125-153. Canada's role on the International Commission for Supervision and Control in Vietnam is studied as a peacekeeping action and an act of foreign policy.

3285. Thomson, Dale C. "Canada-U.S. Relations: What Price Tag for Option Three?" International Perspectives (January-February, 1973): 3-6.

3286. Thomson, Dale C. "Les relations canado-américaines: coexistence ou intégration." ["Canadian-American Relations: Coexistence or Integration."] Politique étrangère 37:2 (1972): 163-184. Canada has traditionally sought to differentiate itself from the United States, and wants to defend itself militarily, socially, and economically, but doesn't want to offend the United States.

3287. Torrelli, Maurice, and Valaskakis, Kimon. "Canada-EEC Relations." International Perspectives (September/October, 1973): 18-22.

3288. Tracy, Nicholas. "Matching Canada's Navy to Its Foreign Policy and Domestic Requirements." International Journal 38:3 (1983): 459-475.

3289. Treleaven, Michael. "Canada, U.S.A., Vietnam, and Central America." International Perspectives 1986 (September-October): 6-9.

3290. Trezise, P.H. "Interdependence and its Problems." International Journal 29:4 (1974): 523-534.

3291. Trudeau, Pierre Elliott. "A Peace Initiative from Canada." Bulletin of the Atomic Scientists 40:1 (1984): 15-19. Pierre Trudeau advocates reducing the threat of war and creating a stable environment for both East and West.

3292. Trudeau, Pierre Elliott. "The Road to Recovery." Atlantic Community Quarterly 16:2 (1978): 139-149. Discussion of short-term problems facing Canada and the U.S., and how they can be resolved, as well as several long-term issues that need to be addressed both in domestic policy and in foreign relations.

3293. Truitt, J.F. "Canada and the Pacific Rim: Least Pacific or Most Pacific?" Pacific Community 8:2 (1977): 259-277. The extent to which Canada is really a "Pacific" nation, as some contemporary writers suggest, is examined using several categories of analysis.

3294. Tucker, Michael. "Canada and Arms Control: Perspectives and Trends." International Journal 36:3 (1981): 635-656.

3295. Tucker, Michael. "Conventional Weapons and Wisdoms: A NATO Dilemma for Canada." International Perspectives (January-February, 1984): 3-6. Although Canada is committed in principle to the defense of Europe, the NATO alliance leaves something to be desired from the perspective of both military strategy and implications for future alignments.

3296. Tucker, Michael. "Trudeau and the Politics of Peace." International Perspectives (March-April, 1984): 7-10. Analysis of Trudeau's October, 1983 "peace initiative."

3297. Turcotte, Claude. "The Trudeau Visit to China." International Perspectives (January/February, 1974): 7-12.

3298. Tutton, Michael. "Chile, Human Rights, and Canada." International Perspectives 1986 (November-December): 20-23.

3299. Vastel, Michel. "Trudeau on Summitry." International Perspectives (November-December, 1982): 10-12. Why Trudeau has been critical of multinational summit meetings.

3300. Wang, Erik B. "Adjudication of Canada-United States Disputes." Canadian Yearbook of International Law 19 (1981): 158-228.

3301. Wilson, W.A. "Of Armaments and Things Nuclear." International Perspectives (January/February, 1978): 16-19.

3302. Winham, G. R. "The Art of Diplomatic Negotiation." International Perspectives (March/April, 1980): 24-26.

3303. Wright, Gerald, and Doran, Charles F. "Canada and the Reagan Administration." International Journal 36:1 (1980-1981): 228-240.

3304. Wrong, Hume. "The Canada-United States Relationship, 1927/1951." International Journal 31:3 (1976): 529-545.

3305. Yee, Herbert S. "Third Party Response in Foreign Policy: Taiwan's Response to Canadian and Japanese China Policies." Asia Quarterly 4 (1979): 309-326. Although the emphasis of this article is on Taiwan's response to Canada's China polity, it also discusses what Canada's China Policy was after Canada announced the establishment of diplomatic relations with the People's Republic of China in October, 1970.

14
"Low" Foreign Policy Issues: Quality of Life

Books

3306. Aitken, Hugh G., et al. *The American Economic Impact on Canada*. Westport, Ct.: Greenwood Press, 1981.

3307. Axline, W.A., et al., eds. *Continental Community*. Toronto: McClelland and Stewart, 1974. Essays on economic and political integration, with analysis of Canadian-American relations in taxes, financial relations, energy policy, and foreign investment.

3308. Buckley, Alan. *The Long-Term Canadian Environment for Foreign Firms: A Political and Social Analysis*. New York: Conference Board, 1981.

3309. Cameron, Duncan. *Canada and the Third World Economic Order*. Ottawa: University of Ottawa, 1982.

3310. Campbell, Dennis, ed. *Legal Aspects of Doing Business in North America and Canada*. St. Paul, Minn.: West Pub. Co., 1987.

3311. Canada. Foreign Investment Review Agency. *A Comparison on Foreign Investment Controls in Canada and Australia*. Ottawa: The Branch, 1979.

3312. Canada. Foreign Investment Review Agency. *Extracts from Provincial Laws and Regulations Affecting Foreign Investment in Canada, November 1972*. Ottawa: Foreign Investment Division, Foreign Investment Review Agency, 1972.

3313. Canada. Foreign Investment Review Agency. Policy Research Division. *Selected Readings in Canadian Legislation Affecting Foreign Investment in Canada*. Ottawa: Research and Analysis Branch, Foreign Investment Review Agency, 1977.

320   Contemporary Canadian Politics

3314. Canada. Parliament. Senate. Standing Committee on Foreign Affairs. _Canada - United States Relations_. Ottawa: Standing Senate Committee on Foreign Affairs, 3 vols., 1975-1982.

3315. Canada International Development Agency. _Canada and Development Cooperation_. Ottawa: Minister of Supply and Services, 1976. Review of CIDA activities in bilateral aid programs and discussion of other CIDA programs and activities.

3316. Canadian-American Committee. _Bilateral Relations in an Uncertain World Context: Canada-United States Relations in 1978_. Montreal: C.D. Howe Institute, 1978. Discussion of setting and major bilateral issues affecting Canadian-American relations, including energy, trade, and investment policy.

3317. Carty, Robert, and Smith, Virginia. _Perpetuating Poverty: The Political Economy of Canadian Foreign Aid_. Toronto: Between the Lines, 1981.

3318. Chafe, Warren, and Clancy, Mary. _Foreign Investment Review Act_. Vancouver, B.C.: Centre for Continuing Education, University of British Columbia, 1975.

3319. Clarke, Robert, and Swift, Richard, eds. _Ties That Bind: Canada and the Third World_. Toronto: Between the Lines, 1982. Essays reviewing Canadian policies toward aid to Third World nations.

3320. Clarkson, Stephen. _Canada and the Reagan Challenge: Crisis and Adjustment, 1981-1985_. Toronto: Lorimer, 1982. How Canadian-American relations have changed under the Reagan administration, with special focus upon economic issues, environmental issues, and military issues.

3321. Cuff, Robert, and Granatstein, J. L. _Ties That Bind: Canadian-American Relations in Wartime: From the Great War to the Cold War_. 2nd ed. Toronto: Hakkert, 1975.

3322. Donnelly, D. K. _CanAmerican Union Now!_ Toronto: Griffin House, 1978. Discussion of the idea of political union between Canada and the United States as a solution to problems of Quebec nationalism and an uncertain direction for Canada's future.

3323. Doran, Charles F. _Economic Interdependence, Autonomy, and Canadian/American Relations_. Montreal: Institute for Research on Public Policy, 1983. Uses trade data to study the effects of economic ties on Canadian-American political relations.

3324. Doran, Charles F. *Forgotten Partnership: U.S.-Canadian Relations Today*. Baltimore: Johns Hopkins University Press, 1984. Detailed discussion of a number of different dimensions of the relationship between Canada and the United States including the psychological dimension, the trade dimension, the political dimension, the environmental dimension, and the energy-supply dimension.

3325. Doran, Charles, and Sigler, John, eds. *Canada and the United States: Enduring Friendship, Persistent Stress*. Englewood Cliffs, N.J.: Prentice Hall, 1985. Essays on Canadian-American relations and culture, defense, environment, and economic issues.

3326. Doran, Charles, and Sokolsky, Joel. *Canada and Congress: Lobbying in Washington*. Halifax, N.S.: Centre for Foreign Policy Studies, 1985. Examination of the rationale and prospects for Canadian lobbying in Washington, and the limits of the effectiveness of such action.

3327. Doxey, Margaret P. *Human Rights and Canadian Foreign Policy*. Toronto: Canadian Institute of International Affairs, 1979. Short paper demonstrating the value that Canada has traditionally placed on human rights when making foreign policy decisions.

3328. English, Harry Edward, ed. *Canada-United States Relations*. New York: Academy of Political Science, 1976. Articles describing Canadian-American bilateral issues, and Canadian-American relations in an international context.

3329. Feldman, Elliot J., and Nevitte, Neil, eds. *The Future of North America: Canada, the United States, and Quebec Nationalism*. Cambridge, Mass.: Center for International Affairs, Harvard University, 1979. Essays dealing with nationalism, regionalism, the crisis of national unity, and Canadian-American relations in the late 1970's.

3330. Fidler, Dick. *Canada: Accomplice in Apartheid: Canadian Government and Corporate Involvement in Southern Africa*. New York: Pathfinder Press, 1977.

3331. Fox, Annette Baker. *The Politics of Attraction: Four Middle Powers and the United States*. New York: Columbia University Press, 1977.

3332. Fox, Annette Baker, Hero, Alfred O., and Nye, Joseph S., eds. *Canada and the United States: Transnational and Transgovernmental Relations*. New York: Columbia University Press, 1976. Essays discussing national attitudes in a number of specific issue areas such as trade, law of the sea, labor, defense, and institutional transnational integration.

3333. Fox, William. _A Continent Apart: The United States and Canada in World Politics_. Toronto: University of Toronto Press, 1985. Study of North-American politics, focusing upon a regional perspective, and examining not only Canadian-American relations, but also relations between Canada and the United States on one hand, and the rest of the world on the other.

3334. Fried, Edward, and Trezise, Philip, eds. _United States-Canadian Economic Relations: Next Steps?_ Washington D.C.: Brookings Institution, 1984. Canadian and American businessmen authored papers discussing trade and investment issues, energy issues, and trade of computer services issues.

3335. Fromm, Paul, and Hull, James. _Down the Drain? A Critical Re-Examination of Canadian Foreign Aid_. Toronto: Griffin House, 1981. Review of Canadian foreign aid policy, suggesting that Canada should not continue with foreign aid in its present form, but should make substantial changes in its policy and its aid packages.

3336. Fry, Earl, and Radebaugh, Lee, eds. _Canada - U.S. Economic Relations in the "Conservative" Era of Mulroney and Reagan_. Provo, Ut.: Brigham Young University, 1985.

3337. Fry, Earl, and Radebaugh, Lee. _Canada - U.S. Trade Relations: Problems and Prospects_. Provo, Ut.: Center for International Studies, 1984.

3338. Fry, Earl, and Radebaugh, Lee, eds. _Regulation of Foreign Direct Investment in Canada and the United States_. Provo, Ut.: Brigham Young University, 1983. Essays covering federal regulation of foreign direct investment, state and provincial perspectives, extraterritoriality and antitrust dimensions of foreign direct investment, merger strategies, and the changing environment for foreign investment.

3339. Ghent, Jocelyn Maynard. _Science, Technology, and Trudeau's Foreign Policy_. Toronto: Canadian Institute of International Affairs, 1978.

3340. Grey, Rodney de C. _Trade Policy in the 1980's: An Agenda for Canadian-U.S. Relations_. Montreal: C.D. Howe Institute, 1981.

3341. Grey, Rodney de C. _United States Trade Policy Legislation: A Canadian View_. Montreal: Institute for Research on Public Policy, 1982.

3342. Gwyn, Richard. _The 49th Paradox: Canada in North America_. Toronto: McClelland and Stewart, 1985. Political-historical analysis of American-Canadian relations, including economic implications of the association.

3343. Hart, Michael M. *Canadian Economic Development and the International Trading System*. Toronto: University of Toronto Press, 1985. Discusses Canada's role in the international trading system, Canada's major trading partners, its economic development policies, and the safeguards used by the Government to maintain stability.

3344. Hay, Keith, ed. *Canadian Perspectives on Economic Relations with Japan*. Montreal: Institute for Research on Public Policy, 1980. History of Canadian-Japanese economic ties, with analysis of contemporary problem areas and issues of concern in the bilateral arrangement.

3345. Hoffman, Gerard H. *Foreign Aid? Yes, but...: A Constructive Critique of the "North-South" Conspiracy*. Toronto: Our Canada Publications, 1981.

3346. Holmes, John Wendell. *Canada, A Middle-Aged Power*. Toronto: McClelland and Stewart, 1976. Review of Canadian foreign policy, international institutions, the "counterweight" theory, and relations within North America.

3347. Hore, John E., ed. *Proceedings of the First Canadian International Futures Research Seminar*. Toronto: Canadian Securities Institute, 1986.

3348. Hutcheson, John. *Dominence and Dependency*. Toronto: McClelland and Stewart, 1978. Political-history of the relation between Canada and the United States, and the effect this relationship has had on Canadian economic development.

3349. Johnson, B., and Zaeher, M.W., eds. *Canadian Foreign Policy and the Law of the Sea*. Vancouver: University of British Columbia Press, 1977.

3350. Langdon, Frank. *The Politics of Canadian-Japanese Economic Relations, 1952-1983*. Vancouver: University of British Columbia Press, 1983. Discussion of early patterns of bilateral trade, and more recent patterns of bilateral economic relations.

3351. Langford, J. A. *Canadian Foreign Investment Controls*. Don Mills, Ont.: CCH Canadian, 1975.

3352. Laxer, Gordon. *Foreign Ownership and Myths About Canadian Development*. Toronto: Department of Sociology, University of Toronto, 1983.

3353. Laxer, R.M. *Canada, Ltd., The Political Economy of Dependence*. Toronto: McClelland and Stewart, 1973.

3354. Levin, M., and Sylvester, C. *Foreign Ownership*. Toronto: Musson, 1972.

3355. Litvak, I.A., and Maule, C.J. The Canadian Multinationals. Toronto: Butterworths, 1981.

3356. Lumsden, I., ed. Close the 49th Parallel, etc.: The Americanization of Canada. Toronto: University of Toronto Press, 1970.

3357. Mahant, Edelgart, and Mount, Graeme. An Introduction to Canadian-American Relations. Toronto: Methuen, 1984. A political history of Canadian-American relations from 1763 through Trudeau years.

3358. Marchak, P. In Whose Interests?: An Essay in Multinational Corporations in a Canadian Context. Toronto: McClelland and Stewart, 1979.

3359. Migué, J.-L. Nationalistic Policies in Canada: An Economic Approach. Montreal: C.D. Howe Institute, 1979.

3360. Moffett, Samuel E. The Americanization of Canada. Toronto: University of Toronto Press, 1972. Discussion of the development of the relations between the American and Canadian people, and analysis of tendencies toward unification and diversification.

3361. Morchain, J., ed. Sharing a Continent: An Introduction to Canadian-American Relations. Toronto: McGraw-Hill Ryerson, 1973.

3362. North-South Institute. In the Canadian Interest? Third World Development in the 1980's. Ottawa: North South Institute, 1980. Discussion of Canadian interests in the question of aid to Third World countries, and strategies that might be followed in the encouragement of Third World development.

3363. Nossal, Kim Richard. The Unmaking of Garrison, United States Politics and the Management of Canadian-American Boundary Waters. Toronto: Canadian Institute of International Affairs, 1978.

3364. Ontario. Legislative Assembly. Select Committee on Economic and Cultural Nationalism. Foreign Ownership: Architecture and Engineering Consulting. Prepared as Part of a Study on Foreign Ownership. Toronto: Select Committee on Economic and Cultural Nationalism of the Legislative Assembly of Ontario, 1973.

3365. Pammett, Jon H., and Tomlin, Brian W., eds. The Integration Question: Political Economy and Public Policy in Canada and North America. Addison-Wesley, 1984.

3366. Paterson, Robert K. Canadian Regulation of International Trade and Investment. Toronto: Carswell, 1986.

3367. Pope, W.H. *The Elephant and the Mouse*. Toronto: McClelland and Stewart, 1971.

3368. Preston, Richard, ed. *The Influence of the United States on Canadian Development: Eleven Case Studies*. Durham: Duke University Press, 1972. Essays discussing a number of different aspects of American influence on Canada including academic study, the conduct of politics, economics, labor relations, and linguistics.

3369. Pringsheim, Klaus. *Neighbors Across the Pacific*. Westport, Ct.: Greenwood Press, 1983. Political history of the development of the political and economic relationship between Canada and Japan, 1877-1978.

3370. Protheroe, David R. *Imports and Politics: Trade Decision-Making in Canada, 1968-1979*. Montreal: Institute for Research on Public Policy, 1980. Analysis of trade decisions made by the Trudeau government during the 1968-1979 years.

3371. Radebaugh, Lee, and Fry, Earl, eds. *Canada-U.S. Free Trade Agreements*. Provo, Ut.: Brigham Young University, 1986.

3372. Redekop, John H., ed. *The Star-Spangled Beaver*. Toronto: Peter Martin Associates, 1971. Essays describing the effects the United States has on Canadian politics, economics, and society.

3373. Reilly, Wayne G., ed. *Encounter with Canada: Essays in the Social Sciences*. Durham, N.C.: Duke University Center for International Studies, 1980. Collection of essays dealing with different issues confronting contemporary Canada, including the politics of language, the idea of national unity, investment policy, the legislative process, public administration, and foreign policy.

3374. Rotstein, A. *The Precarious Homestead: Essays on Economics, Technology, and Nationalism*. Toronto: New Press, 1973.

3375. Runge, C. Ford, ed. *The Future of the North American Granary: Politics, Economics, and Resource Constraints in North American Agriculture*. Ames, Iowa: Iowa State University Press, 1986.

3376. Slimman, Donald J. *The Parting of the Waves: Canada-United States Differences on the Law of the Sea*. Toronto: Canadian Institute of International Affairs, 1975.

3377. Staines, David, ed. *The Forty-Ninth and Other Parallels: Contemporary Canadian Perspectives*. Amherst: University of Massachusetts Press, 1986.

3378. Stairs, Denis, and Winham, Gilbert, eds. Canada and the International Political/Economic Environment. Toronto: University of Toronto Press, 1985. Deals with the international environment, Canada's international policy, and Canadian trade policy.

3379. Stairs, Denis, and Winham, Gilbert. The Politics of Canada's Economic Relationship with the United States. Toronto: University of Toronto Press, 1985. Discussion of free trade, North American continentalism, U.S. foreign economic policy, and prospects for trade liberalization in the future.

3380. Stern, Robert, Trezise, Philip H., and Whalley, John, eds. Perspectives on a U.S.-Canadian Free Trade Agreement. Ottawa: Institute for Research on Public Policy 1987.

3381. Stone, Frank. Canada, the GATT, and the International Trade System. Montreal: Institute for Research on Public Policy, 1984. Traces bilateral and multilateral ties from before the Second World War through to the 1980's. Includes discussion of multilateral alliances, and new dimensions of international trade for Canada.

3382. Swanick, Eric. Canadian Trade Missions: An Introductory Bibliography. Monticello, Ill.: Vance Bibliographies, 1980.

3383. Swanson, Roger F. Intergovernmental Perspectives on the Canada-U.S. Relationship. New York: New York University Press, 1978. Discussion of U.S. and Canadian consular represenation, intergovernmental relations at the state/provincial level, and the function of bilateral Canadian-U.S. organizations.

3384. Teeple, G., ed. Capitalism and the National Question in Canada. Toronto: University of Toronto Press, 1972.

3385. Tremblay, Rodrique. Financial, Industrial, and Trade Interrelationships Between Canada and the United States. Montreal: Université de Montréal, 1981.

3386. Von Riekhoff, Harold, Sigler, John, and Tomlin, Brian. Canada-U.S. Relations: Policy Environments, Issues, and Prospects. Montreal: C.D. Howe Institute, 1979. Changing Canadian-United States relationship, and future possibilities.

3387. Wex, Samuel. Instead of FIRA: Autonomy for Canadian Subsidiaries? Montreal: Institute for Research on Public Policy, 1984. Role of foreign-owned subsidiaries in Canada, their independence from parent organizations, devices the government can use to keep them controlled, and prospects for the future.

3388. Whalley, John. *Canadian Trade Policies and the World Economy*. Toronto: University of Toronto Press, 1985. Examination of Canada's trade policies, its access to foreign export markets, and Canada's links with the global economy.

3389. Whalley, John, ed. *Domestic Policies in the International Economic Environment*. Toronto: University of Toronto Press, 1985. Relations between government and business, especially with regard to the international economic environment. Includes discussion of foreign business investment, trade issues, and how government can act to adjust economic shocks not begun in Canada.

3390. Williams, Glen. *Not for Export: Toward a Political Economy of Canada's Arrested Industrialization*. Toronto: McClelland and Stewart, 1986.

3391. Wright, Richard W. *Japanese Business in Canada: The Elusive Alliance*. Montreal: Institute for Research on Public Policy, 1984. Analysis of bilateral trade relationship, and plans being made for future business relations.

Articles

3392. Abdel-Malek, T., and Sarkar, A.K. "An Analysis of the Effects of Phase II Guidelines of the Foreign Investment Review Act." *Canadian Public Policy* 3:1 (Winter, 1977): 36-49.

3393. Aho, C. Michael, and Levinson, Marc. "A Canadian Opportunity." *Foreign Policy* 66 (1987): 143-155. Analysis of U.S.-Canadian Free Trade discussions.

3394. Albrecht, D.J. "Canadian Foreign Investment Policy and International Politico-Legal Process." *Canadian Yearbook of International Law* 21 (1983): 149-173.

3395. Alper, Donald, and Monahan, Robert. "Bill C-58 and the American Congress: The Politics of Retaliation." *Canadian Public Policy* 4:2 (Spring, 1978): 184-192.

3396. Alper, Donald, and Monahan, Robert. "Regional Transboundary Negotiations Leading to the Skagit River Treaty: Analysis and Future Application." *Canadian Public Policy* 12:1 (1986): 163-174. Background of the negotiations and the structures of conflict resolution used in the negotiations are discussed.

3397. Armstrong, Gregory. "Domestic Factor in Aid Policy." *International Perspectives* (March/April, 1975): 44-48.

3398. Armstrong, Willis C., Armstrong, Louise S., and Wilcox, Francis O. "Atlantic Council Policy Paper: U.S. Policy Towards Canada: The Neighbor We Cannot Take For Granted." Atlantic Community Quarterly 19:3 (1981): 280-295. Suggestions for U.S. policy toward Canada, with specific attention paid to economic policy and defense policy.

3399. Bachand, Denis. "Une évaluation des investissements americains au Québec." ["An Evaluation of American Investments in Quebec."] Études internationales 2:1 (1971): 110-114.

3400. Bagramov, L., and Popov, V. "Libre échange nord-américain et souveraineté du Canada." ["North American Free Trade and Canada's Sovereignty."] La Vie internationale 2 (1986): 74-82.

3401. Balthazar, Louis. "Canada-U.S. Relations: Achieving a Stronger Identity." International Perspectives (January-February, 1973): 7-8.

3402. Balthazar, Louis. "New Atmosphere in Canadian-American Relations." International Perspectives (September/October, 1977): 25-28.

3403. Balthazar, Louis. "Les rélations canada-américaines: Nationalisme et continentalisme." ["The Canadian-American Relations: Nationalism and Continentalism."] Études internationales 14:1 (1983): 23-38.

3404. Banker, Stephen. "How America Sees Quebec." International Perspectives (January, 1983): 13-18.

3405. Barber, C.L. "Looking Outward: A New Trade Strategy for Canada." Canadian Public Policy 2:1 (Winter, 1976): 113-120.

3406. Barry, Donald. "Border Broadcasting and Free Trade." Canadian Public Administration 29:2 (1986): 11-13.

3407. Barry, Donald. "Border Broadcasting: Lessons for Canadian Diplomacy." Queen's Quarterly 93:2 (1986): 381-398.

3408. Barry, Donald. "The Canada-European Community Long Term Fisheries Agreement: Internal Politics and Fisheries Diplomacy." Revue d'Intégration européenne 9:1 (19985): 5-28.

3409. Barry, Donald. "Canadian Policy and US Business Interests." International Perspectives (September-October, 1984): 8-10. Canadian officials should take the effect of "protectionist" legislation on American business interests into consideration when they consider future legislation of this type.

3410. Barry, Donald. "Eisenower, St. Laurent, and Free Trade, 1953." International Perspectives 1987 (March-April): 3-7.

3411. Béliveau, Donald, and Billardon, Jean-François. "La décision d'implication internationale au sein de l'entreprise privée." ["The Internationalization Decision in the Private Firm."] Études internationales 15:1 (1984): 7-60. Seeks to describe the decision process of businessmen when questions of internationalization are, and identifies some of their perceptions of and satisfaction with Canadian and Quebec government programs.

3412. Bilgin, B. "Japan's Changing Industrial Strategy and Its Implications for Japanese Investment in Canada." Pacific Affairs 55:2 (1982): 267-272.

3413. Billa, Krupadanam, J.B. "Canadian-American Relations: Growing Independence of the Lesser Power in a Disparate Dyad." International Studies 18:4 (1979): 615-628. Discussion of Canadian nationalism and where Canada stands in its relationship with the United States.

3414. Boardman, Robert. "Canada and the Community: One Year After." World Today 33:10 (1977): 395-404. The collaboration between Canadian officials and the European Commission still faces obstacles.

3415. Boardman, Robert. "Initiatives and Outcomes: The European Community and Canada's `Third Option'." Revue d'Intégration européenne 3:1 (1979): 5-28.

3416. Bonin, Bernard. "Les facteurs économiques de la politique étrangère du Canada." ["Economic Factors of Canadian Foreign Policy."] Politique étrangère 38:2 (1973): 149-178. Importance of the influence on Canadian foreign policy of traditionally strong ties of the United Kingdom and the United States, and especially of strong economic ties with the latter.

3417. Borgese, Elisabeth Mann. "Law of the Sea: Crossroads Again." International Perspectives 1986 (July-August), 12-15.

3418. Boucher, Marc. "The Politics of Economic Depression: Canadian-American Relations in the Mid-1930s." International Journal 41:1 (1985-1986): 3-36.

3419. Braën, André. "Legal Aspects of Canadian Fisheries on the Atlantic Coast." Canadian Yearbook of International Law 21 (1983): 3-52.

3420. Brecher, Irving. "Canada-U.S. Economic Relations." International Perspectives (November/December, 1975): 29-27.

3421. Brecher, Irving. "The Continuing Challenge of International Development: A Canadian Perspective." Queen's Quarterly 82:3 (1975): 323-343.

3422. Brecher, Irving. "Foreign Aid and Human Rights." International Perspectives (September-October, 1985): 23-26. Whether Canada should link foreign aid to behavior of foreign governments in the area of human rights.

3423. Brillon, Marc. "Political-Legal Interactions in the Gulf of Maine: A Canadian-American Dispute." Journal of International Affairs 37:2 (1984): 357-365. Negotiations and conflict over the Georges Bank fishing area, halfway between Nova Scotia and Cape Cod.

3424. Britton, J.N.H. "Locational Perspectives on Free Trade for Canada." Canadian Public Policy 4:1 (Winter, 1978): 4-19.

3425. Brodhead, Tim. "If Africa is the Question, is NGO the Answer?" International Journal 41:4 (1986): 869-881. Analysis of the role of Canadian Non-Governmental Organizations (NGOs) and their policies in the African aid crisis.

3426. Bromke, Adam. "Relations Between Canada and Poland." International Perspectives (March/April, 1975): 26-31.

3427. Buckley, Suzann. "Reflections on Canadian Imperialism." Canadian Journal of African Studies 15:1 (1981): 46-51. Canada's role as a colonial or imperialist power in the Third World.

3428. Buzan, Barry. "Canada and the Law of the Sea." Ocean Development and International Law 11 (1982): 149-180.

3429. Caccia, Charles. "Looking at Ourselves Through Water." International Perspectives (November-December, 1985): 20-21. American-Canadian relations in the area of water pollution policy.

3430. Calvert, A.L., and Crener, M.A. "Foreign Business Control: The Canadian Experience, 1973-1977." Canadian Public Administration 22:3 (1979): 415-438.

3431. Cameron, David R. "The Political Impact of the Free Movement of Goods, Persons, Services, and Capital on the General Process of Integration: A Comment on the Canadian Case." Revue d'Intégration européenne 3:3 (1980): 357-361.

3432. Cameron, Duncan. "Monetary Relations in North America." *International Journal* 42:1 (1986-1987): 170-198.

3433. Carroll, John E. "Water Dampens U.S.- Canadian Relations." *Bulletin of the Atomic Scientists* 40:1 (1984): 20-25. U.S failure to act in the area of environmental relations is hurting American-Canadian relations in the area of Acid Rain.

3434. Carroll, John E., and Mack, Newell B. "On Living Together in North America: Canada, the United States, and International Relations." *Denver Journal of International Law and Policy* 12:1 (1982): 35-50.

3435. Carstensen, Peter C. "Competition Policy for an Economically Integrated North America." *Law and Contemporary Problems* 44:3 (1981): 81-104.

3436. Charlton, Mark. "The Management of Canada's Bilateral Food Aid: An Organizational Perspective." *Revue canadienne d'Études du Développement* 7:1 (1986): 7-19. Focuses upon the CIDA organzation and role in the food aid distribution process.

3437. Clark, Joseph. "Canada and the Commonwealth." *Round Table* 296 (1985): 306-310.

3438. Clark, Peter. "Hurtling Canada's Dumping Laws." *International Perspectives* (March-April, 1984): 29-32. The importance of the Canadian Anti-Dumping Act for Canada and its implications for other nations.

3439. Clark, Robert. "International Trade Environment." *International Perspectives* (September-December, 1979): 7-12.

3440. Coffey, Colin. "Foreign Investment in Cable Television: The United States and Canada." *Hastings International and Comparative Law Review* 6:2 (1983): 399-432.

3441. Cohen, Maxwell. "Canada and the U.S. -- New Approaches to Undeadly Quarrels." *International Perspectives* (March-April, 1985): 16-22. Formal and informal mechanisms for policy dispute resolution.

3442. Cohen, Maxwell. "Canada and the United States -- Possibilities for the Future." *The Columbia Journal of Transnational Law* 12:2 (1973): 196-212. Historical review of Canadian-American relations, and prospects for resolution of contemporary tensions and problems.

3443. Cohen, Maxwell. "Canadian-American Relations." *International Perspectives* (November/December, 1980): 3-9.

3444. Cohen, Maxwell. "Constants and Variables in Canada-US Relations." *International Perspectives* (November-December, 1980): 3-9 Look forward into the Reagan presidency to anticipate issues of importance in Canadian-American relations.

3445. Cohen, Maxwell. "Le traité canado-américain des eaux limitrophes et la Commission mixte internationale." ["The Canada-United States Boundary Waters Treaty and the International Joint Commission."] *Études internationales* 11:3 (1980): 375-392. Examines the bilateral structures which exist for avoiding and settling disputes in "shared resource planning," examining the Boundary Waters Treaty, and the Great Lakes Quality Agreement.

3446. Cohn, Theodore. "Canadian Aid and Trade in Skim Milk Powder: Some Recent Issues." *Canadian Public Policy* 4:2 (Spring, 1978):213-229.

3447. Cohn, Theodore. "Canadian Food Policy and the Third World." *Current History* 79:460 (1980): 138-153.

3448. Cohn, Theodore. "Food Surpluses and Canadian Food Aid." *Canadian Public Policy* 3:2 (Spring, 1977): 141-154.

3449. Cooper, Andrew Fenton. "Subnational Activity and Foreign Economic Policy Making in Canada and the United States: Perspectives on Agriculture." *International Journal* 41:3 (1986): 655-673.

3450. Cooper, John. "Delimitation of the Maritime Boundary in the Gulf of Maine Area." *Ocean Development and International Law* 16:1 (1986): 59-90. Study of how the 1984 decision in the Gulf of Maine case was determined.

3451. Cowhey, Peter. "Trade Talks and the Informatics Sector." *International Journal* 42:1 (1986-1987): 107-137.

3452. Cowley, George A. "Culture and Foreign Policy." *International Perspectives* (September-October, 1976): 27-32.

3453. Crane, David. "Canada's Energy Policies in a Global Context." *International Perspectives* (July/August, 1973): 32-37.

3454. Crener, M.A. and Hénault, G.M. "International Development: Administrative Look at Transnationals." *International Perspectives* (July/August, 1977): 18-22.

3455. Critchley, W. Harriet. "Canada and the Sea: Maritime Forces and Law of Sea." *International Perspectives* (March/April, 1978): 3-7.

3456. Dalpé, Robert. "Politique commerciale et contrôle de l'investissement étranger: l'expérience canadienne." ["Commercial Policy and Control of Foreign Investment: The Canadian Experience."] Canadian Journal of Political Science 20:2 (1987): 337-361.

3457. Daneau, Marcel. "Les pêches canadiennes: objet de relations internationales complexes et conflictuelles." ["Canadian Fisheries: An Object of Complex and Conflicting International Relations."] Études internationales 18:1 (1987): 127-152.

3458. Delvoie, L.A. "Economic Relations with Arab World." International Perspectives (November/December, 1976): 29-34.

3459. DeMestral, A.L.C., and Legault, L. H. J. "Multilateral Negotiation -- Canada and the Law of the Sea Conference." International Journal 35:1 (1979-1980): 47-69.

3460. Denis, Jean-Emile, Stavrinidis, Christine, and Tessier, Serge. "Les incidences sectorielles et régionales du libre-échange Canada-Etats-Unis." ["The Sector-Based and Regional Consequences of Free-Trade between Canada and the United States."] Études internationales 17:1 (1986): 33-48.

3461. Denis, Paul-Yves. "Le modèle brésilien de développement, la géopolitique, et les intérêts canadiens." ["The Brazilian Model of Developmennt, Geopolitics, and Canadian Interests."] Études internationales 7:3 (1976): 343-358.

3462. DeVoretz, Don, and Maki, Dennis. "The Size and Distribution of Human Capital Transfers from LDCs to Canada: 1966 - 1973." Economic Development and Cultural Change 28:4 (1980): 779-800.

3463. Diebold, William. "Canada and the United States: Twenty-Five Years of Economic Relations." International Journal 39:2 (1984): 389-409.

3464. Dinsmore, John. "Les échanges internationaux du Québec." ["International Exchanges of Quebec."] Études internationales 7:1 (1976): 110-115. The development of the industries in Quebec is discussed in terms of investment, technology, and the external commercial activities undertaken by the province.

3465. Dobell, Peter C. "The Influence of the United States Congress on Canadian-American Relations." International Organization 28:4 (1974): 903-929.

3466. Dobell, Peter C. "Negotiating with the United States." International Journal 36:1 (1980-1981): 17-38.

3467. Dolan, Michael, et al. "Asymmetrical Dyads and Foreign Policy: Canada-U.S. Relations, 1963-1972." Journal of Conflict Resolution 26:3 (1982): 387-422. Analysis of Canadian-American relations, with emphasis upon nations' economies and the extent of their linkages.

3468. Dolan, Michael, and Tomlin, Brian. "Foreign Policy in Asymmetrical Dyads: Theoretical Reformulation and Empirical Analysis, Canada-United States Relations, 1963-1972." International Studies Quarterly 28:3 (1984): 349-368.

3469. Dolan, Michael, Tomlin, Brian, and von Riekhoff, Harold. "Integration and Autonomy in Canada-United States Relations, 1963-1972." Canadian Journal of Political Science 15:2 (1982): 331-364.

3470. Donnelly, Michael W. "Growing Disharmony in Canadian-Japanese Trade." International Journal 36:4 (1981): 879-897.

3471. Donneur, André. "La pénétration économique en Amérique latine." ["Economic Penetration into Latin America."] Études internationales 14:1 (1983): 83-102.

3472. Doran, Charles F. "The United States and Canada: Intervulnerability and Interdependence." International Journal 38:1 (1982): 128-146.

3473. Drobnick, Richard. "Political Risk Analysis for Canada and Mexico." Technological Forecasting and Social Change 26:4 (1984): 315-353.

3474. Drouin, Marie-Josée, and Malmgren, Harold. "Canada, the United States, and the World Economy." Foreign Affairs 60:2 (1981): 393-413. Study of the special relationship between the U.S. and Canada with suggestions for the future.

3475. Drummond, Ian. "On Disbelieving the Commissioner's Free-Trade Case." Canadian Public Policy 12 (1986): 59-67. Review of the Report of the Royal Commssion on the Economic Union and the Development Prospects for Canada, 1985, otherwise known as the MacDonald Report.

3476. Dupuy, René-Jean. "The Law of the Sea Conference." International Perspectives (March/April, 1974): 63-72.

3477. Dworsky, Leonard. "The Great Lakes: 1955-1985." Natural Resources Journal 26:2 (1986): 291-336.

3478. English, H. Edward. "Foreign Investment in Manufacturing." Proceedings of the Academy of Political Science 32:2 (1976): 88-99.

3479. English, H. Edward. "'National Policy' and Canadian Trade." International Perspectives (March-April, 1984): 3-6. What should Canadian trade policy be in future years, and why?

3480. Epstein, William. "Canada and Disarmament." International Perspectives (March-April, 1979): 28-34.

3481. Farquharson, Duart. "Trudeau Abroad: A Short Jaunt to Washington." International Perspectives (January/February, 1975): 8-11.

3482. Fayerweather, John. "Canadian Foreign Investment Policy." California Management Review 17:3 (1974): 74-83. Assesses implications of Canadian actions during the 1972-1973 period having to do with government policy regarding foreign investments, including analysis of the consequences and implications of the Foreign Investment Review Act.

3483. Fayerweather, John. "Elite Attitudes Toward Multinational Firms: A Study of Britain, Canada, and France." International Studies Quarterly 16:4 (1972): 472-490.

3484. Feld, Werner J., and Brylski, Cheron. "A North American Accord: Feasible or Futile?" Western Political Quarterly 36:2 (1983): 286-311.

3485. Feldman, Elliot J., and Feldman, Lily Gardner. "The Special Relationship between Canada and the United States." Jerusalem Journal of International Relations 4:4 (1980): 56-85.

3486. Feldman, Lily Gardner. "Canada and the United States in the 1970s: Rift and Reconciliation." World Today 34:12 (1978): 484-492.

3487. Ferguson, Marjorie. "Broadcasting in a Colder Climate: Canada's Cautionary Tale." Political Quarterly 58:1 (1987): 40-52.

3488. Finkle, Peter Z.R. "Canadian Foreign Policy for Marine Fisheries: An Alternative Perspective." Journal of Canadian Studies 10:1 (1975): 10-23.

3489. Finlayson, Jock. "Canadian Business and Free Trade." International Perspectives (March-April, 1985): 29-31. Advocates new Canadian-U.S. free trade agreements.

3490. Finlayson, Jock A., and Haglund, David G. "Oil Politics and Canada-United States Relations." Political Science Quarterly 99:2 (1984): 271-288.

3491. Fitzgerald, Gerald. "Le Canada et le développement du droit international: La contribution de l'Affaire de la fonderie de Trail à la formation du nouveau droit de la pollution atmosphérique transfrontière." ["Canadian-American Arbitration and the Creation of Law: The Contribution of the Trail Smelter Case to the Development of International Law, Including the Emerging Law of Transboundary Air Pollution."] Études internationales 11:3 (1980): 393-419. Decisions from the Trail Smelter Arbitral Tribunal in 1938 and 1941 have continued to contribute to international law, especially in the area of transboundary air pollution in which the Tribunal indicated a principle of international liability.

3492. Fleming, Peter, and Keenleyside, T.A. "The Rhetoric of Canadian Aid." International Perspectives (September-October, 1984): 18-22. Canadian performance in relation to Third World development is not as strong as government statements and speeches have indicated.

3493. Forest, Pierre-Gerlier. "A Propos de la «troisième option» et de la politique américaine de l'Etat Canadien." ["On the "Third Option" and the American Politics of the Canadian State."] Études internationales 13:2 (1982): 305-322. The special relationship between the United States and Canada, and the need for Canada to be concerned for its own future first.

3494. Fowler, R.M. "Canadian-American Relations." International Perspectives (May/June, 1973): 35-39.

3495. Fox, Annette Baker. "On Living Together in North America." International Journal 36 (1980-81): 1-16.

3496. Fox, Annette Baker, and Hero, Alfred O., Jr. "Canada and the United States: Their Finding Frontier." International Organization 28:4 (1974): 999-1014.

3497. Franck, Thomas M. "International Law in Canadian Practice: The State of the Art and the Art of the State." International Journal 31:1 (1975-1976): 180-193.

3498. Frederick, Michel. "The Delimitation of the Continental Shelf Between Canada and the United States in the Beaufort Sea." Canadian Yearbook of International Law 17 (1979): 30-98.

3499. Freeman, Susan. "Canada's Changing Posture Toward Multinational Corporations: An Attempt to Harmonize Nationalism With Continued Industrial Growth." New York University Journal of International Law and Politics 7:2 (1974): 271-316. Describes historical roots of Canadian economic nationalism, and analyzes initiatives in Canadian industrial strategy.

3500. Fry, Earl. "Sectoral Free Trade." *International Perspectives* (September-October, 1984): 3-7. The establishment of a free trade agreement is in the best interests of both Canada and the United States.

3501. Fry, Earl H. "Surviving Freer Trade with the U.S." *Canadian Public Administration* 29:2 (1986): 8-10.

3502. Gallon, Gary. "The Aid Fix: Pushers and Addicts." *International Perspectives* (November-December, 1983): 11-14. Foreign aid serves a function, but some developing nations are overly dependent upon this aid.

3503. Gallon, Gary. "CIDA - Aiding or Trading?" *International Perspectives* (July-August, 1984): 17-20. The role and function of the Canadian International Development Agency, with special attention to its effect on non-governmental organizations in the Third World.

3504. Gallon, Gary. "Canadian Aid and Environmental Protection." *International Perspectives* (May-June, 1984): 19-21. Canada's two major agencies for development in the Third World, the Canadian International Development Agency, and the Export Development Corporation, have not been as careful as they should have about promoting environmental protection processes in the activities they support.

3505. Garnier, Gerard. "Les entreprises multinationales et l'indépendance éventuelle du Québec." ["Multinational Enterprises and the Eventual Independence of Quebec."] *Canadian Public Policy* 5:1 (Winter, 1979): 59-69.

3506. Garnier, Gérard. "Pouvoirs de décision des filiales québécoises d'entreprises américaines." ["Powers of Decision of Quebec Subsidiaries of American Enterprises."] *Études internationales* 2:1 (1971): 11-43.

3507. Gérin-Lajoie, Paul. "CIDA in a Changing Government Organization." *Canadian Public Administration* 15:1 (1972): 46-58.

3508. Gérin-Lajoie, Paul. "Twenty-Five Years of Development Co-Operation." *International Perspectives* (November/December, 1975): 38-42.

3509. Gilpin, Robert. "Les investissements directs américains et la présence de deux nationalismes au Canada." ["Direct American Investments and the Presence of Two Nationalisms in Canada."] *Études internationales* 2:1 (1971): 44-57.

3510. Gilpin, Robert. "Integration an Disintegration on the North American Continent." *International Organization* 28:4 (1974): 851-874.

3511. Globerman, Steven. "Canada's Foreign Investment Review Agency and the Direct Investment Process in Canada." Canadian Public Administration 27:3 (1984): 313-328.

3512. Gordon, M.J. "A World Scale National Corporation Industrial Strategy." Canadian Public Policy 4:1 (Winter, 1978): 46-56.

3513. Gordon, Sheldon. "Canadian Aid Policy. International Perspectives (May/June, 1976): 21-25.

3514. Gordon, Sheldon. "The Canadian Government and Human Rights Abroad." International Perspectives (November-December, 1983): 8-10. Ottawa's record in this area is not as strong as it could, or should, be.

3515. Gotlieb, Allan E. "Canada-U.S. Relations: The Rules of the Game." SAIS Review 4 (1982): 177-188.

3516. Gotlieb, Allan, and Dalfen, Charles. "National Jurisdiction and International Responsibility: New Canadian Approaches to International Law." American Journal of International Law 67:2 (1973): 229-258. Describes Canadian approaches to international law, especially in the two areas of outer space law and the law of the sea.

3517. Gotlieb, Allan, and Kinsman, Jeremy. "North-South, or East-West?" International Perspectives (January/February, 1983): 25-29.

3518. Gotlieb, Allan, and Kinsman, Jeremy. "Reviving the Third Option." International Perspectives (January-February, 1981): 2-5. The 1980s present new opportunities for Canada to strengthen its trade relationships abroad, apart from with the United States.

3519. Graham, William. "Reflections on United States Legal Imperialism: Canadian Sovereignty in the Context of North American Economic Integration." International Journal 40:3 (1985): 478-509. Canada must continue to pressure the United States to be more responsive to the wishes of other nation-states through a variety of international forums.

3520. Grant, J. "Foreign Investment: Turning Off and Turning On." Canadian Public Policy 9:1 (March, 1983): 32-36.

3521. Grayson, George W. "The Maple Leaf, the Cactus, and the Eagle: Energy Trilateralism." Inter-American Economic Affairs 34:4 (1981): 49-76.

3522. Green, Fitzhugh. "Acid Rain and U.S.-Canadian Relations." Washington Quarterly 9:3 (1986): 103-108.

3523. Greene, Stephen, and Keating, Thomas. "Domestic Factors and Canada-United States Fisheries Relations." Canadian Journal of Political Science 13:4 (1980): 731-750.

3524. Greenwood, T. "Canadian-American Trade in Energy Resources." International Organization 28:4 (1974): 689-710.

3525. Grenier, Raymond. "La «crise globale» et la coopération canadienne au développement de l'Afrique francophone." ["The `Global Crisis' and Canadian Cooperation in the Development of French-Speaking Africa."] Études internationales 5:2 (1974): 367-375. Discusses the various dimensions of Canadian activity in helping French-speaking Africa, as well as some analysis of Canada's financial contributions to this end.

3526. Grenon, Jean-Yves. "Canada and Europe's `Eighteen'." International Perspectives (March/April, 1976): 37-42.

3527. Haglund, David G. "Canada and the International Politics of Oil: Latin American Source of Supply and Import Vulnerability in the 1980s." Canadian Journal of Political Science 15:2 (1982): 259-298.

3528. Hamilton, Richard E. "A Marketing Board to Regulate Exports of Natural Gas." Canadian Public Administration 16:1 (Spring, 1973): 83-95.

3529. Hammer, Heather-Jo, and Gartrell, John W. "American Penetration and Canadian Development: A Case Study of Mature Development." American Sociological Review 51:2 (1986): 201-213.

3530. Handelman, Stephen. "North American Détente at Mid-Term." International Perspectives (November/December, 1978): 19-21.

3531. Harrison, Fred. "New Ways to Trade with U.S." International Perspectives (March-April, 1984): 6-8. Free trade agreements can be signed by "sector" rather than in an all-or-nothing manner.

3532. Hawkins, Gordon. "Implications of Canada as a Seabed Power." International Perspectives (July/August, 1972): 35-39.

3533. Hay, Keith. "Canadian Trade Policy in the 1980s" International Perspectives (July-August, 1982): 16-20. Multilateral trade policy is not going to be as effective in the future as a series of bilateral endeavors.

3534. Hay, Keith, and Davies, Robert. "Declining Resources, Declining Markets." International Perspectives (March-April, 1984): 13-18. Reliance on resource-based trade is detrimental to the future export prospects of Canada.

3535. Haythorne, George. "The International Labour Organization: A Canadian Appraisal After Fifty Years." Canadian Public Administration 14:2 (Summer, 1971): 173-192.

3536. Heeney, Stephen. "Canadian-Japanese Mutual Interests." International Perspectives (January/February, 1975): 15-18.

3537. Helleiner, G.K. "Canada and the New International Economic Order." Canadian Public Policy 2:3 (Summer, 1976): 451-465.

3538. Helleiner, G.K. "International Development Eight Years On." International Journal 33:2 (1978): 395-400.

3539. Henderson, Michael D. "Managed Trade: Look Out, Canada!" International Perspectives (1985): 28-30.

3540. Hérisson, Martin. "Canada's `Third Option'." Nord e Sud 272 (1977): 75-92.

3541. Hocking, Brian. "Canada-U.S. Freer Trade Negotiations. Domestic and International Politics in the Pre-Negotiation Phase." The Round Table 300 (1986): 384-394.

3542. Hodges, Luther H. "Canadian-United States Economic Relations: And Some Constitutional Considerations." Presidential Studies Quarterly 11:1 (1981): 48-51.

3543. Hollick, Ann L. "Canadian-American Relations: Law of the Sea." International Organization 28:4 (1974): 755-780.

3544. Holmes, John W. "Canadian-American Relations -- Vive la Difference." Round Table 285 (1983): 11-24.

3545. Holmes, John W. "The Dilemma of Canadian-American Relations." International Perspectives (May-June, 1972): 3-9.

3546. Holmes, J.W. "Divided We Stand." International Journal 31:3 (1976): 385-398.

3547. Holmes, John W. "The Dumbbell Won't Do." Foreign Affairs 50 3-22.

3548. Holmes, John W. "Impact of Domestic Political Factors on Canadian-American Relations: Canada." International Organization 28:4 (1974): 611-636.

3549. Holmes, John W. "Morality, Realism, and Foreign Affairs." International Perspectives (September/October, 1977): 20-24.

3550. Holmes, John W. "Morality, Realism, and Foreign Affairs." International Perspectives (November/December, 1981): 14-18.

3551. Holsti, Kal J., and Thomas A. Levy. "Bilateral Institutions and Transgovernmental Relations Between Canada and the United States." International Organization 28:4 (1974): 875-902.

3552. Horowitz, I.L. "The Hemispheric Connection: A Critique and Corrective to the Entrepreneurial Thesis of Development with Special Emphasis on the Canadian Case." Queen's Quarterly 80:3 (1973): 327-359.

3553. Houle, F. "The Federal Government of Canada and the World Economy: Strategies of Insertion." Canadian Journal of Political Science 20:3 (1987): 467-500.

3554. Howard, Rhoda. "The Canadian Government Response to Africa's Refugee Problem." Canadian Journal of African Studies 15:1 (1981): 95-116. Canada's actions within the U.N. aid framework, and Canada's policies of admission of African refugees to Canada.

3555. Howard, Rhoda. "Contemporary Canadian Refugee Policy: A Critical Assessment." Canadian Public Policy 6:2 (1980): 361-373. Study of the historical, humanitarian, racial, economic, and ideological factors of Canadian refugee policy.

3556. Hurtig, Mel. "Sharing the Continent: The Need for Equitable Division." International Perspectives (Special Issue, 1976): 10-14.

3557. Inglis, Alex. "Canada and the United States: Recent Statements on the Relationship." International Perspectives (March/April, 1975): 3-12.

3558. Islam, Nasir. "Politics of World Food Scarcity." International Perspectives (November/December, 1976): 18-23.

3559. Jacomy-Millette, Annemarie. "David et Goliath: L'équilibre fragile des relations énergétique canado-américaines á l'aube de la création de Petro-Canada." ["David and Goliath: The Fragile Equilibrium in Relations Regarding Energy Between Canada and the United States at the Dawn of Creation of Petro-Canada."] Études internationales 13:4 (1982): 633-656. Describes the world context within which Canadian energy decisions must be made. Describes evolution of past Canadian energy policies and the National Energy Program.

3560. Jockel, Joseph T. "The Canada-United States Relationship after the Third Round: The Emergence of Semi-Institutionalizd Management." *International Journal* 40:4 (1985): 689-715. Examines the increased use of multilateral authorities in settling differences between the two countries.

3561. Jockel, Joseph, and Sokolsky, Joel. "Washington and Ottawa: The Next Phase." *Round Table* 291 (1984): 316-329.

3562. Johnson, Harry. "Canada-U.S. Relations: The Advantages of Integration." *International Perspectives* (January-February, 1973):9-11.

3563. Johnston, Douglas M. "Coastal Zone Management in Canada: Purposes and Prospects." *Canadian Public Administration* 20:1 (1977): 140-151.

3564. Kaplan, William. "Assistance Under the 1970 UNESCO Cultural Property Convention: Canada's Request to the United States." *Stanford Journal of International Law* 22:1 (1986): 123-152.

3565. Keating, Thomas. "Domestic Groups, Bureaucrats, and Bilateral Fisheries Relations." *International Journal* 39:1 (1983-1984): 146-170.

3566. Keenleyside, T.A. "Canada and the Pacific: Policies for Economic Growth." *Pacific Affairs* 46:1 (1973): 5-28.

3567. Keenleyside, T.A. "Canada-South Africa Commercial Relations, 1977-1982: Business as Usual?" *Canadian Journal of African Studies* 17:3 (1983): 449-467. Analysis of effects of 1977 changes in Canadian foreign relations with South Africa.

3568. Keenleyside, Terence. "Foreign Aid and Human Rights." *International Perspectives* 1987 (March-April): 15-19.

3569. Keenleyside, T.A., Burton, B.E., and Soderlund, W.C. "The Press and Foreign Policy: Canadian Newspaper Coverage of Relations with the United States, October-December, 1982." *International Journal* 41:1 (1985-1986): 189-220.

3570. Keohane, Robert O., and Nye, Joseph Jr. "Introduction: The Complex Politics of Canadian-American Interdependence." *International Organization* 28:4 (1974): 595-610.

3571. Kienet, Alvin. "Decoloniation in the North: Canada and the United States." *Canadian Review of Studies in Nationalism* 13:1 (1986): 57-77. Reviews Native Canadian land claims and proposals for self government.

3572. Kirn, Jackie Krolopp, and Marts, Marion E. "The Skagit-High Ross Dam Controversy: Negotiation and Settlement." Natural Resources Journal 26:2 (1986): 261-290.

3573. Kirton, John. "Canada and the United States: A More Distant Relationship." Current History 79:460 (1980): 117-120.

3574. Kirton, John. "The Politics of Bilateral Management: The Case of the Automotive Trade." International Journal 36:1 (1980): 39-69.

3575. Kirton, John. "An Uncertain Take-Off: The North American Space Industry in the 1980s." International Journal 42:1 (1986-1987): 138-169.

3576. Kirton, John, and Donnelly, Michael. "Japanese Investment: The Answer for Canada." International Perspectives 1986 (March-April): 3-7.

3577. Kreinin, Mordechai E. "North American Economic Integration." Law and Contemporary Problems 44:3 (1981): 7-32.

3578. Kresl, Peter K. "The United States, Canada, and the `Market Mentality'." Journal of Inter-American Studies and World Affairs 14:1 (1972): 3-12. Canadian-American trade relations, and the degree to which Americans take Canada for granted.

3579. Lalonde, Marc. "Canada and the Energy Independence of the Free World." Politique internationale 12 (1981): 201-209.

3580. Lamson, Cynthia, and VanderZwaag, David. "Arctic Waters: Needs and Options for Canadian-American Cooperation." Ocean Development and International Law 18:1 (1987): 49-99.

3581. Langdon, Frank. "La politique économique du Japon à l'égard du Canada." ["Japan's Economic Strategy Toward Canada."] Études internationales 16:3 (1985): 525-545. Although the emphasis of this article is on Japan's policies vis-a-vis Canada, it does describe to some extent Canadian-Japanese political and economic ties.

3582. Langdon, Frank. "Canada's Struggle for Entrée to Japan." Canadian Public Policy 2:1 (Winter, 1976): 54-64.

3583. Lantzke, Ulf. "Energy: An International Problem." International Perspectives (March/April, 1979): 31-34.

3584. Laux, Jeanne. "Public Enterprises and Canadian Foreign Economic Policy." Publius 14:4 (1984): 61-80. Examines the degree to which the federal government can influence foreign economic relations through regulation of public enterprises such as the Canadian Development Corporation, and the Canadian National Railways.

3585. Law, Carl Edgar. "Canada and the Seas: Freedom of the Seas." International Perspectives (July/August, 1980): 13-16.

3586. Leach, Richard. "Canada and the United States: A Special Relationship." Current History 72:426 (1977): 145-149.

3587. Leach, Richard, Riley, Richard, and Levy, Thomas . "State-Province Relations Across the Canadian Border." State Government 48:3 (1975): 150-155. Discussion of the regular meetings of the Governors of six New England states and Premiers of five Eastern Canadian Provinces.

3588. Leach, Richard, Walker, Donald, and Levy, Thomas . "Province-State Trans-Border Relations: A Preliminary Assessment." Canadian Public Administration 16:3 (1973): 469-482.

3589. LeBlanc, Philippe. "Canada at the U.N. Human Rights Commission." International Perspectives (September-October, 1985): 20-22. Canada could do much more for human rights at the U.N. than it is doing at the present time.

3590. LeDuc, Daniel. "Le libre-échange canado-américain: Défi à la souveraineté et au progrés." ["Canadian-American Free Exchange: Challenge to Sovereignty and Progress."] Canadian Journal of Political Science 19:2 (1986):305-324.

3591. Legault, L. H. "A Line for All Uses: The Gulf of Maine Boundary Revisited." International Journal 40:3 (1985): 461-477.

3592. Legault, L. H., and Hankey, Blair. "From Sea to Seabed: The Single Maritime Boundary in the Gulf of Maine Case." American Journal of International Law 79:4 (1985): 961-991.

3593. Léger, Georges Antoine. "Droit de la mer: La contribution du Canada au nouveau concept de la zone économique." ["Law of the Sea: Canada's Contribution to the Concept of an Economic Zone."] Études internationales 11:3 (1980): 421-440. Describes Canada's role in developing a new concept in Oceans Law, the exclusive economic zone, based upon a new application of Canada's approach to the Law of the Sea.

3594. LeMarquand, David. "Preconditions to Cooperation in Canada-United States Boundary Waters." Natural Resources Journal 26:2 (1986): 221-242.

3595. Lemarquand, D, and Scott, A.D. "Canada-United States Environmental Relations." Proceedings of the Academy of Political Science 32:2 (1976): 149-163.

3596. Levy, T., and Munton, D. "Canada and the U.S.: Implications of State-Provincial Relations." International Perspectives (March-April, 1976): 23-28.

3597. Leyton-Brown, David. "Extraterritoriality in Canadian-American Relations." International Journal 36:1 (1980-1981): 185-207.

3598. Leyton-Brown, David. "The Mug's Game: Automotive Investment Incentives in Canada and the United States." International Journal 7:1 (1980): 4-14.

3599. Leyton-Brown, David. "The Mulroney Gamble." International Perspectives (September-October, 1985): 27-30. Whether closer economic ties with the United States are a good thing.

3600. Leyton-Brown, David. "The Multinational Enterprise and Conflict in Canadian-American Relations." International Organization 28:4 (1974): 733-754.

3601. Leyton-Brown, David, and Ruggie, John Gerard. "The North American Political Economy in the Global Context: An Analytical Framework." International Journal 42:1 (1986-1987): 3-24.

3602. Lipsey, Richard. "Will There Be a Canadian-American Free Trade Association?" World Economy 9:3 (1986): 217-238.

3603. Litvak, Isaiah A., and Maule, Christopher J. "Canadian Investment Abroad: In Search of a Policy." International Journal 31:1 (1975-1976): 159-179.

3604. Litvak, Isaiah A., and Maule, Christopher J. "Canadian-United States Corporate Interface and Transnational Relations." International Organization 28:4 (1974): 711-732.

3605. Litvak, Isaiah A., and Maule, Christopher J. "Interest-Group Tactics and the Politics of Foreign Investment: The Time-Reader's Digest Case Study." Canadian Journal of Political Science 7:4 (1974): 616-629. Studies formulation of federal legislation on Canadian magazines and how that legislation was affected by both Canadian and American governmental and corporate action.

3606. Litvak, Isaiah A., and Maule, Christopher J. "The Multinational Corporation: Some Perspectives." Canadian Public Administration 13:2 (Summer, 1970): 129-139.

3607. Lloyd, Trevor. "Canada's Arctic in the Age of Ecology." Foreign Affairs 48:4 (1970): 726-740.

3608. Lyon, Peyton. "Sharing the Continent: The Benevolent Neighbor." International Perspectives (Special Issue, 1976): 14-18.

3609. Lyon, P.V., et al. "Ottawa et le Tiers-Monde." ["Ottawa and the Third World."] International Perspectives (1979): 12-18.

3610. Lyon, P.V., and Leyton-Brown, D. "How 'Official' Ottawa Views the Third World." International Perspectives (January-February, 1979): 11-16. Analysis of Trudeau Government policy toward the Third World, both rhetoric and action.

3611. McAllister, Ian. "Canadian Aid for the Training of Public Servants in Ghana and Zimbabwe." Public Administration and Development 7:3 (1987): 289-307.

3612. McDougall, John N. "Prebuild Phase or Latest Phase? The United States Fuel Market and Canadian Energy Policy." International Journal 36:1 (1980-1981): 117-138.

3613. McFadyen, S. "The Control of Foreign Ownership of Canadian Real Estate." Canadian Public Policy 2:1 (Winter, 1976): 65-77.

3614. McGonigle, R.M., and Zacher, Mark W. "Canada and the Sea: Problem of Marine Pollution." International Perspectives (March/April, 1978): 8-11.

3615. McKie, James W. "An Antimonopoly Policy for North America." Law and Contemporary Problems 44:3 (1981): 105-130.

3616. Maclure, Jeffrey. "North American Acid Rain and International Law." Fletcher Forum 7:1 (1983): 121-154.

3617. McRae, D. "Adjudication of the Maritime Boundary in the Gulf of Maine." Canadian Yearbook of International Law 17 (1979): 292-303. Discussion of the agreement to submit the delimitation of the maritime boundary in the Gulf of Maine to binding settlement.

3618. McRae, D. "Arctic Waters and Canadian Sovereignty." International Journal 38:3 (1983): 476-492.

3619. McRae, D. "The Gulf of Maine Case: The Written Proceedings." Canadian Yearbook of International Law 21 (1983): 266-283.

3620. Maisonrouge, Jacques. "Management and Multinationals: Some Thoughts on Solving the Human Energy Crisis." Canadian Public Administration 20:4 (Winter, 1977): 590-599.

3621. Malmgren, H.B. "The Evolving Trade System." Proceedings of the Academy of Political Science 32:2 (1976): 124-136.

3622. Manuge, Grant. "IDRC at Twelve." International Perspectives (November-December, 1982): 13-16. Status report on the International Development Research Centre, Canada's agency designed to aid the world's poor nations.

3623. Masson, Claude. "La Présence économique américaine au Québec." ["The American Economic Presence in Quebec."] Études internationales 2:1 (1971): 3-10.

3624. Masson, L. "Les impératifs economiques de la politique étrangère du Canada." ["Economic Imperatives of Foreign Policy in Canada."] Études internationales 2 (1970): 6-19.

3625. Matthews, Robert. "The Churches and Foreign Policy." International Perspectives (January-February, 1984): 18-21. Describes the efforts of Christian churches in Canada to influence foreign policy in the area of human rights.

3626. Matthews, Robert, and Pratt, Cranford. "Human Rights and Foreign Policy: Principles and Canadian Practice." Human Rights Quarterly 7:2 (1985): 159-188. Article attempts to suggest the grounds for state interference in the internal politics of another state if this interference is undertaken for the purpose of fighting for human rights. Article then examines Canadian policy with regard to South Africa in this light.

3627. Maule, Christopher. "Foreign Investment in the Pacific Rim." International Perspectives 1987 (January-February): 21-24.

3628. Maule, Christopher, and Vanderwal, Andrew. "International Regulation of Foreign Investment." International Perspectives (November-December, 1985): 22-27. Need for the international community, and Canada, to act to control multinational corporations.

3629. Meisel, John. "Escaping Extinction: Cultural Defence of an Undefended Border." Canadian Journal of Political and Social Theory 10:1-2 (1986): 248-265.

3630. Moroz, A.R., and Back, K.J. "Prospects for a Canada-United States Bilateral Free Trade Agreement: The Other Side of the Fence." International Journal 36:4 (1981): 827-850.

3631. Muirhead, Bruce. "Trade Policy Askew." International Perspectives (July-August, 1985): 8-10. The future of Canadian trade does not lie in Western Europe, but in the Pacific Basin.

3632. Munro, Donald. "Law of the Sea: A Canadian Dilemma." International Perspectives (September-October, 1982): 14-17. Analysis of the Law of the Sea Convention and its implications for Canada.

3633. Munro, Gordon R. "Canada and the Sea: Extended Fisheries Jurisdiction." International Perspectives (March/April, 1978): 12-17.

3634. Munton, Donald. "Dependence and Interdependence in Transboundary Environmental Relations." International Journal 36:1 (1980-1981): 139-184.

3635. Munton, Donald. "Political Problems of Acid Rain." International Perspectives (January/February, 1981): 6-10.

3636. Munton, Donald. "Reagan, Canada, and the Common Environment." International Perspectives (May-June, 1982) : 3-6. The Reagan presidency is not sympathetic to Canadian environmental concerns.

3637. Munton, Donald J. and Poel, Dale H. "Electoral Accountability and Canadian Foreign Policy: The Case of Foreign Investment." International Journal 33:1 (1977-1978): 217-247.

3638. Murphy, C.F. "The Future of North America." Queen's Quarterly 82:3 (1975): 426-433.

3639. Murray, David. "Canadian Business: Trade with Latin America." International Perspectives (November/December, 1980): 28-30.

3640. Murray, J. Alex, and Gerace, Mary C. "Canadian Attitudes Toward the U.S. Presence." Public Opinion Quarterly 36:3 (1972): 388-397.

3641. Naftali, Timothy, and O'Hagan, Peter. "U.S.-Canada Free Trade: A Question of Canadian Maturity." S.A.I.S. Review 6:2 (1986): 39-58.

3642. Nagy, Gretchen E. "Sagebrush and Snowshoes: The Struggle over Natural Resources in Canada and the United States." Law and Contemporary Problems 44:3 (1981): 247-264.

3643. Neville, W.F.W. "Continentalism Fulfilled." Journal of Canadian Studies 5:4 (1970): 58-71.

3644. Niosi, Jorge. "Étude bibliographique: Nord-Sud: Technologie endettement, commerce et firmes multinationales." ["Bibliographic Study: North-South: Indebted Technology, Commerce, and Multi-National Corporations."] Études internationales 14:1 (1983): 165-181.

3645. Nixon, J. Bradford, and Burns, Jeffrey H. "An Examination of the Legality of the Use of the Foreign Investment Review Act by the Government of Canada to Control Intra- and Extra-territorial Commercial Activity by Aliens." International and Comparative Law Quarterly 33:1 (1984): 57-80.

3646. Noel, S.J.R. "Canada and the American Question: A Review Article." Journal of Commonwealth and Comparative Politics 13:1 (1975): 87-92. Review of five books dealing with Canadian-American relations.

3647. Nolan, Cathal J. "The Influence of Parliament on Human Rights in Canadian Foreign Policy." Human Rights Quarterly 7:3 (1985): 373-390. Suggests that the Canadian Parliament has managed -- albeit in a limited way -- to influence the development of Canada's human rights policy in foreign affairs.

3648. Nossal, Kim Richard. "Does the Electoral Cycle in the United States Affect Relations with Canada?" International Journal 36:1 (1980-1981): 208-227.

3649. Nossal, Kim Richard. "IJC and the Garrison Diversion." International Perspectives (November/December, 1978): 22-25.

3650. Nye, J.S., Jr. "Transnational Relations and Interstate Conflicts: An Empirical Analysis." International Organization 28:4 (1974): 961-996.

3651. Ornstein, Michael D. "Assessing the Meaning of Corporate Interlocks: Canadian Evidence." Social Science Research 9:4 (1980): 287-306.

3652. Ornstein, Michael D. "Interlocking Directorates in Canada: Intercorporate or Class Alliance?" Administrative Science Quarterly 29:2 (1984): 210-231.

3653. Page, Don. "Unlocking Canada's Diplomatic Record." International Journal 34:2 (1979): 251-280.

3654. Painchaud, Paul. "Canadian Cultural Diplomacy." International Perspectives (May/June, 1977): 34-39.

3655. Paragg, R.R. "Canadian Aid in the Commonwealth Caribbean: Neo-colonialism or Development?" Canadian Public Policy 6:4 (Autumn, 1980): 628-641.

3656. Passaris, Constantine. "Immigration and Foreign Policy." International Perspectives (November/December, 1976): 23-29.

3657. Peacock, Don. "Negotiating the Pipeline." International Perspectives (January/February, 1978): 12-15.

3658. Pearson, Geoffrey. "Human Rights: Emergence Into International Relations." International Perspectives (July/August, 1978): 9-11.

3659. Pearson, L.B. "Reflections on Inter-War Canadian Foreign Policy." Journal of Canadian Studies 7:2 (1972): 36-42.

3660. Pharand, Donat. "La contribution du Canada au développement du droit international pour la protection du milieu marin: Le cas spécial de l'Arctique." ["Canada's Contribution to the Development of International Law for the Protection of the Marine Environment: the Special Case of the Arctic."] Études internationales 11:3 (1980): 441-466. Describes Canada's Arctic Pollution Prevention Act of 1970, and the intense diplomatic efforts undertaken by the Government under international law to enforce this policy.

3661. Pharand, Donat. "The Northwest Passage in International Law." Canadian Yearbook of International Law 17 (1979): 99-133. Analysis of law dealing with Northwest Passage.

3662. Pickering, John, and Swets, Gina. "Who'll Stop the Rain: Resolution Mechanisms for U.S. - Canadian Transboundary Pollution Disputes." Denver Journal of International Law and Policy 12:1 (1982): 51-91.

3663. Plumptre, A.F.W. Canada and the International Monetary Fund." International Journal 26:1 (1971): 109-121.

3664. Pollock, David, and Manuge, Grant. "The Mulroney Doctrine." International Perspectives (January-February, 1985): 5-8. Describes the tendency to closer Canadian-U.S. economic ties and greater reliance on foreign investment and the private sector in general.

3665. Pratt, Cranford. "Canadian Foreign Policy: Bias to Business." International Perspectives (November-December, 1982): 3-6. Canadian foreign policy often favors business interests over those of other interest groups.

3666. Pratt, Cranford. "Canadian Policy towards the International Monetary Fund: An Attempt to Define a Position." *Canadian Journal of Development Studies* 6:1 (1985): 9-26. Canadian policies toward the IMF need to be changed, but Canada will not take the actions necessary to achieve a more equitable international order and greater human rights.

3667. Rasmussen, Eric K. "The 1978 Great Lakes Water Quality Agreement and Prospects for U.S.-Canada Pollution Control." *Boston College International and Comparative Law Review* 2:2 (1979): 499-520. Analysis of the Great Lakes Water Quality Agreement of 1978, its historical basis, and discussion of implications of the 1978 Agreement.

3668. Regan, Gerald. "Sectoral Free Trade with the U.S." *International Perspectives* (May/June, 1984): 15-17.

3669. Reid, Escott. "Canada and the Struggle Against World Poverty." *International Journal* 25:1 (1969-1970): 142-157.

3670. Rhee, Sang-Myon. "Equitable Solutions to the Maritime Boundary Dispute Between the United States and Canada in the Gulf of Maine." *American Journal of International Law* 75:3 (1981): 590-628. Traces history of the disputes, discusses the relationship between fishery resources and maritime boundaries, and suggests solutions.

3671. Riddell-Dixon, Elizabeth. "Deep Seabed Mining: A Hotbed for Governmental Politics?" *International Journal* 41:1 (1985-1986): 72-94. Explanation of Canadian priorities at the UNCLOS III conference.

3672. Rigaldies, Francis. "The Delimitation of the Continental Shelf Between Neighbour States." *Canadian Yearbook of International Law* 14 (1976): 116-174.

3673. Rigaldies, Francis. "Le statut du golfe de Saint-Laurent en droit international public." ["The Status of the Gulf of St. Lawrence in Public International Law."] *Canadian Yearbook of International Law* 23 (1985): 80-171.

3674. Ristoratore, Mario. "Siting Toxic Waste Disposal Facilities in Canada and the United States: Problems and Prospects." *Policy Studies Journal* 14:1 (19985): 140-148.

3675. Ritchie, Ronald S. "Canada's Energy Situation in a World Context." *International Perspectives* (March/April, 1974): 13-17.

3676. Ritchie, Ronald S. "Canada's Energy Situation in a World Context." *International Perspectives* (November/December, 1981): 19-21.

3677. Robinson, Davis, Conson, David, and Rashkow, Bruce. "Some Perspectives on Adjudicating Before the World Court: The Gulf of Maine Case." American Journal of International Law 79:3 (1985): 578-597.

3678. Rodgers, Raymond S. "Conclusion of Quebec-Louisiana Agreement on Cultural Cooperation." American Journal of International Law 64:2 (1970): 380. Discussion of announcement by two governments of increased cultural links.

3679. Ross, June M. "Limitations on Human Rights in International Law: Their Relevance to the Canadian Charter of Rights and Freedoms." Human Rights Quarterly 6:2 (1984): 180-223. Examines ways of interpreting the Canadian Charter of Rights and Freedoms, 1982, in light of both a number of international documents related to human rights and international jurisprudence in this area.

3680. Rotstein, Abraham. "Canada-U.S. Relations: Shedding Innocence and Dogma." International Perspectives (January-February, 1973):12-14.

3681. Rotstein, Abraham. "Foreign Policy and the Canadian Business Community." International Journal 39:1 (1983-1984): 136-145.

3682. Rotstein, Abraham. "Hidden Costs of Free Trade." International Perspectives (July-August, 1985): 3-7. Whetheor or not Canada joins a free trade arrangement with the United States, Canadian manufacturing is going to be hurt.

3683. Rugman, Alan M. "Canadian Resources and American Interests." Inter-American Economic Affairs 37:2 (1983): 87-98.

3684. Rugman, Alan M. "Free Trade and Canadian Independence." Canadian Public Administration 19:2 (1976): 308-311.

3685. Rutan, Gérard F. "Stresses and Fractures in Canadian-American Relations: The Emergence of a New Environment." Orbis 18:2 (1974): 582-593.

3686. Sadler, Barry. "The Management of Canada-U.S. Boundary Waters: Retrospect and Prospect." Natural Resources Journal 26:2 (1986): 359-385.

3687. Safarian, A.E.. "Foreign Investment in Primary Industries." Proceedings of the Academy of Political Science 32:2 (1976): 75-87.

3688. Safarian, A.E. "Some Myths About Foreign Business Investment in Canada." Journal of Canadian Studies 6:3 (1971): 3-20.

3689. Sanguin, André-Louis. "La zone canadienne des 200 milles dans l'Atlantique, un exemple de la nouvelle géographie politique des océans." ["The Canadian 200-Mile Atlantic Zone: An Example of the New Political Geography of the Oceans."] Études Internationales 11:2 (1980): 239-252. Describes the Third Conference on the Law of the Sea which began in 1973, and the concept of a 200 mile economic zone and its implications in modern political geography.

3690. Sapiro, Miriam. "Investigating Allegations of Chemical or Biological Warfare: The Canadian Contribution." American Journal of International Law 80:3 (1986): 678-681.

3691. Sarbadhikari, P., and Jecchinis, Chris. "The Nature of Canadian International Developmental Aid." International Studies 17:2 (1978): 347-end.

3692. Sarna, A.J. "The Impact of a Canada-U.S. Free Trade Area." Journal of Common Market Studies 23:4 (1985): 299-318. Current patterns of trade are discussed, along with the idea of a free trade area and benefits and potential costs of free trade.

3693. Sauter, John V. "Specialization and Trade: Case Study: The North American Bicycle Market: Mexico, Canada, and the United States." Inter-American Economic Affairs 30:4 (1977): 3-16.

3694. Schlegel, John P. "Twenty Years of Policy Evolution: Canada, the U.S.A., and South Africa." Round Table 301 (1987): 40-52.

3695. Schneider, Jan. "The Gulf of Maine Case: The Nature of an Equitable Result." American Journal of International Law 79:3 (1985): 539-577. The judgment of the case indicated that Canada and the United States will have to work out some compromise arrangements for conservation and management of their shared resources such as are found in the Georges Bank.

3696. Schrank, W.E., Skoda, B., Roy, N., and Tsoa, E. "Canadian Government Financial Intervention in a Marine Fishery: The Case of Newfoundland, 1972, 1973-1980, 1981." Ocean Development and International Law 18:5 (1987): 533-584.

3697. Scott, Anthony. "The Canadian-American Problem of Acid Rain." Natural Resources Journal 26:2 (1986): 337-358.

3698. Scott, Anthony. "Fisheries, Pollution, and Canadian-American Transnational Relations." International Organization 28:4 (1974): 827-850.

3699. Sewell, W. R. Derrick, and Utton, Albert. "`Getting to Yes' in United States-Canadian Water Disputes." Natural Resources Journal 26:2 (1986): 201-206.

3700. Sharp, Mitchell. "The Quarrel of Continentalism." Politique internationale 12 (1981): 211-216.

3701. Sharp, Mitchell. "Sharp on Westell." International Perspectives (January-February, 1985): 3-4. Responds to an article in an earlier issue of International Perspectives wand criticises closer economic ties with the United States.

3702. Shaw, Timothy. "Africa After this Famine." International Perspectives (May-June, 1985):6-10. Canada's response to Ethiopia's crisis.

3703. Shelley, Anthony. "Law of the Sea: Delimitation of the Gulf of Maine." Harvard International Law Journal 26:2 (1985): 646-681.

3704. Spurgeon, David. "A New Approach to Foreign Aid: The IDRC of Canada." Science and Public Affairs (Bulletin of the Atomic Scientists) 28:9 (1972): 33-36. Description of Canada's new International Development Research Center and its goals for creating a new approach to foreign aid.

3705. Spurgeon, David. "IDRC -- A New Style of Aid Agency." International Perspectives (May/June, 1972): 41-43.

3706. Stairs, Denis. "The Political Culture of Canadian Foreign Policy." Canadian Journal of Political Science 15:4 (1982): 667-690.

3707. Staples, David G. "Canadian Policies on Direct Foreign Investment: The Issues Behind the Legislation." SAIS Review 4:2 (1984): 135-148.

3708. Stein, Leslie. "Trade Adjustment Assistance as a Means of Achieving Improved Resource Allocation through Freer Trade: An Analysis of Policies for Aiding the Import-Injured in the U.S., Canada, and Australia." American Journal of Economics and Sociology 41:3 (1982): 243-255. Examines policies of these three countries for compensating individuals injured on account of increased import competition.

3709. Stevenson, Garth. "Foreign Direct Investment and the Provinces: A Study of Elite Attitudes." Canadian Journal of Political Science 7:4 (1974): 630-647. Relation between foreign direct investment and federalism, the degree to which foreign investment threatens the state's power. Studies variation in party positions on issues.

3710. Stevenson, Garth. "The Third Option." *International Journal* 33:2 (1978): 424-431.

3711. Strempel, Ulrich. "Europe as a Test for Canada's Third Option." *Aussenpolitik* 29:4 (1978): 399-420.

3712. Swainson, Neil. "The Columbia River Treaty -- Where Do We Go From Here?" *Natural Resources Journal* 26:2 (1986): 243-260.

3713. Swanson, Roger F. "Canada and the U.S.: Relations Between States and Provinces." *International Perspectives* (March/April, 1976): 18-23.

3714. Taras, David. "Brian Mulroney's Foreign Policy: Something for Everyone." *The Round Table* 293 (1985): 35-46.

3715. Teigeler, Jutta. "Foreign Aid and NGOs." *International Perspectives* 1986 (March-April): 21-24.

3716. Triantis, S.G. "Canada's Interest in Foreign Aid." *World Politics* 24:1 (1971): 1-18.

3717. Tynan, Thomas M. "Canadian-American Relations in the Arctic: The Effect of Environmental Influences upon Territorial Claims." *Review of Politics* 41:3 (1979): 402-427. Certain environmental factors and the unsettled nature of international law focus Canadian attention on the Arctic while the global US policy sees the importance of the Arctic as minor.

3718. Van Roggen, George C. "Canada-U.S. Relations into the 1980s: A Proposal for Free Trade." *Presidential Studies Quarterly* 11:3 (1981): 330-334.

3719. Wagner, J.R. "Congress and the United States - Canada Water Problems: Senator Neuberger and the Columbia River Treaty." *Rocky Mountain Social Science Journal* 11:3 (1974): 51-60.

3720. Warren, J.H. "Sharing the Continent: Third Option Can Work Well." *International Perspectives* (Special Issue, 1976): 5-10.

3721. Wearing, Joseph. "Foreign Ownership: The True North Strong and Fettered." *Journal of Canadian Studies* 7:1 (1972): 51-59.

3722. Weaver, Clyde, and Richards, Peter. "Planning Canada's Role in the New Global Economy." *Journal of the American Planning Association* 51:1 (1985): 43-52. History of Canadian economic planning during the Trudeau era, and a discussion of changes needed to re-envigorate the Canadian economy in the current era.

3723. Weintraub, Sidney. "Canada Acts on Free Trade." *Journal of Interamerican Studies and World Affairs* 28:2 (1986): 101-118.

3724. Weintraub, Sidney. "U.S.-Canada Free Trade: What's in It for the U.S.?" *Journal of Interamerican Studies and World Affairs* 26:2 (1984): 225-244. Discussion of various industrial benefits which would accrue to the United States with a free trade agreement.

3725. Westell, Anthony. "Canada's Investment Capital Moves South of the Border." *International Perspectives* (January-February, 1981): 10-14. The implications of the rush or Canadian corporations to establish themselves in the United States have notbeen fully appreciated.

3726. Westell, Anthony. "Economic Integration with the U.S.A." *International Perspectives* (November-December, 1984): 5-26. Explains failure of the "third option," and argues for closer Canadian-American trading relationship.

3727. Westhues, Kenneth. "Foreign Goods and Nation-States in the Americas." *Canadian Review of Studies in Nationalism* 7:2 (1980): 351-371.

3728. Wex, Samuel. "The Legal Status of the International Joint Commission Under International and Municipal Law." *Canadian Yearbook of International Law* 16 (1978): 276-303. The importance of maintaining the independence of the members of the Commission consistent with the structure of the Commission is a good reason for extending the grant of limited functional immunities in Canada to them.

3729. Wilbur, J.R.H. "Canada and the United States: Trade War in the Depression." *International Perspectives* (March/April, 1975): 16-20.

3730. Wilford, D. Sykes, and Nattress, W. Dayle. "Monetary and Financial Integration in North America." *Law and Contemporary Problems* 44:3 (1981): 55-80.

3731. Wilkinson, Bruce. "Canada-United States Free Trade: The Current Debate." *International Journal* 42:1 (1986-1987): 199-218.

3732. Williams, Douglas, and Young, Roger. "Canadian Food Aid: Surpluses and Hunger." *International Journal* 36:2 (1981): 335-352.

3733. Williams, Glen. "Symbols, Economic Logic, and Political Conflict in the Canada-USA Free-Trade Negotiations." *Queen's Quarterly* 92:4 (1985): 659-678.

3734. Willoughby, William R. "The Canada-United States Joint Economic Agencies of the Second World War." Canadian Public Administration 15:1 (1972): 59-73.

3735. Winham, Gilbert. "Canada at Tokyo Round of Trade Negotiations." International Perspectives (March-April, 1979): 27-30. Implications for Canadian business of Tokyo Round talks.

3736. Wonnacott, Paul. "United States Investment in the Canadian Economy." International Journal 27:2 (1972): 276-286.

3737. Wonnacott, R. "Canada's Future in a World of Trade Blocs: A Proposal." Canadian Public Policy 1:1 (Winter, 1975): 118-132.

3738. Young, Christopher. "Canada and the United States: Special Relations Won't Go Away." International Perspectives (March/April, 1975): 12-16.

Index

Aboriginal peoples: aboriginal rights, 35, 50, 70, 124, 252, 976; electoral rules, 2148; self-government, 967, 977, 995, 996, 1015, 1038, 1048, 1055, 1772; self-government, bibliography, 1050. See also native people
Abortion policy, 308, 380; public opinion, 1851
Acadia: ethnic groups, 1275; nationalism, 1172
Access to information, 120, 121, 140; documents, 852. See also freedom of information
Accountability in government: Employment and Immigration, Canada, and, 744; federalism, 547; public administration, 2538, 2711, 2620; public servants, 326
Acid rain, 339, 786, 3433, 3491, 3522, 3616, 3635, 3662, 3697. See also environmental issues
Administration: courts, 2526; information, 2634; intergovernmental relations and, 604, 605; judicial, 104; public policy and, 477; reorganization, 2609
Administrative accountability, 2627
Administrative agencies and Parliament, 2339
Administrative behavior, judicial control of, 193
Administrative communications, 2632
Administrative courts, 80, 185, 231
Administrative culture, 2696
Administrative environment, 902
Administrative federalism, 294
Administrative information in Quebec, 2722
Administrative law, 67, 107, 186, 2618
Administrative reform, 2621, 2539 2707
Administrative secrecy, 2505a
Administrative state in Canada, 326
Administrative tribunals, 2473
Administrator-citizen relations, 2639
Advertising: foreign investment and, 1419; voting behavior and, 2171
Advisory agencies, 2560
Aerospace industry: government promotion, 919; politics, 1833
Affirmative action, 235, 251, 273, 1918
Africa: foreign aid, 3122, 3425, 3554, 3702; foreign policy with, 3077, 3078, 3123, 3164 3180, 3181,

Africa: foreign policy with, continued, 3182, 3242, 3243, 3244, 3273; Quebec foreign policy and, 3190, 3215, 3240, 3241; refugees and Canada, 848
Age and electoral behavior, 2058
Aged persons and economic security, 515
Aging policy, 816
Agricultural policy, 330, 619, 690, 877, 878, 928; bilateral relations, United States, 3375, 3449; Quebec and elections, 1602
Air pollution, 743, 3491
Airport policy: development, federalism and, 329; expansion, 944
Air transportation regulation, 280, 715
Alberta: elections, 1968, 1846; elections and political parties in legislature, 2142; farm interest groups, 1906; Indian urbanization, 1245; nationalism, 1161; ombudsman and MLAs, 2397, 2629, 2630; political economy of, 1025; political parties, 2192; politics in, 983; Social Credit party in, 1927; social policy, 1209; urban development, 972
Amendment of Constitution, 103, 172, 195, 196, 197, 206, 210, 212, 222, 229c, 227, 229i, 245
American influences upon Canadian law, 265
Americanization issue, 1349. See also foreign policy, United States; continentalism
Analysis of governmental policy, 722
Anti-Inflation Law, constitutionality, 152
Anti-militarism, 2999
Anti-nuclear politics, 1808
Anti-separatism in Quebec, 1666

Apartheid, foreign policy and, 3330. See also South Africa
Appeals, civil, 270
Arab nations: economic relations, 3458; foreign policy with, 2981
Arbitration in public service, 2537, 2573
Arctic: anti-pollution laws, 678; development, 1132; development of oil industry in, 709; eastern, bibliography of, 980; eastern, planning, 1010; ecology, 3607; environmental issues, 3717; foreign policy over, 2972, 3092, 3165; international law, 3660; law, jursidiction over water, 1231. See also North
Arctic Seas, 3027, 3028, 3580, 3618
Argentina, business and politics in economic development, 914
Arms control, 3095 3230, 3294; bibliography, 2985
Arms supply and Parliament, 3060
Arts, government policy on, 405, 649
Asbestos industry, health policies in, 844
ASEAN, 3261
Asia, foreign policy with, 3011, 3112, 3141, 3250, 3261
Assembly, freedom of, and municipal politics, 1269
Asylum, foreign policy and, 3014
Atlantic alliance, 2987, 3019, 3138, 3178, 3233, 3234
Atlantic provinces: federalism, 1059, 1074; public administration in, 2782
Atomic weapons, 3015
Attitudes: electoral behavior, 2087; electoral system in Ontario, 2150; English-Canadians and Quebec Separatism, 1436; mass media toward Quebec Government, 1607;

Attitudes, continued: political support, 1900; public to immigration, 1404; Quebec citizens on Quebec-Ottawa problems, 1475; Quebec citizens toward Constitution, 1657; Quebec Independence, 1383; unions to politics, 1810; youths to poltiics, 1811
Audit legislation, 2602
Auditing, internal, 2558
Auditor General, 2256, 2294, 2414, 2433, 2507, 2601, 2748, 2791
Australia: budget formation process, 353; constitution similar to Canada, 268; constitutional reform, 229c; development of federalism in, 349; farm interest groups in Canada and 1834; federalism and fiscal relations, 682; federalism and inter governmental relations in, 351; federalism and planning, 478; feder alism and resource devel opment, 638, 647; feder alism compared to Canada, 275, 444; health policy in, 610; immigration policy, 838; integovernmental agreements, 953; race relations commis sions, 910; social wel fare, family allowances, 945
Automation and bureaucracy, 2654
Automotive investments, foreign policy and, 3598
Automotive trade, 3574

Backbenchers: 2299; legislation, 2396
Balance of powers, 2611
Bank Act of 1977, 907
Banking policy, 637
Bank of Canada and Inflaation, 576
Bargaining in federal government, 274, 2517, 2518
Beaufort Sea, 3498

Belgium: nationalism in, 1683; religious, linguistic, and class voting, 1387
Bennett, William, Premier of British Columbia, 1989
Bélanger Report, 516
Bibliographies: aboriginal self-government, 1050; arctic regionalism, 980; arms control and disarmament, 2985; bilingualism policy, 434; federalism and intergovernmental relations, 351, 371, 420; foreign policy, 2819, 2820, 2830, 2848, 2877; Governors-General, 2235; human rights, 68; indian policy, 981, 982; international trade, 3644; municipal administration, 974, 2513; Ontario politics, 973; participation, 1747; political parties, 1958, 2005; provincial politics, 1024; provincial regulatory agencies, 2511; public administration, 2488; Quebec and confederation, 1590; Quebec, 1457, 1479, 1511, 1542; research on Parliament, 2402; resource law, 301; Royal Commissions, 2241; trade missions, 3382; voting behavior, 2065; women and politics, 1770, 1793
Biculturalism, 1350, 1351, 1480; in Quebec, 1735. See also bilingualism and biculturalism
Bicultural organizations, 1674
Bicultural relations and cabinet formation, 2238
Bilingualism, 1395; biculturalism, 1337, 1339, 1346, 1410, 1431, 1432, 1482; civil service, 2561, 2574, 2575, 2700; language districts, 1394; legislation 39; Ontario, 959; Parliament, 2321; policy, 621, 1322, 1394. See also language policy

Bill 1, French Language Charter, 1567
Bill 22 in Quebec (language policy), 754, 1729
Bill 101, language rights, and human rights, 217
Bill C-58, 1391, 1392
Bill of Rights, 131, 182; civil liberties, 175; judiciary, 187 Bill of Rights (U.S.), compared to charter of rights, 258
Biotechnology in Quebec, 1618
Board of Broadcast Governors, 2672
Border issues, United States. See United States
Boundary waters, 3429, 3445, 3594, 3686
Bourassa, Robert, 1616
Brazil, economic relations, 3461; foreign policy with, 3100, 3104
Bribes, 2578
Britain: business associations and public policy, 659; constitution compared to Canada, 268; federalism, and devolution, 710; foreign policy with, 2988, 317; oil policy, regulation of, 617. See also United Kingdom
British Colubmia: Constitution and, 43, 44, 45, 52, 53, 1258; culture, and geography, 2220; economics, 1289; elections and communications, 1951, 2221; immigration laws, 785; forest policy, Royal Commission, 1165; legislature, reform, 2462; members of legislature, 2459; New Democratic Party, 1272, 1291, 1962; political economy, 35; political parties, 975, 1989; politics, 1065, 1066, 1223, 1266; public administration, 2814; public opinion and race relations, 1088; public service agencies, 2714;

British Columbia, continued: question period in legislature, 2439; United States and, 3136
British North America Act, 93; constitutional law, 122
Broadcasting: election results, 2176; free trade and, 3406, 3407; policy, 298, 409, 3487
Budgeting, 2595
Budget: (1975) 644; (1976) 769; constraints, federal, 570; deficit financing and inflation, 586; energy programs and, 713, 859; process, 476, 495, 506, 519, 697, 746; provincial, 905; public expenditure and, 706; reform, Saskatchewan 1203, 1280; spending and, 587, 720, 952; zero based, 656
Budget process, 340; accountability of, 358; Canada and Australia, 353; federal government, 388, 389
Bureaucracy, 2557, 2631, 2689, 2690, 2691; aircraft building policy, 2524; attitudes, 2762, 2763; authority, 2781; community influence, 2582; federal capital region, 2563; French Canada, 2542; monetary policy, 2584; Ottawa, in, 2234; Parliament and, 2281, 2339, 2359, 2393, 2449; politics, 2494; public policy, 698; Quebec, 2738, 2739; reform, 454, 2510; representative, 2767
Bureaucrats, 2477; elections and, 2493; politicians and, 2523
Business: government and, 416, 509, 512, 575, 659, 683, 691, 739, 789, 914, 2546, 2554; interest groups, 1840; parliamentary regulation of, 507; regionalism, 1133; regulation, 445, 446, 447, 448

By-Elections, 2110, 2197

Cabinet, 2249, 2263, 2272, 2273, 2274, 2275, 2291; Auditor-General, and, 2256; bicultural Relations, 2238; civil servants, 2284; cabinet decision making, 2254, 2289; Mackenzie King, 2280; prime minister, 2240, 2243; New Brunswick, 2278; operation, 2277; Parliament, and bureaucracy, 2281; Quebec, 1715; staff, 2288
Calgary, urban politics, 966
Campaign activity: political parties, 2098; spending, 2105, 2170, 2173, 2174, 2175
Canada Act, 1982, 229i
Canada Bill, 205
Canada Council, 2741; planning and control, 778
Canada Development Corporation, 543
Canada Development Investment Corporation, 543
Canadian-American relations, 1357, 1406; public opinion, 1360, 1361, 1421. See also continentalism; United States
Canadian Broadcast Corporation, regulation of, 904
Canadian Congress of Labour, 1921
Canadian International Development Agency, 3503, 3507, 3508
Canadian Labour Congress and foreign policy, 1824
Canadian Radio-Television and Telecommunications Commission, 2796
Canadians abroad, protection, 3184
Canadian Security Intelligence Service, 571
Canadian studies, 2885; outside of Canada, 731
Candidate selection, 2053, 2057, 2422; voting results, 2091; women, in elections, 2090

Capitalism, law, and right to work, 137
Capital movements and government control, 958
Capital Region and bureaucracy, 2563
Capitals, federal, 1254
Career Assignment Program, 2742
Career patterns of civil servants, 2697, 2768, 2769, 2770, 2771
Caribbean, foreign aid to, 3655; foreign policy with, 3020, 3105
Catholic Church in Quebec, 1609, 1719
Catholics and Socialism, 1929
Caucus reform in the Conservative party, 2038
Central America, foreign policy with, 3159, 3189, 3289
Centralization and federalism, 873. See also federalism
Charity-state relations, 592
Charter of Fundamental Freedoms of Quebec, 1597
Charter of Rights and Freedoms, 33, 34, 55, 98, 132, 191, 220, 229a, 259; administrative law and, 186; civil rights and, 170; constitutional reform, 84; courts and, 201, 241; discrimination on grounds of age and, 202; federal role, 146; federalism, and the 1984 election, 642, 2077; human rights, 264, 3679; international law, 188; language rights, 69; parliamentary sovereignty, 192; patriation of new constitution, 239; public administration, 2744; Supreme Court, 42, 237, 250; tribal philosophies, 154; United States Bill of Rights and, 258
Checks and balances, 2271
Chile, foreign policy with, 3298

China, economic policy with, 2970; foreign policy with, 2973, 3043, 3225, 3297, 3305
Church and foreign policy, 2992, 3222, 3625
Citizen-administrator relations, 2639
Citizen demands to public administration, 2737
Citizen rights, 55
City politics. See municipal politics
Civil appeals, 270
Civil code in Quebec, 1624
Civil judges in Quebec, 224
Civil law, common law, 225
Civil liberties 71, 72, 170, 173; bill of rights and, 175; emergency powers, 260
Civil servants, 2802; bilingualism in, 2561; control of information, 2587; ministers and, 2284; Ontario, 2768, 2769, 2770, 2771; Ottawa, 2487, 2812; public policy, 381; Quebec, 2521; responsibility, 2751; role, 2765
Clark administration, foreign policy, 2900
Clark, Joe, as Prime Minister, 2250
Class, 1857, 1895; nationalism, 1331; participation, 1847; political ideology, 2023; politics in Quebec, 1552; region, and political culture, 1228; voting, religious, linguistic, 1387. See also social class
Cleavages: elections, 2128, 2129; Ontario Legislature, 2463; party system, 2094
Clerk of Parliament, 2452
Coalitions in Parliament, 2211
Coastline management, 3563
Collective bargaining, 2572, 2594, 2698, 2705, 2706
Collective violence, 1841, 1842, 1843
Colombo Plan, 3269

Colonialism in Quebec, 1686
Columbia River Treaty, 3712, 3719
Combines Investigation Act, 916
Commissioner of Official Languages, 2555
Committees, House of Commons, 2388, 2394, 2404, 2419, 2444, 2445, 2446; autonomy 2343; bureaucracy, 2359; executive, 2424; interest groups, 2450; Public Accounts, 2326; standing, and legislation, 2455
Committees, Ontario legislature, 2461
Common law, judicial review and, 225
Common market of Canada, 370
Commonwealth, foreign policy with, 3000, 3042, 3142, 3155, 3220, 3236, 3262, 3437; Francophonie, 1435
Communications and politics, 1919; policy and federalism, 296, 479; public administration, 2772; space age, 771; Winnipeg businessmen and, 512
Communism in Canada, 1940
Communist Party, 1921, 1925
Community: development, 1230; influence and bureaucracy, 2582; nationalism, 1303
Community Property Law, 148
Complaining, public administration and, 2483
Conditional grants, 905
Confederation, changes in federalism, 471; federalism and, 296; new constitution and, 109; Ontario and, 387; philosophical roots, 333; role of press in debates, 374. See also federalism
Conflict of interest, 2695; members of parliament, 2331, 2382
Congress (U.S.), Canada and, 3326

Index   365

Conservatism, 1912, 2059, 2069, 2086; Anglo-American democracies and, 1306; ideology, 2164
Conservative Government and foreign policy, 2867, 2871
Conservative Party, 1943, 2006, 2184; Brian Mulroney, 1931; caucus reform, 2038; Constitution, 1978; election (1979), 1954; in power, 1979-1980, 1996; leadership, 1988, 2185; leadership convention (1976) 1939, 2117, (1983), 2141; new constitution and, 108; Newfoundland, political culture, 1229; Quebec, 1515; quest for power, 1973
Constituency service of MPs, 2364, 2416
Constituency size, 2179
Constitution, 37, 38, 51, 223; aboriginal rights 35, 70, 106, 252; amendment of, 33, 36, 40, 58, 59, 61, 99, 105, 110, 111, 172, 195, 196, 197, 206, 210, 212, 222, 227, 228, 229h, 229i, 245, 382; biculturalism, 62; British and Canadian, similarities, 268; British Columbia, 1258; British North America Act, 93; Conservative Party and, 108; convention and, 168; economic development, 253, 348; federalism, 91, 109; Foreign Affairs Committee of British Parliament and, 194; future, 89; language rights and, 69; mineral industry, 375; native people, 106; natural resources, 162; patriation of, 229e, 246; poverty reports, 581; Quebec, 100, 115, 116, 229d, 1710; redistribution of resources, 169; reform, 64, 98, 160, 180; Saskatchewan Indians, 143; social policy, 75;

Constitution, continued: Supreme Court, 90; taxing power, 83; Trudeau, Pierre, and, 144; Western premiers, 135, 136; women, 66, 82
Constitution Act, 1982, 232, 282, 303; natural resources and, 103
Constitutional amendment, the Supreme Court, and federalism, 724
Constitutional debate in Canada, 113, 122, 174
Constitutional Development, Northern Territories, finances, 1268
Constitutional evolution and federalism, 442
Constitutional history, 55, 60, 91
Constitutional law, 54, 74, 76, 77, 78, 86, 87, 88, 92, 97, 101, 112, 122, 125, 138; Constitution and, 168; Quebec and, 262; telecommunications regulation, 293
Constitutional reform, 84, 126, 127, 156, 165, 204, 207, 215, 385, 800; aboriginal people, 124; Canada Act, 1982 and, 119, 229i; changes not made, 176; Conservative Party, 1978; Crown and, 222, 229c; economic aspects of, 153, 167, 271; federalism, 161, 220, 221, 462, 464, 465, 471, 729, 730, 756, 886, 923; historical view, 65, 218, 244, 256; individualism, 272; Manitoba and, 216; natural resources, 568; opposition to, 166; patriation, 209; policy making, 163; provincial rights, 267; Quebec, 211; specific changes, 269; Supreme Court, 85; Trudeau, Pierre, and, 142; Western view of, 213
Constitutional rights, 125, 230
Constitutions of Canada, federal and provincial, 139

Consumer law, 145
Consumers' Association of Canada, 654
Continental Shelf, 3498, 3672
Continentalism, 1362, 1363, 1424, 3310, 3314, 3322, 3325, 3329, 3356, 3365, 3368, 3400, 3403, 3406, 3407, 3408, 3409, 3434, 3435, 3507, 3510, 3519, 3530, 3541, 3552, 3556, 3557, 3570, 3572, 3577, 3586, 3608, 3638, 3640, 3643, 3685, 3693, 3699, 3700, 3720, 3727; economics, 3432; environment, 3433; Quebec foreign policy, 1671, 1731. See also Canadian-American relations; United States, foreign policy
Contraception policy, 380
Controller General, 2775
Convention and the new Constitution, 168, 246
Cooperative Commonwealth Federation, 1942, 1948. See also New Democratic Party
Cooperative federalism, 616, 730
Corruption, 1760, 1807; in politics, 1099
Court administration, 2526, 2613
Courts: administrative, 80, 185; Charter of Rights and, 34, 42, 201, 241; discrimination and, 149; environmentalists, and nuclear power, 306; federal, 107, 134; interpreting, 118
Court, Supreme: arbitration, 189; Constitution and, 90; constitutional reform, 85
Creditiste Party, 2161. See also Social Credit Party
Criminal justice, 73, 164
Crisis management, 2508
Crombie, David, and Toronto politics, 985
Cross-national attitudes, 1329

Crown, 2252, 2269, 2270, 2283; bureaucracy, 2642, 2745; constitutional reform and Australia and, 229c; Governor General and, 2245
Crown Corporations, 450, 2473, 2674; legislatures, 2360; public lands, 573
Cruise missile, 2998, 3017, 3046
Cuba, foreign policy with, 3185, 3204
Cultural affairs, 921
Cultural federalism, 296
Cultural relations, foreign policy and, 3452; Quebec-Louisiana, 3678; United States, 3325, 3342, 3357, 3360, 3361, 3372, 3395, 3590, 3629
Cultural sovereignty, 1417
Cultural traditions, women, and political history of, 1334
Culture: geography, and politics, British Columbia, 2220; government policy and, 345, 405; language, 1376; nationalism, 1414; Newfoundland, Conservative Party, 1229; participation, 1412; political, and federalism, 791; politics, 1355; Quebec and Canada, 1588; region, class, and, 1228, 1262; working class, 1328. See also political culture
Cutbacks and public administration, 2657, 2663, 2798

Debates, constitutional, 113
Decentralization: bureaucracy, 2512, 2783, 2803; federalism, 283; Quebec, 1680
Decision-making, 1385
Defense: cruise missiles, 2998; foreign policy and, 2903, 2967, 2968, 3033, 3249; maritime, 3029;

Defense, continued:
nuclear, 2965; organization, 3156; Parliament, 2349, 3060; policy, 2831, 3030, 3034, 3079, 3082, 3114, 3193, 3208, 3209, 3210, 3235, 3238, 3253, 3254, 3255, 3267, 3274, 3288; procurement, 3059; Quebec and, 3135; strategy, 3206
Deficit financing and inflation, 836
De Gaulle and Parti Québécois, 1527
Delegated legislation, 326, 2377, 2408, 2418; in Quebec, 2457
Denmark, foreign policy with, 3211
Dental and medical care, Newfoundland, 545
Deputy minister, role, 2544
Development in Quebec, 1659, 1724
Development programs, federal-provincial cooperation in, 908
Diplomacy, 2846, 3012, 3013, 3109, 3192, 3653, 3654; foreign policy, 2975; law and, 3090; Lester Pearson, 2997, 3080, 3229
Diplomatic immunity, 3094
Diplomatic negotiation, 3302
Diplomatic staff: Africa and Middle East, 3273; United States, 3275, 3276
Diplomats, 3023; attitudes of, 3145; conditions of Foreign Service, 3130
Disability and employment, 2809
Disarmament, 3187, 3194, 3195, 3230, 3231, 3232, 3260, 3294, 3301, 3480; arms control, bibliography, 2985; initiatives, 3070, 3071
Discrimination: Charter of Rights and, 202; courts and, 149; equal pay, 200; equal protection, 219; human rights, 179; legislation against, 81; protection from, 198

Dissent and human rights, 46
Dissolution of Parliament, 2145, 2385, 2386
Distribution of Income, 835
Division of powers. See separation of powers
Documents in foreign policy, 2860
Dominion status, Constitution and, 125
Drug policy, 360

Eastern Arctic planning, 1010
East Germany, foreign policy with, 3259
East-west relations, 3271
Ecology, Arctic, 3607; Eskimo and, 1116; policy, 368; pollution, 954. See also environment
Economic and Regional Development, Ministry of, 2261
Economic backgrounds of politicians, 2391
Economic conditions and electoral behavior, 2084
Economic Council of Canada, 809
Economic development, 598, 814; constitution, 253; federalism, 917; government spending, 313; international economics and, 3343; MacDonald Report, 494, 562, 577, 658, 684, 686, 712, 768, 826, 865, 868; Quebec, 1724; regionalism, and federalism, 302; West, 1271
Economic equalization program, 580
Economic federalism, 271, 284, 423, 426, 484, 612, 613, 627
Economic health and energy, 854
Economic nationalism, 1320, 1408, 3359; Quebec, 1631; 1676
Economic policy, 281, 307, 314, 336, 364, 407, 513, 584, 611, 684, 686, 701, 712, 748, 768, 826, 865,

Economic policy, continued: 868, 1423; British Columbia, 354; constitution, 64, 181, 348; federalism, 400; first ministers' meeting, 404; management of, 410; ownership issues, 399; regionalism, 427; regulation, 403; remedies for, 422
Economic relations, 3693; Arab nations, 3458; Brazil, 3461; Europe, 3414, 3415; federalism, 484, 612, 613, 627; Japan, 3344, 3350, 3369, 3391, 3412, 3450, 3576, 3581, 3582; Latin America, 3471, 3639; Mulroney policy, 3599, 3664; Pacific region, 3566, 3627, 3631; South Africa, 3567; United States, 3306, 3320, 3323, 3324, 3334, 3336, 3337, 3340, 3341, 3342, 3353, 3365, 3371, 3372, 3375, 3379, 3380, 3385, 3393, 3409, 3410, 3418, 3420, 3424, 3451, 3460, 3463, 3472, 3474, 3475, 3484, 3489, 3490, 3500, 3501, 3509, 3519, 3529, 3541, 3542, 3561, 3562, 3574, 3575, 3577, 3578, 3590, 3600, 3601, 3602, 3604, 3615, 3623, 3630, 3641, 3650, 3651, 3652, 3668, 3682, 3683, 3684, 3718, 3723, 3724, 3725, 3726, 3729, 3730, 3731, 3733, 3734, 3736, 3737, 3738
Economic security policy for aged persons, 515
Economics: law and, 1335; nationalism and, 1356; Parti Québécois, 1637; prairie provinces, 1226; Quebec, 1601; Sovereignty-Association, 1460, 1462, 1465
Economy, political, 607; political support, 1886; industry and, 473; interest groups and, 460; Quebec, 1798; right-wing extremism, 2198

Editorials: coverage, 1974 federal election, 2214; elections, (1972) 2203;
External Affairs, and elections, (1972) 2204, (1974) 2204; newspapers and policy, 1845
Edmonton, Alberta, political parties and urban politics, 1212
Education: financing of, 957; foreign policy, 2878; minorities and, 726; nationalism and, 815; provincial politics, 1103; reform in Nova Scotia, 489
Effectiveness of administration, 2552
Efficacy, political, sense of in Canada, 1871
Election Act, public information and, 2172
Election broadcasting in Canada, 2176
Election campaigns, 1956
Election expenses regulations, 1933, 2081
Elections, Federal: (1911), 2107; (1965), 1914; (1968), 1975, 2027, 2030, 2075, 2151; (1972), 1799a, 2004, 2027, 2033, 2216; (1974), 1985, 2178, 2214, 2216 (1979), 1941, 1954, 1963, 1986, 2046, 2073, 2090, 2196, 2201; (1980), 1986, 2090, 2124; (1984) 642, 1955, 1987, 2077, 2119, 2125; Charter of Rights, and federalism, 642; class and ethnic voting in Winnipeg, 2225, 2226, 2227; demographics, 2032; ethnic minorities, 1923; incumbency, 2114, 2115; local candidates, 2057; majority government, 2134; media, 2001, 1755, 2068; occupation, 1974, 2070; opinion polls and, 2109; political parties, 1944, 1945, 2031, 2120, 2180; political party leaders, 1968, 2223; procedures, 2074; Quebec 1950, 2028, 2139; regionalism, 2034

Elections, federal, continued: religious cleavages, 2106; voter registration, 2080; voting patterns, 2035, 2058; women candidates, 2090. See also By-Elections
Elections and bureaucrats, 2493
Elections, Kitchener Ontario, 1285
Elections, provincial: Alberta, political parties in legislature, 2142; British Columbia, 1951, 2220, 2221; New Brunswick, 2014; Newfoundland, 2050; Northwest Territories, 2082; Nova Scotia, 1970, 2022; Ontario, 2116; party identification, 2031; Prince Edward Island, 2212; Quebec, 1523, 1566, 1602, 1697, 2083, 2153; Quebec (1969), 2104; Quebec (1970), 1517, 1967, 2079; Quebec (1973), 1517, 2182; Quebec (1976), 1451, 1454, 1493, 2017, 2089, 2183; Quebec (1981), 1456; Quebec (1985), 2029, 2067, 2118; Saskatchewan, 2130
Elections, Toronto City Council, 2401
Election strategy, 2040
Electoral Behavior: 2189; advertising, 2171; Alberta, 1846; attitudes, 2087, 2150; bibliographic study, 2065; campaign financing, 2105, 2173, 2174, 2175; economic conditions, 2084; editorials, 1972, 2203; issues, 2042; ethnic voting, 2213; external affairs, and editorials, (1972), 2204, (1974), 2204; liberal ideology, 2165; party identification, 2101; political parties, 2202; social class, 2078, 2111, 2162, 2167, 2177, 2199, 2213, 2229, 2230; split-ticket voting, 2159

Electoral boundaries, British Columbia, 1951
Electoral competition in Canada, 1876
Electoral expenses, House of Commons, 2096
Electoral law in Canada, 1934
Electoral process, 1992, 2206; financial support, 2215; political parties, 2037, 2060, 2061, 2149, 2193, 2194; reform, 1961, 2051
Electoral reform: 1458, 2140; Aboriginal voters, 2148; local elections, Winnipeg, 2143; redistribution of seats, 1968
Electoral studies in Quebec, 2088
Electorate and ideology, 2121
Electric power planning: in Ontario, 889; in Quebec, 1461
Elite, political, 1782, 1783, 1862, 2503; business, and policy, 1802; ideology, 1888, 1889; in Quebec, 1901
Emergency powers, 2268; civil liberties, 260
Employers and labor unions in Quebec, 1598
Employment and Immigration, Canada, accountability in, 744
Employment Equity, 810
Employment policy, 305
Employment, public, 2474
Energy: 3528; budget, 713, 859; conservation and transportation, 595; crisis, 707; economics, 854; electric power planning in Ontario, 889; Federalism, and the West, 798; National Energy Program, 694; North American relations, 482; oil lobby, 524, 710; tax policy, 559,
Energy crisis and regional development, 1210
Energy policy, 296, 310, 322, 342, 474, 475, 485,

Energy policy, continued: 531, 542, 750, 840, 872, 920, 931, 3521, 3524; administration, 428; budget, 859; development projects in North, 288; energy crisis, 418; federalism, 382, 461, 813; foreign ownership, 432; foreign policy, 2610, 3453, 3579, 3583, 3612, 3675, 3676; National Energy Program, 466, 753; national policy, 376; natural gas forecasts, 846; petroleum development, 842; prices of energy, 620; Quebec, 1623; regulation, 665, 672, 673, 674, 675, 676, 677; trans-border relations, 924; United States, 3559

Energy resources, Newfoundland's claim to offshore, 488

Energy revenues and redistribution among provinces, 582

Energy subsidies, 947

English-Canadians: nationalism in Quebec, 1474, 1617, 1660

Environmental issues, 3433, 3667, 3674; Arctic, 3717; transboundary, 3595, 3634, 3635, 3636

Environmental policy, 368, 546, 614, 615; economic perspectives, 827; nuclear power and the courts, 306; planning, Ontario, 1147; regulation and, 792, 793; resources, 327; water resources and, 563

Equal opportunity in New Brunswick, 1292

Equal pay: laws, 200, 276; public policy, 486

Equal protection, 219

Equality: ethnic groups, 2047; rights, 57, 199, 219

Equalization, federal-provincial relations, 580, 799, 821

Equity, 556; employment, 810

Eskimo politics, 1116, 1117. See also native peoples

Ethics in public administration, 2551, 2687 2637

Ethnic groups: culture and economics in Quebec, 1630; demands, and nationalism, 1365; equality, 2047; immigration, 1403; indians, 455; influences on Senators, 2353; language, and gender and politics, 1748; minorities and the 1983 election, 1923; nationalism, 1332, 1368, 1374; politics, 1308; pluralism, 1348; politics in Acadia, 1275; politics in French Canada, 1442; politics in the North, 1438; politics in the Northwest Territories, 1222; politics in Nova Scotia, 1373; politics in Quebec, 641, 1704; public administration, 2685, 2813; separatism, 1336; voting and social class in Winnipeg, 2213, 2225, 2226, 2227

European Community, foreign policy with, 3096, 3152. See also Europe

Europe: economic relations with, 3414, 3415; foreign policy with, 3036, 3062, 3087, 3124, 3148, 3160, 3170, 3175, 3176, 3177, 3216, 3217, 3219, 3221, 3228, 3246, 3272, 3287, 3526

Evaluation: policy, 536, 560, 666; public administration 2776

Evidence, exclusion of, 214, 229g

Evolution of federalism, 417

Exchange rate as a policy instrument, 311, 820

Exclusion of evidence, 214, 229g

Executive government, 2244

Executive power, 2424, 2611; planning, 787
Expenditure process, 358, 901. See also budget process
External Affairs: editorials, and elections (1972), 2204, (1974), 2204; Minister of, 2264; Parliament, 2336, 2341, 2375, 2460; public administration, 2761. See also foreign policy
External Affairs Ministry: operation, 2596, 2874, 2875, 2876, 2936; organization, 2917, 2932; specialists, 2892
Extraterritoriality, 3597

Family law, 47
Farm interest groups: Alberta, 1906; Canada and Australia, 1834
Farm lands, taxation of, 544
Fascism, 2024
Federal capitals, 1254
Federal Court Act (1970), 2623; governmental secrecy, 606
Federal Court of Canada, 134; administrative law, 107
Federal financial relations, 867; income security, 781
Federal Freedom of Information Act, 2766
Federalism, 275, 279, 349, 390; accountability, 547; administrative, 294; airport development, 329; Atlantic Canada, 1059, 1074; centralization, 622, 651, 873; changes in, 372, 471, 758, 770; Charter of Rights and, 201, 642, 2077; confederation, 296; conflict management, 760; consociational democracy, 797; Constitution Act, 1982, 91, 303; constitutional evolution and reform, 64, 282, 442, 462, 465, 685, 729, 756, 886;

Federalism, continued: cooperative, 616, 730; crisis of, 414, 510, 618, 688, 856; decentralization, 283, 721, 857; economic issues, 284, 357, 370, 400, 484, 562, 612, 613, 627, 917; energy policy, 461, 798, 813; evolution of, 349, 382, 417; external affairs, 367; fiscal relations, 356, 377, 401, 402, 511, 582, 626, 682, 799, 864, 905; foreign policy, 624, 774, 860, 2889, 2902; fragmentation and political support, 716, 856; Fulton-Favreau formula, 483; health care in Ontario and Quebec, 802; insurance regulation, 487; interest groups, and medical association, 951; intergovernmental relations, 351, 874; intergovernmental relations, bibliography, 371, 420; law, 125; linguistic groups, 685; medicare, 668; modernization theory, 884; monetary policy, 829; multiculturalism, 1420; national unity, 449, 880; natural resource revenues, 431, 875; organization of government, 894; Parliamentary supremacy, 2458; parliamentary system 733; planning, 478; policy development, 325; political parties, 2155; political structures, 443; Prince Edward Island, 2212; problems of, 439, 440, 441; public choice, 444; public servants, 365; Quebec and, 359, 539, 597, 628, 719, 879, 938, 1470, 1481, 1535, 1599, 2187; regional development, 302, 415, 728; regulatory process, 429; resource development, 638, 647; responsiveness, 554, 555; Senate reform, 2347;

Federalism, continued:
separation of powers,
436; society, 882;
sovereignty association,
1521; structural problems, 885; Supreme Court
and Constitutional Amendment, 724; transport
regulation, 430, 950;
types of, 285; Western
disenchantment, 636
Federal language legislation, 408
Federal Privacy Commissioner, 2786
Federal-provincial relations, 392, 437, 438;
communications policy,
479; conflict and, 561,
883; constitutional
reform, 456, 457, 458,
464, 923; cooperation in
development programs,
908; economic relations,
290; energy crisis and
tax policy, 559; equalization, 580, 821; fiscal
relations, 580, 782, 867,
930; health policy, 941;
immigration, 940; natural
resources, 103, 568;
Newfoundland's claim to
offshore energy resources, 488; Ontario,
387; provincial powers,
955; redistributive
power, 930; reform, 922;
Supreme Court, 238;
transportation regulation, 861. See also federalism; individual
provinces
Federal public service,
2501
Federations, design of, 289
Feminism: law, 155; Marxism
and, 1818, 1999; politics, 1920
Finance: municipal, 1248,
1255, 1279; municipal,
Ottawa 1207; Northern
Territories, constitutional development, 1268;
political parties, 2163;
public, 2800; public, in
Quebec, 564, 1604, 1620;
Saskatchewan, 1280. See
also municipal politics

Finances: elections and,
1933, 2081, 2105, 2170,
2173, 2174, 2175, 2215;
Parliament, 2338; political parties, 1981, 2208;
political parties, bibliography, 2005
Finance, Task Force on Public, 590
Financial administration,
2545, 2644, 2667, 2731,
2790
Financing government, 2475
Finland, bilingual language
districts, 1394
Firefighters in municipalities, 1202
First ministers' conferences, 404, 2279
Fiscal administration, 751;
policy outputs, 745
Fiscal federalism, 283,
356, 377, 401, 402, 511,
626, 782, 864, 905, 936;
Australia and, 444; constitution and, 169;
energy revenues redistribution, 582; equalition, 799, 821; federal-provincial relations,
867; New Brunswick economic development and,
426; policy making, 657
Fisheries, 3419, 3423,
3450, 3457, 3488, 3523,
3565, 3633, 3696, 3698;
free trade and, 3408;
jurisdiction over, 578,
579; management of in
Quebec, 522; policies,
828
Fisheries Act, 793
Flanders, ideology in, 2095
FLQ see Front de la Libération du Québec
Food: politics of, 394;
processing and regulation, 548
Foreign affairs. See foreign policy
Foreign Affairs, Ministry
of. See External Affairs
Ministry
Foreign aid, 2861, 3317,
3345, 3502, 3503, 3504,
3507, 3508, 3513, 3669,
3704, 3716; Africa, 3122,
3425, 3525, 3554, 3702;

Foreign aid, continued:
Caribbean, 3655; domestic influences upon, 3397; evaluation, 3335; food, 3436, 3446, 3447, 3448, 3558, 3732; Francophone Africa, 3122; Ghana, 3611; goals, 2926; human rights, 3422, 3568; international development, 3421, 3691; International Development Research Centre, 3622; non-government organizations and, 3715; programs, 3315; Third World, 3319, 3362, 3492, 3609, 3610; foreign aid, training of public servants, 3611
Foreign business controls, 3430
Foreign energy policy, 2610
Foreign investment, 424, 1418, 3456, 3613, 3628, 3707, 3708, 3709, 3710, 3711; controls, 3308, 3311, 3313, 3351, 3352, 3353, 3499; controls, provincial, 3312; foreign ownership, 3354, 3364, 3390, 3509, 3520, 3687, 3688, 3721; foreign policy and, 3637; manufacturing and, 3478; oil industry, 432; policy, 3394; Quebec, 3505, 3506; regulation, 3366; television, 3440; United States, 3338, 3399, 3736, see also economic relations
Foreign Investment Review Act, 916, 3318, 3387, 3392, 3482, 3483, 3511, 3645; Cabinet and, 2249
Foreign policy, 2824, 2825, 2826, 2828, 2829, 2832, 2833, 2834, 2835, 2839, 2842, 2844, 2845, 2851, 2857, 2858, 2859, 2868, 2870, 2872, 2873, 2879, 2883, 2886, 2887, 2893, 2895, 2899, 2901, 2906, 2909, 2916, 2924, 2925, 2927, 2935, 2943, 2952, 2995, 3198, 3199, 3347, 3517, 3518, 3659;

Foreign policy, continued:
acid rain, 3522; Africa, 3077, 3078, 3123, 3164, 3180, 3181, 3182, 3242, 3243, 3244, 3273; agriculture, 3449; annual review, 2880; Anti-Americanism, 2913; approaches to, 2862; Arab nations, 2981; Arctic, 2972, 3027, 3028, 3092, 3165, 3580; Asia, 3011, 3112, 3141, 3250, 3261; asylum, 3014; Atlantic Alliance, 2987, 3019, 3178, 3233, 3234; atlas, 2843; attitudes toward, 1284, 2898; bibliographic essay, 2877; bibliography, 2819, 2820, 2830, 2848; bilateral approaches, 2836, 2974, 3002; Brazil, 3100, 3104; Britain, 2988, 3170; British Columbia, United States and, 3136; business and, 3665, 3681; Canada and Quebec, 2849; Canada's role, 3066, 3067, 3068; Canadian Labour Congress, 1824; Caribbean, 3105; Central America, 3159, 3189, 3289; changes, 2928, 2945; Chile, 3298; China, 2973, 3043, 3225, 3297, 3305; Christian Churches, 2992, 3222, 3625; Clark administration, 2900; class theory, 2921; cold war, 2956; Commonwealth, 3000, 3042, 3142, 3155, 3220, 3236, 3262, 3437; Conservative Government and, 2867, 2871; Cuba, 3185, 3204; cultural relations and, 3452; defense, 2847, 2903, 2967, 2968, 3033, 3249; Denmark, 3211; détente and, 2923; diplomacy, 2846, 2975; disarmament, 3230, 3231; documents, 2821, 2822, 2860; domestic influences upon, 2840, 2850, 2882, 2896, 2915, 2918, 2930, 2941, 2946; East Germany, 3259;

Foreign policy, continued: economic aspects, 2854, 3416, 3584, 3624; economic policy with USSR and China, 2970; energy policy and, 3453, 3559; Europe, 2881, 3036, 3057, 3062, 3087, 3096, 3124, 3148, 3152, 3160, 3170, 3175, 3176, 3177, 3216, 3217, 3219, 3221, 3228, 3233, 3246, 3272, 3287, 3526; federalism, 382, 624, 860, 2902; foreign investment and, 3637; France, 3021, 3063, 3074, 3103, 3212, 3283; Francophonie, 3091, 3158, 3162; goals, 2864, 2905; Greenland, 3128; history, 2837, 2838, 2848, 2853; human rights, 229b, 2423, 3327, 3514, 3589, 3626, 3647, 3658; immigration and, 3656; independence, 3054, 3055, 3056, 3132; India, 2945, 3139, 3237; Indochina, 1954-1972, 2963; Indonesia, 229b; international institutions, 2888; international peace, 1943-1957, 2978; international role of Canada, 2979, 2980; international security, 3052; international treaties, 2982; Israel, 2960, 2969, 2984, 3168, 3200; Japan, 3143, 3166, 3205, 3369, 3536; Jerusalem, 3168; Latin America, 3098, 3099, 3106, 3146, 3191, 3196, 3197, 3202, 3203, 3226, 3527; law of armed conflict and, 3093; Law of the Sea, 3349, 3376, 3417, 3428, 3455, 3459, 3543; leadership, 2947; lesser powers, 2911, 2948; media, 2865, 2939, 3569; Mexico, 3037, 3473; Middle East, 3001, 3009, 3040, 3053, 3097, 3171, 3252, 3273; middle powers and, 3076, 3120, 3121, 3237, 3346;

Foreign policy, continued: military and, 2996, 3224, 3288; morality, 3549, 3550; Mulroney Administration, 2944, 3281, 3714; Namibia, 3186; NATO, 2971, 3039, 3041, 3101, 3115, 3116, 3126, 3127; New Democratic Party, 2890; Nigeria, 3258; Norway, 3133, 3134; nuclear weapons, 3161; Organization of American States, 3065; orientations, 2934; Pacific region, 2962, 2983, 3069, 3110, 3118, 3144, 3151, 3245, 3263, 3264, 3293, 3627; Pakistan, 2957, 3108, 3010; Palestine, 2984, 3200; Parliament, 2336, 2341, 2375, 2460, 2914, 3060; peacekeeping, 3083, 3129, 3284; Poland, 2964, 3179, 3426; political culture and, 3706; protection of Canadians abroad, 3184; provinces and, 2841, 2891, 2904, 2929, 3016; province-state relations, 3587, 3588, 3596; public opinion, 2907, 2912, 2940, 2953; Quebec, 1581, 2866, 2869, 2884, 2897, 2910, 2919, 2922, 2931, 2942, 2949, 2950; Quebec and Africa, 3085, 3190, 3215, 3240; Quebec and France, 1633, 2878, 3153; Quebec and Latin America, 3081; Quebec, and United States, 1450, 1721, 1731, 3218; responsible government, 2937; Rhodesia, 3247; science and technology and, 3339; seas, 3027, 3028; sources, 2827, 2855; South Africa, 3005, 3038, 3086, 3113, 3222, 3223, 3247, 3282, 3330, 3694; Soviet Union, 2956, 2958, 2959, 3073, 3088; state-provincial relations, 3713; style, 2863; superpowers, 3025, 3051, 3061, 3075, 3102; Tanzania, 3247;

Foreign policy, continued:
Third World, 2989,
3239, 3248, 3362, 3427,
3609, 3610; trade, 3058;
Trudeau administration,
2856, 2894, 2938, 2951,
3026, 3048, 3149, 3257,
3481; UNCTAD, 3058;
United Nations, 3018,
3050, 3089, 3107, 3125,
3131, 3147, 3167, 3169,
3232, 3564; United
States, 2881, 2890, 2954,
2955, 2976, 2977, 3003,
3004, 3008, 3049, 3072,
3119, 3150, 3172, 3188,
3227, 3265, 3280, 3285,
3286, 3289, 3290, 3292,
3300, 3303, 3304, 3333,
3348, 3356, 3357, 3361,
3367, 3368, 3377, 3383,
3386, 3398, 3401, 3402,
3403, 3423, 3429, 3434,
3441, 3442, 3443, 3444,
3449, 3450, 3465, 3466,
3467, 3468, 3469, 3485,
3486, 3493, 3494, 3495,
3496, 3498, 3515, 3522,
3543, 3544, 3545, 3546,
3547, 3548, 3551, 3559,
3560, 3571, 3573, 3586,
3591, 3592, 3593, 3594,
3597, 3646, 3648, 3649,
3670, 3677, 3680; Vietnam, 2986, 3004, 3289;
water issues, 3429;
Western Security, 2966;
West Indies, 3020; white
paper, 2823; world
powers, 3024; World War
I, 2994
Foreign service, 2908
Foreign Service Officers,
see Diplomats
Foreign trade 3388
Forest policy: Ontario,
398; Royal Commission,
and British Columbia,
1165
France, foreign policy
with, 3063, 3021, 3074,
3103, 3212, 3283; Quebec
and, 1633, 3153
Francophone Africa, foreign
aid, 3122
Francophone minorities: in
Canada, 1643; New Brunswick, 1221

Francophones in public
service, 2472
Francophonie: Commonwealth, 1435; foreign
policy, 3091, 3158
Freedom of assembly and
municipal politics, 1269
Freedom of information,
117, 128, 150, 184, 249,
373, 852
Freedom of Information Act,
2766
Freedoms, Fundamental,
Quebec Charter of, 1597
Free trade, 1427, 3400,
3424, 3451, 3460, 3475,
3484, 3489, 3500, 3501,
3531, 3541, 3561, 3562,
3590, 3718, 3723, 3724,
3726, 3731, 3733; broadcasting and, 3406, 3407;
United States, 3393,
3400, 3409, 3410, 3630,
3641, 3668, 3682, 3684,
3692
French Canada: 1512, 1521,
1570, 1572, 1589; bureaucracy, 2542; leadership
in, 1699; Mackenzie King
and, 1703; nationalism
in, 1690, 1652; Saskatchewan and, 1180; voting
behavior, 1663
French Canadian Prime Ministers, 2285
French-English culture and
economics in Quebec, 1630
French-English relations in
Canada, 1548
French language: organizations, 3162; politics,
1664, 1665
Front de la Libération du
Québec, 1544, 1612
Fullerton Report, 1340
Fulton-Favreau formula, 483

Gallop Polls and political
parties, 2222
Gardiner, Frederick, and
Toronto politics, 988
Garrison diversion project,
3649
Gas: energy policy, 542,
846; National Energy
Program, 796; regulation
of, 665

Gas pipeline project, 288
Gender: administration, 2467, 2520; differences in politics, 1816, 1822; ethnicity, and language, and politics, 1748; ideology, 2113; political party preference, 2071
General Agreement on Trade and Tariffs, 3381
Geography: language politics, 1378; politics and, British Columbia, 2220
Ghana, foreign aid, 3611
Governmental immunity, 96
Government and universities, 574
Government Information in Quebec, 1679
Government spending, 319; economic development, 313
Governor General: bibliography, 2235; the Crown, 2245; powers, 2265
Great Lakes, 3477;
Greenland, foreign policy with, 3128
Growth, economic, in the West, 1271
Growth of government, 749
Gulf of Maine, 3423, 3450, 3591, 3592, 3617, 3619, 3670, 3677, 3695
Gulf of St. Lawrence, 3673

Hamilton, Ontario, urban politics, 1004
Hartz, Louis, 2152
Hassidic Jews in Quebec politics, 1725
Health and social services, 594, 832: federalism in Ontario and Quebec, 802; lobbying and, 634; public policy analysis, 492; regulation, 534; usage in Ontario, 747
Health insurance, 459, 765, 843, 911, 912
Health, occupational, regulation of, 600
Health policy, 277, 610, 941, 949; asbestos industry and, 844; federalism, 382, 668, 951; legislatures, 2381;

Health policy, continued: lobbying, 1844; medical and dental care, Newfoundland, 545; medicare, 433; New Brunswick, 540; Ontario, 925; Quebec, 366, 1634
Health services: finances, 775; legislative responsiveness, 780; management, 664; Nova Scotia, 623; Quebec, 942
Heeney, Arnold, diplomacy, 3080
Highway employment and provincial elections, 2207
Highway policy, 705
Hockey, Soviet Union, foreign policy, 3073
House of Commons, 2300, 2302, 2303, 2304; bilingualism, 2321; business, 2393; committee system, 2444, 2445, 2446; constituency size, 2179; distribution, 2447, 2448; electoral expenses, 2096; human rights, 2345, 2423, 2451; information, 2378; leaders in, 2456; procedure and reform, 2313, 2340; redistribution of seats, 1968; reform, 2301, 2313, 2332; Speaker, 2324, 2329; standing committees, 2388, 2394, 2404, 2419, 2455; turnover in, 2361. See also Parliament
Housing policy, 395, 421, 652, 887, 888; Métis in Saskatchewan, 1115; public, in Hull, Quebec, 1095, 1594; urban, 1205
Human resource: planning, 2732; Quebec public administration, 2591
Human resources and social policy, 494
Human Rights, 46, 56, 94, 95, 170, 350; bibliography, 68; Chile, 3298; covenants, 178; federalism, minorities and, 337; foreign aid and, 3422, 3568; foreign policy and, 229b, 3327,

Human Rights, continued: foreign policy and, 3514, 3589, 3626, 3647, 3658, 3679; Charter of Rights and, 264; discrimination, 179; language rights, and Bill 101, 217; law, 125
Human Rights Act, 2786
Humor and administration, 2633
Hydro-electric power: in Ontario, 398; in Quebec, 1461, 1662
Hydrogen systems, energy policy, 872

Identity, national. See national identity
Ideological origin of confederation, 255
Ideology, 1938, 1972, 2076; conservatism, 2164; electorate, 2121; elite, 1888, 1889; gender differences, 2113; "Left-Right" scale, 2126, 2166; political parties, 1943, 2156, 2228; public policy, 1890, 2169; Quebec, 1537, 1539, 1629, 1640; Quebec, bibliography, 1542; Quebec and Flanders, 2095; religious, and power, 1700; ruralism and right-wing extremism, 2198; social class, 2023, 2108, 2210; voting behavior, 2165
Immigration, 287, 343, 541, 669, 670, 671, 708, 766, 803, 838, 899, 1286, 1352; accountability in, 744; adaptation, 837; attitudes and, 1345, 1404; British Columbia, 785; ethnicity, 1403; federal-provincial relations, 940; foreign policy and, 3656; labor, 779; professionals, 1433; public attitudes, 1404; Quebec, 1605
Immunity, governmental, 96
Import policy, 3370
Income and political party preference, 2071

Income averaging, 591
Income inequality, 897
Income security and federal finance, 500, 781
Incumbency and elections, 2114, 2115, 2116
Independennce movement, Quebec. See sovereignty-association
Independent administrative agencies, 2515
Indexation of salaries, 584, 718
India, foreign policy with, 3139, 3237
Indian policy, 413, 455, 468, 929, 948, 1168; bibliography, 981, 982; constitutional opposition, 190; constitutional reform, 272; jurisprudence of law of treaties, 263; law and, 129; rights of, 63; Saskatchewan and new Constitution, 143; self-government, 1055, 1166; urbanization in Alberta, 1245. See also aboriginal peoples
Indochina, 1954-1972, foreign policy, 2963
Indonesia, foreign policy with, and human rights, 229b
Industrial policy, 277, 378, 490, 727, 768; federal aid to, 473, 535, 757, 839, 870; planning, 331; public aid to, 286
Inflation act (anti-) of 1975 and Supreme Court, 152, 208, 242
Inflation: Bank of Canada, 576; causes, 660; government deficits, 805, 836; indexation, 718; science policy, 667; unemployment, 702
Influence in Parliament, 2437
Information: access to, 2778; administrative, 2634, 2722; automation, 2673; coordinator, 2734; Freedom of Information Act, 117, 120, 121, 128, 140, 150, 249, 373, 2766;

Information, continued:
Government in Quebec, 1679; House of Commons, 2371, 2378; management in public service, 2528, 2625, 2727, 2728; parliamentary correspondents in Quebec, 1639; quality control, 2736; Quebec public administration, 2528; right of public to, 2587; systems for management, 2603
Information, public, and Election Act, 2172
Innovation in Public Service, 2522
Institute of Public Administration of Canada, 2692, 2750
Insurance, discrimination and human rights, 179; regulation and federalism, 487; unemployment, 801
Integration, political, 1359, 1388; newspapers, 1909
Intelligency agency, proposal for, 240
Interest groups, 1784, 1796, 1797, 1828, 1849, 1853, 1856, 1892, 1893, 1898; farm, 1834, 1906; health policy, 1844; Labour, 1863, 1864; lobbies, 1829, 1830, 1831, 1905; Medical Association, and federalism, 951; Ontario, 1883; Parliament, 1897; peace groups, participation, 1839; political economy, 460; public policy, 1877; public service, 1899; Quebec, 1836; standing committees, 2450. See also pressure groups
Intergovernmental relations, 412, 435, 463, 481, 551, 680, 728, 874, 943, 953; bibliography, 371; federalism, 351; fiscal relations, 936; local and central government, 604, 605, 650; machinery of, 824; transportation regulation, 861

Internal auditing, 2558
International arrangements entered into by agencies, 2761
International development, 3421, 3691
International Development Research Centre, 3622, 3704, 3705
International economic planning, 3389, 3537, 3538, 3722, 3735
International institutions and foreign policy, 2888
International Joint Commission, 3251, 3649, 3728
International Labour Organization, 3535
International law, 3516; Arctic, 3660, 3661; Arctic pollution, 678; Charter of Rights, 188; patriation of new Constitution, 219; Quebec's claim for sovereignty, 262
International Monetary Fund, 3663, 3666
International political economy, 663
International relations, 3378; federalism, 774, 2889; state-owned enterprises, 725. See foreign policy
International trade, 3381, 3439, 3534, 3621; bibliography, 3644
International treaties, foreign policy, 2982
Interpreters, court, work of, 118
Interprovincial relations, 437, 438. See federalism
Inuit land claims, 1011
Investment, foreign, 424. See foreign investment
Irish constitution and similarities to Canada, 268
Israel, foreign policy, 2960, 2984, 3168, 3200; Jerusalem issue, 2969
Issues in general election, 1974, 2178

Japan: economic relations, 3344, 3350, 3369, 3391, 3412, 3470, 3576, 3581, 3582; foreign policy with, 3143, 3166, 3205, 3536
Japanese Canadians, 1381, 1430; racism in World War II, 453
Jerusalem, foreign policy on, 3168
Jews, Hassidic, in Quebec politics, 1725
Jobs, loss of, 177
Judges, civil, in Quebec, 224
Judicial administration, 104, 2615
Judicial admissions of criminal activity, 229f
Judicial Committee of Privy Council, 158, 159, 236, 266
Judicial control of administrative behavior, 193
Judicial, legislative, and executive powers, balance, 2611
Judicial officers, 2613
Judicial review, 254; administrative decisions, 2623; legislative supremacy and, 225
Judiciary and Bill of Rights, 187
Justice, criminal, 73, 164
Justice Development Commission, 2743

King-Byng Dispute, 2265
King, Mackenzie: Cabinet and, 2280; French Canada, 1703; Prime Minister, 2257, 2260; public service, 2797
Kitchener, Ontario, elections in, 1285
Korean Airlines incident, 3044
Korean War, 3270

Labour: immigration, 779; interest groups, 1863, 1864; law, 48; policy, 2013; unions in Quebec, 1598

Lambert Report, 2642, 2733 2735, 2799
Land management in Canada and the U.S., 328
Language: administration, 2585; Constitution and, 232; culture, 1376; geography, 1378; legislation in Quebec, 1534, 1567, 1611, 1621, 1622, 1691, 1693, 1702, 1729, 1733, 1738; municipal politics, 1256; nationalism, 1689; Ontario, 1126; power, 1441. See also bilingualism
Language policy, 959, 1301, 1341, 1664, 1665, 1748, 2146; Bill 22, 754; bilingualism policy, 621, 685; civil service, 2553, 2561, 2699, 2700, 2808, 2813; federal approach, 566; Ontario, 565
Language rights: Constitution and, 69, 408; human rights, and Bill 101, 217; Quebec 261
Languages, Official, Commissioner of, 2555
Language unpermitted in Parliament, 2357
Latin America: economic relations, 3471, 3639; foreign policy with, 3081, 3098, 3099, 3106, 3146, 3191, 3196, 3197, 3202, 3203, 3226, 3527
Law 101 and language legislation in Quebec, 1733
Law: abortions and morality, 308; administrative, 67, 107; American influences upon, 265; community property, 148; constitutiontal, 54, 74, 76, 77, 78, 86, 87, 88, 92, 97, 101, 112, 122, 125, 138; consumer, 145; convention in patriation of Constitution, 246; family, 47; federalism, 125; feminist perspective, 155; indians, 129; international, and new Constitution, 188, 219;

Law, continued:
  international and Quebec's claim for sovereignty, 262; marital, 147; media 41; newspapers, 133; public, 91; right to work, 137; social issues, 391; young persons, 183
Law, administrative, 2618
Law and order, 2794
Law and policy, 470
Law and political parties in Parliament, 2052
Law and politics and economics, 1335
Law, international, and Arctic pollution, 678
Law of armed conflict, foreign policy and, 3093
Law of the Sea, 3349, 3376, 3417, 3428, 3455, 3459, 3476, 3498, 3532, 3543, 3585, 3593, 3632, 3633, 3689, 3703
Leadership: Conservative Party, 1988, 2185; (1976), 1939, 2117; (1983), 2141; conventions, 1946, 1947, 2259; Liberal Party, 2133; (1968), 2186, 2195
Leaders in the House of Commons, 2456
League for Social Reconstruction, 1960
Left, 2160; ideological, 1984, 1993, 1994; nationalism, 2191; urban Canada, 2085
"Left-Right" continuum and political parties, 2064
Legal aid policy problems 277
Legal perspectives of national security, 631
Legal system in Quebec, 1624
Legislation: private member, 2396; standing committees, 2455
Legislative assemblies of provinces, distribution, 2427; Quebec, 1651
Legislative behavior, 2434
Legislative, powers, balance, 2611
Legislative process, 2432; participation, 2390; provincial government, 1235; reform, 2335
Legislative responses to health needs, 780
Legislative supremacy, 225
Legislators and bureaucrats, 2449
Legislators, policy interests of provincial, 491
Legislatures: British Columbia, reform, 2462; Crown Corporations and, 2360; health policy, 2381; Ontario, 2461, 2463; pages in, 2464; provincial, 2316, 2317, 2383, 2384; provincial, officers of, 2425; Quebec, 2372, 2420, 2429;
Lévesque, René: separatists and, 1649; victory of, 1493; view of Quebec, 1528, 1529, 1530, 1531
Liberalism, 2086; voting behavior, 2165
Liberal Party, 1943, 2093; elections, 1954, 1996; history, 1969, 2009, 2010; leadership selection, 2133, 2186, 2195; Ontario, 2219; policy, 1935; prairie provinces, 2000; Quebec, 2083; Saskatchewan, 1998, 2011
Liberties, see civil liberties
Library of Parliament, 2412
Life insurance, taxation of, 557
Linguistic groups: federalism, 685; New Brunswick, 1221; regional cleavages, 979, 1410, 1621; voting, 1387
Lobbying: business groups, 1905; health policy, 634, 1844
Local Elections: political parties in, 2144; reform in Winnipeg, 2143
Local government, 650, 1227, 1243, 1244, 1251, 1252, 1253; decision-making, 1801; northern territories, 1282; Northwest Territories, 1012;

Local government, continued: Nova Scotia, 760; public service, 2501; Quebec, 2746; reform, 1232, 1263

MacDonald Commission, 494, 562, 577, 653, 658, 663, 684, 686, 712, 768, 826, 865, 868, 946
Machinery of government, 2525
Majority Government, 2134
Management in government, 300, 935, 2469; consultants, 2740; control, 2774; eduction, 2600; evaluation, 2516, 2670, 2676; fisheries in Quebec, 522; information systems, 2603; policy, 2491; resources and, Quebec Civil Service, 2521
Manitoba: constitutional reform in, 216; development, 1130; perspective on political rights, 171; politics, 994, 1034; social welfare assistance in, 529
Manpower and public service, 2805
Manufacturing industry and government policy, 532
Maoist Theory in Canada, 2158
Marine Law, 3671, 3672, 3673
Marine Pollution, 3614
Maritime defense, 2967, 2968, 3029
Maritime provinces and regionalism, 1123, 1124, 1199; Western Canada and, 1196
Maritimes, Resource Management Services, 2559
Market and state conflict, 772
Marxism in Canada, 1949; feminism and, 1818, 1999
Mass media attitude to Quebec government, 1607
Media, 1788, 1823; Charter of Rights and, 34; elections, 1755, 2001, 2068;

Media, continued: foreign policy, 2865, 2939, 3569; law 41; parliamentary privilege, 2417; political culture, 1393; public opinion, 1887; regulation, 1391, 1392
Medical and dental care, Newfoundland, 545
Medicare, 433; federalism, 668; Ontario, 925. See also health policy
Member of Parliament, 2306; attitudes, 2369; behavior, 2350; conflict of interest, 2331; constituents, 2416; role, 2368, 2430, 2435, 2436; salaries, 2421; Senators, salaries, 2392; socialization, 2370. See also Backbenchers, Private Members
Members of (provincial) legislature: Alberta, Ombudsman and, 2397; British Columbia, 2459
Mental health services in police force, 740
Merger policy, 2680
Merit and public personnel, 2693
Métis, 63; housing policy, in Saskatchewan, 1115
Metropolitan politics. See municipal politics
Mexico: economic relations, 3693; energy and North American relations, 482, 3521; foreign policy with, 3037, 3473; social structure and public policy, 681
Middle East, foreign policy, 3001, 3009, 3040, 3053, 3097, 3171, 3252, 3273
Middle Powers: foreign policy, 3076, 3120, 3121, 3237; NATO and, 3266; United States and, 3331
Migration, 932
Military, 2990, 2991, 3031, 3032, 3270; cruise missiles, 2998, 3017; foreign policy, 3224; history and politics, 2993;

382 Index

Military, continued:
policy, 3006, 3017, 3064, 3137, 3140, 3157, 3235; United States, 3045, 3320, 3321. See also defense
Mineral policy, 891; Newfoundland's claim to offshore, 488; Ontario, 1194; stockpiling needs, 625
Mining policy, 334; constitutional debate, 375; Ontario, 398
Minister (Cabinet) and Unemployment Insurance, 700
Minister of External Affairs, 2264
Ministerial administration, 2564
Ministerial cabinets in Quebec public administration, 2534
Ministerial comptroller, 2718
Ministerial office staff, 2236
Ministers and civil servants, 2284
Ministers of State, 2253
Ministers, provinicial, 1108
Ministers' staff, 2288
Ministry of State for Economic and Regional Development, 2261
Ministry of State for Science and Technology, 493
Minorities: affirmative action, 273; education of, 726; general election, 1923; human rights, and federalism, 337; language rights 69
Minority government, 2066, 2216; Ontario, 1200; public administration, 2669
Modernization: and federalism, 884; Quebec, 1553, 1646, 1647
Monarchy, 2252. See also Crown
Monetary policy, 829, 847
Money, inflation, and the Bank of Canada, 576
Montesquieu, 141, 229j

Montreal: local government, 1013, 1021, 1041, 1093, 1211, 1241
Morality, law and abortions, 308
Morin, Claude, Quebec foreign policy and, 2922
Mortgage finance and housing policy, 887
Motor vehicle safety, regulation of, 918
Mulroney administration, foreign policy, 2944
Mulroney, Brian: Conservative Party and, 1931; federal-provincial relations and, 392; foreign economic policy, 3599, 3664; foreign policy, 2944, 3281, 3714
Multi-culturalism, 1300, 1318, 1347, 1399, 1410, 1411, 1548; federalism, 1420; language groups, 1379; Quebec, 1658. See also bilingualism-biculturalism
Multinational corporations, 3499, 3600, 3606, 3620; foreign investment and, 3355, 3358; government and, 788; Quebec, 3505, 3506
Multinationalism in Canada, 2852
Municipal administrators, Nova Scotia, 2519
Municipal finance, 1255, 1279; Ottawa, 1207; reform, 1102
Municipal government, public administration, 2747
Municipal labor relations, 2548
Municipal politics, 964, 987, 1006, 1009, 1037, 1040, 1054, 1056, 1062, 1063, 1076, 1077, 1084, 1097, 1098, 1107, 1136, 1145, 1149, 1175, 1227, 1233, 1293; administration, 1020; administration, bibliography, 2513; bibliography, 974; citizen participation, 1267; decision making, 1071; development, 1178; finances, 1096, 1134,

Municipal politics, continued: finances 1150, 1159, 1185, 1190, 1204, 1247, 1248, 1249; firefighters, 1202; freedom of assembly, 1269; government of capital cities, 1072; Hamilton, Ontario, 1004; language, 1256; Montreal, 1021, 1241; Nova Scotia, 968; provincial governments, 1122; Quebec, 1041, 1144, 1193; 1237, 1238, 1239, 1240, 1632; reform: New Brunswick, 1143; reorganization, 1176; social class, 1167; Toronto, 1021, 1068, 1131; Vancouver, 1273; waste collection, 1201; Winnipeg, Manitoba, 1021, 1128, 1197; women, 1189
Municipal-provincial relations, 1260; New Brunswick, 1191

Namibia, foreign policy, 3186
Narcotics legislation, 538
National Assembly, Quebec, 1651
National capital, 1157
National Energy Program, 466, 673, 674, 675, 676, 694, 753, 796
National identity, 1419
National integration, 1166; Quebec separatism, 1685; voting, and political parties, 2100
Nationalism, 1298, 1299, 1302, 1304, 1305, 1307, 1309, 1311, 1314, 1315, 1316, 1317, 1321, 1325, 1326, 1327, 1366, 1367, 1371, 1372, 1375, 1382, 1386, 1415, 1416, 1478, 1943, 2069, 2191, 3373, 3374, 3413, 3493; Alberta, 1161; Canadian-American relations, 1297; class, 1331; culture, 1370, 1401; economics, 1320, 1356, 1408, 3384, 3479; economics in Quebec, 1631, 1676;

Nationalism, continued: ethnic demands, 1332, 1365; federalism, 1397, 1429; internationalism, 1434; political culture, 1295, 1324; Quebec, 1463, 1464, 1468, 1469, 1473, 1478, 1485, 1487, 1491, 1498, 1499, 1508, 1533, 1537, 1538, 1541, 1543, 1545, 1546, 1547, 1561, 1562, 1568, 1574, 1576, 1578, 1579, 1580, 1583, 1584, 1585, 1593, 1595, 1609, 1610, 1613, 1619, 1625, 1631, 1636, 1642, 1644, 1648, 1654, 1655, 1660, 1661, 1666, 1668, 1681, 1683, 1684, 1687, 1688, 1690, 1695, 1706, 1708, 1709, 1714, 1716, 1722, 1736; Quebec, bibliography, 1511; Quebec unions, 1904; regionalism, 1396; social class, 1610; technology, 1310, 1353; transportation, 1402; United States, 1425
Nationalization, 1219
National Research Council, 599
National security, 631, 900; Parliament, 2318; Royal Canadian Mounted Police and, 332. See also security, national
National Socialism in Canada, 2008
National unity, 284, 449, 1380, 1400: Constitution, 456, 457, 458; federalism, 880; Quebec, 1591
Native leaders' attitudes, 1109, 1110, 1111, 1112, 1113, 1168
Native people: Constitution, 106. See also Aboriginal people
Native rights in Canada, 1057
NATO, 2966, 3174, 3206, 3266, 3268, 3295; foreign policy, 2971, 2987, 3039, 3041, 3101, 3115, 3116, 3119, 3126, 3127
Natural gas, 3528; forecasts, 846; policy, 542;

Natural gas, continued: regulation of, 665; revenues, 875
Natural resource policies, 277, 295, 368, 393, 398, 3642; Constitution and, 103, 162; federalism, 431; law, 425
Natural resources: aboriginal peoples, 967; constitutional reform, 568; coordination of shore management agencies, 895; northern land use policy, 1051; regionalism, 1135; regulation of, 552; rent of, 523; revenue sharing, 533; water, and environmental diplomacy, 563
Navy, 3288
Neutron bomb, 3174
New Brunswick: cabinet committee system, 2278; development agreement with Ottawa, 426; elections, 2014; equal opportunity in, 1292; francophone policy, 1221; health professionals in, 540; municipal reform, 1143; provincial-municipal relations, 1191; reform of municipalities, 1148; third parties in, 2147
New Democratic Party, 1926, 1971, 1976, 1977, 2020; British Columbia, 1962, 1989, 1272, 1291; foreign policy, 2890; Manitoba, 1034; platform, 1948; Saskatchewan, 1219
Newfoundland, 1019, 1047, 1214, 1215; confederation, 991, 1087; medical and dental care, 545; offshore energy resources and federalism, 488; political culture, 1229; political economy of, 1043, 1044; political parties, 1224, 1225, 1229; public administration, 2478; voting, fishermen, 2050
Newspapers: editorials and policy, 1845, 1909, 2205; law, 133

New Zealand: Constitution, 268; race relations commissions, 910
Nigeria, foreign policy, 3258
Nominating candidates for Parliament, 2422
NORAD, 3047, 3119, 3206, 3267, 3278, 3279
North: 1137; constitutional development, finances, 1268; development, 990, 1017, 1046, 1060, 1092 1114, 1140, 1154, 1220; ethnicity, 1438; politics, 1086, 1089, 1281, 1282, 1283; public service in, 2628; resource policy, 1051. See also Arctic
North Atlantic Treaty Organization. See NATO
Northern energy development, 288
Northwest Passage, 3661
Northwest Territories, 1141; division of, 1091, 1139; elections in, 2082; ethnic politics, 1222; local government, 1012; public administration in, 2806
Norway: foreign policy with, 3133, 3134; oil policy, regulation of, 617
Nova Scotia: education reform in, 489; election (1970), 2022; ethnic politics, 1373; health services in, 623; local government, 960; municipal administrators, 2519; municipal government, 968; ombudsman, 2787; political socialization in, 1855; public administration, 2662; seats in Parliament, 2447; Royal Commission, 1164
Nuclear attack and Quebec, 3135
Nuclear defense, 2965, 3301
Nuclear exports, 2961
Nuclear policies, 306, 312, 320, 3161, 3194, 3201

Nuclear politics issue, 1808
Nuclear power, regulation, 602, 643, 695, 939

Occupational health, regulation of, 600
Occupational training, federalism, and policy development, 325
Occupation and voting, 1974, 2070
October Crisis, 1471, 1483, 1492, 1501, 1502, 1612; children's attitudes, 1413; public opinion, 1445
Official Languages, Commissioner of, 2555
Official Secrets Act, 631
Oil policy, 485, 617, 750, 3490, 3527; Alberta, 710; Arctic, 709; development policies, 842; energy crisis, 524; foreign ownership, 432; National Energy Program, 796; public revenue, 635; regulation of, 528
Old age pensions, 292
Ombudsman, 469; Alberta, 2397, 2629, 2630; legislation, 632; Nova Scotia, 2787; Quebec, 2531, 2532, 2536
Ontario: attitudes and electoral system in, 2150; bibliography, 973; bilingualism policy, 959; civil servants, 2768, 2769, 2770, 2771; confederation, 387; Conservative Party, 1039; elections, 2151; electric power planning, 889; environmental planning, 1147; governmental reform, 1118, 1208; government reorganization, 1152, 1153, 1173; health care, 802; interest groups, Law Union, 1883; languages policy for, 565, 1126; legislature, cleavages, 2463; legislature, committees in, 2461;

Ontario, continued: legislature, officers of 2425; Liberal Party, 2219; management by results, 2516; mineral policy, 1194; minority government, 1200; Northwest region, 1283; opposition party, role of, 2138; politics, 1035, 1036; property tax, 527; provincial planning, 1246; public administration, 2729; regional development, 1276; urban development, 1142
OPEC and energy policy, 418
Open government, 2579
Opinion polls and elections, 2109
Opinion, public and the sovereignty association referendum, 1705
Organization of American States, foreign policy, 3065
Organization theory and public administration, 2811
Ottawa: municipal finance, 1207; municipal politics in, 1254; public administration, 2747, 2812; Quebec relations, 1675

Pacific region: economic relations, 3566, 3631, 3627; foreign policy with, 2983, 3069, 3110, 3118, 3144, 3151, 3245, 3263, 3264, 3293
Pages in Parliament and legislature, 2464
Pakistan, foreign policy with, 2957, 3010, 3108
Palestine, foreign policy with, 2984, 3200
Parliament, 2325, 2337, 2342, 2354; administrative agencies, 2339; arms supply, 3060; associations, 3163; audit, 2344; behavior, 2314; bilingualism, 2321; bureaucracy, 2281, 2359; coalitions, 2211; Commissions, 2641; committees, 2424,

Parliament, continued: committees, 2444, 2445, 2446; conflict of interest, 2382; control of enterprises, 507; defense policy, 2330, 2349; dissolution of, 2145, 2385, 2386; efficiency, 2379, 2395; federalism, 733; foreign affairs, 2336, 2341, 2375, 2460; human rights, 2345, 2423, 2451; human rights, foreign policy and, 3647; influence, 2327, 2437; information, 2371, 2378; institutions, 2352; international organizations, 3162; leaders in, 2456; literature on, 2355; national security, 2318; nominating candidates for, 2422; pages in, 2464; policy and, 2308, 2323, 2380; political parties, 2052; political support, 2367; power, 2300, 2302, 2303, 2304, 2307, 2334, 2346, 2363; prime ministers, 2271; privilege, 2417, 2428; procedure, 2309, 2310, 2311, 2312, 2319, 2320, 2322; reform, 2301, 2315, 2335, 2340, 2389, 2409, 2410, 2411, 2413 2433; reporting, 2351; representation, 2465; research on, 2402; Research Service, 2453; roles, 2368; Scientific Committee, 2356; seats of Nova Scotia in, 2447; spending, 2338; standing committees and legislation, 2455; television of, 2400; turnover in, 2361; written questions in, 2362. See also House of Commons and Senate

Parliamentary correspondents and information in Quebec, 1639

Parliamentary sovereignty, Charter of Rights and Freedoms, 192

Parliamentary supremacy, 2454; federalism, 2458

Parliamentary Task Forces, 2426

Participation, 1752, 1758, 1761, 1768, 1769, 1778, 1780, 1792, 1821, 1878, 1913, 1914, 1917; Afro-Canadians, 1773; bibliography, 1747; culture, 1412; democracy, 1751, 1774; determinants, 2224; environmental policy, 1759; legislative process, 2390; municipal politics, 1267; political parties, 1861; pressure groups, 1891; Quebec, 1522; students, 1825; unemployment, 1850; women and, 1742

Parti Quebecois, 1463, 1488, 1537, 1575, 1650, 1701, 1995, 2019, 2036, 2055; accomplishments in Government, 1526; American reactions, 3111; criticisms of, 1514; economics, 1637; goals, 1455, 1530, 1531; growth of, 1550; in 1985, 1603; in office, 1555, 1672, 1715; Quebec elections, 2079, 2083; realignment in Quebec, 2041; social change in Quebec, 1698; social class, 1673; White Paper, 1513

Partition, 1571

Party and social class, 1937

Party identification: concept of, 1884, 1885, 2063; elections, 2031

Party leaders and party activity, 1769, 1827

Party organization, 1859

Patriation of Constitution, 98, 194, 209, 229e; Charter of Rights, 239; international law, 219; law and convention in, 246; Quebec and, 229h

Patronage: 1873; in public service, 2797; in Quebec, 1525, 1854

Peace groups participation, 1839

Peace initiatives, 3213, 3214

Peacekeeping, 3083, 3129, 3167, 3277, 3284
Pearse Report, Royal Commission, Forest Policy in British Columbia, 1165
Pearson, Lester, diplomacy, 2997, 3080, 3229
Pension funds, 292, 588
Periodicals, regulation of, 1391, 1392
Personnel and financial administration, 2644
Personnel management in Quebec, 2566 2568
Personnel reorganization, 2725
Petro-Canada, 3559
Petroleum industry. See oil policy
Pipeline (gas) project, 1977, 288
Planning: administration in Quebec, 2527; goal setting, 841, 893; Ontario, 1246; policy-making, 331; public administration, 2665, 2785; public administration in Quebec, 2533, 2588; public policy, 633; public service, 521, 2576; regional, 1250
Pluralism in Canada, 1911
Poland, foreign policy with, 2964, 3179, 3426
Police, 79, 247, 653; administration in Quebec, 2529; mental health services in, 740; politics, 1794. See also Royal Canadian Mounted Police
Policy-making, 299, 317, 318, 341, 379, 569, 811; constitutional reform, 163; federalism, 325; framework, 850; government officials, 892; philosophy of, 601; planning, 818, 841; provincial legislators and, 491; research, 762; structures, 714
Politial parties, third parties in New Brunswick, 2147
Political corruption, 1760
Political culture, 1294, 1295, 1296, 1312, 1313,
Political culture, continued: 1319, 1330, 1338, 1437, 1440, 1762, 1779; federalism, 797; Quebec, 1588, 1653; regional, 1262
Political development in Canada, 386
Political economy, 304, 324, 407, 419, 607, 655, 764; industry, 473; Newfoundland, 1043, 1044; ownership issues, 399; social welfare, 396; tradition of, 759
Political efficacy in Canada, 1871
Political elite, 1862, 2503. See also elites, political
Political integration and newspapers, 1909
Political modernization: Quebec, 1553
Political participation, 1910
Political parties, 1921, 1922, 1952, 1975, 2012, 2188; Alberta, 2142, 2192; bibliography, 1958; British Columbia, 975, 1272; campaign activity, 2098; centralization, 2054; cleavages, 2094; Conservatives in Quebec, 1515; constituency organization, 1902; elections, 2037, 2060, 2061, 2120, 2149, 2159, 2180, 2193, 2194, 2202; Edmonton (Alberta) 1212; federalism, 2155; financing, 1981, 2163, 2208; financing, bibliography, 2005; Gallop polls, 2222; ideology, 1943, 2156; issue awareness, 2042; language, 2146; leaders, 1826, 1827, 2223; local elections, 2144; loyalty, 2025, 2078, 2097; New Democratic Party, 1272; Newfoundland and political parties, 1224, 1225; Nova Scotia, 2022; officials, 1826, 1860, 1907, 1908; organization, 1859, 2099; Parliament, 2052;

Political parties, continued: political recruitment, 1832; preference and income, 2071; provincial politics, 1064, 2007; public administration, 2604, 2562; Quebec, 1444, 1983, 1995, 2018, 2021, 2056, 2104, 2153, 2187, 2209; realignment, 2026; regionalism, 963, 1924, 2002; religious affiliation, 2092; Saskatchewan, 1216, 2130; social class, 2112, 2122, 2167, 2200; structure, 2063; third parties, 2218; Toronto, 2157; (Quebec) Union Nationale, 1505; urban Canada, 1974; voting behavior, 1944, 1945, 2043, 2044, 2045, 2100, 2112; women, 1743, 1826, 1928; workers, 2049. See also specific party names; Third Parties

Political party identification, 1884, 1885, 2123, 2127, 2131, 2132, 2217; cleavages, 2128, 2129; ideology, 2228; instability, 2136; party loyalty, 2102, 2103; voting, 2101, 2137

Political patronage, 1873; in Quebec, 1854

Political realignment, 2026

Political recruitment, 1872, 1875; party activists, 1832

Political rights, Manitoba perspective, 171

Political sects, 1980

Political socialization, 1762, 1779, 1800, 1866, 1867, 1868, 1869, 1880, 1881, 1882, 1885, 1894; Nova Scotia, 1855; Quebec, 1903

Political sociology, 1744

Political structures and environmental politics, 743

Political support, 1767, 1805, 1806; economy, 1886; federalism, 716; Parliament, 2367; political attitudes, 1900

Political theory in Canada, 1938; 1997

Political party organizations, 1964. See also Parties

Pollution: anti-pollution laws in the Arctic, 678; ecology and, 954; pollution control and effects on industry, 784

Population policy, 451

Populism, 2048; Quebec, 2072

Poverty, 530, 1390; Constitution, 581; social policy and, 384

Power, electric, planning in Ontario, 889

Prairie politics, 1005, 1061, 1083, 1259, 1265; economics, 1226; Liberal Party, 2000; regionalism, 1008

Premiers and prime ministers, 2279

Press and politics, 1817; in Quebec, 1720, 1837

Pressure groups, 1784, 1804, 1896; Indian politics, 948; Labour, 1863, 1864; participation, 1891. See also interest groups

Price stabilization, 497, 738

Prime minister: advisors, 2263; cabinet and, 2240, 2243; character, Mackenzie King, 2260; committees in House of Commons, 2343; dissolution of Parliament, 2145; French Canadian, 2285; history, 2237; information for, 2286; Office of, 2255, 2262, 2276, 2290, 2297; Office of and Privy Council Office, 2295, 2296; Parliament, 2271; power, 2231, 2246, 2258, 2265, 2266, 2267, 2268, 2293, 2298; premiers, 2279; U.S. Presidents and, 2242. See also specific individual names

Prince Edward Island, 2212

Privacy, public servants and, 248

Private Members' Bills, 2396
Private sector, regulation of, 687
Privilege: Media, 2417; Parliament, 2428; Yukon Legislature, 2431
Privy Council, Judicial Committee of, 158, 159, 236, 266
Privy Council Office, 2247, 2251, 2282, 2287, 2590; Prime Minister's Office and, 2295, 2296
Progressive-Conservative party. See Conservative Party
Progressivism in the West, 2015
Property tax, 525, 812, 871; Ontario, 527; public policy, 585
Protest groups and civil servant, 2815
Provinces: budgeting and conditional grants, 905; Charter of Rights and, 146; constitutions and federal constitution, 139, 267; controls of foreign investment, 3312; foreign policy, 2841, 2904, 3016; international activities, 2891, 2929; legislative process, 1235; legislators, policy interests of, 491; planning, 2655; powers and federation, 955; public administration, 2583, 2782; public domain, 508; public servants, training, 2622; public service, 2490, 2501; regulatory agencies, bibliography, 2511; social welfare policy, 517, 352.
Province-state relations, foreign policy, 3587, 3588, 3596, 3713
Provincial constitution, British Columbia, 1258
Provincial development, 1290
Provincial elections: highway employment and, 2207; Prince Edward Island, 2212

Provincial legislators, 2364, 2365, 2366
Provincial legislatures: distribution, 2427; officers of, 2425; Yukon, 2431
Provincial-municipal relations, 1260; finances, 1247; New Brunswick, 1191
Provincial planning in Ontario, 1246
Provincial political parties, 2007
Provincial politics, 969, 997, 1073, 1120; Alberta, 972, 983, 1025, 1209; Atlantic Canada, 1074; bibliography, 973, 1024; British Columbia, 975, 1065, 1066, 1223, 1266, 1272, 1289; economic policy, 1289; federalism, 1074; financies, 1182, 1183; Labor, 1223; Manitoba, 994, 1034, 1130; minority government, 1200; municipalities and, 1122; New Democratic Party, British Columbia, 1272, 1291; Newfoundland, 1019, 1043, 1044, 1047, 1214, 1215; Ontario, 973, 1035, 1036, 1039, 1118, 1152, 1153, 1173, 1200, 1208; policy-making, 1070; political parties, 999, 1064, 1106; political parties, Saskatchewan, 1216; prairie politics, 1061, 1083; private enterprise, 1127; public policy, 986; Quebec, see Quebec; reform, 1208; Saskatchewan, 998, 1264, 1280. See also specific provinces
Public Accounts Committee, 2414; Ontario Legislature, 2441
Public administration, 2484, 2495, 2505, 2506, 2509, 2616, 2617, 2626, 2638, 2640, 2643, 2653, 2656, 2659, 2660, 2661, 2668, 2671, 2677, 2678, 2679, 2683, 2709, 2710, 2721, 2730, 2756, 2757, 2758, 2759, 2760, 2793,

Public administration, continued: 2810; accountability, 2538; bibliography, 2488; British Columbia, 2814; Charter of Rights, 2744; citizen demands, 2737; communication, 2772; conformity, 2708; cutbacks, 2657, 2663; decentralization, 2803; effectiveness, 2552; employment and disability, 2809; ethics, 2551, 2637, 2685; evaluation, 2776; finances, 2800; goals, 2550; Halifax, Nova Scotia, 2662; information, 2625, 2778; instruction, 2754, 2755; intergovernmental relations, 604, 605; language, 2585, 2808; Newfoundland, 2478; Northwest Territories, 2806; Ontario, 2729; Ottawa, 2747, 2812; philosophy, 2719; planning, 2553, 2665, 2785; planning in Quebec, 2588; political parties, 2604; power, 2570, 2624, 2684; problems, 2498; profession, 2569; provinces, 2583, 2782; public interest, 2485; public role, 2482; Quebec, 1563, 2470, 2534, 2591, 2636, 2646, 2647, 2648, 2649, 2650, 2651, 2652, 2681, 2780; reform, 2571; regulation, 2784; rewards, 2682; secrecy, 2701, 2801; setting, 2645; study of, 2586; teaching of, 2675; teaching in Quebec, 2530; technology, 2779, 2804; text, 2466, 2480, 2496; values, 2666

Public corporations, 326, 363, 2712, 2713

Public employment, 2474, 2481, 2792

Public enterprises, 2577; financial management, 2545

Public finance in Quebec, 1604

Public housing in Hull, Quebec, 1095, 1594

Public Information and Election Act, 2172

Public interest and public administration, 2485

Public interest groups, 654

Public Interest Laws in Quebec, 1678

Public law, 91

Public management, 2504

Public opinion: Canadian-American relations, 1421; foreign policy, 2940; ideology, 1890; legalization of abortion, 1851; media, 1887; Nazi Trials, 1916; October Crisis, 1445; sovereignty association referendum, 1705

Public planning, 2723, 2724

Public policy, 277, 291, 317, 318, 321, 323, 405, 736, 741, 1763, 1819, 1821, 2468, 2753; analysis, 858; administration, 477; bureaucracy, 698; Canada Development Corporation, 543; civil servants and, 381; decision-making, 609; equal pay, 486; ideology, 2169; instruments of, 956; interest groups, 1877; political development, 386; programs and clients, 520; provincial politics, 986; Trudeau administration years, 819; United States, comparison, 863. See also policy-making

Public sector: bargaining, 274; employees in Quebec, 2549

Public servants: 2686, 2749; accountability, 2620; advisors, as, 2658; the Crown, 2745; ethics, 2687; federalism, 365; personal liability, 2726; political neutrality, 711; political rights, 2580; privacy, 248; provinical, training, 2622; public servant and responsibility, 2764; rights for, 2635

Public service, 2605, 2606, 2607, 2695, 2696, 2697, 2698; accountability in, 2581, 2711; administrative reform, 2539, 2707; bilingualism, 2574, 2575, 2700; British Columbia, 2714; change, 2752; collective bargaining, 2705, 2706; Francophones, 2472; gender, 2467; history, 2489; image, 2818; information management, 2727, 2728; innovation in, 2522; language training, 2553, 2699; local, provincial, federal, 2501; management, 2497; manpower, 2805; political neutrality, 2598; North, 2628; patronage in, 2797; planning in, 521, 2576; power, 2540; provincial government, 2490; Quebec, 2556, 2612; recruitment, 2702; reform, 2541; responsibility in, 2715, 2716, 2717, 2720; training, 2704; unions, 2479; women, 2703. See also public administration

Public Service Employment Act, governmental secrecy and, 606

Public Works Department, reorganization, 2471

QUANGOS, in British Columbia, 2714

Quebec (city): urban renewal, 1151

Quebec (province), 1041, 1452, 1453, 1476, 1600; administrative history, 1645; administrative information in, 2722; administrative law, 67; attitudes toward Constitution 1657; bibliography, 1457, 1479, 1590; bureaucracy, 2738, 2739; Cabinet, 1715; Canada and, 1495, 1516; Charter of Fundamental Freedoms, 1597; citizens who are English, 1474; civil code, 1624; civil judges,

Quebec (province), continued: 224; civil service, 2521; Conservative Party in, 1515; Constitution and, 62, 100, 115, 116, 211, 232, 1710; continentalism, 1671, 1731; decentralization, 1680; delegated legislation, 2457; economic development, 1601, 1724; economic nationalism, 1631; economic relations, United States, 3623; economy, 1798; education policy, 1103; elections, 1523. 2153, (1970), 1517, 2079, (1973), 1517, 2182, (1976), 1451, 1454, 1493, 2017, 2089, 2183, (1981), 1456, (1985), 2067, 2118; electoral platforms in Quebec, history, 1566; electoral reform in, 1458; electoral studies in, 2088; energy policy, 1623; English-Canadian nationalism, 1617; ethnic politics, 641, 1704; federal elections, 1950, 2030, 2139; federalism, 229d, 296, 359, 414, 539, 628, 719, 802, 879, 938, 1302, 1342, 1343, 1481, 1565, 1590, 1599; federalism, and political parties, 2187; fisheries in, 522; foreign cultural relations, Louisiana, 3678; foreign investment, 3505, 3506; foreign relations, 1450, 1581, 1671, 1741, 2849, 2866, 2869, 2884, 2897, 2910, 2919, 2922, 2931, 2942, 2949, 2950 3135; foreign policy, Africa, 3085, 3190, 3215, 3240, 3241; foreign policy, France, 1633, 2878, 3153; foreign policy, Latin America, 3081; foreign policy, United States, 3218; general text, 1586; governmental finance, 1620; government information, 1679; government organization, 1500, 1669;

Quebec (province) continued: government personnel, 1447, 1484; government policy making, 1446; government political institutions, 1628; government politics in, 1449, 1496; health policy, 366, 802, 912, 942, 1634; histories, 1472, 1549; hydro-power, 1461; ideology in, 1537, 1539, 1629, 1640, 2095; immigration policy, 1605; independence of, 879, 1383, 1444; industrial development, 3464; interest groups, 1836; language policy, 754, 1534, 1611, 1691, 1693, 1621, 1622, 1702, 1729, 1733; language rights, 217, 261; law, 125; legislature, 2372, 2420, 2429; local government, 2746; modernization of, 1646, 1647; municipal politics, 1237, 1238, 1239, 1240; municipal reform, 1144, 1193; National Assembly, 1651; nationalism, 1781; ombudsman, 2531, 2532, 2536; Ontario and, 802; Ottawa, relations with, 1470, 1486, 1675; Parti Quebecois and, 2041, 2083; patriation, 229h; patronage in, 1854; personnel management, 2566, 2568; planning administration, 2527, 2533; police administration, 2470, 2529, 2616, 2617, 2681; political culture, 1653; political elite, 1901; political issues, 1536; political participation, 1522; political parties, 1983, 2018, 2019, 2021, 2056, 2104; political practices, 1600; political socialization, 1903; populism and Social Credit, 2072; press, 1720, 837; public administration, 1563, 2484, 2499, 2500, 2528, 2530, 2534, 2588, 2591,

Quebec (province) continued: public administration 2636, 2646, 2647, 2648, 2649, 2650, 2651, 2652, 2780; public finance, 564, 1604; public opinion and, 64, 1475; public sector employees, 2549; public service, 2556, 2612; reform of legislature, 2429; separation of powers, 114; separatism, 597, 1436, 1682, 1685, 1726; Social Credit Party, 2003, 2209; social class and nationalism, 1610; socialist movement, 2062; society, 1577; sovereignty and constitutional law, 151, 262; sovereignty, United States relations and, 3035; Sovereignty Association (anti), 1982; standing committees in, 2415; technocrats, 2535; technological politics, 1635; Union Nationale, 1505; United States and, 1721, 3399, 3404; urban politics, 1013, 1162 voting in general elections, 2028; women in cabinet, 2292; women's movement, 1490, 1865; Workers' Movement, 1696
Question Period, 2438; Victoria, 2439; written, 2362
Quiet Revolution, 1443, 1555, 1565, 1616, 1670,1677, 1694. See also October Crisis

Race relations, 1088
Race Relations Commissions, 910
Racism, 693; and Japanese-Canadians in World War II, 453
Radio-Quebec: function of, 553; policy of, 2567
Rail travel and technology, 742
Railway regulation, 344
Reader's Digest Magazine, regulation of, 1392

Reagan administration, foreign policy, 3303
Reagan, Ronald, relations with Canada, 3320
Realignment, political parties, 2026: elections, 2035; party activists, 1832; Quebec and Parti Quebecois, 2041
Recruitment, political, 1872, 1875, 2702
Redistribution, House of Commons, constituency size, 1968, 2179
Redistribution of income and wealth, 169, 898, 930. See also fiscal federalism
Referendum (on Sovereignty-Association), 1448
Reform: administrative, 2539, 2621; British Columbia legislature, 2462; electoral system, 2051, 2140; House of Commons, 2332, 2340; legislative process, 2335; legislature in Quebec, 2429; Parliament, 2409, 2410, 2411, 2413, 2433; Senate, 2333, 2347
Refugee policy, 309, 541, 596, 804, 3555; African, 848
Regime support, 1858
Regional and Economic Development, Ministry of, 2261
Regional and linguistic cleavages, 979
Regional dependency, 1213
Regional development, 1100, 1257, 1277, 1278; energy crisis, 1210; Ontario, 1276; policy, 1078
Regionalism, 984, 1007, 1018, 1075, 1195, 1217, 1261, 1264, 1274; Atlantic Canada, and federalism 1059, 1074; bibliographies, 980; business development, 1133; constitution and, 1160; corporations, 1186; culture, 1262, 1228; development, 790; disparities in, 1138; Eastern Arctic, bibliography, 980;

Regionalism, continued: economics, 302, 427, 1023, 1121, 1242; federalism, 284, 415, 728, 1058, 1104; foreign policy attitudes, 1284; maritimes, 1123, 1124, 1199; models of, 1129; national growth, 1177; natural resources, 1135; North, 990; planning, 1125, 1250; political parties, 2002; prairie politics and, 1005, 1061; Quebec, 1459; reallocation of resources, 1052; representation in Canada, 1924; West and, 970, 989, 1105
Registrar of Supreme Court of Canada, 2789
Registration of voters in elections, 2080
Regulation, 341, 403; air transportation fares, 280, 715; business policy, 445, 446, 447, 448; cable television, 498, 499; economy, 403; environmental policy, 792, 793; food processing, 548; income and wealth, 898; motor vehicle safety, 918; natural gas, 665; natural resources, 552; nuclear energy, 602, 695, 903, 939; occupational health, 600; oil industry, 528; paramedical professions, 534; public administration, 2784; quasi-judicial organizations, 640; social policy, 735; technology, 630; telecommunications, 293, 583, 862; television, 278; toxic chemicals, 795; transportation, 567, 755, 861, 906, 2492; uranium production, 903. See also subject regulated
Regulatory agencies, 326, 2476; analysis of, 549, 550, 603; failure, 833; provincial, bibliography, 2511

Regulatory commissioners, 2795
Regulatory process, 315; federalism and, 429
Religion: cleavages in elections, 2106; ethnic influences on Senators, 2353; ideology and power, 1700; party choice, 2092, 2146; voting, 1387
Rental housing, 888
Reorganization of public works department, 2471
Repatriation of Constitution. See patriation
Representation Act, 1974, 2448
Representation: economic backgrounds of politicians, 2391; government, 734; in Parliament, 2465
Representative bureaucracy, 2767
Research, government support of, 773
Research Service for Parliament, 2453
Resource development and federalism, 638, 647
Resource Land and Crown Corporations, 573
Resource law bibliography, 301
Resource management services, 2559
Resource policies, 295, 393, 398, 514; Constitution, 64, 103, 162; environment, 327; federalism, 425; non-replenishable resources, and economic theory, 752; oil and gas, 750; policy making, 295; revenues and federalism, 875; taxation and the Supreme Court, 806
Responsibility in public service, 2715, 2716, 2717, 2720
Responsible government: foreign policy, 2937; public servants, 2764
Retrenchment, 2773
Revenue sharing, 505, 533, 582, 635
Rhodesia, foreign policy with, 3247

Rights: aboriginal, Constitution and, 252; Bill of, 131; Charter of, see Charter of Rights and Freedoms; criminal, 230; indian, 63
Rights of aboriginal peoples, 976
Right to know, 120
Right to work, law, and capitalism, 137
Royal Canadian Mounted Police, 102, 123, 243, 332
Royal Commissions: bibliography, 2241; Conditions of Foreign Service, 3130; Economic Union and the Development Prospects for Canada, 1985; Electric Power Planning in Ontario, 889; Forest Policy in British Columbia, 1165; Nova Scotia, 1164; values of, 834. See also MacDonald Commission
Ruralism and right-wing extremism, 2198

Salaries: determination of health and education workers, 822; indexation of, 584; Members of Parliament, 2421; public employment, 2481; Senators, 2392
Sales tax reform, 646
Sampling for election studies, 2135
Saskatchewan: budget reform, 1203, 1280; French-Canadian minority, 1180; housing policy for Métis, 1115; indians and new Constitution, 143; Liberal Party in, 1998, 2011; Lieutenant-Governor, 1146; municipal politics, financing, 1204; New Democratic Party, 1219; political parties, 1216; politics, 998, 1022; voting turnout, 2130
Scale for conservatism in Canada, 1912

Science and technology, Ministry of State for, 493
Science policy, 316, 648, 667, 737, 823
Scotland, nationalism in Quebec, compared, 1736
Seabed mining, 3671
Sea, Law of the, foreign policy and, 3349
Second Chambers. See Senate
Secrecy: administrative, 2505a, 2701 2801; governmental, 606
Security, 3208, 3209, 3210
Security Intelligence Services Act, 653, 900
Security, national, 631, 900; Canadian Security Intelligence Service, 571; control of, 653; in the multi-ethnic state, 825; legal perspectives, 631; political control, 629; Parliament, 2318; Royal Canadian Mounted Police and, 332
Security of Europe, 3138
Security, Western, 2966
Self-determination in Quebec, 1619
Self government by aboriginal peoples, 967, 1772
Senate, 2305, 2373; need for, 2348; procedure, 2387; reform, 2333, 2347, 2358, 2407, 2440, 2442; role of, 2403. See also Parliament
Senators, 2374; ethnic and religious influences, 2353; salaries, 2392
Separation of powers, 37, 141, 355, 436; Constitution and, 233, 234; Quebec and, 114
Separatism, 597, 1082, 1384, 1649, 1682, 1685, 1713, 1726; goals, 1455. See also sovereignty-association
Sexual assault laws, 679
Shore management agencies, coordination of, 895
Skagit-High Ross Dam, 3572
Smallwood, Joey, Newfoundland and, 1224, 1225

Social class: electoral behavior, 2167; ethnic voting in winnipeg, 2213, 2225, 2226, 2227; ideology, 2108; left-right images in voting, 2111; left-wing radicalism, 2210; municipal politics, 1167; Parti quebecois government, 1673; party, 1937; political ideology, 2023; political party choice, 2200; Quebec and nationalism, 1498, 1610; religion, and party choice, 2146; voting, 2112, 2122, 2151, 2162, 2177, 2199, 2229, 2230. See also class
Social Credit Party, 1927, 1953, 1990; British Columbia, 1989; ideology, 1979; Quebec, 2003, 2072, 2209; West, 2015. See also Creditiste Party
Social groups, 1411; Orléans, 1524; politics, 1757
Socialism, 2039, 2069, 2086; Catholics, 1929; ideology, 1965; in Canada, 1942, 2008; in the West, 2015. See also Left
Social issues and law, 391
Socialist groups, 1960
Socialist Movement in Quebec, 2062
Socialist Party, 1943
Socialization, political, 1762, 1779, 1800, 1866, 1867, 1868, 1869, 1880, 1881, 1882, 1885, 1894; legislators, 2370; Nova Scotia, 1855; Quebec, 1903
Social policy, 480, 763, 897; Alberta, 1209; Constitution, 75; human resources, 494; poverty, 384; regulation of, 735, 794; welfare, 47, 352, 396
Social relations and federalism, 882
Social Science Research Council of Canada, 937

Social security policy, 732; emergence of 338; reform, 934; review, 696
Social services, health, 594, 832
Social status, 1411, 1422
Social structure and public policy, 681
Social welfare: assistance in Manitoba, 529; charity-state relations, 592; decision-making, 496; family allowances, 945; income security, and federal finance, 781; minimum income, 807; provinces, 517; public enterprise, 927
Society and politics, 1294; in Quebec, 1577
Solicitor General, 2248
South Africa: economic relations, 3567; foreign policy with, 3005, 3038, 3086, 3113, 3222, 3223, 3247, 3282, 3330, 3694; voting, 1387
Sovereignty Association, 1466, 1467, 1468, 1477, 1497, 1503, 1506, 1508, 1535, 1554, 1556, 1557, 1558, 1559, 1571, 1573, 1614, 1626, 1627, 1667, 1737; economics, 1460, 1462, 1465, 1528, 1529, 1530, 1531; federalism, 1521; foreign policy, 1741; francophones in Canada and, 1643; international law and, 1615; referendum on, 1448, 1494, 1518, 1540, 1582, 1606, 1705
Sovereignty Association (anti), 1982
Sovereignty-association referendum, constitutional aspects of, 151, 297
Soviet Union: economic policy with, 2970, 3088; foreign policy with, 2956, 2958, 2959, 3073
Space industry, 3575
Speaker, 2324, 2329, 2452; Office of, 2398, 2399; power, 2405; selection, 2376

Spending, governmental, 313, 319, 388, 389
Split-ticket voting, 2159
Stabilization of prices, 497
Standing committees: House of Commons, 2388, 2394, 2404, 2419; interest groups, 2450; legislation, 2455; Ontario Legislature, 2461; Quebec, 2415
"Star Wars," 3193, 3235
State-owned companies in Quebec, 1608
Statistics on politics, 1749
Student participation, 1825
Suburbanization, 1389
Summitry, 3299
Superpowers, 3271; foreign policy, 3025, 3051, 3061, 3075, 3102
Support, political, 1767; economy and, 1886; federalism, 716; regime, 1858
Supreme Court of Canada, 203; anti-inflation act of 1975, 208, 242; arbitration, 189; Charter of Rights and Freedoms, 237, 250; Constitution, 85, 90; federalism, and Constitutional amendment, 724; federal-provincial relations, 238; history of, 130; political change, 49; Registrar of, 2789; resource taxation, 806. See also Court, Supreme
Sweden: air pollution control and environmental politics, 743; pension fund programs, 588
Switzerland, religious, linguistic, and class voting, 1387
Sydney, Nova Scotia, urban politics, 1014

Tanzania, foreign policy with, 3247
Task Forces in Parliament, 2426

Taxation: administration, 662; assessment, 572; energy crisis, 559; farm lands, 544; harmonization and federal finance, 526; life insurance, 557; non-residents, 808; policy, 335, 661; power in constitution, 83; property, 525, 585, 812, 871; tax reform, 504, 537, 593, 637, 645, 646, 703, 808
Technocracy and public administration, 2788
Technocrats in Quebec, 2535
Technology: administration, 2599; bureaucracy, 2654; nationalism, 1310, 1353; public administration, 2779, 2804; Quebec, 1635; rail travel, 742
Telecommunications policy, 298; federal-provincial relations, 479; regulation, 293, 467, 498, 499, 583, 862, 915; space age, 771
Television: broadcasting policy, 409; Parliament, 2400; regulation, 278, 498, 499, 904; referendum in Quebec, 1823
Textile industry, 383
Theater and politics in Quebec, 1551
Third Parties, 2181, 2218; New Brunswick, 2147; provincial politics, 1106
Third World: aid policy, 3319, 3609; economic relations with, 3309; foreign aid to, 2989, 3239, 3248, 3362, 3427
Time Magazine, foreign ownership and, 1392, 3605
Toronto, 985, 988, 1287; City Council, election of, 2401; development policy, 1080; municipal politics, 1021, 1131; political parties, 2157; public administration, 2747; urban politics, 965, 1184
Toxic waste disposal, 795, 3674

Trade and commerce: barriers, 757; foreign policy, 3058;overseas trade, 347; policy, 3405, 3533
Trade missions, bibliography, 3382
Training and public service, 2622, 2704
Trans-Canada Highway policy, 705
Transportation policy, 284, 296, 361, 362, 430, 452, 502, 503, 589, 723, 855; energy conservation, 595; federalism, 950; nationalism, 1402; regulation, 567, 689, 755, 861, 906, 2492
Transport Commission, 2492
Treasury Board of Canada, 472, 699, 2590, 2664
Treasury proposals for tax reform, 504
Treaties, 3007. See also NATO, NORAD, ASEAN
Treaties (indian) and jurisprudence, 263
Tremblay Report, 1509
Tribal philosophies and Charter of Rights, 154
Tribunals, administrative, 231
Trucking de-regulation, 755
Trudeau administration and foreign policy, 2856, 2894, 2938, 2951, 3026, 3033, 3048, 3245, 3257, 3291, 3292, 3296, 3299, 3481
Trudeau Doctrine, 3033, 3173
Trudeau, Pierre: actions in government, 1789, 1791; attitudes, 2190; Constitution and, 142, 144; federal-provincial relations and, 392; philosophy of, 346, 1959; policies, 1966; press, 2239; Prime Minister, 2232, 2233

UNCTAD, foreign policy, 3058
Unemployment: insurance, 700, 801; participation, 1850

Union democracy, 1803
Union Nationale Party in Quebec, 1505, 1560, 1712, 2083
Union of Soviet Socialist Republics, see Soviet Union
Unions, labor: attitudes to politics, 1810; public servants, 2479; Quebec and nationalism, 1904
United Kingdom: Canadian Constitution, 194; charity-state relations, 592; equal pay and public policy, 486; race relations commissions, 910
United Nations: foreign policy, 3018, 3089, 3107, 3125, 3131, 3167, 3169, 3232; human rights, 3589
United States: air pollution control and environmental politics, 743; bilateralism with, 3049, 3325; Bill of Rights, 258; border projects, 3363; British Columbia and, 3136; charity-state relations, 592; Congress, Canada and, 3326; Congress, foreign policy, 3465; cultural relations, 3325, 3342, 3360, 3395; economic relations, 3306, 3323, 3324, 3334, 3336, 3337, 3340, 3341, 3342, 3365, 3371, 3372, 3379, 3380, 3385, 3409, 3410, 3418, 3420, 3424, 3451, 3460, 3463, 3472, 3474, 3475, 3484, 3489, 3490, 3500, 3501, 3509, 3519, 3529, 3531, 3541, 3542, 3561, 3562, 3574, 3575, 3577, 3578, 3590, 3600, 3601, 3602, 3604, 3615, 3650, 3651, 3652, 3683, 3718, 3723, 3724, 3725, 3726, 3729, 3730, 3731, 3733, 3734, 3736, 3737, 3738, 3375, 3623; energy policy, 482, 924, 931, 3521, 3524, 3559; environmental relations, 3595; equal pay and public policy, 486;

United States, continued: exclusionary rule and constitution, 214; federalism in, 351; foreign policy, 2955, 2976, 2977, 3003, 3004, 3119, 3150, 3172, 3188, 3227, 3265, 3280, 3285, 3286, 3289, 3290, 3292, 3300, 3303, 3304, 3316, 3320, 3328, 3333, 3338, 3348, 3357, 3361, 3367, 3368, 3377, 3383, 3386, 3398, 3401, 3402, 3403, 3423, 3434, 3441, 3442, 3443, 3444, 3450, 3466, 3467, 3468, 3469, 3485, 3486, 3493, 3494, 3495, 3496, 3498, 3515, 3544, 3545, 3546, 3547, 3548, 3571, 3573, 3586, 3591, 3592, 3593, 3594, 3597, 3646, 3648, 3649, 3670, 3677, 3680; foreign policy, acid rain, 3522; foreign policy agriculture, 3449; foreign policy, Arctic Waters, 3580; foreign policy, bilateral institutions, 3551, 3560; foreign policy, dispute resolution, 3147; foreign policy, fisheries, 3523; foreign policy, Law of the Sea, 3376, 3543; foreign policy, Quebec, 3218; free trade, 3393, 3400, 3630, 3641, 3668, 3682, 3684, 3692; health policy system, 949; influence of, 3307; joint organizations, foreign policy, 3008; middle powers and, 3331; military issues, 3045, 3320, 3321; nuclear power plants, regulation, 643; province-state relations, 3587, 3588, 3596; Quebec sovereignty and, 3035, 3111; race relations commissions, 910; social security policy, 732; tax reform, 639; trucking deregulation, 755
Unity. See national unity
Universities: federalism, 574; government relations, 851, 853;

Universities, continued: research and federal funds, 869
Uranium and government regulation, 903
Urban development, 971, 1026, 1027, 1028, 1029, 1030, 1031, 1032, 1033, 1042, 1067, 1079, 1081, 1142, 1163, 1181, 1218, 1236; Alberta, 972; federal relations and, 1049; municipal licensing, 1178; planning, 961, 962, 978, 1009; transportation policy, 1045
Urban politics, 1000, 1001, 1003, 1016, 1069, 1085, 1090, 1101, 1119, 1188, 1206, 1236; aldermen, 1094; Calgary, 966; Edmonton political parties, 1212; financial relations, 1159; housing policy, 1205; intergovernmental relations, 1002; law, 48; management, 1053; Montreal 1013, 1093, 1211; new left, 1170; policymaking, 993, 1198; political parties 1974; Quebec, 1013, 1162; Sydney, Nova Scotia, 1014; Toronto, 965; urban reform, 1171; water supply, 1187
Urban renewal, Quebec City, 1151

Vancouver and metropolitan politics, 1273
Vietnam and United States, foreign policy, 2986, 3004, 3289
Violence, collective, 1841, 1842, 1843
Voter registration in elections, 2080
Voting behavior, 1970; 1979 election, 2046; 1968 and 1972 elections, 2027; advertising, 2171; class, religious, linguistic, 1387; francophone minorities, 1663; national integration, 2100; party identification, 2101,

Voting behavior (continued): 2137; political parties, 1944, 1945; Toronto City Council, 2401; turnout, Sakatchewan, 2130. See also elections

Wage and price controls, 738, 777, 830
Wage discrimination and women, 2502
Wales nationalism and Quebec, 1716, 1736
Waste collection, 1201
Water issues: jurisdiction, Arctic, law, 1231; North America, 3572
Water quality: Agreement, 3667; management, 896
Water resources management and environmental diplomacy, 563
Welfare policy: legislation, 47; reform, 369, 934; social, federal and provincial dimensions, 352
West Africa, foreign policy with, 3123
Western Canada, 1022; development, 1169, 1192, 1271; disenchantment and federalism, 636; economics, 1105; energy, and federalism, 798; maritimes and, 1196; Progressivism in, 2015; regionalism and cooperation, 1158; separatism, 1082; Social Credit in, 2015; socialism in, 2015
Western premiers and the Constitution, 135, 136
Western view of Constitutional reform, 213
West Germany: federalism and international relations, 774; nuclear power plants, regulation, 643
West Indies, foreign policy with, 3020
White Paper on Sovereignty Association, criticism of, 1513

Winnipeg, 1021, 1128 1156; businessmen and political communication, 512; electoral reform in local elections, 2143; ethnic voting and social class, 2213, 2225, 2226, 2227

Women in politics: affirmative action, 1918; attitudes in Quebec on partisanship, 1809; bibliography, 1770, 1793; cabinet in Quebec, 2292; candidates in 1979 and 1980 elections, 2090; Constitution and, 66, 82; cultural traditions and political history of, 1334; municipal politics, 1189; participation, 1742, 1746, 1750, 1753, 1754, 1756, 1765, 1771, 1776, 1777, 1786, 1790, 1813, 1816, 1879, 1936; party officials, 1826; political parties, 1743, 1928; public service, 2703; Quebec, 1490, 1865; rights, 1812; wage discrimination, 2502. See also gender

World War I, overseas policy in, 2994

Written questions in Parliament, 2362

Yukon legislature, privilege, 2431

Zimbabwe, foreign aid, 3611

About the Compiler

GREGORY MAHLER, Associate Professor of Political Science, the University of Vermont, has published numerous studies and articles on topics in contemporary politics. His books include *New Dimensions of Canadian Federalism* and *Comparative Politics: An Institutional and Cross-National Approach.*